VOLUME-TO-WEIGHT CONVERSIONS
FOR SELECTED INGREDIENTS

The figures for dry ingredients are given as rough ranges because they depend on how densely the ingredients are packed into the spoon or cup. The imprecision becomes more evident as the volume measure increases.

INGREDIENT	1 TEASPOON	1 TABLESPOON	¼ CUP	½ CUP	1 CUP
FLUIDS					
Water	5 grams	15 grams	60 grams	120 grams	240 grams
Milk	5	15	60	120	240
Cream, heavy	5	15	58	115	230
Lemon juice	5	15	60	120	240
Oil	4.5	14	55	110	220
Butter	4.5	14	56	112	225
Shortening	4	12	48	95	190
Corn syrup	7	20	84	165	330
Honey	7	20	84	165	330
Vanilla extract	4	12			
Alcohols, unsweetened (vodka, rum brandy)	4.5	14	56	112	225
SOLIDS					
Salt, granulated	6.5	20	80	160	320
Salt, flaked	3.5–5	10–15	40–60	80–120	160–240
Sugar, white granulated	4.5	13	50	100	200
Sugar, brown	4–5	12–15	48–60	96–120	195–240
Sugar, powdered	2.5	8	30	60	120
Flour, all-purpose	2.5–3	8–9	30–35	60–70	120–140
Flour, bread	2.5–3	8–10	32–39	65–78	130–155
Flour, cake	2.5	7–8	29–32	58–65	115–130
Flour, whole-grain	2.5	8	30–32	62–65	125–130
Cornstarch	2.5–3	8–9	30–35	60–70	120–140
Rice (standard rice cooker measure = 140 grams)					190
Beans, medium					190
Lentils, small					200
Cocoa	2	6	22–24	45–48	90–96
Baking soda	5	15			
Baking powder	5	15			
Yeast, dry, (1 packet = 7 grams)	3	9			
Gelatin	3	9			

KEYS TO
GOOD
COOKING

Also by Harold McGee

On Food and Cooking

The Curious Cook

KEYS TO GOOD COOKING

A Guide to Making the Best
of Foods and Recipes

HAROLD McGEE

THE PENGUIN PRESS   NEW YORK   2010

THE PENGUIN PRESS
Published by the Penguin Group
Penguin Group (USA) Inc., 375 Hudson Street, New York, New York 10014, U.S.A. •
Penguin Group (Canada), 90 Eglinton Avenue East, Suite 700, Toronto, Ontario,
Canada M4P 2Y3 (a division of Pearson Penguin Canada Inc.) • Penguin Books Ltd, 80 Strand,
London WC2R 0RL, England • Penguin Ireland, 25 St. Stephen's Green, Dublin 2, Ireland
(a division of Penguin Books Ltd) • Penguin Books Australia Ltd, 250 Camberwell Road,
Camberwell, Victoria 3124, Australia (a division of Pearson Australia Group Pty Ltd) •
Penguin Books India Pvt Ltd, 11 Community Centre, Panchsheel Park, New Delhi – 110 017,
India • Penguin Group (NZ), 67 Apollo Drive, Rosedale, North Shore 0632, New Zealand
(a division of Pearson New Zealand Ltd) • Penguin Books (South Africa) (Pty) Ltd,
24 Sturdee Avenue, Rosebank, Johannesburg 2196, South Africa

Penguin Books Ltd, Registered Offices: 80 Strand, London WC2R 0RL, England

First published in 2010 by The Penguin Press,
a member of Penguin Group (USA) Inc.

Copyright © Harold McGee, 2010
All rights reserved

LIBRARY OF CONGRESS CATALOGING-IN-PUBLICATION DATA
McGee, Harold.
Keys to good cooking : a guide to making the best of foods and recipes / Harold McGee.
p.   cm.
Includes bibliographical references and index.
ISBN 978-1-59420-268-1
1. Cookery.   2. Food.   I. Title.
TX651.M269   2010
641.5—dc22   2010017303

Printed in the United States of America

1   3   5   7   9   10   8   6   4   2

DESIGNED BY NICOLE LAROCHE

To Florence and John

CONTENTS

INTRODUCTION

Cooking can be one of the most satisfying things we do in life. It's a chance to make things with our own hands, nourish and give pleasure to people we care about, and choose exactly what we eat and make part of ourselves. It's also a way to explore the astounding creativity of the natural world and thousands of years of human culture, to taste foods and traditions from all over the planet at our own table. This endlessly rewarding quality is what has kept me delving into cooking for more than thirty years.

Cooking is especially rewarding when it goes well! It's true, as we're frequently reminded, that the only way to become a good cook is to cook, and cook, and cook some more. But many of us don't manage to cook that frequently, and frequent cooking can also be cooking by rote, habitual and mediocre. The surest way to cook with pleasure and success—whether you're a beginner, a weekend gourmand, or an accomplished chef—is to cook with understanding.

This book is designed to help you cook better by explaining what foods are, how cooking changes them, which methods work best, and why.

Keys to Good Cooking is not a cookbook. Recipes we have in abundance, in print and on the Web, from across the globe and across the centuries, from professionals and celebrities, families and friends. Instead, this book is a guide to help you navigate through the ever-expanding universe of recipes and arrive at the promised land of a satisfying dish.

It's easy to get lost along the way. Some recipes give reliably good results, but many don't. Some are sketchy and leave us guessing how exactly to proceed. Others are intimidatingly long and detailed. Different recipes for the same dish may give contradictory directions and explanations. Some place faithfulness to tradition above realistic handling of today's ingredients. And many perpetuate old misconceptions and flawed methods.

Even good recipes are no guarantee of success. At best they're an incomplete description of a procedure that has worked for the recipe writer. Whenever we cook from a recipe, we have to interpret and adapt it for our kitchen, our ingredients, and our experience. And the process of interpretation and adaptation is just as important to success as the recipe itself. A good recipe can be badly made.

Happily, it's also true that we can redeem a flawed recipe by seeing its flaws and correcting them as we adapt it.

Keys to Good Cooking is meant to be a constructively critical companion to your recipe collection, and a guide to the kitchen, gadgets, ingredients, and techniques with which you turn recipes into foods. It's a concise summary of our current understanding of food preparation. It provides simple statements of fact and advice, along with brief explanations that will help you understand *why*, and apply that insight whenever you cook. It will help you evaluate recipes, recognize likely flaws or problems, and make adjustments and corrections as you go. And I hope it will help you put aside recipes, improvise and experiment, and come up with your own ways of doing things.

The first six chapters of this book describe the range of tools and pantry ingredients available to the home cook, how heat and basic cooking methods work, and the essentials of kitchen safety. These subjects aren't likely to be at the top of your need-to-know list, and you may figure you already know what you need.

But because we usually equip our kitchens and pantries piecemeal, and only pay attention in emergencies to how the oven works or doesn't, it can be a real eye-opener to pause and take a closer look at these things. Once you think about how heat actually flows into and out of our foods as we cook, you'll understand why standard stew recipes often dry out the meat, why a medium-hot oven can scorch baked goods, and what you can do to make sure you don't have those problems again. And did you know that thorough cooking not only can't kill some tough forms of bacteria that sicken us, it actually awakens them into rapid growth? Watch those leftovers! The most important kitchen facts are often the least obvious.

So I suggest reviewing these early chapters every once in a while to get better acquainted with foods and appliances and cooking methods, no matter how familiar they seem. And take the time to read through chapter 6, "Cooking Safely." Tens of thousands of Americans are made ill by food every day, many of them due to unnecessary mistakes made by cooks who could and should know better.

The remaining chapters are organized by ingredients and kinds of preparations. Read the introductory sections to find out how to recognize and handle good ingredients. Then, when you're cooking a particular dish, go to the paragraph or two devoted to that kind of preparation. Review the facts and the various possibilities before you start cooking, to help you choose a recipe or make adjustments to the one you've chosen, and just to get organized. If a problem or question arises as you go, if a step needs clarification, check again.

To keep this book a manageable size, it covers cooking basics, not advanced techniques or fine points. And because a cook in the kitchen needs to get back to cooking pronto, I've tried to make the information as quickly accessible as possible. I've kept statements brief and to the point, repeated them when necessary to save the trouble of hunting down cross-references, and highlighted key words to make them easy to spot on the page.

Key subjects and important facts to keep in mind are indicated in boldface.

Directions and important actions are indicated in italics.

---

ere's an example of how I hope you'll use this book. Let's say Thanksgiving is coming up, you haven't roasted a turkey since last Thanksgiving, and you've seen a recipe for brining the turkey to keep it moist. You might start by looking at the introduction to cooking meat on p. 238:

No matter what you read in recipes or hear pronounced by people who should know, keep these simple truths in mind:

- **Searing meat does *not* seal in its juices, and moist cooking methods do *not* make meats moist.** Juiciness depends almost entirely on how hot you cook the center of the meat. If it gets much hotter than 150°F/65°C, it will be dry.
- **Meat overcooks quickly. Low heat slows cooking and gives you the greatest control over doneness.**
- **Most recipes can't predict correct cooking times.** There's no substitute for checking meat doneness yourself, early and often.

Then you could read the summary of brining pros and cons on p. 246:

Brining is the immersion of meat in a weak solution of salt and water, with or without other flavorings, for hours to days before cooking. Injecting brine into the meat interior speeds the process. The salt penetrates the meat, seasons it, and improves its ability to retain moisture and tenderness.

Brines of a certain strength, 5 to 10 percent salt by weight, also cause the meat proteins to absorb extra water from the brine, making the meat seem exceptionally juicy when cooked. Very lean poultry and pork can benefit from this extra moisture, especially when they're overcooked.

Brine selectively. Brines have drawbacks: they dilute the meat's own flavorful juices with tap water, and usually make the pan juices too salty for deglazing into a sauce.

And then you could look at the basics of roasting birds, which begin this way on p. 258:

Whole birds are a challenge to roast well. Their breast meat is low in connective tissue and best cooked to 150°F/65°C for chickens and turkeys, 135°F/57°C for duck and squab. But their leg meat is high in connective tissue and best cooked to 160°F/70°C, and their skin is best cooked to 350°F/175°C to make it crisp and brown.

To roast birds well:

* *Don't stuff the body cavity or rely on a pop-up thermometer.* Stuffing must be heated to 160°F/70°C to kill bacteria, so the breast meat will be overcooked and dry. Pop-up indicators pop only when the breast meat is already overcooked.

Now you can decide for yourself whether you want to have a brine-moist turkey or an edible pan sauce, a moist breast or an in-bird stuffing, and you can add a cooking thermometer to your pre-Thanksgiving shopping list (and consult p. 45 for advice on thermometers).

You'll notice that the pages of this book have plenty of blank space. That's because the words on them aren't the last, just the first. The margins and line spaces are there for you to fill with new information and ideas as they come along, and especially with notes specific to your kitchen, your tastes, your discoveries—your own personal keys to good cooking.

I hope that your copy of this book will quickly become well stained and marked up, and will long help you cook with insight, pleasure, and success.

KEYS TO
GOOD
COOKING

Good
cooking
starts with
a good
under-
standing

1

GETTING TO KNOW FOODS

Good cooking starts with a good understanding of its raw materials, the foods we cook.

We're all familiar with the foods that we regularly buy and eat, and the more we cook, the better we get to know them and the way they behave. But foods have histories and inner qualities that aren't obvious from our everyday encounters with them, and that determine their value and behavior. The more fully we know our foods, the better we can choose them and cook with them.

I first encountered the inner world of foods decades ago as a student, when I headed to an unfamiliar section of the library and found shelf after shelf devoted to the science of food and agriculture. I browsed in them, and at first was startled and amused by what I saw: photographs taken through the microscope of meat fibers and the way they shrank as they cooked, microbes growing in yogurt and cheese, the oil droplets jammed against each other in a bit of mayonnaise, gossamer-thin gluten sheets in bread dough. But soon I was mesmerized. And though I'd stopped studying science years earlier, I found myself drawn into what was going on behind *these* scenes, into the nature and behavior of the protein and starch and fat molecules that they were constructed from. It was thrilling to begin to understand why meats get juicy when cooked just right and dry when overcooked, why milk thickens into yogurt and cheeses have so many textures and flavors, why well-formed bread dough feels almost alive to the touch.

The language and ideas of science are less familiar than our foods are, and I know that their strangeness can be off-putting. Try to put up with them anyhow, and don't worry about the details. Just start by knowing that there *are* details, and that they can help you understand cooking and cook better. Then, when a question comes up, when you really want to know more, use the brief explanation in this book as an entry point to the world of details that's out there to explore.

WHAT FOODS ARE

Foods are complex, dynamic, and fragile materials.

Most foods come originally from living plants and animals, which are nature's most intricate and active creations. Some—fresh fruits and vegetables, fresh eggs, shellfish from the tank, yogurt—are still alive when we buy them.

Living things are fragile. They thrive in the right conditions, die and decay in the wrong ones. Their tissues can be damaged by physical pressure, by excessive heat or cold, by too little fresh air or too much, and by microbes that start consuming them for food before we can.

Most foods are produced on farms or ranches or in factories far distant from our kitchens. Before we can buy them, they have been raised, harvested, prepared and packaged, transported to the market, unpacked, and displayed—and require careful temperature control and gentle handling throughout to minimize their deterioration.

Our food plants and animals have been bred and selected over thousands of years and come in countless different varieties, each with its own advantages and disadvantages.

The quality of a food is a general measure of how well it fulfills its potential for providing nourishment and the pleasures of flavor, texture, and appearance.

Food quality depends on many factors. These include the variety of plant or animal the food comes from, how that plant or animal lives, and how the food is handled in its progress from farm to plate.

HOW FOODS ARE PRODUCED

Cooks today can choose foods from a wide and sometimes confusing range of production systems.

Most foods are produced in "conventional" large-scale industrial systems that are designed to minimize production costs and food prices, and maximize shelf life. Conventional foods are produced and shipped from sources all over the world, wherever labor and other costs are low enough to offset the costs of transportation.

Most meats come from farm animals raised largely or entirely indoors, with little living space, on manufactured feeds that often include materials the animal wouldn't normally eat (fish meal, rendered animal remains and waste), antibiotics to stimulate growth and control disease, and sometimes with growth-stimulating hormones.

Most fruits, vegetables, grains, and cooking oils come from plants grown with industrial fertilizers, herbicides, and pesticides. Some crops have been genetically modified with modern DNA technology, which may reduce herbicide and pesticide use.

Most fish and shellfish are produced in aquaculture, the water-animal version of intensive meat production, in confinement and on formulated feeds. Some fish and shellfish are still harvested from the wild.

Most prepared foods are made from conventional ingredients, and usually include texture stabilizers, natural or artificial flavor concentrates, and preservatives. They're industrial approximations of the original kitchen product, designed to minimize price and maximize shelf life.

Conventional systems have important drawbacks. Conventional agriculture and meat production, and aquaculture, can cause damage to the environment, the spread of antibiotic-resistant bacteria, and unnecessary animal suffering. Harvesting wild fish and shellfish has depleted many populations to dangerously low levels.

Alternative production systems attempt to remedy various drawbacks of conventional systems. Many foods are now advertised or certified to have been produced:

- **organically,** without the use of industrial fertilizers or pesticides, genetically modified crops, or most industrial additives, and with minimal use of antibiotics;
- **sustainably,** without damaging effects on the local or global environments, or on wild populations;

- **humanely,** with consideration for the quality of life of farm animals;
- **fairly,** with farmers in developing countries receiving a good price;
- **selectively,** without the use of genetically modified crops, certain hormones or antibiotics or feeds, or preservatives or other additives; or with the use of high-quality or heritage varieties;
- **locally,** with fewer resources spent on transportation.

Food production terminology is neither precise nor tightly regulated. The terms are loose at best, and because some justify higher prices, they may be used to mislead or deceive.

Be skeptical about alternative production claims, but not cynical. All food choices, even casual ones, influence the agriculture and food industries and the people who work in them, and have a cumulative impact on the world's soils, waters, and air.

CHOOSING FOODS

Good cooking calls for good ingredients. Cooking can mask the defects of mediocre or poor ingredients, but it can't make the best foods with them.

Foods land in our shopping carts with a history. Their genetic background, their variety or breed, and everything they go through from farm to display case influence their quality and what we can do with them.

Think about your priorities and choose foods consciously. If production practices and their consequences matter to you, then check the credentials of the suppliers and buy accordingly.

No particular production method is a guarantee of food quality. Both conventional and alternative foods can be mistreated or spoiled during the harvest or later handling.

Learn to read the signs of quality in the foods you shop for. The chapters in this book describe what to look for in each food.

Check the ingredient lists on prepared foods to know what you're really buying.

Care for the foods you buy to preserve their quality. A long hot car ride from the store can cause damage as much as mishandling at any other stage.

INSIDE FOODS: FOOD CHEMICALS

As with all material things, including our bodies, foods are composed of countless invisibly small structures called *molecules*. We eat so that food molecules will become our body's molecules.

Molecules come in various families or kinds, and we call those kinds *chemicals*. Many chemical names—proteins, enzymes, carbohydrates, saturated and unsaturated fats—are familiar from nutrition guidelines and packaged food labels. They're becoming common cooking terms because they can help cooks understand what their methods are actually doing to change foods.

The major chemical building blocks of foods are water, proteins, carbohydrates, and fats. These chemicals, and the changes they undergo during cooking, create the structures and textures of our foods.

Water

Water is the primary chemical in fresh foods of all kinds, and a major ingredient in most cooked dishes. The cells of all living things are essentially bags of water in which the other molecules are suspended and do their work.

Water is what makes foods seem moist. Its loss is what can make them seem unpleasantly dry or pleasantly crisp.

Water is also an important cooking medium. We cook many foods in hot water, or in the watery fluids from other foods.

Water can be acid, alkaline, or neutral—neither acid nor alkaline. Acidity and alkalinity affect the reactions of other food molecules and are important factors in cooking. Acid liquids include fruit juices and vinegar, and taste sour. Alkaline ingredients include many city tap waters, baking soda, and egg whites, and taste flat.

The boiling point of water is an important cooking landmark. It's instantly recognizable as bubbling turbulence, and it marks a specific temperature, 212°F/100°C at sea level (lower temperatures at high altitudes), that is hot enough to kill microbes, firm meats and fish, and soften vegetables.

The boiling point of water is an important cooking limitation. It is too low to develop the rich flavors of roasting and frying, which develop increasingly quickly above 250°F/120°C.

Water in foods can slow their cooking. When foods are heated in the hot dry air of an oven or barbecue, their surface moisture evaporates and cools them.

Proteins

Proteins are the main building blocks in meats and fish, eggs, and dairy products.

Proteins are the sensitive food chemicals, easily changed by heat and by acidity, and the reason that meats and fish are tricky to cook well.

Picture proteins as separate long threads, more or less folded up, crowded together in a watery world.

Proteins coagulate when the temperature rises to 100 to 140°F / 40 to 60°C and the threads unfold and stick to each other, forming a solid mass of stuck threads with water pockets trapped in between. This is why heating causes meat and fish flesh to get firm and liquid eggs to solidify.

Coagulated proteins dry out when they are cooked hotter than their coagulation point and stick more tightly to each other. This is why meat and fish flesh quickly get hard and dry, why eggs get rubbery, and why precise temperature control helps cook these foods just right.

Acidity can also cause proteins to coagulate, even at low temperatures. This is why acid-producing bacteria set milk into yogurt and an acid marinade firms and whitens pieces of fish in ceviche.

Enzymes are active proteins: proteins that change other chemicals around them, and so change food qualities. Meat enzymes make meats tender and more flavorful. Some fish enzymes turn fish mushy and unpleasantly fishy. Enzymes in fruits and vegetables cause discoloration and destroy vitamins.

Cooking inactivates enzymes and prevents them from changing foods further, because like other proteins they're sensitive to heat and acids.

Gelatin is the exceptional insensitive protein. Instead of its molecules staying separate at low temperatures and sticking together irreversibly at high temperatures, they cluster together to form a solid gel when cool, melt when heated, and can be repeatedly gelled and melted.

Carbohydrates

Carbohydrates are the main building blocks in foods from plants: vegetables, fruits, grains, and so on.

Sugars and starches are carbohydrates that plants use to store energy, and that we can digest, absorb, and use for energy.

Fiber is the common name for the other carbohydrates that plants use to build the walls of their cells, and that we can't digest and absorb well. They include pectins, gums, and cellulose.

Carbohydrates are not as sensitive and easily changed as proteins. When heated, most of them simply absorb water and dissolve. This is why ordinary cooking softens plant foods, and why precise temperature control is not important in cooking most of them.

Carbohydrates are also extracted from plants and used as purified ingredients.

Sugars contribute sweetness to foods. In large amounts they also create a thick body—as in syrups—or a creamy or brittle solidity, as in candies.

Starch is a bland carbohydrate, the main chemical in grain flours and also sold in pure form. Starch molecules are long threads, and plants pack them into dense granules, the familiar powdery particles of cornstarch and other pure starches. When cooked in liquid, the granules absorb water and release the long threads, creating thick body in sauces and solid structure in baked goods. Starches from different sources—

wheat, corn, potato, arrowroot, tapioca—have special qualities that suit them to different cooking uses.

Pectin is a bland carbohydrate whose long molecules thicken jams and jellies.

Agar, xanthan gum, guar gum, and locust bean gum are bland carbohydrates from seaweed, microbes, and seeds whose long molecules are also used to thicken and stabilize sauces, ice creams, and gluten-free baked goods.

Fats

Fats and oils are chemicals in which animals and plants store energy. They're commonly extracted and used as purified ingredients. Unlike proteins and carbohydrates, they are fluids, and provide a delicious moistness to foods. Unlike water, they can be easily heated to temperatures far above water's boiling point, and help create the characteristic flavors of roasting and frying. They also carry aromas better than water, and help flavors linger in the mouth during eating.

Fat and *oil* **name different versions of the same chemical**.

Fats are solid at room temperature and melt into a liquid beginning around body temperature. They come mainly from meats, and include butterfat and lard.

Oils are already liquid at room temperature, and solidify only when chilled. They're mainly extracted from seeds—canola, soy, corn, peanut—and from the olive fruit.

Food fats and oils are mixtures of different chemical fats.

Saturated fats are fats that tend to be solid at room temperature and resistant to staling, thanks to the rigid structure of their molecules.

Unsaturated fats are fats that tend to be liquid at room temperature and prone to staling and off flavors, thanks to the flexible structure of their molecules.

Hydrogenated fats are unsaturated fats that have been chemically modified to make them saturated, more solid and resistant to staling.

Trans fats are unusual unsaturated fats that behave like saturated fats. Small amounts occur naturally in butter, beef, and lamb; large amounts occur in hydrogenated oils and shortenings. They're unhealthful and are being eliminated from manufactured foods.

Omega-3 fats are highly unsaturated fats found mainly in seafood and in walnuts and canola oil. They appear to be especially healthful and are being added to many foods.

Meat fats are solid at room temperature because they have a high proportion of saturated fats. Poultry fats and pork fat (lard) are softer than beef and lamb fat because they contain more unsaturated fats.

Vegetable and fish oils are liquid at room temperature because they contain a high proportion of unsaturated fats.

Oils and melted fats don't mix with water unless they're helped by other ingredients. When combined, they form temporarily separate droplets. Fats and oils are less dense than water, so their droplets rise to form a layer above the water.

Emulsions are creamy mixtures of oil and water with droplets of one suspended in the other. Added egg yolk and other ingredients can coat the droplets and make a stable mixture that feels thicker than water or oil alone.

FOOD TEXTURES

Food texture or consistency is what a food feels like in the mouth: how hard or soft it is, and how it feels as we chew it, move it around, and swallow it. Texture is created by the main food building blocks, and by how the cook handles them.

Most cooking problems involve texture, not flavor.

Liquid foods may be thin and watery or thick and velvety, smooth or rough or lumpy, oily or creamy.

Solid foods may be hard or soft, moist or dry, chewy or tender, leathery or crisp.

Most pleasant textures result when the building blocks are evenly integrated with each other, and in the right proportions. Unpleasant textures result when the building blocks are segregated from each other or fall out of balance.

Meats, fish, eggs, and custards are tender and moist when moderate heat causes their proteins to bind loosely to each other and to water. They become tough and dry or curdled when excess heat causes the proteins to bind tightly to each other and squeeze water out.

Vegetables are tender and moist when brief near-boiling heat causes their cell wall carbohydrates and starch to bind less tightly to themselves, and to absorb water. They become mushy when prolonged heat causes the plant cells to lose their structure and fall apart.

Breads, cakes, and pastries are pleasantly firm when their carbohydrates have absorbed the right amount of moisture, too dry or too soft otherwise.

Sauces are smooth when starches or fats or proteins are evenly dispersed in the sauce liquid. When these ingredients are not evenly dispersed, sauces are lumpy or curdled or oily.

Bird skins and bread crusts are crisp when they've had all their water cooked out of them and the solid structures have no flexibility; as they reabsorb moisture and gain slight flexibility, they become leathery.

To understand texture changes, try to picture in your mind what is happening to the food's building blocks as you cook.

FOOD FLAVORS

Flavors are the major source of our pleasure in eating. They come from specific chemicals in foods, usually present in tiny amounts, which we are able to sense with our taste and smell receptors.

Good cooks hone their ability to analyze food flavors, recognize how they can be improved, and make adjustments.

Flavor is a combination of taste and smell. We sense taste on the tongue, and smell, or aroma, in the nose.

There are five basic tastes.

- **Saltiness** comes mainly from sodium chloride, in foods and added in the form of salt crystals.
- **Sourness** comes from acids of several kinds, especially citric and malic acids in fruits, acetic acid in vinegar, and lactic acid in fermented foods such as yogurt and cheese, cured sausages, and sauerkraut. Acids stimulate saliva flow and contribute to the mouthwatering quality of foods and drinks.
- **Sweetness** comes mainly from various kinds of sugars found in plants and in milk. There are many different chemical sug-

ars, all with names ending in *-ose*. Table-sugar sucrose is sweeter than corn-syrup glucose and milk-sugar lactose, but less sweet than honey's main sugar, fructose.

- **Savoriness,** also called by the Japanese term *umami,* is the brothy, round, mouthfilling taste caused by monosodium glutamate (MSG) and a few other chemicals. It's strong in meat stocks, soy sauce, aged cheeses, mushrooms, and tomatoes.

- **Bitterness** is the characteristic taste of chemicals that some plants make to deter animals from eating them. This is why it takes getting used to, and why not all people enjoy it. Bitterness is strong in chicories, brussels sprouts, and mustard greens, and an important part of coffee, tea, chocolate, and beer flavors. Added salt greatly diminishes bitterness.

Pungency and astringency are other important mouth sensations. Pungency is the heat and bite of black and chilli peppers, ginger, raw garlic and onion, and mustard, wasabi, watercress, and arugula. Astringency is the drying, rough effect caused by tannins in strong black tea or red wine.

There are hundreds of different aromas in foods. Aromas are what individualize foods and give them their specific flavor identities. All fruits have sweet and sour tastes, but only apples smell like apples, peaches like peaches.

There are many different aroma qualities in foods, which may smell not just fruity, meaty, fishy, eggy, nutty, or spicy, but also flowery, grassy, earthy, woody, smoky, leathery, and barnyardy.

Food aromas are always mixtures of aroma chemicals. Like chords in music, food aromas are an integrated combination of several individual chemical notes. Coriander seed and ginger share a lemony note in their spiciness; ripe banana has a note of clove.

When we combine ingredients in cooking, we create new aroma mixtures. Herbs and spices give us dozens of notes to fill out the flavor harmony of a dish.

Heat changes food flavors. Cooking gives meats and fish stronger flavors than they had when raw. It makes onions and garlic milder, cabbage stronger. Mustard greens lose their pungency and gain bitterness.

Cooking can add new flavors to foods. Frying in oil or fat creates a characteristic flavor from changes in the fat molecules.

High heat or prolonged heat creates especially delicious "browned" flavors. When a food turns brown in the frying pan or oven, or on the grill, it's a sign that heat has caused flavorless proteins and carbohydrates to react together to form hundreds of taste and aroma molecules. The browning reactions are most productive at temperatures above the boiling point of water, so foods brown best when heat dries out their surfaces.

SEASONING FOODS

To season a food is to balance and adjust its flavors to give the greatest possible pleasure to the people who will eat it.

Good seasoning is the cook's responsibility. It can't be specified in a recipe, because ingredients and cooking procedures are too variable.

People perceive flavors differently. This is a matter of inescapable biology, not arbitrary preference. People inherit different sets of chemical receptors, and may be hypersensitive to some tastes or smells, completely blind to others. Some people are born with more taste buds than others. And everyone's overall sensitivity to taste and smell declines in later life.

A good cook allows for differences in flavor perception. Discuss them openly to learn whether you're especially sensitive or insensitive to particular flavors, and then take that self-knowledge into account when you season foods. Don't be offended when people ask to season your food for themselves.

Tastes provide the foundation of flavor, and aromas are its free-form superstructure. To season a food is to balance its basic tastes and fill out its aromatic possibilities.

Always check the seasoning toward the end of cooking. Food flavors evolve during the cooking process. Flavor integration or "melding" is desirable, but often involves the loss of appealing flavor notes.

Season foods while they're at serving temperature. Flavor perception is strongly affected by temperature. Saltiness, bitterness, and most aromas are accentuated in hot food.

To season a food, taste it actively. Ask yourself questions such as these:

- Is there enough salt to avoid blandness?
- Would the acid of some lemon juice or vinegar make the flavor brighter and more mouthwatering? Acidity is especially undervalued as a general flavor booster and balancer.
- Is there enough savoriness or sweetness to carry the aroma?
- Would some pungency from pepper add a desirable edge?
- Have desirable aromas faded away or become masked? Should they be revived by adding a fresh round of those aromatics? Should the aroma be filled out with a complementary herb or spice, or butter, or grassy olive oil?

2

BASIC KITCHEN RESOURCES

Water, the Pantry, and the Refrigerator

Water and the foods we've always got on hand are so familiar that we seldom give them a second thought. It's worth giving them that and more for the very reason that they enter into almost everything we cook.

Water is the lifeblood of cooking, a universal ingredient as well as a medium for heating foods, cooling them, and cleaning up. But there's a lot more to it than H_2O, and the water that happens to come out of the tap doesn't always give the best or most wholesome results.

The pantry is a set of foods and ingredients that keep well and that we keep on hand because we cook with them regularly. It includes prepared foods in cans and jars; dry grains, beans, flours, and pastas; cooking fats and oils; and flavorings and seasonings, herbs and spices. The pantry usually expands without our planning it, and can turn into a very mixed collection of old and new, stale and fresh, flavorless and flavorful. It's good to take stock regularly and cull it.

I've found one way to do some pantry maintenance that can also be pleasurable and stimulating. Occasionally I'll just stand in front of my crowd of flavorings, open one container after another, and taste or sniff. Not with any particular cooking in mind, but just to refresh my memory of the things I've got and what they're like, to enjoy each for its own qualities, and to set aside the faded for replacement. Malt vinegar and balsamic, black pepper and long pepper, plain brown cane sugar and winey brown palm sugar, vanillas from Madagascar and Tahiti and Mexico: they're all absorbing on their own as the distinctive flavors of specific places and cultures, and as possible elements in what I'll put together for my own table in the coming weeks. A world of sensations on a couple of shelves.

WATER IN THE KITCHEN

Pure water itself is plain H_2O. But all actual waters—whether from a well, a city supply, or a bottle—contain small quantities of dissolved minerals, organic substances, and air. These minor components in water can affect the flavor, color, texture, and long-term healthfulness of ingredients cooked in it.

Tap water is usually adequate for cooking, but some foods may turn out better if you filter it or check its composition and adjust it.

Have your tap water tested for lead if your dwelling is old, newly plumbed, or part of a multiunit building. Lead is a potent nerve poison that is especially damaging to children, accumulates in the body, and is commonly found in drinking water thanks to the past use of lead in plumbing. In the United States even today, "lead-free" fixtures may legally contain some lead.

Let the cold tap run for 1 to 2 minutes or until cold if you haven't drawn any water for hours. Even a mostly plastic plumbing system can release undesirable amounts of lead, copper, and zinc from faucet fixtures into the water as it sits in the pipes.

Use cold tap water for most cooking jobs. Water hot from the tap may carry more dissolved metals from the plumbing pipes, and off flavors from sitting in the hot-water tank.

Use hot tap water for steaming or in a water bath, when the water doesn't come in direct contact with the food.

Check the taste of your tap water. Run the cold water for a minute, fill a glass, let it warm to room temperature, and taste it. If the taste is unpleasant, try to improve it with a water filter.

Check the pH and hardness of your water and make adjustments if necessary. Get this information from the water quality report for your city's system. Or get pH test papers or a pH meter from a scientific supply company.

Water pH is a measure of acidity. The ideal pH for most cooking is a neutral 7. If it's less than 7, it's slightly acid and may speed the discoloration of green vegetables when they're boiled. If it's above 8 and alkaline, it will taste flat, will brew flat-tasting tea, and may cause pale vegetables and grains to turn yellow.

To adjust the pH of your water for cooking, add a little baking soda to make acid water more alkaline, or a little lemon juice, sour salt (citric acid), or cream of tartar to make alkaline water more acid.

Water hardness is a measure of calcium and magnesium content. Too much of either can cause a bitter taste, the yellowing of rice and other pale foods, scum formation on brewed tea, and slowed softening of boiled vegetables and grains.

If your water is hard enough to cause any of these problems, use bottled water for making tea, and steam sensitive foods rather than boiling them. Water softeners replace "hard" minerals with sodium. Softened waters vary widely in sodium content and taste.

To make clean-flavored ice, start with good-tasting water and clean ice trays. Once frozen, store ice cubes in an airtight container. Before using, rinse them for a few seconds in running water. Ice often sits in the freezer long enough for its surface to absorb unpleasant odors.

STORING FOODS

The aim in storing foods is to keep them on hand while slowing their natural deterioration and maintaining their quality as long as possible.

Stale foods are foods whose flavor and/or texture have deteriorated noticeably, but that are still edible. Cooking can often remedy staleness. Reheating softens stale bread and recrisps pastries, nuts, and fried snacks.

Spoiled foods are foods whose flavor and/or texture have deteriorated to the point that we consider them inedible. This judgment is subjective. Spoiled foods can still be nutritious and safe to eat, but off flavors and mushiness are warning signs that foods may be infected with harmful microbes.

The enemies of freshness and long shelf life are heat, light, and air.

Heat and light energy, oxygen, moisture, and microbes cause foods to go stale and to spoil.

Most foods keep best when stored in cold, dark, airtight conditions.

Storing Foods at Room Temperature

Pantries, cupboards, and cabinets at room temperature are cool enough for storing dry, canned, and cured foods, and a few fresh root vegetables that are naturally slow to spoil. Dry foods will keep for months; hermetically sealed in cans for a year or more. Salt and refined sugars keep indefinitely.

Keep storage shelves as cool as possible. Don't use toasters, countertop ovens, or other portable heating appliances directly underneath them. Pull appliances out from under food-storage cabinets before using. Avoid storing food in cabinets under the sink, next to the dishwasher or refrigerator, or above the stove top.

Store dry pantry ingredients in opaque containers, or in windowless cabinets. Glass bottles and jars look attractive but allow light to enter and stale the contents.

Paper and cardboard packaging and thin plastic bags can impart off flavors to dry foods, and offer little protection from moisture, oxygen, and insects. Choose products that are packaged in tough plastic bags, or transfer foods from the original packaging to glass or plastic canisters.

Canned foods often have a strong flavor from the high temperature at which they're processed. They can be delicious; European connoisseurs prize the best and carefully age canned seafood and meats for several years.

Canned vegetables and fruits often include large amounts of salt, citric acid, sugar, and other additives to give flavor and maintain texture. Read labels before buying.

Refrigerate leftover canned foods in glass or plastic containers to avoid reactions between food, oxygen, and the exposed metal edge. If you keep food in the can, cover the opening with plastic wrap, not aluminum foil, which will corrode.

Mark the storage date on packages and cans, place new items behind old ones on the shelf, and use the oldest items first.

There's no reliable rule for predicting the shelf life of pantry foods. Properly prepared and stored foods will not become dangerous to eat while stored unopened. They slowly slide from edible to barely edible to inedible. Different people will define these stages differently. Manufacturers' expiration dates are usually conservative.

Taste long-stored foods for yourself, and use them quickly if they're edible. Once opened, any packaged food will deteriorate much faster.

Storing Foods in the Refrigerator and in the Freezer

The refrigerator and the freezer are appliances in which we chill or freeze foods that would quickly spoil at room temperature. They also extend the shelf lives of many pantry ingredients.

Refrigerators and freezers help us store foods longer by removing heat energy from them. This slows the chemical changes that cause staling and spoilage.

Most fresh ingredients and cooked foods require chilled storage to slow the growth of microbes that cause spoilage and food-related illness.

Some prefrozen vegetables and seafood can be of higher quality

than their fresh versions if they've been frozen within hours of the harvest and kept properly frozen until they're cooked.

Cooked dishes usually freeze better than their raw ingredients. Ice crystals cause tissue damage and juice loss in raw meats and fish, vegetables and fruits, but have less noticeable effects on cooked tissues.

Check refrigerator and freezer temperatures regularly with a thermometer, and adjust the thermostat if necessary. Clean the door gaskets and cooling coils regularly.

Keep the coldest refrigerator area between 32 and 35°F/0 and 2°C for especially perishable ground meats, fish, chicken, and milk. Lowering the temperature from 40°F/5°C to 35°F/2°C can double their shelf life.

Keep the freezer as cold as it will get, ideally 0°F/−18°C or lower.

Avoid habits that warm refrigerators or freezers. Open the doors as briefly and seldom as possible. Cool cooked foods at room temperature or in an ice bath before putting them in the appliance. Temperature variations gradually damage texture and flavor even in frozen foods that remain frozen.

Enclose foods in solid plastic or glass containers to minimize odor transfer among foods and the appliance air and walls. Use glass containers to store strongly flavored or colored foods, which leave persistent residues in plastic. If you use flexible plastic bags, choose standard thick-walled bags for freezer storage, or special bags for vacuum packing.

Minimize exposure to air within storage containers. Use the smallest possible container, or a flexible bag that you squeeze to the food's contours by hand or with a vacuum-packing machine. Press flexible plastic wrap or waxed paper onto the food surface, or coat with a thin layer of oil.

Allow dry spices or herbs, grains or flours to warm to room temperature before opening the package. Moisture in the air condenses on cold objects, and will damage food flavor.

FATS AND OILS

Fats and oils have many uses in the kitchen, from simply anointing with flavor and richness, to frying, to structuring cakes and pastries. Fats are solid at room temperature; oils are liquid.

There are many different fats and oils to choose among, with different flavors and consistencies. Unrefined oils, extracted from their source without removing all impurities, generally have more flavor than their refined equivalents.

Flavorful animal fats include butter from cow's milk and lard from pigs, and softer chicken, duck, and goose fats.

Lard is softer than butter and goes rancid more easily. Check labels and avoid hydrogenated lard, which is more stable but contains trans-fatty acids.

Flavorful plant fats include coconut, palm, and cocoa fats, and margarine, an imitation of butter made with vegetable fats.

Flavorful plant oils include olive, sesame, walnut, almond, and hazelnut oils. Their distinctive flavors are changed by heat, and best preserved when the oils are added at the end of cooking.

Olive oils vary widely in quality and price. "Extra-virgin" designation and price are no guarantees of quality. Good inexpensive oils are mild in flavor and right for cooking. Good expensive oils tend to be strongly flavored, sometimes pungent enough to make you cough, rich in antioxidants, and best used as a condiment.

Mostly flavorless plant oils include canola, corn, cottonseed, peanut, soy, safflower, and grapeseed oils. Vegetable shortening is a flavorless plant fat, created by chemical modification of refined vegetable oils. These neutral oils are good for frying foods without adding flavor.

Fats and oils slowly break down and become rancid. Exposure to light, warmth, and/or air causes them to develop stale, cardboard, paint aromas and a harsh taste.

Liquid oils are especially prone to rancidity, while solid fats are more stable.

Use the freshest fats and oils possible. Check use-by dates, and buy them in small quantities so they don't sit in your pantry for weeks or months.

Store fats and oils tightly sealed in a cool dark place. Refrigerate especially vulnerable tree nut oils and lard, and also butter and margarine, which contain traces of water and milk solids. Butter and margarine can last for several days at room temperature if protected from air and light, for example in a butter keeper that immerses the fat surface in water.

Wrap solid fats tightly to the surface, preferably with impermeable foil. Don't leave a gap between fat and wrap, where air can cause rancidity.

When using stored fats, scrape the surface layer away and discard it. This is where rancid flavors accumulate.

Taste oils and fats before cooking with them. Off flavors will get into the food, and are also a sign that the oil or fat will deteriorate further during cooking.

Refined and fresh oils tolerate higher frying temperatures than unrefined and stale oils. All fats and oils deteriorate and smoke at pan temperatures much above 400°F/200°C. Butter, margarine, and some vegetable shortenings contain other substances that lower their smoke point to around 350°F/175°C. For frying, choose shortening without added flavors and emulsifiers.

Home-rendered poultry and pork fat contain impurities that encourage rancidity. Wrap them closely, refrigerate or freeze them, and use them within a few weeks.

Keep oil left over from deep-frying only if it's still relatively light and thin, and has been strained to remove food particles. Discard if it's dark and viscous. Used or long-stored oils will smoke at a lower frying temperature than fresh oils.

Nonstick sprays combine a small amount of vegetable oil with emulsifiers and other chemicals that help prevent food from adhering to pan surfaces. Most sprays begin to brown and smoke at around 350°F/175°C.

THE FLAVOR PANTRY

Most pantry items are sources of flavor that make the foods we prepare more delicious.

Building and refining the flavor of a dish means adjusting the balance among the basic tastes and drawing on the flavor pantry to create a full, harmonious aroma.

Collect a broad palette of tastes and smells in your pantry, keep it easily accessible and organized, and use it actively and creatively. When a dish seems not quite right, when it "needs a little something," scan your collection, refresh your memory with tastes and sniffs, and imagine.

Salts

Salt is an essential seasoning for nearly all foods. It even heightens the flavor of sweets. Salt is a mineral—sodium chloride—and keeps indefinitely. It's sold in many different forms. Salt is also a defining ingredient in many prepared pantry foods, including soy sauce, miso, anchovy paste, and fish sauce.

Granulated table salts are sometimes fortified with potassium iodide, a mineral that helps prevent iodine deficiency diseases. They often include small amounts of a silicate anticaking agent, essentially a powdered sand, to prevent the crystals from sticking to each other.

Kosher salts and pickling salts do not include iodide or anticaking powders, and so will make a pickling brine without any cloudiness. They come in large, flat crystals that are easier for the cook to pinch, sprinkle, and see on the food surface when seasoning.

Sea salts are harvested from the ocean, as much ordinary salt is. They may be more or less refined. Moist sea salts include trace magnesium and calcium minerals that may provide a slight bitterness.

Rock salts are coarse and chunky, not necessarily pure enough for human consumption, used as a coolant in ice cream makers, and as a decorative bed on which to present shellfish and other foods.

Fleur de sel, or "flower of salt," is harvested from the surface of salt ponds in large, flat crystals. It's expensive and intended as a last-minute condiment, to provide visual appeal and a crunch as it dissolves into momentarily intense saltiness.

Seasoned or seasoning salts supplement basic saltiness with added flavors, including spices, herbs, monosodium glutamate, sugar, and smoke.

Colored salts combine sodium chloride with colored minerals, from red clays to black sands, that add little or no flavor. An exception to this rule is "black salt" from India, a light gray-pink and with a strong eggy smell.

Salt substitutes replace some sodium chloride with potassium chloride. They taste less salty and more bitter than salt.

All salts without added flavors taste about the same, especially in food. Exotic origins can be very interesting to the mind but don't register on the palate.

Different salts can differ importantly in their density, or how much a given volume weighs. A spoonful of table salt may weigh twice as much as a spoonful of flaky kosher salt, and produce double the saltiness when added to a food. Different brands of kosher salt may vary in the amount of salt per spoonful by more than a third.

Measuring salt correctly is one of the biggest challenges in cooking from recipes. Many recipes specify volumes of salt but not the kind of salt, and so don't really tell the cook exactly how much salt to use. It's always best to specify salt quantities by weight, not volume.

Try to make sure what kind of salt your recipe calls for if it uses volume measures. If you don't use the same kind of salt, then adjust for the difference in density. If the recipe doesn't specify salt brand, then start with a smaller volume and add more to taste. For salt brines, find a recipe that specifies either salt brand or weight.

Different people often experience the same level of salt differently. This can be a matter of perception, not just preference. Someone who likes a lot of salt may not be able to taste it as well as other people.

Get an idea of your salt sensitivity and take it into account when you cook. Season a dish with other people and compare your perceptions.

Curing salts are not salts for everyday kitchen use. They are a mixture of sodium nitrite, nitrate, and regular sodium chloride. They're used to make sausages and other cured meats, where nitrite and nitrate prevent the growth of botulism bacteria and preserve meat color.

Label curing salts clearly and use them carefully. The nitrites in curing salts are toxic in large amounts. They are sometimes dyed pink and called pink salt to distinguish them from table salt. Don't mistake pink curing salts for pink-colored specialty table salts.

Acids

Acids are substances that taste sour, or tart. They're a characteristic, balancing, and refreshing taste in almost all fruits, in fermented drinks and dairy products, and in many sauces and dressings.

Most food acids are just sour, with no aroma. The exception is acetic acid, which gives vinegar its characteristic smell.

Lemon and other citrus juices are the most common acid ingredient, but not well suited to the pantry because the fruits and their sour juices are perishable. Citrus juices are best squeezed fresh and added to a dish just before serving. They're usually damaged by cooking heat and deteriorate quickly in the refrigerator.

Verjus is the tart juice of unripe grapes, an uncommon alternative to citrus juices, and also perishable.

Vinegars are water solutions of acetic acid, and keep for years at room temperature. They come in different strengths. Standard malt, cider, and distilled vinegars are usually 5 percent acetic acid. Some Asian vinegars are 3 to 4 percent, while wine vinegars may be 7 percent.

Check vinegar labels for acetic acid contents before substituting vinegars in a recipe, and adjust quantities accordingly.

Vinegars often have complex tastes and smells because they're made by fermenting flavorful alcohols.

- **Cider, malt, wine, and sherry vinegars** taste like their sources.
- **Distilled vinegar** is pure acetic acid in water, and has no other flavors.
- **Balsamic vinegar** has a distinctive aroma, intense sweet-sour taste, and dark color thanks to its unique production method, which can take years. It comes in a very expensive original form, a cheap industrial imitation, and a number of grades in between.

- **Chinese black vinegar** is made from roasted fermented rice and is rich flavored and somewhat salty.
- **Japanese rice wine vinegar** is made from unroasted fermented rice and has a delicate flavor.
- **Flavored vinegars** are made by steeping various herbs or fruits in vinegar.

Dried acid fruits are pantry acids that keep for years and also provide some fruit flavors. Find them in ethnic markets.

- **Tamarind** is the soft, dark brown pulp of a tropical tree pod, sour and sweet and savory from browning in the sun, used in Indian and Mexican cooking.
- **Amchur** is powdered unripe mango, used in Indian cooking.
- **Sumac** is the powdered red fruit of the sumac bush; it's tannic as well as sour, and used in Middle Eastern cooking.

Pure acids, crystallized from fruits or fermentations, are handy for giving a simple acid accent to foods, with no aroma or added liquid. They're all available from suppliers for home brewing.

- **Ascorbic acid, or vitamin C,** is an antioxidant and especially valuable for preventing the discoloration of cut or pureed fruits and vegetables. It's much more effective than lemon juice or citric acid. Ascorbic acid is a pure form of the vitamin found in many fruits. If you want to use a vitamin C supplement in cooking, check the label to make sure that it doesn't include other nutrients or fillers.
- **Citric acid,** or sour salt, can often be found in the specialty or kosher section of supermarkets. It's a pure form of the acid found in lemons.
- **Malic acid** can be found in health-food stores. It's a pure form of the acid found in apples.

- **Tartaric acid, or cream of tartar,** is a pure form of an acid found in grapes and wines. It's frequently used in baking to make stable egg foams for meringues and cakes, and to react with baking soda to produce leavening carbon dioxide.

Sugars and Syrups

Sugars and syrups are crystalline and liquid sources of sweetness, the one taste that all humans enjoy from the moment they're born. Most are extracted from the fluids of various plants and trees.

Refined sugars are crystals of pure sucrose, washed free of all other plant residues. They provide simple sweetness.

Unrefined and partly refined sugars are sucrose crystals that retain a coating of molasses, the syrupy dark by-product of cooking down and crystallizing plant juices. Generally, the darker the color, the stronger the flavor, which is rich and complex.

Different forms of sugar have different densities, so that spoonfuls will weigh different amounts. In cooking it's the weight of sugar, not the volume, that counts.

If you substitute a different form of sugar for the kind specified in a recipe, check to make sure that you use the correct weight.

- **Table sugar,** pure granulated sucrose, may be made from sugarcane or sugar beets. Usually there's no difference, but beet sugar can sometimes have a slight off flavor.
- **Extra-fine, or baker's, sugar** is finely ground table sugar. The smaller crystals dissolve more rapidly into uncooked preparations such as meringues.
- **Confectioners', or powdered, sugar** is very finely ground sugar combined with a small percentage of cornstarch, and mainly

used to make icings. It's fluffy; substitute 1¾ volumes for 1 volume of granulated sugar.

- **Brown sugar** is granulated sugar with a fine coating of molasses syrup that makes the crystals cling together in a soft mass, and that can dry out on the shelf to form hard lumps. Standard brown sugar is manufactured by adding molasses to fully refined sugar.

- *To resoften brown sugar,* heat lumps in the microwave oven for 20 to 30 seconds at a time until soft, or seal them for some hours in a plastic bag with a piece of apple or slice of fresh bread.

- **Muscovado, turbinado, barbados, demerara, piloncillo, and whole sugars** are partly refined cane sugars that retain a coating of molasses from the original cane juice. They usually have stronger flavors than standard brown sugars.

- **Palm sugar and jaggery** are unrefined crystals from the sap of Asian sugar palm trees, coated with a brown molasseslike residue that's distinctively winey.

- **Date sugar** consists of ground dried dates, and includes tiny fragments of the fruit. It doesn't dissolve completely as other sugars do.

Syrups are concentrated water solutions of various sugars, usually glucose and fructose. Traditional syrups provide a range of distinctive aromas as well as some acidity. Thanks to their water content, larger volumes of syrup are usually required to substitute for granulated sugar.

- **Honey** is the nectar of flowers, concentrated and transformed by the honeybee into the original sugar syrup. "Varietal" honeys from specific plants have distinctive flavors. Honey contains fructose and glucose sugars instead of table-sugar sucrose. It is sweeter than table sugar volume for volume, browns faster when heated, and retains moisture better in baked goods.

Honey slowly crystallizes into a grainy paste when stored. Reliquefy it by warming gently.

- *Don't feed honey to children less than one year old.* They're susceptible to bacterial spores in it and can become very ill.
- **Most traditional syrups** are boiled-down plant saps. Darker colors mean more intense caramel flavors. Maple syrup, mainly sucrose, and birch syrup come from trees, cane syrup and sorghum syrup come from large grasses, and agave nectar, mainly fructose, comes from a cactuslike desert plant. Malt syrup is made from germinated barley grains; its primary sugar maltose is less sweet than sucrose or fructose.

  "Pancake syrup" and other imitations of maple syrup are made from corn syrup and artificial flavorings.
- **Molasses** is the dark, thick residue left from refining cane sugar into crystalline sucrose. Its flavor is strong and distinctive, less sweet than pure sugar, somewhat bitter and acid. Pomegranate molasses is the boiled-down juice of the pomegranate fruit, sweet and tart.
- **Corn syrups** are manufactured from cornstarch. They are part glucose sugar, part starchy thickener, so they provide the thickness of a concentrated sugar syrup with only modest sweetness. Unlike the other syrups they have no interesting flavor of their own and are often flavored with vanilla. They're a useful structural ingredient in baking and candy making.
- **High-fructose corn syrups** are corn syrups whose glucose has been partly converted into sweeter fructose.

Sugar substitutes come in two different types:

- **Intensive sweeteners** provide sweet taste in very small quantities and with few or no calories. Artificial intensive sweeteners include saccharin, aspartame, sucralose, and acesulfame. Rebaudiosides are natural sweeteners extracted from the stevia plant. All of these sweeteners except aspartame retain their sweetness when cooked. Aspartame can sicken people who have a genetic disease called phenylketonuria.

- **Bulking agents** provide the physical mass of sugar with fewer calories and with less sweetness. Xylitol, a bulking agent derived from plant fiber and sold in health-food stores, has a cooling effect when it dissolves on the tongue.

Savory Seasonings

Savoriness is the mouthfilling, mouthwatering taste found in concentrated meat broth, aged cheeses, tomatoes, and cooked mushrooms. It's also called by its Japanese name, *umami*. Savoriness is created mainly by an amino acid, glutamate, and partner substances called ribonucleotides.

MSG, or monosodium glutamate, is a crystalline powder that has a savory and salty taste. Despite its reputation for causing the "Chinese restaurant syndrome" of facial flushing and headache, numerous medical studies have found no evidence for this.

There are many ingredients and condiments that are especially rich in glutamate and its partners, and valued for their savory, mouthfilling quality. They include:

- Canned meat and vegetable broths, packaged demi-glace, concentrated meat extract, bouillon cubes;

- Cured anchovies and anchovy paste, Italian colatura, Japanese bonito flakes (katsuobushi), Asian fish and oyster sauces and shrimp pastes;
- Mushrooms, especially dried shiitakes and porcini, yeast pastes (Vegemite, Marmite), dried seaweeds, especially Japanese kombu;
- Worcestershire sauce, soy sauce, liquid amino acids (also from soy), miso, fermented black beans.

Soy sauce may include wheat as well as soybeans, and comes in several different types. Chinese brands are usually darker and stronger than Japanese brands. Tamari sauce is made with little or no wheat, "white" soy sauce with little soy.

Check soy sauce labels to make sure that the sauce has been fermented. Traditional and more flavorful soy sauce is made slowly by fermentation; "chemical" soy sauces are made very quickly using strong acids.

Bitter, Pungent, and Cooling Seasonings

Bitterness, pungency, and coolness are not especially pleasant sensations in themselves, but they provide a pleasing edge when combined with other flavors.

Bitterness is an important taste component of coffee, tea, and chocolate flavors, of quinine or tonic water, and in vermouth, Fernet-Branca, and other aperitif alcohols.

The main pantry sources for bitterness are bitter alcohols and preparations called bitters, extracts of spices and wood barks used mainly in cocktails. They have strong aromas in addition to the taste. Some Chinese teas are selected for their extreme bitterness.

Pungency is not a taste, but a feeling of burning irritation that can be pleasantly painful. It's produced by various chemicals in onions and garlic, in olive oil, and in a few plants that we use as pantry spices and as the basis for countless "hot sauces." There are several different kinds of pungency.

- **Pepper and ginger pungency** burns only the mouth or whatever body surface the food touches.

  White and black pepper, green peppercorns, chillis (many varieties of red "peppers," cayenne, paprika, pimientos), and ginger burn the mouth. Pepper pungency survives cooking.

- **Mustard pungency** burns the nose and lungs as well as the mouth. It's volatile and is carried on the breath and through the air. Cooking diminishes mustard pungency.

  Mustard seeds and their various preparations, horseradish root, and Japanese wasabi root all sting the nose and lungs.

  Wasabi powder is usually horseradish powder combined with green food coloring. Authentic fresh wasabi root is available in Japanese groceries; grate it just before using.

- *To avoid a coughing fit from excessive mustard pungency,* or to recover from one, inhale only through the nose and exhale only through the mouth.

- **Sichuan pepper pungency** is a buzzing, numbing sensation in the mouth, caused by Sichuan peppercorns, Japanese sansho powder and leaves, and Australian mountain pepper. It survives cooking.

All pungent flavorings can irritate the eyes and lungs when they're heated during cooking or dishwashing.

When handling chillis, wear protective gloves or be careful afterward to wash hands thoroughly with soapy water. Residual irritants on the fingers can burn whatever part of the body you touch next.

When cooking with pungent spices, turn on exhaust fans and open windows.

When cleaning cutting boards, knives, and containers, begin with cold water and scrape and rinse chilli residues gently down the drain with minimal splashing. This will minimize the creation of irritating vapors.

To relieve a mouth burning from hot chillis, sip a noncarbonated cool liquid. The irritants causing the burn can't be washed off, but lowering the mouth temperature reduces the pain. The prickling of strong carbonation increases it. To relieve chilli-burned skin, cool it with refrigerator-temperature objects or tap water. Don't use ice, which can cause cold-induced pain and injury.

Cooling is a sensation caused in the mouth by the menthol in peppermint and spearmint. It's especially evident when breathing in through the mouth. Pantry sources of menthol are mint extracts and mentholated candies.

Aromatic Spices and Herbs

Spices and herbs provide aromatic accents in cooking. There are dozens from all over the world to try out.

Spices are ideal pantry items. They're mainly plant seeds, barks, and roots, generally become more concentrated and intense when dried, and keep well.

Use whole spices whenever possible, and grind just before using. Once ground, spices lose aroma and stale quickly.

To deepen spice flavors, heat them briefly in a dry pan or in oil until they smell nutty.

Many herbs are much better fresh than dried. Herbs are green leaves and tend to lose aroma and become haylike with time.

Good dried herbs include bay laurel, oregano, rosemary, sage, savory, and thyme, all tough Mediterranean plants tolerant of dry conditions.

Store dried herbs and spices in airtight containers that are either opaque or kept in the dark.

Sample bottled spices and herbs when you've just bought them and then regularly afterward, and replace them when their aroma has faded. Whole spices keep well for about a year, but herbs and ground spices for only a few months.

Common herbs in cooking include carrot-family chervil, cilantro, dill leaf, and parsley; mint-family basil, marjoram, mints, oregano, rosemary, sage, and thyme; dried onions and garlic; lemon verbena and lemongrass; aniselike tarragon, and bay laurel.

Common aromatic spices in cooking include carrot-family anise, caraway, celery seed, coriander, cumin, dill, and fennel; tropical allspice, cardamom (green, white, black), cinnamon and cassia, clove, ginger and galangal, grains of paradise (a distant relative of cardamom), nutmeg and mace, star anise, turmeric, and vanilla; mainly pungent chillis, peppers (black, white, long, cubeb, green peppercorn), mustard and horseradish and wasabi, and Sichuan peppercorn and sansho from Japan; pinelike juniper berries; garlicky asafetida; dried citrus peels; sweet-smelling fenugreek and licorice; and nutty poppy seeds and sesame seeds.

Spice and herb mixes that give a distinctive regional flavor include quatre épices and bouquet garni from France, garam masala and panch phoran from India, shichimi from Japan, ras el hanout and chermoula from northern Africa, five-spice powder from China, and za'atar and zhug from the Middle East.

Flavored Ingredients and Flavor Extracts

Flavored ingredients and flavor extracts are means of infusing aromas into foods instantly, often just before serving. Most flavored ingredients are stable, but flavored oils are prone to rancidity. Keep them refrigerated.

Flavored oils, vinegars, alcohols, salts, and sugars are widely available and of variable quality. Make them yourself by infusing or mixing the unflavored base material with herbs, spices, citrus peels, and similar ingredients.

Be cautious when making flavored oils, beware of noncommercial flavored oils, and store all in the refrigerator. Deadly botulism bacteria are commonly found on plants, including herbs and spices, and thrive in the airless environment under room-temperature oil. Be sure your recipe addresses this hazard.

Commercial flavor extracts are concentrates and used in very small quantities. They're usually made with alcohol, and mix easily with water-based ingredients and sauces. Vanilla and almond extracts are the most common flavor extracts today.

Check extract labels carefully to see whether they were made from complex natural ingredients or from "flavors" or "flavorings," which indicates a simplified approximation of the natural ingredients. Approximated and artificial extracts are less expensive but often taste wrong.

Add extracts a drop or two at a time and taste the food to check intensity. Add toward the end of cooking so that aroma isn't cooked out and wasted.

Liquid smoke is a water extract of smoke, and it can be spray-dried to make smoke powder. Smoke itself contains cancer-causing chemicals, some of which may persist in extracts. If liquid smoke contains any sediment, let it settle and use only the liquid above it.

Alternatives to liquid smoke include smoked salts, smoked chillis (pimentón, chipotle), and black cardamom.

Hydrosols are water-based aroma extracts of herbs and other plant ingredients. They're easily diluted in water and are especially useful in flavoring drinks. Orange flower water and rose water are ancient examples from Middle Eastern cooking.

Essential oils of perfumery quality are increasingly available for kitchen use. They're highly concentrated and offer unusual nonfood aromas, including woods, leather, and tobacco. Most mix best with food oils and fats, but can also be dispersed in water-based sauces.

Cooking Alcohols

Alcohols are liquids that contain ethyl alcohol, a substance that yeasts produce from sugars during the fermentation of grape juice, cooked grains, and other materials. Alcohols include wines, beers, and sakes ranging from 4 to 15 percent alcohol, and distilled products—brandies, whiskeys, rums, vodkas—that may be 40 percent alcohol or more.

Alcohol itself is sweet and aromatic, but irritating at the high levels in distilled products. It also reacts with other ingredients during cooking to extract and create additional flavors.

Most alcohols carry other flavors, including acidity, sweetness, savoriness, and a wide range of aromas from the fermentation process and sometimes from added flavor ingredients.

Cooking wines are usually fortified to a minimum alcohol content around 18 percent; otherwise they would quickly spoil after opening. Madeira, marsala, sherries, and Chinese shaoxing rice wine share a nutty aroma thanks to controlled oxidation, which stabilizes the wine flavor against change during storage.

Refrigerate leftover table wines to prevent them from spoiling before you cook with them.

Cooking does not eliminate all alcohol from a dish made with wine or spirits. Stews and flambés may retain enough to cause adverse reactions in people who are sensitive to alcohol.

Brandy, rum, vodka, and other strong alcohols will ignite when hot and exposed to a flame.

Flambé with caution. Lower the pan heat and turn off the stove-top hood; otherwise the flames can be pulled into the hood filter.

It's easier to cook well when you have the right tools

3

KITCHEN TOOLS

t's easier to cook well when you have the right tools for the various tasks that cooking entails, the cleaning and cutting and mixing and holding and heating.

Some utensils and appliances are clearly better suited than others for particular tasks, but the choice of kitchen tools is also a personal matter, not dictated simply by performance. Some cooks are minimalists and take pride in doing the most with the fewest possible tools. Others are connoisseurs of gadgetry and enjoy amassing a collection that may be more shown off than employed. And most cooks just know what they like. Copper pans are very expensive and not *that* superior to aluminum, cast iron is a pain to maintain, clay pots are breakable. But I love the heft and luster of my one copper sauté pan, the years of seasoning on my cast iron, and the deeply saturated umber, sparkles of mica, and handmade roughness of my country French clay. These tools may not help me cook better, but they do help me cook with more pleasure.

To date there are no perfect pans that heat evenly, release foods instantly, clean with a swipe, and last forever. But utensils continue to evolve. The last few years have brought new ceramic pan materials that can tolerate direct stove-top heat. And there are now new families of pan coatings that don't break down into toxic materials when accidentally overheated, and that are getting better at preventing foods from sticking despite constant use and wear. Even minimalists can welcome a new generation of tools that are easier on the food, the cook, and the environment.

MEASURING TOOLS

When we cook, we combine ingredients and heat them until they've been transformed to our satisfaction. Proportions, cooking temperatures, and cooking times all affect the outcome.

Measuring tools are often helpful, and sometimes essential, to control food proportions and the heating process.

Scales are essential for cooking with precision. Weight is a direct measure of an ingredient itself. By contrast, the volume taken up in a measuring spoon or cup includes variable amounts of empty space. A teaspoon of granular salt can contain twice as much salt as a teaspoon of flake salt.

Weighing with a scale is also quicker and less messy than measuring volumes with cups and spoons.

Invest in a good digital scale that reads in grams, has a capacity of at least 1 kilogram (2.2 pounds), reads in increments of a tenth of a gram, and is accurate to 1 gram. Weigh and write down the weight equivalents of volume measures you use frequently—cups of water, spoons of salt—and use them to convert recipes that don't give weights.

Measuring cups and spoons indicate the volume of space taken up by a material and any air that comes along with it. Measuring cups for dry ingredients are usually made from opaque metal or plastic, and are meant to be filled level with the top edge. Measuring cups for liquids are usually transparent glass or plastic, marked in fractional quantities, and meant to be filled level with the appropriate mark.

Choose metal measuring spoons and cups that are rigid and won't dent.

Choose liquid measuring cups that are narrow and tall, so that small volume differences translate into large changes in the level of the ingredient. Laboratory-style graduated cylinders are ideal.

Thermometers measure the heat content of foods and various kitchen materials and appliances. They come in several types.

- **Instant-read thermometers** with moving needles rely on the expansion of metal with heat. They're inexpensive, slow to register the temperature, not very accurate, and require frequent checking for accuracy. Oven-ready versions can be left in a hot oven to measure its temperature or the temperature inside a roast.

- **Digital probe thermometers** have an electronic temperature sensor at the tip of the probe. They're inexpensive, faster, accurate, and require occasional checking. Oven-ready versions separate the probe and dial with a long wire, so that the probe can be in the closed oven while the dial stays on the stove top.

- **Infrared, noncontact, point-and-shoot thermometers** measure the infrared radiation emitted by an object's surface. They're moderately expensive, very fast, accurate, and require occasional checking.

- **Frying, candy, and chocolate thermometers** are specialty tools designed for particular temperature ranges, and often come with useful clips to attach them to pans. Many are liquid-filled glass tubes mounted on a metal scale. Make sure that the tube can't slide back and forth on the scale, a common defect that compromises accuracy.

Choose a digital probe thermometer to measure interior food temperatures and the temperature of hot water. Check its accuracy periodically by measuring the temperatures of crushed ice, 32°F/0°C, and boiling water, 212°F/100°C at sea level (subtract 2° from 212°F for every 1,000 feet of elevation, 1° from 100°C for every 300 meters of elevation).

Choose an infrared thermometer to measure the temperatures of cooking *surfaces*—oven walls, frying pans, pizza stones—and deep-frying oil, as well as different areas in the refrigerator and freezer. Don't use it with hot water, whose surface is significantly cooled by evaporation, or with glass, metal foil, or bare stainless steel pans, which give falsely low readings. To measure the temperature of a shiny pan, place a drop of oil on it and aim the thermometer at the oil.

Timers keep track of how long a cooking activity has been going on. It takes time for heat to transform food, and perhaps the most common cooking error is to heat food too long, or not long enough, simply because the cook gets distracted and forgets.

Use timers as a reminder to check food before it's overcooked and to measure the duration of cooking steps.

WORK SURFACES

Much kitchen work is done on countertops and tables, which are valuable long-term furnishings. We protect their surfaces with thin sheets of other materials.

Cutting boards are made from various kinds of wood, wood composites, and plastics. Wood cutting boards are easier on knife edges than plastic. Avoid glass boards. Both wood and plastic can be properly cleaned to eliminate harmful bacteria.

Keep several cutting boards to save the trouble of cleaning one repeatedly as you prepare a meal. It's important to avoid the possible contamination of one ingredient with another, and proper cleaning takes time.

Place a damp towel under a cutting board to prevent it from sliding around on the countertop as you work.

Large wood boards and stone slabs are useful and sometimes essential in baking and in candy and chocolate work. An oversize wood board makes an easily cleaned surface for kneading bread. Thin but weighty marble or granite slabs have a hard surface and high heat capacity. They help keep pastry doughs cold and flaky as they're made and shaped, and steadily cool melted chocolate and scalding-hot candy syrups so the cook can control their crystallization and texture.

Pastry cloth is a stiff, tightly woven cloth that can be dusted with flour and used as a nonstick surface on which to roll out pastry dough or nestle bread dough rising in a basket or bowl.

KNIVES AND OTHER CUTTING TOOLS

Food preparation often requires the cook to divide large masses into smaller pieces, from boning a leg of lamb to grating cheese. Sharp metal edges are the best tools for this task.

Knives come in many different materials, styles, and qualities. Read about the choices and try a number before investing in expensive ones. A large "chef's knife," a smaller paring knife, and a honing tool to re-align knife edges will serve most needs. Serrated edges are good for cutting fragile tomatoes and cakes and brittle bread crusts.

Choose knives made of stainless steel for the easiest care. Carbon steel is softer and easier to sharpen, but loses its edge faster, discolors, and can give a metallic taste to acidic fruits. Ceramic blades are brittle and difficult to sharpen.

Keep knife edges sharp. Dull knives compress and damage foods instead of cutting cleanly, and are more likely to glance off the food and cut a finger. Take a minute to hone knives before every use, and sharpen them once or twice a year. Sharpening, or grinding and reforming the edge, requires sharpening stones or devices, practice, and time. Some cookware stores offer sharpening services.

Handle knives with care. Don't hit the blade with other utensils or bowl or sink edges. Use cutting boards, and don't cut directly on stone or steel countertops. Wash knives by hand, dry them quickly and thoroughly, and store them in a sleeve guard, rack, or block to protect their edges.

Kitchen shears are handy for cutting various foods without a cutting board, including herb leaves from stems, whole chickens into parts, cooked leafy vegetables, and pizza slices.

Mandolines or Japanese slicers make it possible to cut vegetables and fruits rapidly into very thin slices and regular shreds. Use the plastic attachment or a towel to hold food pieces and avoid slicing fingers.

Peelers that remove the outer layer of vegetables and fruits have a small, suspended, flat blade that can be pushed or pulled along the food surface. They're hard to sharpen but inexpensive; keep several.

Mezzalunas consist of one or two curved blades that are quickly rocked back and forth on a cutting board to chop such ingredients as herbs and chocolate. The curved blades are hard to keep sharp.

Graters scrape foods into shreds, from coarse to fine. Box-shaped graters should be stiff enough not to deform when you press on their sides. Smaller, very sharp planelike graters cut extremely fine, delicate shreds. Use fine graters only at the last minute, especially with hard cheeses and truffles; the shreds give up their aroma quickly and often clump together again.

Specialized cutting tools include zesters for removing the aromatic but paper-thin pigmented skin of citrus fruits, apple corers, melon ballers and ice cream scoops, french-fry and cheese and hard-boiled-egg slicers, and the multiple-blade Jaccard for piercing and tenderizing meats.

Can openers cut through metal lids using a sharp metal edge. They're prone to dulling and failure, so keep inexpensive backups handy. When you open cans, examine can edges and carefully remove any metal shards before emptying the contents. Wash the opener's cutting edge well after each use, to prevent the growth of microbes and contamination of the next can.

Keep bandages and antibiotic cream in the kitchen. Knives, cutters, and can edges often cut cooks.

HAND TOOLS FOR GRINDING, MIXING, AND SEPARATING

Cooks can call on many simple hand tools to break foods down and either mix or separate their component parts.

Mortars and pestles pound foods, crushing them stroke by stroke. The pestle heads cover only a small area, so they require many strokes and long effort to get an even puree.

Ricers press cooked potatoes and other soft vegetable chunks in one motion directly through a perforated metal cup, producing an even puree with minimal disruption of the tissue.

Food mills simultaneously crush and strain soft foods when the hand-turned metal blade forces them through a perforated metal screen. Metal-on-metal contact at the central pivot can leave residues in the food; check the underside of the screen as you work and remove any gray material. Some new models have residue-free plastic pivots.

Hand-cranked coffee and spice grinders crush seeds into more even-size particles than the standard electric propeller grinder. They take longer but offer greater control.

Citrus juicers squeeze fluid and some solid cell debris out of the fruit's inner pulp.

Strainers, sieves, slotted spoons, skimmers, and colanders let fluids or pressed soft materials flow through their holes while retaining solids on the metal, metal wire, cloth, or plastic grid. Smaller holes produce a smoother fluid, but take longer to drain. Plastic colander surfaces shed water faster than metal.

Fine cheesecloth and paper or metal coffee filters are especially small holed strainers, good for separating whey from yogurt, or grit from shellfish cooking liquids or the water used to soak dried mushrooms. Most supermarket cheesecloth is too coarse and should be folded into double or quadruple thicknesses for these jobs. Use coarse cheesecloth to bundle herbs for easy removal from stocks and stews.

Salad spinners push water off washed leaf surfaces with centrifugal force. They're quick and effective but can bruise delicate leaves, which may be better tossed gently in a dry kitchen towel.

Wire whisks and egg beaters mix fluid ingredients with each other, and incorporate air bubbles into cream and eggs to make whipped cream, meringues and soufflés, and sabayons. Large balloon whisks and nested whisks within whisks speed air incorporation.

Siphons are metal canisters that force gases into cream, eggs, and other liquids, and turn them into foams. They're filled with the liquid ingredient and pressurized with cartridges of carbon dioxide or nitrous oxide. The gases dissolve in the liquid, and form bubbles in it when the liquid is released from the nozzle. Siphons can also carbonate water or pieces of fruit placed inside them.

Sprayers or atomizers break liquids up into tiny droplets that can be applied as a fine even mist to foods and surfaces. Use a water sprayer to make low-moisture pastry doughs, an oil sprayer to coat cooking surfaces, doughs, and salads with the thinnest possible film, and sprayers of bleach or vinegar solutions to sanitize countertops, cutting boards, and sinks.

ELECTRIC GRINDERS, MIXERS, AND PROCESSORS

Kitchen appliances with electric motors apply very strong physical forces to foods very rapidly. They make short work of otherwise time-consuming jobs, but their power can also damage foods.

Spice and standard coffee grinders chop hard seeds into particles with a whirling metal blade. They produce an uneven mix of particle sizes unless they're run long enough to reduce everything to a fine powder.

Burr grinders use a mechanism that essentially sieves particles as they're ground. They produce more even particles whose size can be adjusted.

Handheld electric mixers can whip cream and egg foams at much higher speeds than a manual whisk. The whisk attachments themselves are small and not ideal for incorporating a lot of air.

Stand mixers are versatile appliances that efficiently mix, whip, or knead large volumes of ingredients. They usually have attachments for grinding meat and milling grain, which are useful for making fresh hamburger meat and sausages, and especially flavorful breads and polenta.

Stand blenders draw ingredients into a small volume where their blades cut and shear, and mix them into an increasingly fine, silken puree or emulsion. They require caution when blending hot foods, whose steam can build up, force the lid off, and spew the food onto the cook and the kitchen.

To blend hot foods safely, fill the blender less than halfway, loosely cover the hole in the lid with a towel to allow steam to escape, start on low speed, and increase speed gradually.

Immersion or stick blenders turn a set of blender blades at the end of a shaft that can be inserted directly into cooking pots, serving bowls, and measuring cups. They're less efficient than a stand blender, and the cook has to move the blade around in the pot to pulverize all the contents. They usually can't make as smooth a puree as a stand blender, but they're much more convenient.

Food processors and their assorted blades can chop, grate, slice, pulverize, puree, and knead foods. Their broad, horizontal spinning blade doesn't work as well as the small, angled blender blades on small volumes of food, which can get thrown beyond or below the reach of the blade. And they can't produce as fine a puree as a blender, or an evenly sized chop.

Juicers grind all kinds of food into a pulp, then strain them to separate the solid fibers from the fluids. Some juicers can make fine-textured nut butters.

HANDLING TOOLS

The most versatile tools for handling foods are the hands. Fingers can mix ingredients with great thoroughness, provide immediate sensory information about doneness, consistency, and coverage, and place foods precisely on the plate. To use the hands but avoid direct contact with food, wear disposable thin gloves made of polyethylene, vinyl, nitrile, rubber, or latex. Latex offers the best touch sensitivity but can cause allergic skin reactions.

Kitchen towels, pot holders, and thick gloves insulate hands from hot pots and pans. Cloth hand guards can cause burns if they get wet, and ignite when exposed to flame. Rubberlike silicone pot holders and gloves repel water and are slower to burn.

Choose handling tools with long handles to keep fingers away from hot pans, burners, and grills.

Use spoon rests or small plates to hold handling tools on the stove top between uses and reduce cleanup.

Spoons stir liquids or small solid pieces, and hold small amounts for tasting or transferring. Ladles are better designed for transferring large volumes. Spoons made of wood, plastic, or silicone don't change the food temperature as much as metal spoons do, and don't get as hot to the touch, but they can retain food flavors and transfer them to another dish.

Spatulas, palette knives, and scrapers support, scrape, stir, spread, and fold liquid and semiliquid foods. Spatulas and palette knives support broad solid pieces of food and lift them from cooking surfaces. They're best for gentle handling because they don't put direct pressure on the food, though the cook can use them to exert pressure and improve the contact between food and pan. Plastic spatulas don't scratch nonstick surfaces, but they quickly wear into a rough edge at the tip, and will melt if left perched on a hot pan. Silicone spatulas can tolerate temperatures up to 450°F/230°C.

Forks impale pieces of food so that they can be moved. Piercing food causes local damage, which may result in visible holes and slight juice loss. Impaling a delicate material such as cooked fish may break it apart.

Tongs and chopsticks pick up solid foods by squeezing them from two sides. The squeezing pressure may break the delicate structures of such foods as cooked fish, fried crusts, and softened vegetables.

Tweezers, forceps, and needle-nose pliers grip small objects and are useful for the precise placement of delicate ingredients and for removing small bones from fish.

Skewers and toothpicks provide a handle for solid food pieces, and can hold pieces together (the legs on a whole chicken; pieces of meat and vegetables in shish kebab). They're also handy for probing the insides of cakes and custards to see whether they're cooked through.

Brushes spread thin coating films of fluid onto foods and cooking utensils. Brush bristles often trap and soak up food residues that can become rancid between uses. After each use, rub brush bristles vigorously in hot soapy water, then rinse them well and dry them quickly. Brush bristles made with rubberlike silicone are heat resistant and can be cleaned in the dishwasher.

Funnels direct a broad flow of liquid into a narrow flow. Use them for filling bottles and other containers that have a small neck. They may be metal or plastic, and the handiest have a grooved shaft that allows air to escape easily from the container as it fills.

Bulb basters and pipettes exploit air suction to draw up liquid from a small space and place it somewhere else. Use them to draw meat juices up from underneath the fat in a roasting pan, or to remove vinegar from under the floating "mother" in a vinegar barrel.

Gravy or fat separators are medium-size containers with a side spout projecting from the very bottom. When you pour the pan juices from a roast into them and wait a few minutes, fat floats to the top and the meat juices sink to the bottom, where they can be separated off through the spout.

FOILS, WRAPS, AND PAPERS

Kitchen foils, wraps, and papers are thin sheets of material for protecting food surfaces during storage or cooking.

Kitchen foil is made from aluminum, a soft metal that conforms to food surfaces, blocks contact with air, conducts heat well, and tolerates relatively high heat. Very high grill heat can weaken and damage foil.

Use foil to fine-tune heating in the oven. Foil reflects heat radiation. Place loosely over food in the oven, or on the rack above or below, to shield it from the heat of the oven surfaces while allowing the gentler heat of the air to continue the cooking.

Place foil on top of grills and pans to superheat them by reflecting escaping heat back onto them. A sheet on the charcoal grill as the coals reach their maximum heat will turn food residues into ash. A sheet on a heating griddle or wok will make it significantly hotter than it could otherwise get.

Don't use foil to wrap acidic foods or cover steel or cast-iron pots. Aluminum corrodes in contact with acid or with nonaluminum metal containers, develops holes, and dissolves into the food. Insulate foil from direct contact with corrosives using a layer of plastic wrap or waxed paper.

Plastic wraps and preformed plastic storage bags are petroleum products, usually polyethylene, and often include trace substances that can migrate into fatty and oily foods. Some have an unpleasant smell. They tolerate boiling water, but break down and generate toxic fumes at oven temperatures.

Plastic wraps conform more tightly to a food surface than foil, but aren't as strong an air and odor barrier. Thick-walled freezer bags are better air barriers than thin wraps. When available, polyvinyl chloride (PVC) and polyvinylidene chloride (PVDC) plastics are much better oxygen barriers than polyethylene, but carry even higher environmental costs.

To reduce cork taint, the off flavor of a wine with an infected cork, gently stir a piece of plastic wrap and the wine together for a few minutes. The plastic will absorb the off flavor.

Plastic vacuum-pack and "boil-in" bags are made from plastics that tolerate boiling water. They are denser and tougher than storage bags, more effective air and odor barriers, and are useful in controlled low-temperature cooking (sous vide).

Roasting and oven bags are made from nylon and can tolerate oven temperatures between 300 and 400°F/150 and 200°C. They contain a food and its aromas while transmitting heat or microwave radiation from the oven. Foods brown and crisp slowly in oven bags due to the moderate cooking temperature and moist atmosphere inside the bag.

Parchment paper is made from plant fibers treated with sulfuric acid and silicone to make it stiff, water resistant, and tolerant of oven temperatures up to 450°F/230°C. Use it to line cake pans and baking sheets, as a floating cover to control evaporation during braising, and to bake individual servings of foods in packets (en papillote).

Waxed paper is tissue paper impregnated with paraffin, which repels water and melts like candle wax at moderate temperatures. Use it for wrapping foods or as a temporary surface on which to place sticky or oily items.

Butcher paper is a paper layered with a water-repellent plastic lining, used for wrapping raw meats and fish.

Brown or kraft paper protects surfaces during the butchering of meats and other messy procedures, but contains manufacturing residues and should not be left in prolonged contact with food. Don't use brown paper bags for cooking microwave popcorn or anything else.

MIXING CONTAINERS, STORAGE CONTAINERS, AND RACKS

Mixing and working bowls are usually made of glass, ceramic, stainless steel, or plastic.

Glass and ceramic bowls are heavy and move around less on the countertop than other bowls do, but they're brittle and breakable. They heat up and cool down slowly.

Stainless steel bowls are light and rugged, and transfer heat quickly.

Plastic bowls are light and rugged, and transfer heat slowly. Their surfaces are more easily scarred than ceramic or metal, can absorb food odors and pigments, and tend to retain oils and soaps.

To minimize bowl movement when working, place a moist kitchen towel between the bowl and the countertop.

Storage containers are usually plastic or glass. The most versatile can be moved directly between the freezer or refrigerator and the oven.

Plastic containers absorb flavors and pigments from hot foods and are harder to clean than glass.

Insulated plastic picnic coolers are invaluable shopping tools. Use coolers to provide temporary cold storage for fish and shellfish, ice cream, and other delicate perishables when you transport them from the store.

Racks are flat frameworks of wire or metal bars that support containers and foods and allow air to circulate across their bottom surfaces. Racks air-cool foods more evenly than solid sheet pans or countertops. They prevent crisply baked or fried surfaces from trapping the food's inner moisture and getting soggy.

POTS AND PANS

Pots and pans are the containers in which we heat foods. They're available in many different materials and designs.

Try to accumulate a range of pan shapes and sizes so that you can find good matches for the kind of cooking you like to do. Tall pots are good for boiling and steaming, broad pots are good for concentrating liquids, straight-sided skillets for braising, slope-sided pans for sautéing, sideless griddles for flipping, hemispherical woks for stir-frying, flat sheet pans for baking.

Pan size strongly influences the cooking process. A pan that's too small or large for its burner won't heat evenly. A pan that's too small for its contents won't heat its contents fast or evenly enough for a good result. On a frying pan that's too large for its contents, the bare areas can scorch and spoil the flavor.

Avoid metal pans with plastic or wooden handles that can't tolerate oven temperatures. A number of meat, fish, and grain dishes are best started on the stove top and then finished in the same pan in the oven.

Heat diffusers help even out and moderate heat from the burner before it gets to the pot or the pan.

Lids help to control the movement of heat and food moisture out of the pot.

Perforated spatter guards intercept much of the oil spatter generated during frying, while allowing moisture to escape so that the pan temperature remains high and the food can brown.

Foods frequently stick to pots and pans during cooking. High heat causes food proteins and carbohydrates to form bonds with the pan surface.

Sticking is desirable when it leaves a flavorful residue in the pan that can be turned into a sauce.

Sticking is undesirable when the food can't be lifted from the pan without damaging its structure or appearance. This is mainly the case with delicate eggs and fish.

Sticking is reduced on grill-like, dimpled, and irregular pan surfaces that reduce direct contact between food and pan. They also reduce browning and flavor development.

Nonstick coatings are plastic or hybrid materials applied to pans that resist forming bonds with foods. They're not as durable as metals or ceramics, degrade with the stresses of heating and scraping, eventually lose their nonstick properties, and sometimes flake off into the foods cooked in them.

Silicone is a rubberlike material that is made into flexible, nonstick, easy-release baking pans and baking-sheet liners.

Read pan instructions carefully for safe temperature limits. Teflon and related fluorocarbon coatings decompose into toxic gases at temperatures above 500°F/260°C. Silicone degrades in the same temperature range, but without releasing toxic gases. Newer composite ceramic-silicone surfaces are safe to 800°F/430°C.

Handle nonstick pans and liners gently and carefully. Don't leave them on heat unattended, or use in high-temperature broiling or recipes that call for the pan to be heated until smoking. Avoid sharp-edged metal spatulas and abrasive cleaners.

Ceramic Pots and Pans

Earthenware, stoneware, and glass are brittle ceramic materials, and conduct heat poorly and slowly. This means that they heat up unevenly, and may crack if placed directly on a burner or moved from the oven to cold water. Once hot, they release heat to the food slowly and evenly. Their surfaces normally don't cause color or flavor changes in foods.

Glass transmits high oven heat to foods faster than opaque ceramics, because it's transparent to heat radiation as well as to light.

Have artisanal pots tested to see whether they release lead. Some traditional clays and glazes are still made with lead-containing minerals that can cause serious illness.

Use ceramic pots for baking and braising in even oven heat, for keeping foods warm after cooking and when they're served, and for refrigerating and reheating.

Use low heat with ceramics on the stove top, and a metal heat diffuser to spread burner heat over the entire bottom surface. Some new ceramic pans tolerate direct burner heat without cracking, but most cannot.

Use unglazed baking stones to bake free-form breads and pizzas. They conduct heat evenly and absorb dough moisture to speed the crisping of the bottom crust. Glazed surfaces heat well but don't absorb moisture.

A cloche is a combination baking stone and domed cover, which can make an enclosed oven within the oven, trap steam from bread dough, and produce an airier bread with a glossy, crackly crust.

Metal Pots and Pans

Metals are durable materials and conduct heat faster than ceramics, but can affect food flavor and color.

Aluminum is lightweight and a very good heat conductor, properties that make it a good all-around choice for most cooking tasks. Its surface reacts with acidic and sulfur-containing foods to produce off flavors and colors. Anodized aluminum has been treated to form a less reactive ceramiclike surface layer of aluminum oxide.

Copper is heavy and a superb conductor, ideal for heating foods quickly and evenly. But its surface tarnishes in the air and releases metallic-tasting copper into acidic foods. The traditional tin lining applied to copper pots is fragile and not easy to replace. Most copper cookware is now lined with stainless steel. It's expensive.

Cast iron is heavy and a relatively poor heat conductor, a combination that makes it excellent at maintaining its temperature once it's heated. Its surface rusts and causes off flavors in some foods unless it's protected by a layer of enamel (a ceramic material) or by seasoning to produce a resinlike protective layer. Some cast-iron pans are now sold preseasoned.

To season a cast-iron pan, clean and dry it thoroughly, coat with a thin layer of cooking oil, heat over a high burner until it smokes, then cool and wipe out excess oil. After using the pan, wipe it as clean as possible, use minimal water, detergent, and scouring to remove any residue, dry thoroughly, and burnish with a small amount of oil.

Carbon steel is a softer relative of cast iron that's formed into thinner sheets. It's also a relatively poor heat conductor and prone to rusting, but inexpensive and used in woks and restaurant sauté pans. Season and clean carbon steel as you do cast iron.

Stainless steel is a poor heat conductor, but its surface doesn't tarnish or produce off flavors. It's almost always used in combination with other metals that heat more evenly.

Composite pots and pans combine two or more materials to provide good heat conductivity and a relatively unreactive surface in the same utensil. Most have either an aluminum or copper base covered by stainless steel.

Choose composite pots whose conductive material extends up into the sides. A conductive base plate alone will scorch foods along its outer edge.

Heat is the essential but invisible ingredient in cooking

4

HEAT AND HEATING APPLIANCES

Heat is the essential but invisible ingredient in cooking, the one that we can't easily measure out with a scale or spoon. It's what we add to raw foods to transform them into safe, nourishing, tasty dishes. Heat is a form of energy, and it's always on the move, flowing out of foods even as we pour it in.

It's important to add the right amount of heat to the foods we cook. Too little won't transform them enough, and too much turns them curdled, dry, tough, or burned. But it's tricky to get heat right. The appliance settings that we usually rely on are often inaccurate, and sometimes irrelevant to the heating that actually goes on.

Some years ago I decided that I'd been burned often enough by bad recipes and my own bad assumptions. I equipped myself with a couple of reliable aids: a digital instant-read thermometer for measuring temperatures inside foods, and a point-and-shoot infrared thermometer for measuring the temperatures of food and utensil surfaces. Then I started to scrutinize my cooktop and oven and pots, and follow the flow of heat as I cooked.

What I learned surprised me and helped me work with heat more effectively. Low-power electrical and induction burners can heat foods faster than high-power gas, because more of their energy goes into the pot and less into the kitchen air. Foods can scorch in an oven set to a moderate temperature, because the oven's heating elements superheat their vicinity when they cycle on to maintain the temperature. A pot of stew in a low oven may cook calmly and gently or boil violently, depending on whether the lid is ajar so that evaporation can cool the contents, or closed so that the heat just builds and builds.

Try exploring the temperature landscape of your kitchen as you cook foods in different ways. You'll learn a lot about how heat works and how to control it better, and you'll know through your own eyes and nose and fingertips, not just through the words in a book.

HEAT AND TEMPERATURE

All change in the world is driven by energy.

Heat is the penetrating form of energy that moves into and through foods. It transforms foods by agitating their molecules, breaking up some structures and creating new ones. When cooked foods cool down, they lose the heat energy that transformed them, but they remain transformed.

Temperature is a manifestation of the heat energy in a material, whether a food, a frying pan, or a gas flame. The higher the temperature of a pan or pot of water, the more heat energy it has to pour into a food, and the more change it causes.

We measure temperature with thermometers, and using one of two different scales: degrees Fahrenheit or degrees Celsius. One Celsius degree equals 1.8 Fahrenheit degrees. The freezing point of water is set at 32° on the Fahrenheit scale, 0° on the Celsius scale. The boiling point of water at sea level is 212°F or 100°C (and lower by about 2°F/1°C for every 1,000 feet/300 meters of elevation).

The boiling point of water is the one visible temperature landmark that can be recognized without a thermometer. Water at the boiling point constantly forms and releases visible bubbles of steam. Its temperature remains constant while it bubbles because steam formation soaks up all the heat energy coming from the burner.

Cooks do most of their heating in three temperature ranges.

- **Temperatures well below the boiling point of water,** between 130 and 160°F / 55 and 70°C, cause just enough change to kill most microbes and firm delicate eggs, meats, and fish without drying and hardening them.

- **Temperatures around the boiling point of water,** 212°F/100°C, provide enough energy to kill most microbes, soften vegetables, and set doughs and batters. But they dry out and harden eggs, meats, and fish.

- **Temperatures well above the boiling point,** 300°F/150°C and above, crisp food surfaces and cause the development of brown colors and rich flavors.

Precise temperature measurement and control are important in cooking meats, fish, eggs, chocolate, and candies, where a degree or two can mean a noticeable difference in the quality of the result.

Temperatures in this book are rounded off to the nearest 5°F when precision is not important, to make them easier to remember. They're specified to the degree when a degree makes a difference.

HOW HEAT MOVES
IN COOKING

Heat energy always flows from areas of high heat to lower heat. It flows into foods in two basic ways.

Contact heat transfers energy to food by direct contact with a hot surface or with hot water, oil, steam, or air. Hot air heats foods slowly because it's much less dense than other materials. We can safely put a hand in a hot oven for a few seconds, but not into hot water or oil.

Radiated heat transfers energy to food from a distance, by invisible light called infrared radiation. This is the heat we feel when we hold a hand above a hot frying pan or sit in the sun. All objects, even cold ones, radiate at least some heat energy. Materials hot enough to glow visibly, including the sun, flames, coals, and electrical elements, are radiating large amounts of heat.

We sometimes cook foods with contact heat and radiated heat at the same time. In an oven, the heating elements and walls all radiate heat energy, and may transfer more heat to food than the hot oven air does.

Foods cook through when heat from their surface is conducted to their center. With the exception of microwave ovens, heating devices heat food surfaces, and the food surfaces in turn heat their interiors.

We usually pour heat energy onto food surfaces faster than it can be conducted to the center. This is why we can use 3,000°F/1,650°C coals to heat a steak to a crisp, brown 500°F/260°C surface and a moist 130°F/55°C interior.

We cook more evenly when we match surface heating with heat conduction through the food. This is one benefit of slow, low-temperature cooking.

Heat moves out of pots and foods during cooking whenever they're hotter than their immediate surroundings. A pot on the stove top is hotter than the air above it and gives the air some of the heat that it absorbs from the burner.

Heat moves out of foods or hot liquids during cooking whenever they evaporate moisture. Evaporation absorbs and carries energy away from the food or liquid, and cools it. A moist roast or a water bath in the oven will stay much cooler than the hot air around it.

HEAT FROM KITCHEN APPLIANCES

Kitchen cooktops and ovens provide heat energy from several different sources.

Gas flames radiate the heat produced when oxygen in the air breaks down the natural gas molecules into carbon dioxide and water. The flames themselves burn at around 3,000°F/1,650°C.

Electrical elements conduct and radiate heat produced from the movement of their electrons when they're energized by electrical current. They can reach about 2,000°F/1,100°C.

Halogen elements are specialized lightbulbs that radiate heat produced by wire filaments when they're energized by electrical current. Halogen gases in the bulb help the filaments burn hotter and longer than ordinary lightbulbs. Halogen elements can reach temperatures above 1,000°F/540°C.

Induction elements heat with radio waves that energize the electrons in iron-containing pans placed on them.

Microwaves are radio waves that heat foods by directly energizing the food molecules.

Heating power is measured in BTUs and watts. The heating power of gas appliances is rated in BTUs, electrical appliances in watt-hours, or watts for short. One thousand watts is the equivalent of 3,400 BTUs. Most household electric cooktops are rated at the equivalent of 3,000 to 5,000 BTUs, most gas burners at 9,000 to 15,000 BTUs, and high-powered commercial burners at 35,000 BTUs and above.

Don't rely on power ratings to judge the cooking performance of a cooktop or oven.

Low-power electric appliances often heat foods faster than higher-powered gas burners because they're more efficient. Much more of their heat output goes into the food, and less into the kitchen air.

Thermostats are electrical devices that set and maintain ovens and other appliances at a specific temperature.

Check the accuracy of your appliance thermostats regularly with a thermometer. Find out what thermostat settings correspond to a few temperature landmarks, and adjust your cooking settings accordingly.

STOVE-TOP BURNERS

Most stove-top burners heat pots and pans by both direct contact and heat radiation.

Burners waste a lot of energy. More than half the energy of a gas flame escapes around the sides of the pot and heats the kitchen instead. Electrical elements waste about a third of their energy. Induction cooktops are by far the most efficient. They waste about a fifth of their energy.

Cover pots and pans with lids as they heat up to heat them more quickly and efficiently, and to a higher temperature than usual. Lids prevent them from immediately losing much of their heat to the kitchen air.

Gas burners are easiest to control. The flame size can be adjusted instantly and judged by eye.

Electric burners, both exposed metal coils and recessed halogen bulbs, change their heat output more slowly in response to turning the dial, and the change is usually not visible except for the position of the dial.

To lower the heat instantly when cooking on an electric burner, simply lift the pan off the burner.

Induction burners can change their heat output instantly, but with no visual indicator except the position of the control dial. They also require the use of pots whose base includes magnetically active steel or iron, or a separate metal disk that acts as such a base for aluminum or copper pots.

HOT-AIR OVENS

Kitchen ovens are heated metal boxes that in turn heat foods placed inside them.

Conventional ovens heat their air and walls either by a gas flame from underneath, or by electrical elements underneath or within the box. The heating elements and walls radiate their heat toward the air and food, and the hot air heats the food by colliding directly with it.

Ovens can be tricky to cook in. Their effective temperature only occasionally coincides with the temperature you set the thermostat to. A pan of food receives different amounts of heat from the air, the walls, and the heating elements themselves, which cycle on and off and can scorch foods at moderate thermostat settings.

Take time to learn the idiosyncrasies of your oven. All ovens heat unevenly, and have hot and cold spots. Use an infrared thermometer to spot-check temperatures. Use a digital oven thermometer to see how the temperature fluctuates when the heating elements cycle on and off.

Gas ovens are vented to allow the escape of water vapor and carbon dioxide generated in the flame. They allow cooking moisture to escape as well, which helps promote the drying and browning of food surfaces.

Electric ovens don't generate heating gases, are more tightly sealed than gas ovens, and retain cooking moisture better. This is an advantage in baking breads, and a factor that speeds the cooking of other foods.

Convection ovens are gas and electric ovens with a fan that forcibly circulates the hot air in the oven. Forced-air circulation evens out heat throughout the oven, increases the rate at which the hot air collides with the food, and speeds cooking substantially.

Broilers are gas flames or electrical elements arranged in ovens to heat foods directly from above, over a distance of a few inches. They vary widely in heat output and cooking rates.

MICROWAVE OVENS

Microwave ovens heat foods with radio-wave energy, which foods absorb and turn into heat energy. Microwaves are not a form of food irradiation or radioactivity. They do not cook from the inside out.

Microwaves pass through nonmetal containers and penetrate foods

to the depth of about an inch. By contrast ordinary direct heating and heat radiation heat containers first, then the food surface, from which the heat is then slowly conducted into the food interior.

Microwave ovens heat more quickly and efficiently than other appliances because the radio-wave energy penetrates and is absorbed directly by the food, not by the air or the container.

Microwave ovens usually offer less direct and precise heat control than conventional ovens because the power output of most ovens is fixed. The cook can only set when and how often the microwave generator turns on and off. Newer microwave ovens offer truly adjustable power settings and can heat more gradually and gently.

Food quantities affect microwave cooking more than conventional cooking. Microwave ovens take significantly longer to cook larger quantities of food, because the fixed output of microwave energy is being absorbed by more food material and its heating power is diluted.

Multifunction or hybrid ovens combine electrical elements, convection fans, and microwaves to cook large pieces of food especially quickly. Some produce best results with built-in heating programs for different kinds of food.

COUNTERTOP APPLIANCES

Small heating appliances usually offer the advantage of heating more efficiently or with less supervision than the stove top or oven.

Electric kettles boil water faster and more efficiently than any stovetop burner, and shut off automatically.

Electric skillets have a thermostat for setting and maintaining the cooking temperature.

Pressure cookers have tightly fitted lids that retain steam and build up pressure. They cook foods especially quickly at temperatures around 250°F/120°C, well above the boiling point of water on the stove. They're available as self-powered countertop appliances, or as specialized pots for stove-top use.

Countertop or toaster ovens are small electrical ovens that heat up quickly to cook small amounts of food. Small ovens frequently scorch foods even at low oven settings because the electrical elements that heat the oven are very close to the food and get very hot.

Slow cookers heat and hold foods at temperatures somewhat below the boil, and can be left unattended for many hours.

Choose a slow cooker with an adjustable thermostat to make moist braises and stews. Models with fixed high and low settings usually over-cook meats.

Rice cookers automatically heat rice and other dry grains to the boil, maintain a simmer until the food has absorbed all the water, then reduce the heat to keep the cooked food warm. They're reliable, convenient, and can also make porridges and more elaborate grain dishes.

Immersion circulators are a combination of a thermostat, heater, and water pump. Placed in a pot or tub of water, they keep the water at a set temperature for precision low-temperature bath cooking, which produces perfectly done meat, fish, and eggs.

Water ovens are kitchen water baths, a specialized kind of slow cooker that you fill with water. Foods are enclosed in plastic bags and then immersed in the water, whose temperature is set with the oven thermostat. Like immersion circulators, water ovens make it possible to heat meat, fish, and eggs at low cooking temperatures to produce the exact doneness desired. Water ovens that don't actively circulate the water won't heat as precisely or quickly as an immersion circulator.

Deep fryers heat oil to temperatures well above the boiling point of water, high enough to crisp and brown foods. Deep-frying is easily done in an ordinary pot, but deep fryers offer thermostatic temperature control and the convenience of a draining basket and container for oil storage.

Choose a deep fryer with a high power and/or efficiency rating. The faster a fryer can recover its temperature after cold food is added to the oil, the quicker the food fries and the less oil it absorbs.

Indoor grills cook foods on metal bars that may be heated directly or that suspend the food above an electrical heating element.

Clamshell grills press the food between two heated surfaces. They heat foods nearly twice as fast as a frying pan.

Food dryers provide controlled heat at temperatures that are below the minimum setting of most ovens, but are better for removing moisture without actually cooking.

Gas torches are useful touch-up tools for quickly applying high browning heat to meats, fish, and such sweet dishes as crème brûlée. They're also good for starting charcoal fires quickly. Use a torch sparingly, to avoid scorching and leaving distasteful gas residues on the food.

Choose an inexpensive hardware-store torch kit that includes a flame-spreading attachment for broader coverage.

Hair dryers and heat guns can dry out food surfaces and keep sugar work warm.

OUTDOOR GRILLS AND SMOKERS

Outdoor grills offer controlled versions of cooking with fire, either with glowing charcoal or with burning natural gas. Electric grills heat with glowing metal elements. Covered grills offer more control over heating than open, hibachi-style grills.

Choose a cooker with a large cooking area for barbecuing or slow-cooking roasts, so that the meat can be kept far away from the high radiant heat of the coals or flame.

Choose a cooker with a large dial thermometer in the lid, so that you can monitor the temperature of the closed chamber at a glance.

Charcoal grills can brown and deeply flavor food surfaces in a matter of seconds, or slowly and gently imbue them with a distinctive smoky aroma of smoldering charcoal and wood. They cook mainly by direct heat radiation if the grill is uncovered, by a combination of direct radiation and hot air movement if it's covered.

Gas grills use aroma-free gas flames to heat the air and metal or ceramic surfaces, which then reradiate their heat to the food. Gas grills can't achieve the extreme temperatures possible on a charcoal grill, and require the addition of hardwood chips or burning of the food's own juices to produce distinctive aromas.

Electric grills cook over glowing metal rods, and don't provide charcoal-level heat or aromas.

Rotisserie attachments rotate large pieces of meat on a motorized spit. They have two advantages: they cause juices to cling and cook onto the meat surface rather than dripping off; and they expose the meat to short bursts of high surface-browning heat, then longer periods of low heat to cook it through gently.

Smokers cook foods slowly and gently with hot, smoky air. They shield food from the direct heat of coals or heating elements.

Turkey fryers are portable high-power gas burners for use outdoors. They're handy for high-heat wok cooking and any kind of frying that generates obnoxious fumes and spatter.

5

COOKING METHODS

There are many ways to cook an egg or a steak or a potato, and countless variations on each of them. A recipe will specify one way, usually without much detail. "Simmer for 10 minutes." "Grill for 5 minutes, then turn and continue for 4 minutes." "Bake at 400° until done."

Following directions may give us a good egg or potato, but it doesn't help us learn from what we're doing and adjust to get an even better result. Exactly how hot is a simmer, or does it not matter? Should I do anything different if my steaks are a little thinner than the recipe calls for? Is there something I can do to get my baked potato skin to come out crisp instead of leathery?

These are the kinds of questions that I've been asking for thirty years, and still ask pretty much every day I'm near the kitchen. I've tried to pack these pages with good general information and answers, but they're far from being the last word. I hope they'll encourage you to ask many more questions about what's going on in your own kitchen with the foods you care about. That's how you'll develop a deeper understanding of what you're doing, and cook with ever better results.

This chapter describes simmering, grilling, baking, and the other basic methods that we use for heating foods. It summarizes the ways of transferring heat that underlie these methods, how they work, what they're good and not so good at doing, and keys to getting the best results with them. Later chapters will refer you to sections of this chapter when they apply directly, or will build on this chapter to provide more detailed guidance for particular foods.

MEASURING

All cooking starts with the measurement of ingredients and temperatures, even if it's just by eye and touch. Sometimes precision isn't important, and sometimes it's essential. A few drops more or less of water won't make a difference in a stew, but it will in a pastry dough.

Have a good set of measuring tools: a digital scale for weights, rigid cups and spoons for volumes, and digital probe and infrared thermometers for measuring the temperatures inside foods and on food and utensil surfaces.

Become familiar with metric measures, which are much easier to use than the spoon-cup-ounce system and encourage greater precision. See the inside covers of this book for conversion tables.

Measure ingredients by weight instead of by volume whenever possible. Weight is a direct measure of how much of an ingredient there is, no matter how coarse or fine, loosely or tightly packed. Volume is a measure of how much space the ingredient occupies, including air pockets between particles, and this can vary tremendously.

Translate your favorite recipes into more convenient and reliable form by annotating their measures with the metric weight equivalents.

When you measure by volume, hold measuring cups at eye level, and level the contents, to read the scale accurately. Double-check recipes for measuring details: for example, whether to use dense granular salt or lighter flake salt, whether flours or fine sugars should be sifted.

When you measure temperature, hold the thermometer in place until its reading is steady. Instant-read dial thermometers actually take 20 seconds or more to register temperature accurately, and need at least the bottom 1 inch/2.5 centimeters of the probe to be in contact with the food.

Noncontact infrared thermometers are handy but have important limitations. They need to be held within a few inches of the object and carefully aimed at it, and will give an incorrectly low reading for hot liquids (because evaporation cools the liquid surface) and for shiny glass or metal containers (because their surface emits less heat radiation than a seasoned or coated surface).

To measure the temperature of a shiny pan, put a drop of oil midway from the center to the pan edge, aim the thermometer at the oil, move it back and forth while pulling the trigger, and use the highest temperature reading. Don't oil the entire surface until it has reached the cooking temperature.

SERVING FOODS RAW

Raw foods highlight the flavors of the ingredients themselves, which are usually more delicate and light than cooked flavors. Raw vegetable textures are crunchier than cooked, and meat and fish textures are firm and chewy, neither as moist nor as tender as they can be when cooked just until their juices flow.

Raw foods are not necessarily more nutritious than cooked foods. There's no good evidence of any health benefit to keeping foods below 118°F/48°C, a practice reputed to "preserve enzymes." Cooked foods are often more readily digested and their nutrients better absorbed.

Take special care to serve only the freshest and cleanest foods raw. Because they're not exposed to microbe-killing temperatures, raw foods are only as safe as the ingredients used to prepare them. Handling and holding foods at warm temperatures will encourage the growth of microbes and increase the risk of foodborne illness. Know where your ingredients come from, clean them as thoroughly and handle them as little as possible, and keep them cold until just before serving.

MOIST AND DRY HEATING METHODS

The many methods for heating foods fall into two broad groups that produce different qualities.

Moist heating methods cook food with hot liquid water or water vapor. Boiling, braising, poaching, steaming, and pressure-cooking are moist methods. Their maximum temperature is limited to the boiling point of water, 212°F/100°C at sea level, and around 250°F/120°C in a pressure cooker.

Dry heating methods cook food with hot air or oil or metal, or by heat radiation from very hot flames, coals, or metal surfaces. Baking, frying, and grilling are dry methods. They expose foods to temperatures well above the boiling point, often 400°F/200°C or hotter.

Dry heating methods can dry out food surfaces and turn them crisp and brown. Dryness and high temperatures encourage food proteins and sugars to react with each other and form brown pigments and distinctive, rich flavors.

Moist heating methods generally don't encourage these browning reactions, and don't develop the same richness of flavor.

Moist heating methods do not guarantee that foods will come out moist. In fact the quickest way to dry out meats and fish and eggs is to boil them.

The key to moist, tender foods is careful temperature control, no matter what the cooking method.

HEATING IN WATER: BOILING, BRAISING, POACHING, WATER BATHS, LOW-TEMPERATURE COOKING, AND SOUS-VIDE COOKING

Cooking in hot water is simple, versatile, and quick. Water can hold a lot of heat and transfers it to foods faster than oil, steam, or air. Boiling in salted water is a common way to cook many vegetables, grains, and pastas. Lower-temperature poaching and braising in broths, juices, and other flavorful liquids work well for eggs, fish, and meats.

Move slowly and carefully when handling pots full of hot water. Hot water can cause burns in a fraction of a second, and gives off scalding steam when poured into the sink.

Use pot lids to save time and energy and control temperature when cooking in water. Evaporation from the water surface has a cooling effect. Heat a pot to the boil in half the time by putting the lid on to prevent evaporation. Prevent a braise in the oven from boiling by leaving the lid ajar to allow evaporation, or only partly covering with a temporary lid cut from parchment paper.

The boiling point of water is the easiest cooking temperature to recognize and maintain. Plain water boils—bubbles—at a specific temperature, 212°F/100°C at sea level, and won't ever get hotter than that, even if it's over a high flame or in a hot oven.

Turn the heat down and leave the lid ajar once you've added food to the pot and it has returned to the boil. A rolling boil is no hotter than a gentle one, and it's more likely to cause foaming over. A partly open lid allows some cooling and helps deflate any foam.

Boiling water instantly kills nearly all microbes on food surfaces, and is good for making foods as safe to eat as possible.

Blanching, parboiling, and scalding are terms for brief exposure to boiling or near-boiling water, to cleanse food surfaces and partly cook them in preparation for other cooking processes.

When cooking vegetables directly in boiling water, salt the water generously to reduce the loss of flavorful and nutritious substances into the water. Salt does not raise the boiling point enough to affect cooking times. Add less salt to the water for dry grains and pastas, which will absorb more than vegetables do.

Avoid the boiling point for cooking most meats, fish, eggs, and large vegetables. Boiling water overcooks their outsides while the insides cook through.

Simmering, poaching, and braising are loosely defined terms for cooking in water at temperatures below the boil, as low as 130°F/55°C. These methods are often applied to heat-sensitive meats, fish, and eggs, which boiling temperatures harden and dry out. The water temperature is critical for producing the desired texture, but isn't obvious visually.

Simmering usually involves water just below the boil that bubbles occasionally; poaching involves hot water that doesn't bubble at all.

Braising usually means cooking meats partly immersed in liquid that will become their sauce, in a covered pot.

Always check simmering, poaching, and braising temperatures with a thermometer, and adjust as needed. Temperatures near the bottom of the pot may be significantly higher than near the top, especially if the cooking liquid has been thickened at all. Ovens on a low setting often provide more consistent and even heat than stove-top burners.

Don't trust standard braising recipes or slow-cooking appliances to cook meats at the ideal temperature. Most cook too close to the boil and produce dry results. See p. 265 for improving meat braises.

Water baths or bains-marie are arrangements for heating sensitive foods gently and evenly by immersing them in a container of water in the oven. Custard dishes and cheesecake pans are placed in a baking dish or pot filled with enough water to come partway up their sides. The water moderates the oven heat thanks to evaporation from its surface, which keeps the temperature well below the boil even in a hot oven.

Low-temperature cooking is the shorthand term for heating foods just at the temperature we want them to reach for ideal doneness, usually in a water bath whose temperature can be precisely controlled. It's especially valuable for meats, fish, eggs, and other heat-sensitive foods whose textures are best between 130 and 150°F/55 and 65°C, and are easily dried out at standard cooking temperatures. The food is sealed in a protective plastic bag or wrapping, then immersed in a water oven, or in a pot of water whose temperature is monitored and maintained either manually by the cook or automatically by an immersion circulator.

The advantage of low-temperature cooking is that it guarantees a particular doneness throughout the food, because the food is cooked at exactly the temperature that produces that doneness. Once it reaches that temperature, the food can be held in the water bath for some time without any risk of overcooking. This means that cooking times are much less critical than they are in all other methods that cook at higher temperatures.

The disadvantage of low-temperature cooking is that it doesn't create the rich, savory surface flavors that high-temperature frying and grilling do. To get the best of both low and high temperatures, simply cook foods until done, allow them to cool somewhat, and then quickly fry or grill them just long enough to flavor the surfaces and reheat the interior.

Understand and avoid the potential hazards of low-temperature cooking. Low cooking temperatures are slower to kill the bacteria that cause foodborne illness, and tight wrapping makes it possible for botulism bacteria to grow. Use recipes that explain the hazards, and follow their instructions exactly. Be especially careful when maintaining the temperature yourself. In general, it's simplest and safest to serve low-temperature foods immediately.

To cook foods at low temperature:

- *Heat the water oven or a large pot of water* up to the desired temperature. A large volume of water will hold its temperature better than a small one.

- *Seal the food in a plastic ziplock storage bag,* pressing out as much air as possible by immersing it in the water just up to the zipper and then zipping it; or vacuum-pack using a home vacuum-packing machine. Eggs in the shell don't require a protective bag.

- *Immerse the bag in the bath* and heat until the food is cooked through evenly. Low temperatures heat slowly, so allow more time than usual: 30 to 60 minutes for eggs, an hour or so for steaks and chops. If you're not using a water oven or circulator, stir the water regularly, monitor the temperature frequently with an accurate digital thermometer, and heat or add hot water as necessary to maintain it.

- *Make sure that the food remains fully immersed* in the cooking water and surrounded by it. Air and vapor pockets in a bag can cause it to float, and water flow or crowding can push bags against each other or the pot sides.

Sous-vide cooking is a version of low temperature cooking in which the foods are vacuum-sealed in plastic bags (sous vide is French for "under vacuum"). Vacuum sealing in a professional chamber machine can speed the infusion of flavors into a food, compress fruits and vegetables to give them a dense, meaty texture, and remove all air from the package, so that the food heats more evenly and keeps longer after cooking. Household vacuum-packaging machines don't create a strong enough vacuum to infuse or compress foods, can't be used with liquid ingredients, and leave some air in the package.

HEATING WITH WATER VAPOR: STEAMING AND DOUBLE BOILERS

Steam is hot water vapor. It cooks foods in the same temperature range as liquid water, but somewhat more slowly because water vapor is less dense than liquid water. Steam is as hot as the water it's rising from. Most steaming is done at the boiling point, but it can be done more gently over simmering water.

Steaming requires a pot to contain the food and a small amount of water, a lid to contain the steam, and a basket or improvised stand that will fit in the pot and hold the food above the water.

Double boilers are arrangements for cooking gently with indirect steam heat. A double boiler consists of a pot or bowl nested on top of a pot of simmering water. Steam from the water heats the bottom of the cooking pot, which can be lifted away to stop the heating quickly.

Steaming uses much less water and energy than boiling, and leaches less nourishment and flavor from foods. It only takes a few cups of boiling water to fill a large pot with steam for 15 to 30 minutes.

Steaming is well suited to the simple cooking of any vegetable, and to shellfish and thin pieces of fish. It's also good for reheating many foods.

Pile the food very loosely on the steaming rack to allow the steam to circulate throughout. In a large pot, you can stack bamboo or metal baskets and steam more than one food at a time. Place the more delicate foods at the relatively cool top of the stack.

Make sure you have enough water in the pot so that it won't boil dry. Just a few seconds of smoke from the charring bottom can ruin the food's flavor.

Bring the covered pot to a boil over high heat, then reduce the heat to maintain a moderate boil for the remainder of the cooking time. A high rolling boil doesn't produce a higher steam temperature, but it does speed evaporation and the chances of boiling dry.

Open steamer lids away from you, and don't put your hand above or in the pot. Steam can cause a blistering burn in a fraction of a second. When checking doneness or removing food, turn off the heat and use tongs.

Self-steaming in a packet, or cooking en papillote, is a very flexible version of steaming that doesn't require a pot. Food is enclosed in one of many different wrapping materials and the packet then cooked with any source of heat, from a campfire to a microwave oven. When the trapped moisture on the food surfaces gets hot enough, it forms steam and helps cook the food through. If the external heat comes from a fire or grill, it may create some browning or charring aromas inside the packet.

Common packet wrappings include lettuce, cabbage, banana and lotus leaves, corn husks, parchment paper, foil, dough, salt, and clay.

HEATING AT HIGH PRESSURE: PRESSURE-COOKING

Pressure-cooking heats foods with hot water or steam at above-boiling temperatures, around 250°F/120°C. It's much faster and more efficient than ordinary stove-top cooking. A pressure cooker is a special pot that seals tightly and traps hot steam to build the pressure and temperature. Recent designs use a spring to regulate pressure, and do a better job than older weight-regulated types at retaining cooking vapors and ensuring that pressure can't build to unsafe levels.

Pressure-cooking is especially useful for cooking dishes that otherwise take hours: dry beans, meat stocks, stews of tough meat. It's also used to sterilize home-canned vegetables and fruits. The high temperatures kill the tough spores of botulism bacteria that survive ordinary boiling.

Avoid pressure-cooking most meats. The high temperature does tenderize tough connective tissue, but also squeezes out the meat's moisture and leaves it dry and stringy.

Be careful not to fill pressure cookers more than about two-thirds full, and include some oil to suppress the foam that's sometimes generated by dry beans and grains. Excess liquid and foam can clog the pressure valve and create unsafe pressures or messy boilovers.

Reduce the heat to low once the cooker develops full pressure. It takes very little heat to maintain the boil in a sealed pot. To avoid excess pressure on a slow-changing electric burner, remove the cooker from the burner for a minute or so.

Check recipe timings carefully, and set a timer when you pressure-cook. Foods heat through very quickly, so a few minutes too many can overcook them badly.

Reduce the cooker pressure slowly to keep food structures intact and prevent boilovers. Rapid cooling or steam release causes water throughout the cooker to boil violently. This can blow apart beans and potatoes and force liquid through the vents. Instead, simply turn off the heat and let the pressure drop on its own.

To simplify cleanup, use the pressure cooker as a pressure steamer. Pour some water into the cooker, place the food and any water it will need to absorb in a solid bowl, and then place the bowl in the cooker. The food will cook in the bowl, and you can just rinse the cooker out.

HEATING ON METAL: PANFRYING AND PAN ROASTING, SAUTÉING, AND STIR-FRYING

Panfrying and sautéing are methods that heat foods by contact with a hot metal pan, usually lubricated with a thin coating of fat or oil that also aids heat conduction, one surface at a time. The pan temperature is well above the boiling point of water, hot enough to dry the surfaces of many foods and form a brown, flavorful crust.

Panfrying, often shortened to *frying,* is the term usually applied to cooking large pieces of food for some time on each side, turning them with a spatula or tongs.

Pan roasting is a combination of panfrying and oven roasting: you brown thick cuts of meat or fish in the frying pan, and then put the pan in a preheated oven to finish heating the food through from all sides. Finishing in the oven leaves the cook and stove top free for other duties, and heats the food through more gently and evenly than frying alone.

Sautéing, from the French for "jump," is the term usually applied to cooking small pieces of food with frequent shakes or stirs of the pan. Sauté pans have higher sides than frying pans to keep food pieces from jumping out.

Frying is best suited to medium-thick pieces of food that will cook through in about the same time it takes to brown the surface. Thicker pieces can be browned at high frying temperature and then cooked through on lower heat.

Frying spatter can burn the hand and arm, and smaller oil droplets can slowly rain down all over the kitchen.

To minimize spatter and mess, make sure foods are as dry as possible, or coated with flour or breading. Turn on stove-top ventilation and use a screenlike spatter guard over the pan. Keep eyeglasses clean by wearing a baseball-style cap; most eyeglass spatter falls from above onto the inner lens surfaces.

Foods can stick to the pan when they leak sticky starch or proteins, or when prolonged heat turns the frying oil sticky. Nonstick cooking sprays can reduce this problem but develop off flavors at relatively low frying temperatures.

To minimize sticking on a pan without a nonstick surface, preheat the pan without cooking fat or oil. Use unclarified butter, which contains nonstick materials naturally, but only at low frying temperatures. Dry food surfaces thoroughly, or coat with flour or breading. Don't try to lift the food until it has had time to develop a brittle crust. Turn and lift using a spatula with a sharp metal edge that can slip under the crust.

To panfry or sauté:

- *Warm thick cuts of meat* and poultry pieces to room temperature to speed heating and minimize overcooking.
- *Dry food surfaces, or coat in flour or breading* to minimize spatter and sticking and speed browning. Coatings prevent the food surface itself from browning, but add crunch and flavor. Toss chopped vegetables in oil to precoat them.
- *Choose the appropriate pan,* large enough to hold the food without crowding, but not so large that vacant surfaces will scorch oil and escaping juices. A crowded pan won't maintain high enough heat to vaporize the food's juices, and the food will stew in them.
- *Heat the pan on a moderate burner without oil* to 350 to 375°F / 175

to 190°C. Verify the temperature with an infrared thermometer, or with a drop of water that should skitter on the surface before it boils away. Add oil or fat to coat the pan surface, where it should ripple with the heat. If frying on lower heat with unclarified butter, add it to the cold pan and heat until it stops frothing and becomes fragrant, around 300°F/150°C. Add the food and keep the burner on high to restore the pan's heat as it's lost to the food.

- *Adjust the heat as you go to maintain a lively sizzling,* the sound of moisture being vaporized, and to avoid scorching. To lower the heat quickly, especially on an electric stove top, move the pan off the burner, then change the burner setting and return the pan.

- *If sizzling and browning do stop and liquid accumulates* while cooking heat-sensitive meats or fish, remove them from the pan, raise the heat to boil off the liquid, and add the food back when the liquid has evaporated. If this happens with mushrooms, eggplant, or other vegetables, just leave them in the pan, raise the heat, and boil off the liquid.

- *Don't move or turn larger pieces of food for several minutes,* until surfaces have a chance to dry fully and detach from the pan surface. When you move or turn the food, make full use of all areas of the hot pan surface. Once both surfaces have browned, turning the food frequently slows further browning but speeds and evens heating through.

Blackening is an extreme, high-temperature version of panfrying that gives foods a very dark and aromatic crust. Blacken only in a well-ventilated kitchen or outdoors; the extreme heat generates smoke.

To blacken, coat a piece of meat or fish with butter and then powdered seasonings, heat a cast-iron pan over high heat, covered with a lid or piece of foil, until it smokes, and place the food in the pan.

Stir-frying as it's done in China is a high-temperature, rapid version of sautéing that produces a characteristic and delicious flavor. The ideal pan is the bare steel wok, whose curved sides make it easy to keep the pieces of food moving. Use nonstick woks only for moderate-temperature sautéing; their coatings degenerate on high heat. Do true stir-frying only in a well-ventilated kitchen or outdoors; it generates a lot of oil spatter and fumes.

To stir-fry:

- *Cut food into small pieces* that will cook through in 1 to 2 minutes.
- *Dry the food surfaces.*
- *Heat the wok over high heat until it begins to smoke,* covered with a lid or piece of foil to retain heat. To reduce sticking with a kind of last-minute pan seasoning, heat the wok with some oil, then discard the oil once it smokes.
- *Add the cooking oil, then the food,* and stir the food constantly until it's done.

HEATING IN OIL: DEEP- AND SHALLOW-FRYING AND OIL POACHING

Deep- and shallow-frying are methods that heat foods primarily by contact with hot oil, not with the hot metal surface of ordinary frying. Oil can get far hotter than water's boiling point, and does a good job of crisping and browning many different foods. Deep- and shallow-frying increase the fat content of foods, but if well done they may add less fat than everyday pan frying.

Deep-frying immerses foods completely in hot oil. It forms a brown, flavorful crust over whole pieces while the insides heat through. It can be applied to everything from millimeter-thick potato sticks to whole turkeys.

The disadvantages of deep-frying are the large volume of oil required, and the potential hazard of spilled oil, which can burn skin and catch fire.

Shallow-frying is a low-oil alternative in which the food is fried in just enough oil to come halfway up its side, and then turned to cook the other side.

Oil poaching is an alternative to low-heat water poaching. The oil remains well below the boiling point of water, and doesn't crisp or brown the food surface. Compared to water poaching, it extracts less flavor and nourishment into the surrounding liquid, imparts its own or added flavors to the food, and heats the food more gradually.

To deep- or shallow-fry:

- *Choose a deep pot or saucepan* that can hold more than double the quantity of oil to be used, to accommodate the food to be added and the vigorous bubbling of water vapor when the food is added. Use a clip-on frying thermometer or a countertop electric fryer with thermostat.
- *Choose fresh refined cooking oils* low in polyunsaturates. Fresh and light-bodied oils drain best and cling least to fried surfaces. Refined oils are better than most unrefined or highly unsaturated oils at tolerating high frying temperatures and resisting breakdown, smoking, and off flavors. Good frying oils include

refined peanut oil, cottonseed oil, olive oil (though it contributes a distinctive flavor), low-polyunsaturate types of sunflower oil, and solid but trans-fat-free vegetable shortening. Carefully rendered animal fats—lard, tallow, duck fat—are flavorful alternatives.

- *Cut food into evenly sized pieces and dry thoroughly,* or coat in flour, breading, or batter. The drier the food, the less it will foam and spatter and the faster it will brown. Coatings protect the food surface itself from the hot oil. To help batters adhere, lightly flour the food before dipping it in the batter. To help breadings adhere, lightly flour the food, dip it in milk or beaten egg, then coat it with the breading.

- *For an especially crisp crust,* make batters with rice or corn flour or cornstarch replacing some wheat flour, include some double-acting baking powder, or replace up to half of the liquid with vodka.

- *To get the irregular, lacy crust of Japanese tempura batter,* mix ice-cold water briefly and incompletely with the flour and egg just before frying. This minimizes the formation of tough gluten and the time required to crisp the crust. Make fresh batter for every few batches.

- *Don't use a batter for more than 4 hours.* The moist ingredients and repeated dipping of raw foods can lead to unsafe levels of bacteria.

- *Heat oil up to the cooking temperature over moderate heat;* a very hot pan bottom accelerates oil breakdown. Don't let the pot handle project over the stove-top edge where it can be bumped into and cause a spill of hot oil.

- *Add food to the oil without splashing, in small batches* to avoid cooling down the oil excessively and obstructing free oil circulation. Raise the heat to return it to the frying temperature as quickly as possible, then turn heat down to maintain the cooking temperature and steady bubbling of vaporized moisture. Don't cover the pot; evaporating food moisture will fall back into the oil and cause spattering.
- *Monitor the frying closely* and remove or turn the food when it has colored as desired. As the bubbling gets quieter, the oil temperature rises and the food browns faster. The first batch of any food will cook more slowly than subsequent batches; as oil is used and begins to break down, it heats and browns foods more rapidly.
- *Remove food with a wire strainer and shake gently over the fryer, then blot immediately.* Foods absorb more oil as they're cooling down than they do during frying.

To hold fried foods and keep them crisp, place the pieces on a rack or on bunched paper towels with plenty of air spaces. Avoid crowding or piling, which traps their steam and causes sogginess.

To reuse frying oils, filter them through cheesecloth to remove all food residues, and store in a cool place. Discard them when they become unpleasantly flavored, viscous, dark, or fume at frying temperatures.

OVEN BAKING AND ROASTING

Oven baking is a method that cooks foods with hot air and with heat radiation from the oven walls and heating elements. Baking temperatures range from below the boiling point of water to well above it, low enough to cook gently and evenly, and hot enough to dry food surfaces and form a brown, flavorful crust.

Oven baking takes longer than most other methods because hot air heats foods much more slowly than water or oil. This slow and all-enveloping heat allows us to cook foods in the oven unattended for hours, and have a longer period of time during which meats and other sensitive foods remain properly cooked, not overdone.

Gas and electric ovens cook somewhat differently. Gas ovens don't retain moist cooking vapors as well as electric ovens, which can make them slower to cook and cause less rising and lightness in baked goods.

Convection ovens speed and even out heating by force-circulating the hot air with a fan.

To adapt standard oven recipes for a convection oven, reduce the baking temperatures by 25 to 50°F / 15 to 30°C.

Countertop or toaster ovens save energy when baking small amounts of food, but readily scorch foods because their heating elements are close to the food and turn on frequently.

To avoid scorching foods in small ovens, preheat the oven well above the desired baking temperature, place the food on the lowest rack position, farthest from the heating elements, shield it loosely with a piece of foil, and reset the thermostat to the baking temperature.

Check the accuracy of your oven thermostat, and learn the oven's heat landscape. Preheat the oven until the heating elements cycle off, then scan the interior with an infrared thermometer. If the racks and side walls are much hotter or cooler than the thermostat setting, then set the thermostat to appropriately lower or higher temperatures than recipes call for.

Leave room for hot air to circulate around foods. Don't put large baking sheets on more than one rack unless there's a convection fan to force air circulation.

An oven set to a moderate temperature can scorch baked goods and vegetables. The effective oven temperature can repeatedly rise far above the thermostat setting when the heating elements cycle on to keep the oven hot.

To get the most even oven heat for baking, minimize the need for the heating elements to turn on. Preheat the oven well above the final cooking temperature to compensate for the initial temperature drop when you put the food in. Set baking stones in the oven to help it retain heat.

Reduce excessive heat radiation from the oven floor or ceiling by using foil or baking sheets as shields to prevent overcooking. The hottest areas in an oven are near the oven floor, where at least one heating element is located, and the ceiling, where heat rises and collects (and where there may be another electrical element).

Use a low oven, 160 to 220°F / 70 to 105°C, for cooking grains, dried beans, and braises and stews. The oven heats pots more evenly than the stove top and won't crust or scorch the bottom. Prevent pots from boiling by leaving lids ajar to allow evaporation.

Pan materials affect how quickly and evenly foods bake in the oven. Dull and dark metal pans transmit heat more rapidly from oven to food than shiny pans that reflect heat. Thin pans heat unevenly. Ceramic pans collect and build up heat more slowly than metal pans, but retain heat well for serving. Clear glass pans transmit heat radiation directly to food as well as conduct heat to it, and heat more quickly than other nonmetal pans.

Don't depend on recipe timings for baking. Ovens, pans, and ingredients are too variable. Always check doneness for yourself, and start checking early.

BROILING

Broiling is a method that browns and cooks foods with the strong radiation from a gas or electric heating element just above the food's upper surface. Broiling works best for moderately thick cuts of meat or fish and flat-lying vegetables such as asparagus, or to quickly color and flavor the surface of prebaked dishes, including gratins and crème brûlée.

Broiler heat and browning power weaken drastically as the spacing between food and heating element increases. Too large a distance will increase the browning time to the point that it overcooks the food interior. This is the most common error in broiling.

Preheat broilers until the metal elements glow, to speed browning and avoid overcooking.

Oil lean foods lightly to speed browning and improve browned flavors. Wipe off any excess to avoid flare-ups in the broiler.

Place the food surface close to the heating element, as little as 1 inch/2.5 centimeters away, and monitor browning frequently once it begins, every minute or less. Turn or remove the food as soon as the browning is as deep as you want it. If necessary, finish cooking through in the hot broiler compartment with the broiler turned off, or in the oven.

GRILLING

Grilling is a high-temperature, fast method of cooking foods from below with a combination of heat radiation and hot air from glowing coals, or gas or electric heating elements.

The high heat of grilling contributes the flavors of fire, smoke, and extreme browning. Carelessly applied, it scorches foods and covers them with soot and other toxic substances.

Open flames and glowing coals are hazardous. They generate poisonous carbon monoxide gas, and can cause burns and fires. Grill in an open, well-ventilated area outdoors, use long-handled utensils and protective gloves, and have a fire extinguisher nearby.

Gas and electric grills only approximate charcoal grills. They produce heat without the smoky aromatics of burning coals, aren't powerful enough to reach the same temperatures, and can take so long to brown the food surface that the interior ends up overcooked.

Charcoal grills cook mainly with direct heat radiation as long as the coals are glowing underneath the food and the grill is open. When the coals die down or they're placed to one side of the food, hot air does more of the cooking. Closing the grill lid traps the hot air and turns the grill into an oven.

Use hardwood charcoal, which doesn't contain the binders and other additives that formed briquettes do. Use a chimney-style starter instead of petroleum lighter fluid, which can leave bad-tasting residues. To start coals very quickly, ignite them with a gas torch.

Create a low-heat area on the grill with few or no coals underneath, for the gentle indirect heating through of thick foods whose surfaces have already been well flavored over high heat.

To superheat the metal grill to burn off cooking residues and quickly produce grill marks on food, place sheets of aluminum foil over the grill for a few minutes just before cooking. Cast-iron grills accumulate more heat than light stainless steel and mark foods better.

Avoid fat flare-ups and charring, which deposit soot, harsh flavors, and carcinogens on foods. Trim extra fat from meats, and blot oil from marinated vegetables. Monitor foods on the grill constantly.

To prevent food from sticking to the grill, dry the food well, lightly oil the grill and the food just before cooking, and don't try to move the food until it has cooked long enough for the surface juices to dry, harden, and detach.

To speed the cooking of steaks and chops and cook surface and interior evenly, turn them frequently, every minute or less.

Avoid contaminating grilled meats and fish with their raw juices, which may carry harmful microbes. Don't baste or sauce toward the end of cooking with the same liquid you applied at the beginning. Set some aside, cooked if necessary, for finishing. Put the grilled food on a clean dish, not the same one that held the raw food.

Countertop clamshell grills also cook largely with heat radiation, but from two metal plates a fraction of an inch away from the food, which is suspended on grill-like ridges. The two plates are heated to frying temperatures and cook simultaneously from top and bottom. Clamshell grills cook quickly, but without the flavors created by true high-temperature grilling.

SMOKING

Smoking is a method of flavoring foods with the aromas of smoldering wood or other plant materials, including spices and teas. Smoke also has antimicrobial and antioxidant properties and can help preserve foods, though the smoke flavor itself deteriorates with time.

Hot-smoking flavors foods while cooking them. Cold-smoking flavors foods while keeping the temperature low enough to avoid cooking.

The best wood smoke aromas come from particular woods heated to particular temperatures. Hardwoods—especially hickory, oak, and fruit-tree woods—produce aromatics also found in vanilla, cloves, and other spices. They do so at smoldering temperatures, 570 to 750°F / 300 to 400°C, well below the temperature at which wood burns. Pine and other evergreen woods contain resins that create harsh aromas and soot.

For the best smoke flavor, prevent the aromatic materials from burning by controlling their temperature or air supply. Soak wood or spices in water before placing them on glowing coals, or wrap them airtight in foil with small slits to allow smoke to escape. Close grill vents to the point that flames die down to coals from lack of air.

To hot-smoke outdoors, use a dedicated smoker, or set up a standard grill as you would for barbecuing.

To hot-smoke in the kitchen, use a stove-top smoking box, or line a wok or other pan and lid with kitchen foil. Place a foil packet of sawdust, ground spices, tea, or other aromatics on the pan bottom, and the food on a rack. Cover the pan tightly and heat it on medium heat until you can smell smoke. Continue smoking for a few minutes, then turn the heat off and let the pan cool down, covered, until smoke no longer leaks from its edge.

Finish cooking the food in the oven if necessary.

To cold-smoke foods, use a smoker designed for that purpose. Cold-smoking large cuts of meat and fish requires two separate but connecting chambers, one hot and containing the smoke source, the other around room temperature and containing the food. For quick, light cold-smoking of small cuts and prepared dishes, use a handheld food smoker that burns sawdust or aromatics and can aim a narrow smoke stream into a covered dish.

MICROWAVE COOKING

Microwave ovens heat foods directly, deeply, quickly, and efficiently with radio waves that pass through nonmetal containers and penetrate into foods to a depth of an inch or more.

Microwave ovens work well for heating small quantities of food that might scorch on the stove top, and thin cuts of fish and most vegetables, whose nutrients they preserve better than boiling. They're also good at heating water, popping popcorn, making hot cereals, reheating leftovers, melting butter and chocolate, and softening ice cream.

Microwave ovens spare the use and cleaning of pots and pans by heating foods in their storage or serving containers. Plastics, glass, and most ceramics don't absorb microwaves well, and so don't get any hotter than the food they contain. Containers identified as microwave-safe can be taken directly from refrigerator to microwave oven to table.

Don't place used plastic food containers or to-go food packaging in the microwave. They may soften and release chemicals into the food. Always make sure that plastic containers are marked as safe for microwave use.

Avoid putting metal containers or utensils in the microwave. Metals reflect microwaves and turn their energy into electrical currents. Metal containers shield the food inside and prevent microwaves from heating it efficiently. Small gaps between metal objects, or their nearness to oven walls, can cause sparking and burning. Forks and decorated china dishes are almost guaranteed to spark.

Do use metal foil to shield the thin edge of a fish fillet and other delicate parts of a dish for more even heating. Just be sure to leave large spaces between foil pieces and the walls.

Microwave ovens have power settings, not temperature settings. The power settings on some ovens simply determine whether full-power microwaves are emitted constantly or are cycled on and off. Newer ovens offer control over microwave intensity, which allows more gentle heating.

Use high power with care and check cooking progress frequently. Penetrating microwaves can burn the interior of baked goods and nuts while leaving the surface looking unchanged. Melting butter can erupt when the water that separates beneath the fat suddenly boils. A cup of water can superheat past the boiling point without bubbling, then suddenly erupt and scald when the cup is moved.

Use low power settings for greater control and delicate heating, including toasting spices and nuts, and the gentle reheating of coffee to retain its aroma.

Allow more cooking time for large quantities of food. The more food there is in the oven, the more the available energy has to be shared, so there's less energy for any given portion of food to absorb.

Loosely wrap or cover foods. Microwaves mainly energize the water in foods, and can quickly dry them out. Cover foods loosely, with plastic wrap or lids slightly ajar, to help them retain moisture and to surround them with steam that will intercept the microwaves and moderate their heating. Don't cover containers tightly, or the developing steam within will burst the covering or container and make a mess.

Move foods around during cooking either by hand or with an automatic turntable. Microwaves tend to cluster in certain spots within the oven and heat unevenly.

COOKING AT HIGH ALTITUDES

Many cooking methods and recipes must be adjusted at altitudes 1,000 feet/300 meters or more above sea level. Because the air pressure is lower there, water boils at lower temperatures, food surfaces lose more heat to evaporation and transmit heat more slowly, and leavenings produce bigger bubbles earlier in baking. It often takes several trials to adapt a recipe for high altitudes. Specific solutions depend on altitude, cooking method, and dish.

Most foods will take longer to cook. For many egg, meat, fish, and vegetable dishes, simply allowing for enough time is the only necessary adjustment. A pressure cooker is especially useful at high altitudes for speeding the cooking of dry beans and whole grains.

Baked goods, custards, and fruit preserves require more complicated adjustments because they either won't set at the appropriate stage of cooking, or won't set at all. The solution generally involves increasing the liquid ingredients and flour, decreasing the sugar and leavening, and cooking at a higher temperature for a longer time.

6

COOKING SAFELY

F
ood safety is the sobering side of cooking, the subject that food lovers would rather ignore, and no cook can afford to. The basic facts are simple and stark. Harmful microbes are frequently present on foods. They can't be completely removed by washing, and some can survive cooking. Salads and many other nourishing foods are eaten raw or lightly cooked and can make people sick. Food temperatures high enough to quickly kill all harmful microbes also kill deliciousness. And foods cooked to be safe may remain safe for only a few hours unless we act to protect them. A moment's carelessness can undo the greatest care.

These simple facts touch every household. The U.S. Centers for Disease Control estimate that unsafe food sickens nearly 200,000 people every day and kills a dozen.

It is possible to prepare foods that are both delicious and safe. This takes care and effort, and working with guidelines that are not so simple, because foods and microbes are not simple. But anyone who cooks should make the effort, for their own sake as well as for others.

My father likes his hamburgers rarer than rare—"Wave it near the grill," he would say—and he regularly suffered for it. Ground meats are among the foods most frequently contaminated with harmful microbes. When he moved close enough for me to cook for him, I told him that I would take care of his hamburger habit, and developed a way to prepare the meat to ensure its safety even when it's barely cooked (see p. 240). Ever since, both of us have been able to relax and enjoy our burgers without a second thought.

Don't be put off by the many dos and don'ts below. They're just specific applications of a few basic habits. Keep raw foods cold and clean. Cook them properly. Serve cooked foods promptly. Chill leftovers promptly. Start looking over your own shoulder with safety in mind as you cook, and you'll come up with your own checklist of the many small actions that can make a difference. It'll become second nature to think about making foods safely and safe as well as delicious.

COOKING SAFELY

The main hazard in the cooking process is physical injury from sharp edges, powerful machines, and high heat.

Kitchen injuries are usually the result of foreseeable accidents. A few commonsense habits will reduce the odds of an accidental injury.

Wear long sleeves, pants, and shoes when you cook, to protect skin and limbs from hot oven edges, scalding spills, and dropped knives and glass.

Unplug cutting, grinding, and blending machines before handling their blades.

Keep knives sharp, and put them down well away from countertop edges. Dull knives require more pressure and may move unpredictably before penetrating the food.

Always use knives on a cutting board, and cut away from fingers. Keep the cutting board from shifting during use by placing it on a moist towel.

Keep towels, pot holders, and mitts handy to grip hot pans, handles, oven racks, and microwave containers.

Make sure that towels, pot holders, and mitts are dry or made of waterproof materials. Even a little moisture can transmit heat rapidly from hot metal and cause burns and dropped pots. Blistering burns result when skin is exposed for a few seconds to 140°F/60°C, and instantaneously at 160°F/70°C and above.

Turn pot handles over the stove top to avoid colliding with them and causing spills.

Before moving a hot container, make sure that the way is clear and there's a heat-resistant surface to place it on.

Lift lids off hot pans back edge first, to allow steam to escape away from you. When emptying a pot of cooking water into the sink, pour slowly to minimize steaming.

To minimize the splatter of hot oil, thoroughly dry foods before frying. Cover the pan with a splatter screen.

Fumes from high-temperature cooking can cause immediate discomfort and chronic illness. They contain irritating and toxic chemicals.

Equip your stove with a hood and exhaust fan that vent to the outdoors, especially if you do a lot of frying or oven roasting. Many stove-top hoods filter some fumes and spatter from the air but recirculate the rest back into the kitchen. Open the kitchen windows to dilute fumes with fresh air.

DEALING WITH CUTS, BURNS, AND FIRE

It's important and easy to prepare for the aftermath of kitchen accidents.

Equip your kitchen with small and large gauze bandages, antibiotic wound cream, and a fire extinguisher rated for kitchen use (class K or class B fires). Read the directions for using the extinguisher, and check the pressure gauge regularly. Keep it near the door you would escape through in the event of a fire.

If you cut yourself, hold the cut under cold running water to wash away food debris. Dry with a clean towel and apply antibiotic cream and a bandage. If necessary, hold the cut above heart level to reduce blood flow.

If the cut won't stop bleeding, get emergency medical help.

If you burn yourself, hold the burn under cold running water for several minutes, or apply a cloth cooled repeatedly with cold tap water, or cool the skin on a can taken from the refrigerator. Protect the burn with a gauze bandage. If the burn is large or if signs of infection develop, get medical help.

Don't put ice cubes or frozen gel packs onto a burn. Extreme cold can cause additional skin damage. Moderate cooling minimizes damage and pain and speeds healing.

If the burn is severe, get emergency medical help and keep the burn covered with a moist cloth.

In the event of fire, try to put out the flames by smothering them with a fire extinguisher or salt. Water will only spread burning oil and can create the hazard of electrical shock. If the flames are confined to a pot, cover it with the lid.

If you can't put out a fire in a few seconds, evacuate the kitchen and call 911.

FOODBORNE ILLNESS, OR "FOOD POISONING"

The main hazard in the foods we cook is "food poisoning," foodborne illness caused by microbes that either infect us or sicken us with the toxins they leave in foods. Toxins usually sicken us within a few hours, while infections may take a day or more to make us feel ill.

Microbes are everywhere in the kitchen, on foods and work surfaces, in the sink, in the air, and on the cook. Microbes are invisibly small bacteria, molds, yeasts, viruses, and parasites (some wormlike parasites are big enough to see). They can be present on foods by the millions without causing obvious signs of spoilage. People can carry microbes and spread them without being affected by them.

Foodborne illness is caused by microbes whose names are familiar from the news—E. coli, salmonella, listeria, botulism bacteria—and others that are less familiar but just as harmful (campylobacter, staphylococcus, vibrio, Bacillus cereus, noroviruses). They're found in many different foods, but most often in foods from animals: meats, fish and shellfish, eggs, and dairy products.

A few bad microbes in a food can quickly multiply into many thousands. One cell in a piece of warm, moist food can divide into two every

20 minutes, and produce several thousand cells in just 4 hours. A few bacteria are seldom enough to cause illness, but a few thousand can be plenty.

Microbes multiply at temperatures in the microbe growth zone, between 40 to 130°F/5 to 55°C. Most microbes don't grow at temperatures close to the freezing point. They grow quickly at room temperature, very quickly at body and warm food temperatures, then more slowly as the temperature approaches 130°F/55°C, where they begin to die. We can control their numbers by keeping foods out of the microbe growth zone: by storing them cold, cooking and eating them hot, and chilling leftovers right away.

The higher the food temperature, the faster microbes die. Most bacteria die in a couple of hours at 130°F/55°C, a few minutes at 140°F/60°C, and instantly at 170°F/75°C and above.

Viruses, often the culprit in illness caused by shellfish, are destroyed only at temperatures close to the boil, 212°F/100°C. If a food is contaminated with viruses, even cooking that renders it tough may not make it safe to eat.

Some dormant microbe spores survive very high heat and revive as the food cools down. These can grow in food and cause illness even though the food has been fully cooked. This is why it's important to keep leftovers hot or refrigerate them promptly.

Ordinary cooking can't eliminate all microbes and toxins in food. The only way to guarantee microbe- and toxin-free food is to pressure-cook it for hours and consume it immediately. Such food would also be pleasure free.

MAXIMIZING SAFETY FOR VULNERABLE PEOPLE

Safety is more important than any other consideration when you cook for people who are especially vulnerable to physical illness: young children, pregnant or nursing women, the elderly, and anyone who is already ill or taking medication. Even antacids lower our resistance to food-borne illness.

There are several ways to make eating as safe as possible.

Don't serve raw salads or any raw fruits or vegetables that can't be peeled. Wash foods thoroughly before peeling.

Serve pasteurized milks and fruit juices. Don't serve soft cheeses.

Don't serve raw or undercooked meats, fish or shellfish, eggs, or dairy products.

Don't serve fresh oysters, mussels, or clams in any form. All of them can carry viruses and toxins that survive cooking.

Cook most foods to a minimum temperature of 160°F/70°C at their center, intact cuts of meat to 140°F/60°C. Check temperatures with an accurate thermometer.

Boil home-canned foods for 10 minutes.

Once foods have been cooked, hold them at room temperature for no more than 4 hours, or 1 hour if it's warm. For longer serving times, hold the foods hot, at a minimum of 130°F/55°C.

BALANCING FOOD SAFETY
WITH FOOD QUALITY

Many foods are most delicious when eaten raw or lightly cooked. Green salads and sushi are delicious raw foods. Cooked fish gets dry if heated to a temperature above 120°F/50°C, beef above 140°F/60°C, and egg yolks above 145°F/63°C.

Most people in good health accept the risk of eating some foods raw or lightly cooked. That risk can be greatly reduced by following the guidelines below.

To further minimize the risk of eating lightly cooked foods, compensate for low cooked temperatures by holding the temperature for a longer time. Check temperatures with an accurate thermometer.

Microbe numbers are greatly reduced by holding foods covered at an internal temperature of 130°F/55°C for at least 2 hours, 135°F/57°C for at least 40 minutes, 140°F/60°C for at least 15 minutes, and 150°F/65°C for at least 5 minutes.

GUIDELINES FOR
PREPARING SAFE FOODS

There are three general rules for limiting the risk of foodborne illness:

- *Start with wholesome ingredients, and avoid contaminating them with harmful microbes.*
- *Keep perishable raw foods and leftover cooked foods colder than 40°F/5°C.*

- *Cook foods thoroughly enough to kill most harmful microbes, and serve them promptly.*

Many specific practices follow from these general rules.

Buy foods that appear to be wholesome, with no visible damage or bad smells. Check sell-by dates. If they're from a refrigerated case or a freezer, make sure they're actually cold or frozen. Avoid moldy or discolored foods (mold-ripened cheeses excepted), or packages that are leaking. Avoid or discard bulging cans, cracked or open jars, or any sealed containers that show other signs of microbial growth, including unusual bubbling or clouding.

Transfer perishable refrigerated and frozen foods to your refrigerator promptly. Perishables include raw meats, fish, shellfish, eggs, dairy products, and precut vegetables and fruits. Bag cold and frozen foods together to keep them as cold as possible. If there will be a delay, bring along a cooler and some ice. Don't let perishables sit in a warm car or kitchen for hours.

Store perishable foods at or below 40°F/5°C, in the cold rear of the refrigerator. Check refrigerator temperatures regularly with a thermometer and adjust the thermostat if necessary. Open the door as seldom and briefly as possible. Leave foods in the cold until just before you prepare them.

Thaw frozen foods in the refrigerator or in ice water. Don't thaw at room temperature, which allows food surfaces to become warm enough for microbes to grow.

Keep hands, work surfaces, and tools as clean as possible throughout cooking. Cooks can contaminate otherwise sound food by careless handling.

Wash hands and wrists with soap and warm water, rubbing all surfaces vigorously. Before you wash, use a nailbrush to clean under nails. Repeat hand washing during the cooking process whenever hands are exposed to microbes by handling food, opening doors, answering phones, reaching into pockets, covering coughs and sneezes, using the toilet, and touching other people or pets. Dry hands on clean towels, either disposable or used only for that purpose. To avoid repeated hand washing, wear disposable plastic gloves while handling food.

Rinse foods in running water, and scrub away obvious soiling. Washing doesn't eliminate microbes, but can reduce their numbers and the contamination that can occur when peeling produce or even opening dirty cans. Don't use soaps, which can leave residues on the food.

Avoid placing produce or meats in the sink. Use a clean container instead. If you have to use the sink to rinse large amounts of food, sanitize it with a vinegar or bleach solution immediately beforehand and afterward.

Have one cutting board just for meats and fish, and a separate one for other ingredients, so you can prepare a meal without being tempted to skip cleaning between uses. Use large boards with a channel around the edge to avoid spilling pieces or juices. After preparing foods, rinse boards and knives thoroughly, then wash them with hot soapy water and dry. For added protection, sanitize cutting boards with a solution of 1 part distilled vinegar to 2 parts water.

Don't cough or sneeze over foods, or dip fingers in food to taste. When checking seasoning, use a clean spoon for each taste.

Clean thermometer shafts with soapy water between temperature checks.

If you moisten a food with a marinade or sauce while it's cooking and also want to serve it with the finished food, cook the liquid thoroughly just before serving.

Put cooked foods on clean dishes, not on the uncleaned dishes that held the raw ingredients.

Heat foods steadily. Make sure that the food reaches microbe-killing temperatures within 6 hours. Don't let them linger at warm microbe-multiplying temperatures.

Make sure that you cook foods as thoroughly as you intend to.

Use a thermometer to verify cooking and food temperatures.

When cooking in the microwave, make sure that all portions of the dish reach the correct temperature. Microwave ovens can heat unevenly.

For the safe preparation of particular foods, see the chapters that follow.

SERVING FOOD SAFELY

Serve foods as soon as possible after finishing their preparation. This is especially important for gently cooked egg, meat, and fish dishes, and dishes made with cream.

Allow roasted meat a rest period before carving, but once it's carved, serve it immediately. Carve on a scrupulously clean cutting board.

To make salads that combine cooked with raw ingredients, such as potatoes or pasta or beans with fresh herbs, cool the cooked ingredients before combining, to minimize the growth of microbes on the herbs. Include vinegar in the dressing to help discourage microbe growth.

Don't allow foods to remain at room temperature or in the microbe growth zone—40 to 130°F/5 to 55°C—for more than 4 hours, 1 hour on a hot day.

To serve foods over several hours at parties or buffets, reserve portions in the refrigerator or in the oven, held covered at or above 130°F/55°C, and serve as needed in fresh dishes. Don't refill emptied dishes without washing them first. Or serve foods directly from a hot chafing dish or cold from a bed of ice.

Don't follow the 5-second rule. Food dropped on the floor is contaminated immediately. If you can't remove the contaminated surface, discard the food.

Inform guests of ingredients that may not be obvious and that are common causes of allergic reactions, which can be serious. These include nuts and grains, tree fruits, dairy products and eggs, and shellfish.

GUIDELINES FOR HANDLING LEFTOVERS

Refrigerate or freeze leftover cooked foods as soon and as quickly as possible, within 4 hours of cooking. If a dish has been left out overnight, discard it.

Don't put large amounts of warm food directly into the refrigerator or freezer. It may end up spending a long time in the microbe growth zone, and will heat the chilled foods around it, compromising their quality.

Divide large volumes of warm food among smaller containers to speed cooling.

Immerse the containers in cold or ice water first, to further speed cooling and minimize warming of the refrigerator or freezer.

Use most refrigerated leftovers within a few days.

Thaw frozen leftovers in the refrigerator or immersed in ice water.

Reheat cooked leftovers to a minimum of 160°F/70°C, covered to avoid heat loss from evaporating moisture.

When in doubt about the safety of a food, throw it out. Illness is more costly than discarded food.

CLEANING UP AND SANITIZING

Cleaning up removes food residues and microbes so that new foods can be prepared and served safely.

Sanitizing is the process of treating kitchen work surfaces to reduce the numbers of microbes on them and make them safe for contact with food. Microbes persist on apparently clean sinks and dry counters, draining racks and boards, on faucets, even in dishwashers.

To minimize the trouble of cleaning up, use pan lids, spatter guards, and spoon rests to keep foods and processes contained.

Rinse, soak, and clean as you cook. Food residues will come off all surfaces with less work, soap, and water if they don't have a chance to dry.

Hot tap water and detergents are effective at detaching and rinsing away most food residues from surfaces. Undercooked eggs and uncooked doughs harden in high heat and soften better in warm water.

Dishwashers are a time-saving and thorough way of cleaning dishes and utensils. Make sure your hot-water heater supplies the necessary water temperature for proper cleaning, in the range of 120 to 150°F / 50 to 65°C.

Use lye oven cleaners carefully for baked or charred residues on ovens, outdoor grills, and nonaluminum pots. Lye is caustic and can damage skin and clothes.

Bacteria thrive in moist sponges and in scouring pads, cloths, and brushes, which spread them to other surfaces when used to "clean." A sour smell is a telltale sign of large bacterial populations.

Use quick-drying cloths and brushes for most cleaning, sponges only for soaking up puddles of water.

Replace kitchen linens every day or two, and launder in hot water. Use separate towels for drying hands and surfaces.

Sanitize your kitchen work areas regularly with vinegar, household chlorine bleach, or boiling water. It's especially important after handling raw meats, poultry, fish, and fruits and vegetables that grow in close contact with the soil. Treat faucets and refrigerator door handles also.

To sanitize work surfaces:

- *Scrub the surfaces with soap and hot water, rinse and dry.*
- *Spray or wipe down the surfaces with a diluted solution* of distilled vinegar, 1 part to 2 parts water, or household bleach, 1 teaspoon/5 milliliters per quart/liter of water. Use vinegar for wood cutting boards, which chlorine will discolor.
- *Allow the surfaces to dry,* and then rinse or wipe off with clean wet cloths. Ventilate the kitchen well and leave the room while bleach acts; it forms toxic volatile organic compounds.

To sanitize cleaning sponges, pads, and cloths, hold them in a pot of boiling water for 5 minutes; or soak in bleach or vinegar solution; or wet, wrap loosely in plastic wrap, and microwave until steaming.

Run your dishwasher's high-temperature sanitizing cycle regularly, if it has one.

7

FRUITS

Fruits offer everyday inspiration to the cook when they remind us how needlessly delicious and beautiful foods can be. Fruits are the only foods we have that were designed to be both tasty and eye-catching for us—and for our fellow plant-eating animals. And with no cooking required, just the self-preparation we call ripening. Plants make fruits appealing, bright and sweet and juicy, so creatures that can move around will eat them and spread their seeds far and wide.

Mission accomplished.

Truly delicious fruits aren't necessarily easy to come by, especially if you pick not from the tree but from the supermarket bin, where they're seldom ripe and at their best. I feel lucky to have gorged on wild black-berries as a child, and to have planted peach and nectarine and cherry and fig trees whose fruit I could let linger before harvest until they were soft and ripe to the core. These remain touchstones of deliciousness for me, as do the tastes of my visit a few years ago to the national collection of apple varieties in Geneva, New York, where I sampled more apple flavors in a day, anise and banana and rose amazingly among them, than I had in all the rest of my life. If you don't have a garden, or a gardening neighbor, or a nearby national collection, then seek out farmer's markets or make a picking expedition, and gather some touchstones of your own.

Inspiringly ripe fruits can also be a challenge to the cook: what can you make with them that will be an improvement over giving them a wash, a plate, and a napkin? Well, the texture of a dried apricot, velvety outside and chewy within, the distractionless intensity of a seedless raspberry puree, the slow-developing ruby color of simmered quince, the natural spiciness of apples cooked for a few minutes into a sauce. Just to begin with.

FRUIT SAFETY

The main hazards posed by fruits reside on their surfaces.

Bacteria, viruses, and chemical residues can end up on fruit surfaces during growth in the field, harvest, processing, shipping, and sale. Fruits carrying harmful bacteria regularly cause serious outbreaks of illness. You can't always recognize contaminated fruits by their appearance or smell.

Washing can't eliminate all microbes or chemical residues from fruits. To minimize their hazards, peel fruits and/or cook them.

Don't serve raw unpeeled fruits to people who are especially vulnerable to illness.

Prepare all fruits with care, especially those that grow on or near the ground. Wash soiled melon rinds with soapy water before cutting into them.

Wash fruits thoroughly in copious water. If you don't use them immediately, dry them to discourage surface microbes.

Trim away moldy or discolored parts along with a wide margin of healthy-looking flesh.

Serve peeled or cut raw fruits promptly. To keep them for more than an hour or two, refrigerate them. Sprinkle with strongly acid lemon or lime juice to slow the growth of microbes.

Keep precut fruits refrigerated until just before serving.

Dried fruits treated with sulfites can cause life-threatening reactions in people who suffer from asthma or allergies. If this is a concern, check labels and buy fruits dried without sulfites.

FRUIT RIPENING

Fresh fruits are alive and at their best when they're fully ripe. Ripening is the natural process by which mature fruits soften and develop flavor. Once fully ripe, many fruits continue to change and become overripe—too soft and unpleasantly flavored—and prone to spoiling.

Most fruits are harvested and sold before they're fully ripe, so they'll be firmer and less easily bruised, and will keep longer before spoiling.

Fruits generally ripen in one of two different ways.

Plant-ripening fruits don't develop much flavor after they're harvested from the tree or vine, and should taste good when you buy them. They include citrus fruits, most berries, grapes, cherries, melons, pineapples, and plums.

Delayed-ripening fruits continue to develop flavor and soften after harvest. These fruits are best held for several days until they soften and their flavor peaks. They include apricots, avocados, bananas, kiwis, mangoes, pears, peaches and nectarines, persimmons, and tomatoes. Apples also soften and sweeten with time but are usually preferred while they're still crisp.

To speed ripening, keep delayed-ripening fruits in a warm place to quicken their metabolism and enclose them in a paper or perforated plastic bag, if possible with an already softening piece of fruit, to concentrate their ripening gas, ethylene. Don't keep them in an airtight bag, which will suffocate them.

SHOPPING FOR FRUITS

With a few exceptions, the best-quality fresh fruits are those that have been ripened fully on the tree or plant, handled with care not to damage their soft flesh, and brought to market within a day or two.

Most supermarket fruits are picked hard and unripe and shipped hundreds or thousands of miles.

Buy local fruits in season whenever possible. Out-of-season fruits come from far away and are picked before their full flavor has developed.

Taste samples before buying. Looks can be deceiving, and bargain fruits are often on the edge of spoiling. Heirloom and novel varieties are often more flavorful than the standard mass-produced types, but not always.

Beware of glossy supermarket fruits, which are often coated with wax to maximize shelf life. A matte surface that becomes shiny with rubbing has retained the plant's natural wax, and can be a sign of fresher fruit.

Choose small- to medium-size fruits with bright colors and a firm, full appearance. Very large fruits are often watery and less flavorful. Heft fruits and choose those that feel heavy for their size.

Choose plant-ripening fruits that appear to be the ripest: full-colored, soft, and aromatic.

Avoid fruits that look wrinkled, leathery, dented, bruised, slimy, or moldy. At farmer's markets, avoid fruits that have been sitting in full sun and gotten hot to the touch. Prolonged high heat harms fresh fruit.

Examine berry baskets from the bottom and sides, and avoid those with signs of damage, leaked juices, or mold.

Don't put heavy items on top of fresh fruits in shopping carts or bags. Physical pressure damages them and speeds spoilage.

Precut fruits are convenient but vulnerable to spoilage, especially after the package is opened.

Frozen fruits can equal or better the flavor quality of fresh, especially delicate berries that spoil quickly after harvest. But freezing damages their texture, which becomes soft and leaky.

Choose frozen packages from the coldest corners of the freezer, and just before you check out, to minimize partial thawing. Bring a picnic cooler to transport frozen foods home.

Dried fruits come in two forms. Some are treated with sulfites to preserve their color, flavor, and vitamins. Nonsulfited fruits are usually brown and have a more generic raisiny flavor. They're safer to serve to people with asthma or allergies.

Buy canned fruits sold in their own juices, not in a sugar syrup.

Traditional fruit preserves are high in sugar to produce their thick consistency. Many preserves that claim to have less or no added sugar are made with concentrated grape and other juices, and contain as much sugar as standard preserves.

STORING FRUITS

Fresh fruits are alive and breathing. They exhale moisture, which encourages mold growth and spoilage if it's trapped on their surfaces. Berries are especially fragile due to their active metabolism and thin skins.

The aim in storing fruits is to slow the inevitable growth of spoilage microbes, and sometimes to slow the fruits' metabolism.

To keep most fruits for a few days, remove them from bags or baskets and place them in a single layer on a surface lined with moisture-absorbing cloth or paper. Piling traps moisture, causes dents and bruises, and speeds spoilage.

Keep fragile berries for a day at room temperature, spaced apart on a platter or baking sheet lined with cloth or paper. To keep them longer, refrigerate in a plastic basket enclosed in a gently inflated plastic bag, to reduce contact between bag and berry surfaces.

To delay mold growth on berries, especially if you see it beginning on some berries in a basket, heat a pot of water to 125°F/52°C, immerse and gently move the berries around in the water for 30–45 seconds, then allow them to dry in a single layer.

To keep most ripe fruits for more than a few days, refrigerate them, enclosed in a produce drawer or plastic bag to slow moisture loss.

Keep tomatoes at cool room temperature, to avoid flavor losses caused by temperatures below 50°F/10°C.

Don't refrigerate fruits until they've ripened fully. Cold temperatures can damage their ability to ripen.

To restore the flavor of refrigerated fruits, remove them from cold storage at least several hours before using them. Cold suspends aroma production and release in fruits.

To freeze raw fruits for use within a few weeks, wash and cut them up if necessary, toss cut fruits with powdered vitamin C (ascorbic acid) to reduce browning and off flavors, and place on a baking sheet in the freezer until hard. Store the frozen pieces wrapped tightly to prevent off flavors from freezer burn or the freezer itself. Or freeze the pieces immersed in a container of medium to heavy sugar syrup (5 to 10 tablespoons/75 to 150 grams sugar per cup/250 milliliters water).

To freeze fruits for more than a few weeks, "blanch" them first by dropping them into boiling water for a few minutes. This inactivates fruit enzymes and prevents them from slowly creating off flavors and destroying nutrients.

To keep dried fruits for more than a few weeks, wrap them airtight and store in the refrigerator. Dried fruits slowly brown and lose flavor.

THE ESSENTIALS OF COOKING WITH FRUITS

Fruits are filled with sugars, acids, sensitive pigments, and active enzymes that can complicate their preparation.

Always start by washing fruits thoroughly, even if you're going to remove their peels. A knife can easily transfer surface contamination to the inner flesh.

To aid the peeling of tomatoes, stone fruits, and citrus fruits, blanch in simmering water: 10 to 15 seconds for thin skins, a minute for thicker citrus skins.

Use stainless steel or ceramic knives to cut fruits. Carbon steel will cause off tastes and colors.

Cut fruits to roughly the same size so that pieces will cook through at the same time.

To minimize the oxidation and brown discoloration of susceptible cut or peeled fruits while you're preparing them, protect their surfaces with antioxidant vitamin C (ascorbic acid), the most effective treatment, or with an acid that slows the responsible browning enzyme. Immerse them in ice water containing dissolved vitamin C (a crushed 250-milligram tablet per cup/250 milliliters), or citric acid (sour salt) or lemon juice (1 gram citric acid or 1 tablespoon/15 grams lemon juice per cup/250 milliliters). Or toss them in powdered vitamin C or citric acid, or lemon juice. Fruits susceptible to browning include apples, bananas, peaches, and pears.

Use cut or peeled fruit immediately, or cover it closely and refrigerate.

Use stainless steel, enamel, ceramic, or nonstick utensils to cook fruits. Contact with bare aluminum or iron turns some pigments blue and green and imparts a metallic taste.

When exposed to dry heat, fruits brown and scorch quickly thanks to their high sugar content. Use moderate temperatures when baking, frying, and grilling.

Some raw fruits contain enzymes that liquefy gelatin-based jellies and can make milk and cream taste bitter. These include fig, melons, pineapple, and kiwi. To make a jelly with these fruits, cook them through to disable their enzymes before combining with the gelatin, or use canned fruits, or make the jelly with protein-free agar.

Fruit acids and tannins curdle milk and cream, especially when they're warm or hot.

Dried fruits absorb water from other ingredients. If this isn't desirable, as in making baked goods, presoak them in water or another liquid, or briefly steam them.

RAW FRUITS AND FRUIT JUICES

Raw fruits and juices are fragile, best served immediately or immediately chilled.

Prepare raw fruits with carefully cleaned hands, utensils, and cutting surfaces.

Wash the fruit thoroughly and cut away any bruised or moldy areas.

Combat brown discoloration in fruits prone to it, especially apples, pears, and bananas, by treating pieces with vitamin C or acids (see the preceding page).

Juicing extracts the flavorful and nutritious fluids in fruits, leaving behind most of the solid structural materials, or fiber. The thorough mixing of fruit enzymes and other materials with the air makes juices especially quick to lose flavor, color, and nutrients.

Use raw cut fruits or juices immediately, or cover them closely and refrigerate. To slow juice deterioration, immediately add 1 gram vitamin C to each quart or liter of juice.

To freeze fruit juices into ices and sorbets, see p. 463.

FRUIT PUREES, SAUCES, BUTTERS, AND PASTES

Pureeing breaks up fruit flesh and individual fruit cells, and creates a thick fluid that can serve as a flavorful ingredient or sauce. The fruit's solid structural materials give body to the watery fluids.

For fine-textured, silky purees, use a blender. Food mills and processors usually produce a coarser result. For the finest texture, pass purees through a strainer.

To minimize the browning of light-colored fruit purees, including apple, banana, peach, and pear, prechill fruits and dust pieces with powdered vitamin C before pureeing.

Serve fresh purees quickly, or press plastic wrap directly onto the surface and refrigerate or freeze. Fresh pureed fruit is an unstable mixture of enzymes and other materials that react with oxygen, and it quickly deteriorates.

To freeze fruit purees into ices and sorbets, see p. 463.

Cooking fruit purees removes water, thickens their consistencies, and intensifies flavor.

Fruit butters, pastes, and cheeses are purees cooked thick enough to become spreadable or solid. They're usually made with apples, pears, quinces, and guavas, and take hours of gentle heating to cook off much of their moisture without scorching.

To avoid scorching a puree, heat it in a broad pan with occasional stirring in an oven at 225°F/110°C. Or on the stove top, turn down the heat gradually as it becomes more concentrated, and stir and scrape the bottom increasingly often. Purees move more slowly as they thicken, and stick and scorch more easily on the pan bottom.

Start cooking apple, pear, and quince purees with the whole fruit, minus stems and dried flower remains at the bottom, and strain skins, seed, and core when the fruit breaks down. Skins and seeds add flavor.

DEHYDRATING FRUITS AND FRUIT PUREES

Dehydrating fruits and fruit purees preserves them indefinitely, intensifies their flavor, and gives them a pleasantly chewy texture. Dehydrated purees are often called leathers.

Heat fruits and purees at very low oven temperatures, 130 to 160°F/55 to 70°C, to avoid hardening the surface before the inner moisture has escaped, and to avoid damage to color and flavor. For the greatest control, use an electric food dryer.

Cut fruit into thin slices, and spread purees into a thin layer, to speed drying.

Refrigerate dried fruit pieces and leathers, wrapped airtight, to maintain their flavor and texture. They slowly turn brown, lose aroma, and toughen.

POACHING FRUITS, COMPOTES

Poaching fruits in sugar syrup stabilizes their color and flavor, and can either firm their texture or soften them to make a compote. Compote liquids often include fruit juices whose acidity can slow and control softening.

Cut fruits into equal-size pieces so that they'll cook evenly. Presoak or precook dry fruits in liquid to remoisten them.

Adjust the syrup's sugar concentration to the task. Use a low-sugar syrup, 3 or 4 volumes water to 1 volume sugar, to soften firm fruits and make a compote. Use a high-sugar syrup, 2 or 3 volumes sugar to 1 volume water, to firm the surface of soft fruits.

Keep the syrup at a gentle simmer to avoid damaging the fruit surfaces, either on the stove top or in a moderate oven.

Check the fruit's firmness frequently, and remove from the heat promptly to avoid overcooking. Both softening and firming take just a few minutes.

BAKING AND FRYING FRUITS

Baking and frying are different methods for applying dry heat to fruits, removing moisture, softening them, concentrating and developing their flavor, and creating sweet caramel aromas.

Baking cooks slowly and evenly with the oven's hot air and walls, and tends to concentrate the juices in the fruit.

Frying cooks more rapidly through contact with hot fat or oil and the metal pan, and reduces leaked juices to a sticky brown syrup.

Butter contributes caramel aromas to fruits cooked with it, and works especially well for frying fruits or greasing a baking dish.

Bake and fry at medium to low heat. Fruits are high in sugar, and brown and scorch easily.

To bake whole fruits, pierce or partly peel them so that they won't burst during baking.

GRILLING AND BROILING FRUITS

Grilling and broiling expose fruits to the high temperature of a flame or glowing electrical element. They create a dark brown or charred surface and characteristic flavor.

Fruit surfaces brown and char quickly thanks to their high sugar content. The darker that sugars are cooked, the less sweet and the more bitter they get.

To even out the browning of the fruit surface, lightly oil or butter it before cooking.

The key to good grilled or broiled fruit is to balance rapid surface browning with slower heating through.

Cooking rates depend on the intensity of the heat source, the distance between the heat source and fruit, and the fruit's sugar content.

For maximum flexibility in grilling, have one area very hot for browning, and a second moderately hot area for heating through. Color the fruits as desired over the very hot area, then finish cooking over the moderate area.

Check fruits frequently during broiling to make sure they don't blacken excessively. If they're well colored before they heat through, finish the cooking in the oven.

CANNING FRUITS

Canning cooks and preserves fruit pieces, purees, and juices indefinitely by isolating them completely and heating them hot and long enough to kill all microbes.

Improperly canned fruits will deteriorate quickly, and can be dangerous. If the heat treatment is insufficient or the handling careless, it can encourage the growth of potentially fatal botulism bacteria.

Follow well-established guidelines carefully. Consult the U.S. Department of Agriculture's *Complete Guide to Home Canning and Preserving,* available in print or on the USDA Web site, www.usda.gov, or make sure that your recipe includes these steps:

- *Prepare the jars and lids in boiling water.*
- *Heat the fruit preparation or the liquid portion of it to a boil.*
- *Seal the hot fruit preparation in the hot jars airtight.*
- *Heat the jars fully immersed in boiling water or in a pressure canner.* Timings vary depending on the jar size and kitchen altitude. High-temperature pressure canning is essential for a few low-acid fruits (figs, papayas).
- *Check the cooled jars to make sure the lids are bowed in the center and the seal remains airtight.*

MAKING JAMS, JELLIES, AND SUGAR PRESERVES

Jams, jellies, and other traditional sugar preserves treat fruit with a combination of thorough heating and enough added sugar to discourage the growth of spoilage microbes.

Sugar is usually the main ingredient in fruit preserves. Preserves that contain 60 to 65 percent sugar by weight are most stable and set into the traditional spreadable solid consistency. Lower sugar levels make thinner preserves that require refrigeration to slow spoilage by molds.

Acidity and pectin content also determine the consistency of jams and jellies. Pectin is a natural thickening agent in fruits, and it requires high acidity in order to set. A fruit may have enough acid and pectin to set on its own, or may need supplementing with one or both.

Count on adding pectin to many berries, stone fruits, and tropical fruits. Pectin is sold in powdered and liquid form. To test for adequate pectin, prepare the fruit by simmering, then mix 1 spoonful with 3 spoonfuls of denatured rubbing alcohol. If the fruit liquid forms a solid mass, it contains enough pectin to make firm preserves.

There are two main cooking steps in making fruit preserves, simmering the fruit alone, and then boiling it with sugar.

First simmer the fruit alone or with water to free the fruit fluids and thickening pectin from the flesh. Supplement if desired by including pectin-rich apple cores or lemon pith.

To make a clear jelly, strain the simmered fruit and water through several layers of cheesecloth by gravity alone, without pressing down on the fruit solids. Pressing will make a cloudy jelly.

Then cook the fruit or its strained liquid with sugar and any pectin preparation at a rolling boil, and evaporate excess water until the mixture reaches 217 to 226°F / 103 to 108°C (at sea level). The temperature indicates that the mixture has evaporated enough water and reached the correct sugar concentration.

For the freshest flavor and greatest pectin-thickening power, keep the cooking periods as brief as possible. Prolonged high heat and acidity break down pectin.

To speed evaporation and minimize cooking time, maximize the area of fruit mix exposed to the air. Cook small batches in a wide pan. Use a pan with high sides, to prevent the mix from boiling over.

To test the mix when it has boiled at the correct temperature, place a drop on a cold spoon or plate, and refrigerate for 2 to 3 minutes. It should set.

If the test drop fails to set, call the mix a fruit sauce and enjoy the more immediate flavor release it provides compared to a jam. Or combine more pectin and/or acid with a small amount of the mix, add to the pot, and reboil.

To store preserves indefinitely at room temperature, pack in sterilized jars and process them in boiling water. Times depend on jar size and kitchen altitude. Consult the U.S. Department of Agriculture's *Complete Guide to Home Canning and Preserving,* available in print or on the USDA Web site, www.usda.gov.

To store preserves for only a few weeks in the refrigerator, pour them into clean plastic or glass containers and cover.

Uncooked and low-sugar jams are preservelike spreads that are not true preserves, and must be refrigerated. They're made with special packaged pectins. They are quicker to prepare, contain a higher proportion of fruit to sugar, and retain more fresh-fruit flavor.

To make uncooked or low-sugar jams, follow the directions that come with the specially treated pectins that make these spreads possible.

PRESERVING FRUITS IN ALCOHOL

High-alcohol spirits can preserve and flavor fruits, and be flavored and colored by them. Vodka and brandy are common choices. Wine and sherry don't have enough alcohol to preserve fruits, so store wine-fruit mixtures in the refrigerator.

Keep fruit completely submerged in the alcohol. Weigh the raw fruit, and use at least the same weight of spirits that contain around 40 percent alcohol, so that the mixture will be about 20 percent alcohol. Inadequate alcohol may allow the fruit to spoil.

PICKLING FRUITS AND PRESERVING LEMONS

Pickling flavors fruits in a sweet-sour mixture of sugar, vinegar, and spices, and preserves them for days to months in the refrigerator, months when canned.

To pickle fruits, clean the fruits thoroughly, cut into pieces, bring to a simmer with the other ingredients, and cook until somewhat tender, which may take hours. Pickled fruits retain some firmness thanks to the high acid and sugar of the pickling liquid.

Store finished pickles in the refrigerator, or can them.

Preserved lemons are pickled in a mixture of salt and their own highly acid juices.

To make preserved lemons, wash unwaxed lemons well, partly cut them into four connected quarters and crowd them into a jar, sprinkle them liberally with salt, top up the jar with lemon juice, cover, and keep at room temperature for several weeks, until the lemons soften and develop a rich aroma.

Make sure that all of the lemons are always fully submerged in liquid.

Store preserved lemons in the refrigerator to maintain their texture and aroma, or at room temperature for continued softening and flavor development.

COMMON FRUITS: APPLES TO WATERMELON

Apples come in many varieties, some dense and crisp, some porous and mealy, some with distinctive flavors, some firm and some mushy when cooked.

Keep apples in the refrigerator to maintain their flavor and texture.

To preview an apple's cooked texture, microwave a few slices just until soft, or briefly bake them. Varieties that hold their shape well when baked whole include Cortland, Empire, Jonagold, Northern Spy, and Rome. McIntosh apples become very fragile when cooked in any way.

Apricots quickly pass from ripe to mushy. To rescue mushy apricots, cook them for a few minutes into a thick sauce, or cut them in half and dry them in a low oven.

Dried apricots come in two main market styles: pale and deep orange. Choose the deep orange type for the best flavor and nutritional value. Both are treated with sulfites. Less common sulfite-free apricots are brown and have a generic raisiny flavor.

Bananas require holding at room temperature in order to ripen. Don't refrigerate them until they're fully ripe. Refrigeration will darken the skin but not the ripe flesh.

Plantains are varieties of banana that don't get as sweet or soft when they ripen.

For cooking, use firm, slightly unripe bananas, or replace them with plantains.

Berries—blackberries, blueberries, raspberries, strawberries—are small, mostly fragile fruits that can go moldy in hours. Use them as soon as possible after buying them, and rinse just before using.

Berries freeze quickly and well on baking sheets for later cooking. When frozen, slide them into a plastic freezer bag, squeeze the air out, and seal tightly. All berries will leak juices when thawed.

Cherries keep best when they're picked with the stem on. Sweet varieties are the most common; sour cherries (morello, Montmorency) are a different species with a distinctive flavor, and are preferred for pies.

Intensify the flavor in cooked cherry dishes by leaving the pits in. But serve with a warning!

Citrus fruits—grapefruit, lemons, limes, oranges, mandarins, pomelos—are high-acid fruits whose segmented interior is filled with small, separate juice sacs.

Most citrus aroma is in the outer peel or zest, the thin colored layer dotted with oil glands that lies above the bitter white pith. Use the zest by peeling it off with as little pith as possible. Add it to dishes or flex pieces of peel to spray skin aromatic oils onto the juice or other foods.

Choose citrus fruits that feel heavy and firm and have a thin flexible peel. The climates of California and Texas often produce especially deep colors and flavors. If you'll be using the peel, choose fruits that haven't been coated with wax.

To squeeze out the most juice from a citrus fruit, prepare the fruit by pressing down while rolling it on a cutting board. This weakens the skin and inner fruit structure.

Use juice made from seedless navel oranges within a few hours. It slowly becomes bitter. Valencia and other juice oranges don't have this problem.

Cranberries keep for weeks refrigerated thanks to their high acidity and antimicrobial compounds. Their high pectin content produces a thick sauce with just a few minutes of cooking.

Pick through cranberries carefully and discard soft berries. The strong off taste of just a few can spoil a batch of sauce or a dish.

Dates are most commonly available dried, but worth seeking out fresh and enjoying in their crunchy and moist soft stages. Keep fresh dates in a single layer at room temperature.

Figs are very perishable thanks to their high moisture content, low acidity, and a small opening in some varieties (Brown Turkey, Mission) that exposes their moist interior to insects and microbes. They can be spoiled inside without obvious external signs.

Eat fresh figs within a day, or refrigerate or cook them.

To ensure against serving or cooking spoiled figs, cut them in half to check their interior.

Grapes are usually harvested before they're fully ripe, when they have a crisp texture and will keep well for weeks in a cold refrigerator.

For more flavorful grapes, choose "green" grapes that have ripened enough to turn yellow, or especially flavorful varieties, including muscat and Concord.

Kiwi fruits are firm and tart and decorative, with a beautifully patterned cross section, and become softer, sweeter, and more aromatic as they ripen.

Kiwi fruits contain oxalate crystals that irritate the throat when the fruits are juiced, pureed, or dried. Raw kiwis liquefy gelatin jellies.

Mangoes are shipped unripe from several tropical regions of the world and can improve in sweetness and aroma in the kitchen. They come in many different varieties, some very fibrous, others almost custardlike in texture.

Don't refrigerate these tropical fruits until they've fully ripened at room temperature.

Melons (not including watermelons) fall into two groups:

Winter melons (honeydew, casaba, canary, crenshaw) usually have white or green flesh and can keep for more than a month at cool room temperature.

Summer melons (cantaloupe, musk, Persian) usually have orange flesh, are especially aromatic, and keep for up to two weeks.

Choose melons that are heavy, with little or no green color in the skin, and that give slightly when pressed at the stem end and flower ends. Summer melons should have a pleasant aroma, but winter melons will have little or none.

Wash melons in warm, soapy water before cutting, and minimize contact between flesh and skin as you handle them. They grow on the ground and can carry microbes on their surface.

Nectarines are a fuzzless version of the peach, less susceptible to molds and bruises, and with a firmer texture and more intense flavor.

Buy nectarines in season from local producers. Cold storage before they're ripe produces a dry, mealy texture.

Choose nectarines that feel heavy, and refrigerate only after they've ripened.

Papayas are tropical fruits, and come in two types: small and yellow-fleshed, and larger and salmon-pink. Unripe papayas are bland but crisp, shredded for salads in Thai cooking. Ripe ones are soft and aromatic. Raw papayas liquefy gelatin jellies.

Choose papayas with little or no green in the skin and with evident soft spots, which often develop before the inner flesh is fully ripe.

Store papayas at room temperature. Refrigerate only after cutting up.

Papaya seeds taste like nasturtium flowers and can be used for their mild pepperiness.

Peaches are among the most fragile tree fruits; they bruise and mold easily. Handle them gently, and don't pile in the fruit bowl.

Buy peaches in season from local producers. Cold storage before they're ripe produces a dry, mealy texture.

Choose peaches that feel heavy, and refrigerate only after they've ripened.

Pears are best when harvested hard and ripened at a cool room temperature. When harvested after ripening begins, they become mealy.

Buy pears in season from local producers. Cold storage before they've ripened turns them brown and mushy at the core.

Ripen hard pears at cool room temperature. Warmth makes them mealy. Refrigerate only after they've ripened, and keep them for another day or two; ripe pears deteriorate quickly.

Persimmons have a mild flavor and come in two very different types. Pointed-bottom Hachiya types are inedibly astringent until the fruit becomes very soft. Flat-bottom Fuyu types are not astringent and can be eaten crisp.

To remove astringency from firm Hachiya persimmons, vacuum-pack the fruits and keep them warm, at about 100°F/40°C, for 24 hours.

To make a traditional dark persimmon pudding, leaven with baking soda and cook for hours. For an orange pudding, leaven with baking powder and cook just until done.

Pineapples are tropical fruits, harvested before their prime and shipped long distances. They continue to soften in the kitchen but don't become more flavorful.

Different parts of the fruit have different flavor balances. The bottom is the sweetest, and the outer layers are the tartest.

Choose pineapples with yellow skin and evident aroma, and no signs of moldiness on the bottom, the first part of the fruit to ripen.

Don't use fresh pineapple in dishes that include gelatin or milk products. Its enzymes prevent gelatin from setting and make milk products bitter. Cooking eliminates the enzyme activity.

Plums come in two families. Japanese varieties are usually round, very moist, and tart-skinned. European varieties are elongated, dryer, and sweeter. Pluots are meaty, large plum-apricot hybrids.

Use European plums in baking. Japanese varieties are too watery.

Beware of eating too many plums or prunes at one sitting. They contain laxative sugars.

Pomegranates have a leathery skin enclosing dozens of small, delicate fruitlets, each containing red juice and a seed.

To extract pomegranate fruitlets with minimal mess, score the skin with a knife, then hold the whole fruit under water, peel the skin away, and gently push fruitlets off the inner membranes.

Quinces are fragrant relatives of the apple and pear, with a flesh that stays hard and astringent until heated, and cooks down into a firm sliceable mass (Italian cotognata, Spanish membrillo).

To deepen quince flavor, include the peel in the dish, and strain out if desired.

To develop a translucent ruby-red color in off-white quince slices, cook them gently for hours in a light sugar syrup.

Rhubarb is not a true fruit, but the tart, fibrous, celerylike stalk of a large-leaved bush. Some varieties are red, others green. Store it like other vegetables, in the refrigerator.

Choose firm, thin stalks with small fibers. Strip tough fibers from larger stalks.

Keep red rhubarb intensely colored and all rhubarb neatly intact by minimizing cooking liquid and cooking time. Rhubarb starts to disintegrate when cooked for more than a few minutes.

Watermelons now come in various flesh colors, with and without developed seeds. Even "seedless" watermelons have small, immature seeds. Watermelons don't develop more flavor after harvest.

Choose watermelons that are heavy for their size and have a light yellow background skin color, an indication of fruit maturity.

Wash watermelons in warm soapy water before cutting. They grow on the ground and can carry microbes on their surface.

Don't store watermelons in the refrigerator for more than a few days. They're a warm-climate fruit and will soften.

8

VEGETABLES AND FRESH HERBS

Vegetables aren't sweet and soft and easy to love the way fruits are. It takes a cook to make tubers, stalks, and leaves lovable. That's because plants not only didn't design them to be delicious as they did fruits, many tried their best to protect them by making them really unpleasant.

The flavors of most vegetables—and of the fresh herbs that we use to add flavor to dishes—are actually there to serve as chemical warnings and weapons and deter insects and other creatures from eating them. This is more obvious for such strong-flavored foods as garlic and onions and their relatives, bitter chicories, mustard greens and radishes and the other members of the cabbage family, and chillis. But even the "green" flavors of lettuces and spinach and artichokes, and the earthy aromas of mushrooms and beets, come from chemicals that irritate and repel. We can enjoy all these foods because cooking alters and disarms or disguises their weaponry, or in the case of herbs, because we eat them in small quantities as accents rather than a main course.

Apart from seed-carrying fruits that we treat as vegetables, notably the tomato, most vegetables don't ripen the way fruits do. They're edible when they're a freshly sprouted seed and remain edible until they've become too fibrous to chew. Much of the produce we see in markets, farmer's markets included, has been harvested late in its edible life, for maximum mass and durability. Until I had a chance to grow some vegetables myself and chew on them every day or two through the season, I hadn't noticed that big romaine lettuce leaves often taste rubbery, or realized how unlike their usual oversize versions midsize chard and collards are, tender and sweet and mild after just a few minutes of cooking.

So it pays to be just as picky with vegetables as with fruits if you want to make the most of their wonderfully various flavors, textures, shapes, colors, and possibilities for cooking and serving.

VEGETABLE AND HERB SAFETY

The main hazards from vegetables and herbs are microbes, which can end up on and embedded in vegetables and herbs during growth in the field, harvest, washing, packing, and sale. Vegetables and herbs carrying harmful bacteria cause outbreaks of illness every year.

You can't always recognize contaminated vegetables or herbs by their appearance or smell, or by their apparent cleanness, even in prepacked bags.

Washing can't eliminate all microbes from vegetables and herbs. The only way to guarantee their safety is to cook them.

Don't serve raw vegetables or herbs, including salads, to people who are especially vulnerable to illness.

Prepare and serve raw vegetables and herbs with care. Trim away moldy or discolored parts with a wide margin and rinse them thoroughly in copious water.

Keep prepared raw vegetables chilled until you serve them, including packaged precut vegetables.

Minimize contact between herb leaves and their cut ends, especially if the ends have been kept wet and hospitable to microbes. Cut or twist off the stems before washing and chopping the leaves.

Wash hands, knives, and cutting boards with warm, soapy water after handling raw vegetables and herbs.

Potatoes accumulate toxic compounds in response to light, and celery in response to stress.

Don't use potatoes that have turned green without first peeling deeply to remove toxic alkaloids near the surface. Don't use green potatoes to make stuffed potato skins.

Discard badly wilted celery, which may contain compounds that cause skin rash.

SHOPPING FOR VEGETABLES AND HERBS

Fresh vegetables and herbs are alive and breathing, and any that grow above the ground should look like it. (Root vegetables and onions look dormant and are.) The best-quality fresh vegetables are the most recently harvested and most carefully handled.

Extra-large vegetables are usually the most mature, and can be coarse in texture and flavor.

Tiny "baby" or "micro" vegetables are immature, mild in flavor, and expensive.

Choose vegetables and herbs with deep colors, a firm, full appearance, and freshly cut stems. Fresh but slightly wilted leafy vegetables can be a good choice because they're more flexible and less easily cracked and damaged during handling than stiff leaves. They're easily rehydrated by soaking in water.

Avoid vegetables and herbs that look dull, wrinkled, dented, bruised, slimy, moldy, or that have brown, dry cut stems, or that have started to sprout. At farmer's markets, avoid vegetables and herbs that have been sitting in full sun and are hot to the touch.

Precut vegetables are convenient but more vulnerable to spoilage than intact vegetables, and are often wilted. Refresh them in ice-cold water before using.

Frozen vegetables can equal or better the quality of fresh, especially vegetables that lose flavor and tenderness rapidly after harvest. These include green peas and lima beans, and sweet corn.

Choose packages of frozen vegetables from the coldest corners of the market freezer, and just before you check out. Bag frozen foods together, and transport them home in a cooler. Repeated thawing and refreezing damages the quality of frozen foods.

STORING FRESH
VEGETABLES AND HERBS

Fresh vegetables and herbs gradually deteriorate as they use up their limited water and food reserves. The aim in storing them is to slow their deterioration by slowing their metabolism and moisture loss.

Tomatoes and avocados are fruits and need to ripen before we slow their metabolism. Speed their ripening by enclosing them in a paper bag to concentrate the ripening gas, ethylene, and keeping it in a warm place.

Keep most vegetables and herbs in the refrigerator, enclosed in a produce drawer or plastic bag to prevent moisture loss. Before storing, remove damaged portions and rubber bands or ties. Remove more perishable and nutrient-consuming green tops from root vegetables. Partly inflate plastic bags to minimize direct contact with produce, which traps its exhaled moisture and causes local waterlogging. Produce should be moist but not wet.

Keep cold-sensitive vegetables and herbs at cool room temperature to prevent damage or sprouting. These include tomatoes, unripe avocados, onions and garlic, basil, and potatoes to be used for frying, which when chilled accumulate sugars that cause them to brown too quickly.

To store herbs with fleshy stems, including parsley, cilantro, and dill, remove metal or rubber bands, cut off the lower stems, wash, roll in a moist paper towel, and refrigerate in a plastic bag. Or strip off the lower leaves, recut the stems to make a fresh surface for absorbing water, immerse the stems in water in a glass, and enclose the glass and herbs in a partly inflated plastic produce bag.

Keep most herbs in the refrigerator, cold-sensitive basil at room temperature.

To keep dry-climate herbs, including bay leaves, oregano, rosemary, sage, and thyme, rinse them well, then spread them on a plate to dry over a few days at room temperature. To dry them faster in a humid climate, use a low oven or dehydrator.

To freeze vegetables, blanch them first to inactivate plant enzymes that cause off flavors, colors, and vitamin loss. Wash them, cut into pieces that will heat through quickly and evenly, and drop into boiling water for 2 to 3 minutes. Chill immediately in ice water, then pat dry and freeze. Store the pieces wrapped tightly in plastic wrap to prevent off flavors from freezer burn or from the freezer itself.

To freeze fleshy herbs, rinse and pat them dry, freeze quickly on a plate or baking sheet, then wrap them tightly in plastic wrap. This preserves flavor reasonably well, but the herbs will turn dark and limp and wet when thawed.

To preserve herbs under oil or flavor oil with herbs, be careful to guard against the growth of botulism bacteria, which thrive in air-free conditions. Rinse herbs thoroughly and dry them. Premarinate garlic cloves in vinegar. Keep the containers in a cold corner of the refrigerator that stays below 40°F/4°C. Use herbs and oils within a few weeks.

SPROUTS AND MICROGREENS

Sprouts and microgreens are very young vegetables, only a few days old. They're milder in flavor than mature vegetables, delicately crisp, and usually eaten raw.

Sprouts are a common cause of foodborne illness. Bacteria readily grow on the moist surfaces of germinating seeds.

Don't serve raw sprouts to people who are vulnerable to illness.

To make sprouts or microgreens:

- *Buy seeds intended for sprouting and eating,* not planting. Garden seeds may be treated with toxic protective chemicals.
- *Soak the seeds in water* for several hours, then rinse and drain.
- *Keep the seeds in a sprouting jar,* cool and shielded from light, until they're ready in several days. Rinse and drain the seeds several times a day to prevent the accumulation of microbes.

Eat sprouts and microgreens promptly, or store in the coldest corner of the refrigerator and cook thoroughly before eating.

RAW SALADS

Raw salads are simple to make but reward attention to details with better texture.

Wash salad leaves, fresh herbs, and other ingredients in several changes of water until the water remains clear and gritless. Trim or discard damaged leaves.

Reduce leaf size by tearing gently or using a sharp knife. Avoid squeezing and dull knives, which damage leaves and produce dark edges and patches. Cut other vegetables into bite-size pieces.

Crisp leaves and other ingredients by immersing them for up to 15 minutes in ice water. Both water and cold increase plant tissue stiffness.

Chill the dressing in the refrigerator or freezer to thicken its consistency and help it cling to the leaves. Chill the bowl to keep the salad cold as it's prepared and served.

Dry leaves thoroughly using a spinner and/or towel.

Apply the dressing just before serving, and use just enough to coat the ingredients lightly.

To dress a salad that will be served over a long period, use a mayonnaise or other water-based dressing, which wilts and darkens the leaves more slowly than oil-based vinaigrettes.

To distribute just enough dressing quickly and evenly, feel and toss the leaves with your fingers (after washing your hands with warm, soapy water).

THE ESSENTIALS OF COOKING VEGETABLES AND HERBS

Cooking generally softens vegetable texture, deepens flavor, increases the availability of some nutrients while reducing the levels of others, and eliminates microbes.

High temperatures and minimal cooking times usually produce the best results. Vegetable tissues soften slowly at around 190°F/85°C, and faster at the boil. Overcooking turns most vegetables mushy and unpleasantly aromatic. Thin leaves are done in just a minute or two.

Some vegetables are slow to soften or never get completely soft when cooked. Beets, water chestnuts, bamboo shoots, lotus root, and many mushrooms remain firm naturally. Potatoes and some other vegetables can be usefully made to do so by holding them at around 140°F/60°C before boiling them. Acid cooking liquids will also slow the softening of most vegetables.

To cook vegetables well, taste them frequently, and stop the cooking as soon as they reach the desired texture.

Cut vegetables to roughly the same size so that pieces will cook through at the same time.

To slow discoloration of cut or peeled vegetables prone to browning, including potatoes and artichokes, drop the pieces into ice water containing dissolved antioxidant vitamin C (250 milligrams per cup/250 milliliters), or acidulated with lemon juice or citric acid (1 tablespoon/15 grams juice or 1 gram acid per cup/250 milliliters). Or toss with powdered vitamin C, lemon juice, or citric acid.

Cut green vegetables into pieces that will cook through in 5 minutes or less. The chlorophyll pigments turn dull if cooked much longer. Cut mature leaves from their thick stalks and midribs so that they can be cooked separately and more briefly.

"Shocking" green vegetables in cold water right after cooking isn't necessary to "set the color." It's a restaurant method that prevents the continued cooking and color dulling that can occur when hot vegetables are simply piled in a colander after boiling or steaming. Shocked vegetables have to be reheated to serve them hot, and reheating can dull color too.

At home, cool just-cooked vegetables to nondulling serving temperature by transferring them to the serving dish and tossing them with any other ingredients.

Acids of any kind dull green chlorophyll. Dress green vegetables with acidic ingredients (vinegar, tomatoes, or lemon or other fruit juices) at the last minute.

To prevent a wrinkled surface on many cooked vegetables, including asparagus, green beans, carrots, and corn, coat them right after cooking with a little oil or butter. This prevents the hot vegetable from losing evaporated moisture and shrinking.

Cook most frozen vegetables without thawing. For spinach and other delicate leaves that cook very quickly, thaw just enough to break the block apart into small pieces.

Herbs are seldom cooked on their own, either because their flavors are too strong or they're too easily lost in cooking.

Purees of parsley retain their colors and flavor well, while cilantro loses its aroma and basil darkens. Blanching for a few seconds in boiling water helps retain green colors, and cilantro aroma, but diminishes basil aroma.

Brief frying crisps most herb leaves and leaves them translucent while taming the pungency of sage and oregano and retaining some native aroma in basil and parsley. A few seconds in oil at 350°F/175°C is enough for most leaves. Avoid pressing the leaves against the pan bottom, which browns them.

BOILING VEGETABLES

Boiling cooks vegetables by direct contact with water at about 212°F/100°C. The boiling point of water decreases, and cooking times increase, at elevations much above sea level.

The advantage of boiling is that it cooks vegetables quickly, which helps preserve vitamin C and the bright green color of chlorophyll.

The disadvantages of boiling are the time and energy it takes to bring a large pot of water to the boil, and the loss of nutrients leached out by the cooking water.

Don't cut vegetables too finely before boiling. Cut surfaces release more flavor and nutrients to the water.

Start with a large volume of water so that its temperature won't drop too far when the vegetables are added. Six quarts or liters are enough for 1 to 2 pounds/0.5 to 1 kilogram of vegetables.

Add salt to the cooking water, as much as 2 tablespoons/30 grams granulated or 4 tablespoons flake per quart or liter, to reduce the leaching out of vegetable components and speed the softening of plant cell walls. Salt does not raise the boiling temperature significantly or toughen vegetables.

Bring the water to a hard boil first and bring it back to the boil as fast as possible after adding the vegetables, to inactivate damaging enzymes quickly. Partly cover the pot to reduce cooling caused by evaporation and reduce the heat to maintain a steady boil.

Check the vegetables often by probing with a knife tip or tasting, and remove them as soon as they're soft enough.

To keep green vegetables looking vibrant, boil them for less than 10 minutes. If necessary, cut them into small pieces that cook quickly.

Green vegetables stay green longer in neutral or alkaline water. If yours turn dull in 5 or 10 minutes, then try adding small amounts of baking soda to the cooking water. Too much soda will quickly turn them mushy.

Some vegetables are best partly cooked at temperatures below the boil that firm their texture.

To boil potatoes and other starchy vegetables, start them in cold water slightly acidified with lemon juice or cream of tartar, and heat them gradually up to 180 to 190°F/80 to 85°C. This method helps the vegetable surfaces stay intact while the pieces cook through.

To keep root vegetables firm and intact for tossing in a vegetable salad, precook pieces in water at 130 to 140°F/55 to 60°C for 30 minutes. Chill them in ice water for 30 minutes, then boil until tender.

Freshly drained boiled vegetables lose moisture and shrink as they release steam. To stop wrinkling, cool and toss the vegetables with just enough oil to coat them.

STEAMING VEGETABLES

Steaming cooks vegetables with water vapor, whose effective temperature is the boiling point of water. The food is held on a rack above boiling water in a closed pot.

Steaming has two advantages over boiling. It's much more efficient because it requires heating only a cup or two of water instead of a potful. And it leaches fewer nutrients and flavor substances from the vegetable tissues.

Steaming has two disadvantages. It takes slightly longer than boiling because steam is less dense than liquid water. And it can't soften some old and tough vegetables as well because it doesn't dissolve their cell walls as effectively.

Start with enough water to avoid boiling it all off and scorching the pot bottom. If cooking takes more than 10 minutes, check the water level occasionally and if necessary add more water hot from the kettle.

Bring the water to a boil before adding the vegetables to the steamer. Temperatures below the boil cause greater vitamin loss and chlorophyll discoloration.

Don't cram vegetable pieces into the steamer. This causes uneven exposure to the steam and uneven cooking.

Arrange vegetables loosely, in a single layer, or open pile, or on separate stacked steaming racks, to allow the steam access to all surfaces. Leaf vegetables quickly collapse into a dense pile. Check them after a minute or two and tease them apart.

Cover the pot with a tight-fitting lid to trap the steam.

Use moderate heat to keep a steady thread of steam escaping from the lid edge. High heat won't increase the steam temperature.

To check doneness safely, turn the heat off, lift the lid away from you, and let the steam escape. Then use long tongs or a protective mitt to avoid exposing your hand to the pot interior. Steam can cause a serious burn in an instant.

Freshly steamed hot vegetables evaporate moisture and wrinkle. To stop wrinkling, cool and toss the vegetables with just enough oil to coat them.

MICROWAVE COOKING VEGETABLES

Microwave ovens heat with high-frequency radio waves that penetrate an inch or so into food. They pass mostly unabsorbed through glass, ceramic, and plastic, so vegetables can be microwaved directly in serving containers.

Microwaving is a very efficient and rapid way to cook small portions of vegetables, and preserves their vitamins and flavor better than boiling or steaming.

The disadvantage of microwaving is that doneness is more troublesome to check.

Cut the vegetables in pieces less than 1 inch / 2.5 centimeters thick, so that they'll cook through evenly. Whole artichokes and ears of corn can be microwaved intact.

Toss them with some water and oil or butter to prevent them from drying out as they cook.

Place them in a single layer or loosely piled for even exposure to the microwaves.

Cover the dish loosely with a lid or other dish or plastic wrap to retain the steam created during the cooking, which speeds heating and prevents drying out. Avoid direct contact between plastic wrap and food and the possible transfer of plastic residues. Don't cover the dish airtight, or steam pressure will build up and burst the covering off.

Cook vegetables on high power to speed heating.

Use a turntable for even heating, or stop cooking every few minutes to stir and even out heating.

Lift the covering with caution to avoid being burned by escaping steam.

PRESSURE-COOKING VEGETABLES

Pressure-cooking heats vegetables with liquid water and/or steam at temperatures far above the boiling point, around 250°F/120°C. It softens vegetables very quickly compared to other cooking methods.

Pressure-cooking works best with firm vegetables such as beets and carrots that take more than a few minutes to cook, and dishes that are meant to be soft textured, including purees. It doesn't work well with large whole vegetables, whose outsides usually overcook while the centers heat through.

The disadvantages of pressure-cooking are the speed with which vegetables can overcook, and the trouble it takes to reduce the pressure, check doneness, and resume cooking if necessary.

Always use a timer, and stop the cooking immediately when it goes off. To keep pieces intact, let the pot temperature and pressure fall slowly. Rapid cooling and depressurizing will cause internal boiling in the foods and break them apart.

BRAISING AND STEWING VEGETABLES

Braising and stewing cook vegetables in flavorful liquids that are part of the dish. These methods soften the vegetables while imbuing them and the liquid with each other's flavors.

Vegetables often come out poorly done when cooked with meat. Traditional long braising at a simmer to tenderize the meat can turn vegetables mushy. Modern braising at lower temperatures can leave vegetables underdone.

For the best braised vegetables, take as much care with their texture as with the meat's.

In traditional braising near the boil, check vegetables cooked from the beginning often and remove them when they're properly done, each in turn if there are several vegetables. Return to the braise just before serving. Or add fresh vegetables for the last 30 minutes of cooking.

In modern meat braises cooked at 150 to 160°F/65 to 70°C, either precook the vegetables at a simmer before adding the meat, or remove the meat when it's done and raise the liquid temperature to finish the vegetables.

MASHING AND PUREEING VEGETABLES

Mashing and pureeing are ways to disintegrate vegetable tissues into a mass of cell fragments and fluids, using mortars, food mills, food processors, and blenders. Depending on the proportion of fragments to fluids, the result is a soft, lumpy paste like mashed potatoes, or a thick, even fluid like cauliflower puree.

To make the smoothest paste and puree textures, cook foods until very soft, process in a blender, and pass through a fine strainer. Don't worry about overcooking; it's important to break down the food's structure thoroughly.

Don't use machines to process or blend potatoes and other starchy vegetables. Their blades shear apart starch granules and produce a thin, gluey mass.

Tomatoes are watery and produce purees that separate into thick and thin portions.

To make an evenly thick tomato puree, remove the excess water. Simmer as long as needed in an open and wide pot, on the stove top or in a moderate oven. Or strain off the watery portion, reduce it quickly in a small saucepan, and then add it back to the thick portion. Or halve and predry fresh tomatoes in a low oven before pureeing.

Pesto is a puree of green herbs, usually fresh basil leaves, thinned with oil and often including garlic, nuts, and cheese. Breaking leaf tissues can change flavor and cause discoloration.

To retain more original herb flavor in pesto, crush the leaves coarsely in a mortar so that small pieces of leaf tissue remain intact.

To reduce discoloration in pesto, use leaves only, not stems. Blanching the leaves for a few seconds in boiling water will reduce discoloration but also mutes basil flavor.

FRYING, SAUTÉING, SWEATING, GLAZING, AND WILTING VEGETABLES

Frying, sautéing, sweating, glazing, and wilting are all ways of heating vegetables in a metal pan with a small amount of fat or oil.

Frying and sautéing cook vegetables in an uncovered pan at temperatures high enough to vaporize their moisture instantly, so that their surfaces dry out, turn brown, and develop characteristic fried flavors. In sautéing, small pieces are kept moving to cook them evenly and quickly.

Frying vegetables evenly requires close attention. As they cook they release sugary juices that can quickly scorch.

Stir-frying is sautéing done very quickly at very high temperatures, which create distinctive flavors.

Sweating softens vegetables at low pan temperatures so that their surfaces remain moist and unbrowned.

Glazing cooks vegetables in two stages: first in a covered moderately hot pan with some oil or fat but little or no added liquid, essentially steaming them soft with their own moisture; then uncovered, to boil off most of the moisture and leave them with a creamy clinging layer of emulsified moisture and oil.

Wilting tender leafy greens softens and collapses them and reduces their volume by half or more by heating them briefly in a hot oiled pan. Don't worry about heaping them high in the pan; they quickly cook down.

There are two ways to fry vegetables. One is to keep the pan temperature high, not crowd the pan, and make sure that no liquid accumulates. The other, often warned against in cookbooks, is to crowd the pan, let the vegetable fill it with liquid, then heat until the liquid evaporates and the vegetables fry in the oil. The second method works well with notoriously leaky mushrooms and eggplant, which absorb less oil than they do if fried completely dry.

To fry or sauté vegetables dry:
- *Dry the vegetables* of excess surface moisture.
- *Preheat the pan alone* to 400°F/200°C, and add oil and then the vegetables.
- *Start with the burner on high,* and adjust to keep the sizzle of rapid water vaporizing constant.
- *Leave the pan uncovered,* or use a perforated spatter guard, or adjust the lid so that water vapor can escape. Turn or stir the vegetables frequently to cook them on all sides.

To fry vegetables in minimal oil:

- *Add a small amount of oil along with the vegetables to the cold pan,* cover, and turn on the heat to medium.
- *When liquid accumulates,* uncover and increase the heat to boil the water off.
- *When you hear the oil sizzling,* turn the heat back down and stir until evenly browned.

To stir-fry vegetables:

- *Use an uncoated metal wok,* which can tolerate high temperatures and is well shaped to keep the food moving constantly. Most nonstick surfaces shouldn't be heated to stir-frying temperatures.
- *Preheat the wok or pan on high heat* to 450 to 500°F / 230 to 260°C, so that a test drop of oil immediately begins to smoke.
- *Add oil, then vegetables cut small* enough to cook in a minute or two.
- *Stir the vegetables constantly* until they're cooked through.

DEEP- AND SHALLOW-FRYING VEGETABLES AND HERBS

Deep- and shallow-frying cook vegetables at moisture-vaporizing, browning temperatures in enough oil to immerse them completely, or to come partway up the sides. They produce a crisp crust around a moist interior if the vegetable surface is porous enough to dry out and harden, or if it's coated with a batter or breading.

The key to good frying is to adjust the oil temperature to the piece size and the time it takes to cook through. Fry at 350 to 375°F / 175 to

190°C for small pieces that cook through in a few seconds or minutes, 325 to 340°F/160 to 170°C for larger, slower pieces.

Fry in fresh neutral-flavored oil for the best flavor and least oily crust.

Use a fryer or pot large enough that the oil won't bubble over when the food is added.

Don't crowd the pot with vegetables, which will drop the oil temperature too far, slow the frying, and produce an oily result. Fry in small batches.

Check the oil temperature often and adjust the heat to maintain it at the desired temperature. The early cooking of a given batch requires more heat to maintain the temperature than later stages. Later batches fry faster than early batches cooked at the same temperature; accumulating impurities transfer heat to the food more efficiently.

To minimize oiliness on the vegetable crust, use fresh oil, shake each finished piece as you remove it from the oil, and blot it on paper towels immediately. The food absorbs most of the oil as it begins to cool.

Breadings and batters coat vegetables and provide a brown, crisp crust.

To help any coating adhere to moist vegetables, dust the vegetable surfaces with flour.

To help dry breadings adhere to vegetables, dip the floured pieces into wet milk or sticky eggs, then into the breading.

To get a crisper, lighter batter crust:

- *Replace some wheat flour in the batter with rice or corn flour,* to reduce the formation of crust-toughening gluten.
- *Include some double-acting baking powder,* to create bubbles during the frying and a more porous surface.
- *Replace up to half the liquid with vodka,* whose alcohol reduces gluten formation and boils off quickly to dry the crust.

To get an irregular tempuralike crust, barely stir together ice-cold water, egg, and flour, and use this batter immediately. When it gets too thick, make a fresh batch.

BAKING OR OVEN ROASTING VEGETABLES

Heating vegetables in the oven cooks them relatively slowly, by means of hot air and radiation from the oven surfaces, at temperatures ranging from 200 to 500°F/90 to 260°C. Low temperatures dry out and concentrate flavor; high temperatures produce a brown, flavorful surface enclosing a moist interior.

The key to good baking is to adjust the oven temperature to the piece size and the time it takes to cook through.

Coat the vegetable pieces with oil or fat, which speeds cooking, surface crisping, and flavor development. Without oil, surfaces will get leathery and stick to the pan.

Place the vegetables in a shallow pan to heat them evenly from the top and sides. Bottom surfaces will essentially fry in contact with the pan, and brown faster than the top and sides.

Turn the pieces occasionally to even out their browning.

Use high oven temperatures with care. Many vegetables contain enough sugars to scorch on the edge or bottom where they contact the baking pan or absorb heat blasts from the cycling heating elements.

To dry and concentrate vegetable flavor rather than brown, use low oven temperatures, 200 to 250°F/90 to 120°C, or a dehydrator. Slice vegetables very thin on a mandoline to make crisp baked chips.

GRILLING AND BROILING VEGETABLES

Grilling and broiling expose vegetables to very high temperatures from flames or coals. The heat source is below in grilling, above in broiling. These methods create a flavorful, dark brown or slightly charred surface.

Charring produces carcinogens as well as flavor, so it's best to limit it and trim away burned areas before eating.

Coat the vegetables lightly with oil to produce a crisp surface, not a leathery one.

For maximum control in grilling, have one area very hot for browning, and a second moderately hot for cooking through. Color the vegetables as desired over the very hot area, then finish cooking over the moderate area.

For maximum control in broiling, start the vegetables close to the heat source and watch carefully; as soon as they color, turn them, repeat, and then lower away from the heat to cook through, or finish cooking in the oven.

Cooking times are unpredictable. They depend on the intensity of the heat source, the distance between source and vegetable, and vegetable thickness.

Cut vegetables in thick pieces for more flexibility in balancing flavor and moistness. Thin cuts, ½ inch/1 centimeter or less, will cook through very quickly, sometimes before the surface is browned.

To prevent vegetables from sticking to the grill, keep the grill clean, preheat well before cooking, oil the vegetable surface, and let the vegetables brown thoroughly before trying to turn them.

Cook vegetables in husks, skins, or wrapped in foil to retain more moisture and reduce scorching while still picking up the aroma of fire.

CANNING VEGETABLES

Canning cooks and preserves vegetables indefinitely by isolating them completely and heating them hot and long enough to kill all microbes. Because most vegetables are less acidic than most fruits, they require high-temperature canning in a pressure cooker.

Improperly canned vegetables deteriorate quickly and can be dangerous. If the heat treatment is insufficient or the handling careless, it can encourage the growth of potentially fatal botulism bacteria.

Follow well-established guidelines carefully. Consult the U.S. Department of Agriculture's *Complete Guide to Home Canning and Preserving,* in print or online at www.usda.gov, or make sure your recipe includes these steps:

- *Prepare the jars and lids in boiling water.*
- *Heat the vegetable preparation or the liquid portion of it to a boil.*
- *Seal the hot vegetable preparation in the hot jars airtight.*
- *Heat the jars in a pressure canner.* Timings vary depending on the jar size and kitchen altitude.
- *Check the cooled jars to make sure the lids are bowed in the center and the seal remains airtight.*

To eliminate worries about botulism in home-canned vegetables, boil the vegetables for 10 minutes before serving to destroy any toxin that might be present.

QUICK-PICKLING VEGETABLES

Quick-pickling is an accelerated alternative to pickling by fermentation, which takes weeks. Quick-pickling flavors vegetables with added salt or sugar, the acid in vinegar, or the alcohol and acid in wine. It makes vegetables that retain some of the crunchiness of raw vegetables, but are more tender and keep longer.

The pickling process can be as short as an hour for shredded or thin-sliced vegetables, or go on for days for thicker pieces. Vegetables may be pickled raw or cooked, at room temperature or in the refrigerator.

Clean vegetables thoroughly before pickling.

Presalt watery vegetables and squeeze out excess moisture before pickling, to reduce dilution of the vinegar or wine.

Blanch thick pieces in boiling water to soften them and speed penetration of the pickle.

Use unrefined sea salt, whose minerals help preserve crispness, as do alum and pickling lime.

Store finished pickles in the refrigerator.

To keep pickled vegetables for more than a few days, heat them to 185°F/85°C for 30 minutes, then cool and store tightly covered in the refrigerator.

Acid-pickled vegetables don't soften normally when heated. When cooking with them, anticipate that they'll retain some crispness.

FERMENTING VEGETABLES

Fermentation, the original slow method of pickling, preserves vegetables with the acid produced by microbes that grow in a salt brine over a period of weeks. It produces pleasantly sour, softly crunchy vegetables with a characteristic fermented aroma. Whole cucumbers (traditional pickles) and cabbage (sauerkraut, kimchi) are commonly fermented vegetables.

The key to good pickles and sauerkraut is to recruit only the correct fermentation microbes. The wrong microbes produce bad flavors and turn the vegetables soft and slimy.

Use unreactive plastic, ceramic, or enamel containers.

Wash the vegetables and containers thoroughly to remove undesirable microbes. Scrape away the flower ends of cucumbers, which can cause undesirable softening if left intact.

Measure out the salt and water for the brine carefully. The brine strength determines which microbes will grow in it. Most pickling brines are 5 to 8 percent salt by weight. If adding salt directly to shredded vegetables to produce a brine from their juices, aim for 1 to 3 percent of the vegetable weight.

Use pickling or kosher salt to avoid a cloudy brine. Anticaking powders in table salts don't dissolve.

Keep the vegetables completely covered by the brine, shielded from the air and its microbes. Weigh them down with a plate, or restrain them in a perforated plastic storage bag.

Keep the brine surface protected from the air. Press plastic wrap or some other shield directly onto the fermenting surface. Molds can grow on unprotected brine surfaces and cause spoilage.

Keep the fermenting container at cool room temperature, ideally 60 to 65°F / 15 to 18°C. Warm temperatures tend to speed acid but not aroma production, and increase the chance for spoilage.

Check the liquid regularly for surface contamination, and scoop off any mold growth.

Discard the fermentation if it develops off flavors or the liquid becomes very cloudy. Some cloudiness is normal.

Store finished pickles in the refrigerator.

COMMON VEGETABLES: ARTICHOKES TO TURNIPS

Artichokes are the flower buds of a thistle, with a dense, fleshy "heart" surrounded by scalelike leaves. They require trimming, and the cut surfaces quickly discolor unless they're immersed in cold water with a dissolved tablet of vitamin C or plenty of lemon juice.

To speed the steaming of whole artichokes, cut across the top of the leaf cluster to expose the inner leaves. Artichokes also cook quickly in a pressure cooker or microwave oven.

Arugula, or rocket, is a small-leafed cabbage relative whose flavor ranges from mild to hot-mustard pungent. Cooking converts the pungent substances into bitter ones. Salty seasonings reduce bitterness.

Asparagus spears are very active-growing plant shoots. After harvest they quickly lose their sweetness and tenderness and develop a fibrous sheath from the cut end. White asparagus has a milder flavor than green and toughens faster.

Buy asparagus as fresh as possible from the field, and store it in the coldest part of the refrigerator.

Choose thick spears for the highest proportion of tender flesh to fibrous sheath.

To restore some sweetness, soak asparagus for 1 hour in cold water with 1 to 2 teaspoons sugar per cup water/5 to 10 grams per 250 milliliters.

To minimize toughness, cut off fibrous bottoms before cooking, or peel the bottom half deeply. Always peel white asparagus. Snapping is not a reliable way of separating fibrous from tender portions, and wastes a significant amount.

To make use of trimmed bottoms, slice into 1-millimeter thin rounds and serve raw or added at the last minute to a soup or stir-fry.

Avocados are semitropical, chilling-sensitive fruits that are harvested hard and ripen off the tree. Some varieties are soft and rich in oil; others firm and lean, better for slicing than mashing.

Choose avocados that fill their skin and are either firm and unripe or give slightly to pressure, in the early stages of ripening. Avoid overripe soft fruits with loose areas of skin.

Let avocados ripen fully at room temperature before refrigerating, which would damage their ripening systems. Speed ripening by putting avocados in a paper bag with a ripe banana.

Prevent avocado purees like guacamole from turning brown and developing off flavors by pressing wax paper or aluminum foil into the surface. Scrape any discolored patches from the surface before using.

Fresh beans come in many types in addition to the familiar supermarket green beans. Purple beans turn green when cooked. Flat or romano beans have a distinctive flavor and creamy cooked texture. Asian yard-long beans are an entirely different species, drier and meatier. Fresh fava beans and edamame are immature fava and soy seeds, moist when briefly cooked. Fresh shelling beans are like their dried older versions but cook more quickly.

Buy deep-colored, firm beans and use them quickly. Their sweetness and tenderness decline quickly during storage.

Cook beans less than 10 minutes to retain their bright green color.

Beets are deeply pigmented roots that stay somewhat firm no matter how long they're cooked.

To preserve the color patterns of variegated beets, serve in thin raw slices. Cooking damages cells and spreads pigments.

Save and cook beet greens separately. They're very much like chard, tender and nutritious, but are more perishable than the roots and consume their nutrients.

Cook beets with skins on to reduce loss of pigments. Peel soon after cooking when the skin is easier to remove.

Don't worry about bloodlike redness in the toilet for a day or two after eating beets; the body passes a portion of the beet pigments unchanged.

Bitter greens include broccoli rabe, brussels sprouts, collards, dandelion greens, escarole, kale, and mustard greens. Their bitter components are apparently healthful phytochemicals.

Lessen the bitterness of bitter greens by boiling them in copious water and dressing them with salt or salty ingredients (soy sauce, anchovy paste), which mask our perception of bitterness.

Broccoli and broccoli rabe are relatives of cabbage that form masses of flower buds. Broccoli rabe is more bitter than broccoli, with slender stalks and smaller bud clusters.

Choose firm, tight, dark green broccoli heads. Avoid woody-edged stalks. Peel the stalks if their skin is tough.

Cook broccoli and broccoli rabe just long enough to make them tender, 10 minutes or less. Prolonged cooking turns the delicate green buds mushy and produces an increasingly strong and unpleasant sulfurous aroma.

To minimize cooking time for tougher broccoli and to cook buds and stalks evenly, separate the bud shoots from the main stalk. Cook the stalk separately, or cut into small, quickly cooked pieces.

Brussels sprouts are a relative of cabbage that form miniature cabbage-head leaf clusters.

Choose tight, compact, dense sprouts with a stem end that looks freshly cut. Avoid loose, light-feeling sprouts.

Cook brussels sprouts just long enough to make them tender. Prolonged cooking produces an increasingly strong and unpleasant sulfur aroma.

To speed cooking, cut a deep X into the stem end, or cut in half, or pull apart into separate leaflets.

To minimize the bitterness of sprouts, cut them in half or pull them apart and then boil to leach out bitter compounds (and other healthful substances).

Cabbage comes in several forms, from dense green or purple heads, to pale and light Asian napa. The deeper the pigmentation, the more nutrient-rich the cabbage.

Cook cabbage just long enough to make it tender; prolonged cooking makes its sulfurous aroma increasingly strong and unpleasant.

To speed cooking, cut heads into halves or quarters, or chop or shred.

To keep red or purple cabbage from turning blue, cook with an acidic ingredient such as wine, vinegar, or apples.

To make a crisp salad of raw cabbage, soak the chopped or shredded leaves in ice water before dressing them.

Carrots are roots that have a snappy bite when raw, and cook into a very smooth puree. The outer regions are more concentrated in flavor and healthful carotene pigment than the water-carrying core, which can be fibrous in old carrots.

Choose thin, uncracked carrots for the best flavor. Carrots with their greens still attached are fresher than others but should be trimmed of the greens before storing. Prepared "baby" carrots are cut from large carrots. Their white surface fuzz consists of harmless dried cell layers.

Peel carrots, even if they look clean. The outer layers can be bitter and carry off flavors.

Cauliflower is a cabbage relative that forms masses of immature flower tissue that may be white, orange, or purple. Cooked until soft, it makes a very smooth puree.

Choose dense, evenly colored heads with no darkened areas.

To serve cauliflower pieces intact, break into pieces first and then cook them just long enough to make them tender. Prolonged cooking turns cauliflower fragile and makes the sulfurous aroma increasingly strong and unpleasant.

To make a smooth puree, cook a few minutes longer until soft, and process in a blender.

Celery is a cluster of crunchy leaf stalks.

Choose celery bunches that are firm and undamaged. Discard cracked or bruised outer stalks. Stress during growth and handling causes celery to accumulate chemicals that can blister the skin when exposed to sunlight.

To maximize the crispness of raw celery sticks, soak them in ice water.

To remove the stringiness of celery stalks, use a peeler to remove the ridges on the outer stalk surface.

Celery root is the swollen underground stem of a celery relative, gnarled with small roots. Serve it shredded raw and crunchy, roasted in pieces, or cooked to a smooth puree.

Choose celery roots that feel heavy for their size, with smooth surfaces that will require the least peeling.

Peel celery root deeply to remove fibrous roots.

Keep cut pieces in water acidulated with vitamin C or lemon juice until they're cooked. Celery root discolors easily.

Chard is a large leaf vegetable from relatives of the beet. It's rich in oxalates, which can exacerbate kidney stones. Some varieties have colored stalks and veins that leak their pigments when cooked.

Choose chard leaves that aren't cracked and don't have brown edges. Chard is often sold overmature and in need of serious trimming.

Cook young chard very briefly, for just a minute or two. It's very tender.

To remove some oxalates, boil chard rather than steaming or stir-frying.

To maintain and contain the colors of colored chards, cook them separately and combine with other ingredients at the last minute.

Collards are the large, open, somewhat bitter leaves of a cabbage relative.

Choose collard leaves that don't have prominent white veins or cracks. Collards are often sold overmature, with tough veins that require over-cooking the rest of the leaf.

Cook collards just long enough to make them tender. Prolonged cooking makes the sulfurous aroma increasingly strong. Traditional long-cooked collards benefit from the balancing strong flavor of smoked ham.

To reduce the cooking time for collards, remove tough white stalks and veins and use only the green leaf, or shred whole leaves before cooking. Or cook until the green portion is tender and the stalks still crisp, then roll leaves together and cut crosswise into thin shreds.

Corn is the massed immature seeds of the maize plant. The kernels may be white, yellow, or red-purple.

Buy corn as fresh as possible, keep it refrigerated, and use it quickly. Modern varieties don't lose their sweetness as fast as earlier ones, but do still toughen during storage.

Choose young corn with small kernels for tenderness, older corn with tougher kernels for more flavor.

Cook corn on the cob long enough to heat the outer kernels to close to the boil. A pot of boiling water is the usual method. Steaming and microwaving also work well and are more efficient. Microwave or grill in the husk to retain moisture, heat, and flavor.

Sauté corn kernels on moderate or low heat to avoid scorching their sugary juices.

Use corn cobs to flavor stocks or soups.

Cucumbers are melon relatives, refreshingly moist and crisp, usually added to salads but also good when briefly sautéed.

Standard American cucumbers are short and thick, with large seeds, some bitterness, tough-skinned and often waxed to extend shelf life. American pickling varieties are small, short, thin-skinned, and unwaxed.

"European" or hothouse varieties are long and thin, have a thin unwaxed skin, small seed rudiments, and no bitterness. Middle-Eastern and Asian types are similarly elongated but smaller.

Choose cucumbers that are firm and dense, with no shrunken areas. To serve with the dark green skin, buy unwaxed cucumbers.

Dandelion greens in markets are usually a bitter lettuce relative, not true dandelions.

To reduce the bitterness of dandelion greens, boil them in a large pot of water. They usually soften very quickly. Season them with salt to reduce the perception of bitterness.

Eggplants are spongy-fleshed fruits related to tomatoes and potatoes. Long, thin Asian varieties are tender; standard large purple varieties have more large seeds and are prone to developing brown areas.

Bitterness is not common in modern eggplants, with the exception of orange Turkish and pea-size Thai varieties that are prized for it. Salting does not remove bitterness, but does mask bitter tastes.

Refrigerate eggplants for only a few days. They're semitropical and don't keep well in cold storage.

To prevent spongy eggplant flesh from absorbing a lot of oil during frying or baking, compact it by precooking briefly in microwave, or salting slices in a colander until wilted and then rinsing off excess salt.

If eggplant does absorb a lot of oil, continue to heat slowly until the flesh shrinks and releases some of it.

Endive, escarole, and frisée are lettuce relatives with dense, crunchy, somewhat bitter leaves.

Choose the youngest, lightest-colored heads for tenderness and mild flavor.

Choose Belgian endive that is completely white, and refrigerate in an opaque paper bag. Exposure to light causes it to become green, less sweet, and more bitter.

Fennel is a version of the anise-flavored herb plant that forms a large, crunchy, swollen stem. The leaf stalks projecting from it are permanently fibrous. It's often served in thin raw slices or slow-cooked in larger pieces.

Garlic is a pungent underground bulb, a relative of the onion. Its pungency varies, depending on variety, season, and age. Elephant garlic is a milder leek relative, not a true garlic. Black garlic is a processed form of garlic from Asia, nonpungent, sweet-tart and savory, with a molasseslike aroma.

Choose heavy and hard garlic heads, with no signs of sprouting or of shrinking or mold in the outer cloves.

Store in a cool dark place. Refrigeration reduces flavor. Stored garlic slowly dries out and browns faster when cooked.

Don't store plain chopped garlic under oil. Such garlic can cause botulism. Presoak the garlic in vinegar or lemon juice, cover garlic and acid with oil, and store in the refrigerator.

Garlic can be either bitingly pungent or mild depending on how it's handled.

To maximize pungency, crush or puree it raw.

To minimize pungency, slice and blanch the cloves in boiling water or milk, or cook them intact.

For a milder aroma, sauté garlic in butter rather than in vegetable oil.

When sautéing onions and garlic, add garlic to the pan toward the end of cooking. Garlic is less moist than onion and browns and scorches more quickly.

Don't worry if garlic preparations turn green or blue. Acids cause this harmless color change, which is prized in some Chinese pickles.

Kale is the large, elongated, somewhat bitter leaves of a cabbage relative.

Cook kale just long enough to make it tender. Prolonged cooking makes the sulfurous aroma increasingly strong.

To reduce the cooking time, remove tough stalks and use only the green leaves, or shred whole leaves before cooking. Or cook until the green portion is tender and the stalks still crisp, then roll leaves together and cut crosswise into thin shreds.

Kohlrabi are the swollen stems of a cabbage relative, moist and crunchy when raw, moist and soft when cooked briefly, not starchy.

Choose smaller kohlrabi. Large stems can have a tough woody skin.

Leeks are the pungent underground stalk and leaves of an onion relative. The inner leaves and root end have the strongest flavor.

Cooked leeks and especially their tops exude a thick slippery fluid that gels when chilled, and can help thicken soups and stews.

Choose leeks with the largest proportion of white stalk.

Cut and wash lower leek stalks thoroughly. Their many layers trap grit when soil is heaped around them to keep the stalk white.

Use the tougher, stronger-flavored tops as a green vegetable, sliced thin and cooked briefly.

Lettuces are clusters of mild tender leaves, best suited to serving raw in salads. They come in many varieties. Dark open-head leaves are more nutritious than pale closed-head leaves. Those with red color are more astringent.

Choose lettuces with fresh-looking, moderate-size leaves, and few or no blackened areas or brown edges. Avoid badly wilted heads and overmature, coarse leaves.

Refrigerate lettuce and other salad greens close to 32°F/0°C, enclosed in a plastic bag to minimize moisture loss.

Wash lettuce leaves in several changes of water before using. They grow low to the ground and can be gritty.

To crisp lettuce leaves, immerse them for 15 minutes in ice water.

Mushrooms are structures that bear the tiny seedlike spores of soil-dwelling funguses. There are many different species with distinctive, often meaty flavors, including chanterelles, morels, oyster mushrooms, porcini, and shiitakes.

Dried mushrooms have intense, concentrated flavors, especially the savory taste called *umami,* and are a useful pantry ingredient.

Common white and brown mushrooms are variants of the same species, and are sold at several different ages and sizes, from small "buttons" to hand-size "portobellos." The larger and more prominent the brown gills are under the cap, the more flavorful the mushrooms.

Mushrooms aren't made from the same structural materials as most vegetables, and behave differently in the kitchen. When heated, they release copious amounts of water that can slow cooking to a crawl. And most mushrooms retain some chewiness no matter how long they're cooked.

Choose mushrooms that have been least damaged in handling. For the most flavor, choose old mushrooms that are beginning to deteriorate and trim damaged areas.

Use mushrooms promptly; they have a rapid metabolism and deteriorate quickly.

Refrigerate mushrooms close to 32°F/0°C in a paper bag or towel loosely wrapped in a plastic bag, to retain but absorb the copious moisture they exhale.

Wash dirty mushrooms just before cooking. Brief immersion in water won't remove flavor or waterlog them.

Remove older fibrous stems and cook them separately in stocks, or chop finely for a stuffing.

To sauté mushrooms, either don't crowd the pan, so that the juices instantly vaporize and the mushrooms brown quickly; or do crowd the pan so that the mushrooms exude and cook in their juices before browning. Juice-cooked mushrooms need less oil to coat their shrunken surfaces, and absorb less oil when they brown.

To cook with dried mushrooms, rehydrate them in enough hot water to cover, until moist and soft throughout. Strain the flavorful soaking liquid of any grit and use it too.

Mustard greens are the large, open, pungent leaves of a cabbage relative. Raw, they have a mustardlike heat. Cooked, they are heat-free but bitter.

Cook mustard greens just long enough to make them tender. Prolonged cooking makes their sulfurous aroma increasingly strong.

To make mustard greens less bitter, boil in copious amounts of water rather than steam or stir-fry, and salt generously.

Okra is a hollow seed-bearing semitropical fruit. It accumulates a water-retaining mucilage that gives a slippery, slimy consistency to its juices.

Choose small okra that feel flexible. Large fruits are usually stiff and unalterably fibrous.

Store okra in a relatively warm part of the refrigerator.

To minimize okra sliminess, cook them whole, fry or bake them, and use in dishes with little or no added liquid.

To take advantage of okra mucilage, include sliced okra to give body to soups and stews.

Olives are the small fruits of a Mediterranean tree. They accumulate oil, are intensely bitter and astringent when raw, and are processed in several different ways to make them palatable.

Canned black olives are treated with lye and heated, and have a slippery consistency and distinctive flavor.

Cured black and green olives have usually been fermented in a brine, and are salty and tart.

Use cured olives within a day or two, or refrigerate for up to a week. Yeasts grow on refrigerated olives and limit their shelf life. To keep olives longer, refrigerate them immersed in brine or oil.

Onions are pungent dormant bulbs, relatives of garlic. Green onions are the stem and leaves of actively growing plants. There are many varieties. "Sweet" onions aren't especially sugary, but are much less pungent than other onions and good for eating raw.

Cooking and pickling reduce onion pungency.

Choose brown-skinned storage onions for long keeping and strong flavor. White-skinned Spanish onions and red onions are more perishable than storage onions.

To minimize eye-watering pungency during cutting and chopping, chill onions for 30 minutes in ice water, or several hours in the refrigerator. Work quickly and clear the cutting board often; the chopped pieces quickly warm up again.

To minimize harshness in raw sliced or chopped onion, and in salsas made with them, soak or rinse the pieces in cold water to wash out damaged surface cells.

To caramelize onions, cook them partly covered on low heat in fat or oil for a long time, stirring frequently, occasionally adding water or wine or stock to lift stuck juices back onto the onion pieces. Onion juices contain sugar and readily brown and scorch. Be careful to stir constantly if using higher heat to speed the cooking.

Parsnips are a carrot relative, also a root but pale and less dense.

Choose medium-size parsnips without darkened spots or cracks. Large parsnips can have a large, woody core.

Store parsnips in the refrigerator.

Count on cooking parsnips more briefly than carrots and other vegetables. They soften and brown faster, and are more prone to drying out.

Peas are immature green seeds and pods of the pea plant. English peas have a stringy pod and only the seeds are eaten. Snow peas and snap peas are edible pods and don't require shelling.

Choose English peas of medium size in crisp, brittle pods. Large peas from mature pods are starchy and coarse. Refrigerate and use promptly; they lose flavor with time.

Frozen peas are a convenient, good-quality alternative to unpredictable fresh peas.

Choose snow and snap peas with deep green, firm, uncracked pods. Refrigerate.

Cook all peas briefly, just long enough to brighten their color and soften them.

Peppers, bell and chilli, come in many varieties, both fresh and dried. Some are pungent to varying degrees, some not pungent at all ("sweet"). Individual chillis of the same variety also vary in pungency.

Choose fresh chillis that are uncracked, unwilted, and deep colored.

Store fresh chillis in a warm part of the refrigerator, enclosed in a plastic bag to retain moisture.

To reduce the pungency of hot chillis, carefully cut them open and remove the inner pith supporting the seeds. The pungent chemical capsaicin is concentrated there, and easily spreads onto nearby surfaces.

Wash hands and utensils thoroughly with soapy water after handling pungent peppers. Start washing with cold water to avoid launching capsaicin into the air, then finish with hot. Avoid touching the eyes or other sensitive areas for some time. Capsaicin is persistent.

To relieve a mouth burning from hot chillis, cool the mouth with a cold noncarbonated drink. You can't remove capsaicin from the tongue once it has gotten into the cells; you can only relieve the symptoms. They fade in a few minutes.

To remove the tough skins of fresh chilli peppers, bake them in a hot oven to soften the flesh and then pull away the skins; or scorch their skins over a gas burner or a hot grill, let them finish softening enclosed in a plastic bag or squeezed together between two plates, and scrape or rinse away the surfaces. Rinsing causes some flavor loss but is effective at removing unhealthful charred residues.

To reconstitute dried chillis, rinse off dust, dry them, toast them briefly to develop flavor, either in a dry frying pan on medium heat or in a hot oven, then barely cover with hot water and keep submerged until soft.

Potatoes are starchy storage tubers. There are many varieties, most of which keep well for weeks at cool room temperature. "New potatoes" are harvested before they're mature, and should be used promptly or refrigerated.

Choose "mealy" varieties—russets, blue and purple types—if you want a dry, crumbly, or fluffy texture, for french fries or for baked and pureed potatoes that will absorb flavorful liquids or fats.

Choose "waxy" varieties—with red, white, or yellow skins—if you want a firm, dense, moist texture for pieces to be served intact, in salads or gratins.

Choose firm, unblemished potatoes, without bruises or cut marks.

Avoid potatoes with any green color. Green surfaces and sprouts contain bitter and toxic alkaloids.

Store potatoes at cool room temperature and in the dark, to prevent greening. At warm room temperatures, potatoes will sprout and decay. At refrigerator temperatures below about 45°F/7°C, they convert some starch into sugar, and can brown too quickly and scorch when fried.

Trim away green areas and cut out internal black spots, which are bruises from rough handling and often bitter.

To cook potato chunks that will stay intact when tossed for potato salad, firm their texture with a preheating treatment. Hold them for 30 minutes in hot water at 130 to 140°F/55 to 60°C, then chill them in ice water for 30 minutes. Then boil them as usual until they're tender. Allow them to cool before tossing with dressing; hot potato flesh is more fragile.

To make baked potatoes with a crisp skin, oil or butter potatoes before baking unwrapped in a hot oven, 425 to 450°F/220 to 230°C. Baking without oil or in foil produces a leathery skin.

To make crunchy oven-roasted potatoes, peel or cut potatoes into pieces, boil or steam them until done, then dry them, coat with fat or oil, and finish them in a hot oven, 450°F/230°C.

To make a smooth potato puree, press cooked potatoes through a potato ricer or food mill, add other ingredients, and stir together by hand. Use solid chunks of butter, which disperse more evenly into the potatoes than premelted butter. Whip with a whisk to aerate and lighten. Don't use a food processor or blender, which break starch grains and produce a thin, gluey result.

To make crisp french fries, cook them in separate stages: one to soften them, and one or more to crisp and brown their surfaces. Don't use potatoes that have been refrigerated; they will brown too quickly and deeply.

- *To cook french fries in two stages,* cut the potatoes into strips, soak them in ice water for 30 minutes, then blot dry and fry twice: first at 250 to 325°F / 120 to 163°C until limp, then at 350 to 375°F / 175 to 190°C until brown.
- *For french fries that remain crisp longer, cook them in three stages.* Cook the potato strips in simmering salted water until limp, allow them to cool and dry until they're tacky to the touch, then fry twice: first at 340°F/170°C until they just begin to color, then at 365 to 375°F / 185 to 190°C until brown.

Radicchio is a red-leaved lettuce relative, somewhat bitter and also astringent thanks to the red pigment.

Choose heads that feel heavy for their size.

Radishes are pungent storage roots of a cabbage relative. They come in a wide range of sizes, colors, and degrees of pungency.

Choose radishes that are unbruised and heavy for their size. Remove their spoilage-prone green tops before refrigerating.

Scrub and rinse well before serving raw.

To make overpungent radishes more palatable, remove the peel, which contains much of the responsible enzyme. Cooking eliminates their pungency.

Rutabagas are the swollen stems of a cabbage relative, not as starchy as a potato but usually boiled and mashed.

Peel rutabagas deeply before cooking. They're often coated with wax to improve shelf life.

Shallots are a pungent, purple variety of onion that's small and fine structured. Handle as you would other onions.

Spinach is a beet relative with small, mild, and usually tender leaves. It contains oxalates, which kidney-stone sufferers avoid.

Choose small, flat, fresh-looking leaves. Avoid thick leaves with prominent ribs and veins unless you'll be cooking them; these varieties are too chewy for salads.

Wash spinach leaves thoroughly, several times if necessary, to remove all of the sand that it's usually grown in.

To crisp for raw salads, immerse spinach in ice water for 15 minutes.

Always cook more spinach than you think you'll need. Cooking reduces the volume of its packed leaves by three-quarters.

Cook spinach very briefly, a minute or less, just until collapsed. Squeeze the collapsed mass to drain away excess water that would bleed onto the plate or dilute a sauce.

To remove some oxalates, boil spinach in unsalted water instead of wilting, stir-frying, or steaming.

Sprouts are few-day-old seedlings, usually of mung beans, soybeans, and alfalfa. Warm, moist sprouting conditions encourage microbes, so raw sprouts carry a risk of causing illness.

Choose sprouts that look and smell fresh, with few brown or wilted areas.

Use sprouts promptly or keep in the coldest part of the refrigerator. Wash and drain them thoroughly.

Don't serve raw sprouts to anyone especially vulnerable to illness.

Squashes are seedy cucumber relatives. Fresh summer squashes include zucchini and are moist and perishable. Dry winter squashes include pumpkins and keep for months unrefrigerated.

Choose small summer squashes to avoid coarse flesh and large seeds.

Store summer squashes in a warm part of the refrigerator, near the door; colder temperatures can damage them.

Choose winter squashes that feel dense and have no soft spots.

For the sweetest flavor, buy and serve winter squashes soon after the fall harvest.

Store winter squashes at cool room temperature.

Cut winter squashes carefully on a solid, open surface. Their flesh is hard and can catch and release a knife blade unpredictably.

To cook dense squash quickly for purees, cut them in half, scrape out seeds and strings, place them cut side down on a plate, and microwave until soft.

Sunchokes or Jerusalem artichokes are tubers of a sunflower relative. They're crisp and moist, not starchy, and rich in an indigestible but healthful carbohydrate called inulin.

Don't serve or eat large quantities of sunchokes at one meal. Too much inulin can cause gassy discomfort.

Choose sunchokes that are firm and unbruised, and store in the refrigerator.

To turn inulin into sugars and sunchokes sweet and brown, bake sunchokes in a low 200°F/93°C oven for 8 to 10 hours.

Sweet potatoes are the starchy tubers of a semitropical vine, no relation to the standard potato. Orange-fleshed varieties are very sweet and rich in vitamin A. White- and purple-fleshed types are less sweet and contain little vitamin A.

Choose firm unbruised sweet potatoes.

Store sweet potatoes at cool room temperature, 55 to 60°F / 13 to 15°C. Don't refrigerate, which causes development of a hard core that cooking can't soften.

To make sweet potatoes especially sweet, bake slowly in a low oven to give sugar-producing enzymes a chance to work.

To minimize the sweetness of sweet potatoes, heat them through quickly by microwaving, pressure-cooking, boiling, or steaming.

Tomatoes are savory fruits that are richest in flavor and nourishment when fully ripened. Unripe tomatoes are tasty and nutritious in different ways, enjoyable as a crisp vegetable raw, pickled, or cooked.

Choose tomatoes that are deeply colored for their variety (some are pale or green when ripe), and slightly soft, without very soft or damaged spots. Avoid tomatoes in refrigerated produce cases.

Store tomatoes at cool room temperature. Don't refrigerate, which removes much of their aroma. If tomatoes have been refrigerated, leave them at room temperature as long as possible before using them.

Don't discard the jelly surrounding the seeds, which is the part most concentrated in savory and tart flavor. When cooking with tomatoes, strain out the seeds after cooking, not before.

To peel a tomato, use a knife to cut a small X at its bottom, immerse it briefly in simmering water until the corners of the cut curl up, then remove it and pull on the skin corners.

Intensify the flavor of tomato puree by adding small amounts of acid and sugar, and by adding a few fresh tomato leaves and cooking briefly just before serving. Despite their reputation, tomato leaves are not toxic.

To make the smoothest sauce from canned tomatoes, choose brands whose ingredient list doesn't include calcium, which firms texture. For persistent chunkiness, choose tomatoes with calcium added.

Truffles are expensive mushroom relatives, usually cooked very briefly or just warmed to preserve their unique aromas. Black truffles smell earthy, while white truffles have garlicky notes.

Choose firm, dense, pleasantly aromatic truffles, or premium canned truffles, from a reputable source. There are a number of truffle species, and most are far less flavorful than the black winter truffles from France and white truffles from Italy.

Store truffles refrigerated, enclosed in an airtight container alone, or with rice, eggs, or other ingredients that can absorb their aroma.

Avoid shaving truffles into very thin shreds on a plane grater, which immediately releases most of their aroma to the air. Invest in a truffle shaver that produces larger shavings.

Be wary of expensive truffle oils, read their labels, and use sparingly. Most are strengthened with artificial flavors and can overwhelm other ingredients.

Turnips are moist, nonstarchy roots from a cabbage relative.

Choose smaller turnips that are firm and smooth skinned. Large turnips can be coarse fleshed and woody. Remove and keep any greens separately, and store turnips in the refrigerator.

For the mildest flavor, cook turnips briefly. Long cooking produces a strong sulfurous aroma.

9

MILK AND DAIRY PRODUCTS

M ilk is the first food we taste as newborns, sweet and mild and warm. The milks and milk products that we cook with are primal in another way. They bring together basic food materials, sugars and proteins and fats, in a minimally structured form. And that allows us to use them for all kinds of construction projects of our own.

We can enjoy milk as is, or cook it into sauces, or foam it to make a cappuccino. We can thicken its proteins with acid from friendly lactic bacteria to make yogurt and buttermilk, or use just a squeeze of lemon juice and some heat to make fresh cheese. When its fat droplets have been concentrated into cream, we can make crème fraîche or cream sauces or ice cream, or whip the cream gently into a light foam, or whip it hard to break open the fat droplets and make dense, rich butter. We can cook cream or butter with sugar until the mix turns into caramel or butterscotch.

Milk and milk products are remarkable stuff, but often the stuff we buy in stores isn't what it could be. Low-fat milks are modified to replace fat with protein concentrates; creams are stabilized with very high heat and homogenization and added gums; butters are flavored instantly with an approximation of the aromas created by lactic bacteria.

Like many people, I too got in the habit of drinking low-fat protein-added milk, and I used the same milk when I started making yogurt regularly. At some point I bought whole milk for a change, and was surprised by how much better the yogurt tasted. The milk too. No longer were they foods that I consumed out of habit and the idea that they were good for me, the colder and less flavorful the better. They had become delicious in their own right.

Milk and dairy products are worth shopping for the way we do any food we really care about: by finding and buying the ones that taste best. And their protean nature is easy and rewarding to play with. Make your own yogurt or butter just once and you'll enjoy them as never before.

DAIRY PRODUCT SAFETY

Fresh dairy products are highly perishable. Spoilage bacteria readily grow in them, sour and curdle them, and produce unpleasant flavors. Careless handling at any stage can contaminate them with various disease bacteria, including salmonella, listeria, and E. coli.

Keep all fresh dairy products refrigerated to minimize the growth of disease and spoilage bacteria.

Pasteurized milk has been cooked to 145 to 171°F/63 to 77°C to effectively eliminate disease bacteria and greatly reduce the numbers of spoilage bacteria. Pasteurization is no guarantee of safety. Pasteurized milk can become contaminated when it's cooled, packaged, or processed into other dairy products.

Raw milk has not been heated to kill disease bacteria. It is heavily regulated and generally safe, but does carry some risk of foodborne illness.

Fresh-fermented dairy products, including yogurt, buttermilk, sour cream, and crème fraîche, are more resistant to contamination thanks to acids produced by healthful bacteria that ferment them.

UHT (ultrahigh temperature) and sterilized milks are stabilized dairy products, not fresh. They have been heated to very high temperatures to kill nearly all bacteria, and have a strong cooked flavor. Some UHT and sterilized milks are specially packaged to avoid contamination and keep for months at room temperature.

Cheeses vary widely in their resistance to contamination and their safety records. Fresh and soft cheeses are moist enough to support the growth of disease and spoilage bacteria. Drier hard cheeses resist bacterial growth thanks to concentrated salt and acid, but may rarely become infected by toxin-producing molds.

Avoid serving fresh or soft cheeses to the very old, very young, or the ill.

If new mold begins to grow on any cheese, trim that area deeply, or discard the whole piece.

Lactose intolerance is the inability to digest lactose, the sugar found in milk. It's often mistaken for an allergy to milk. Many people outgrow the ability to digest lactose, and may suffer abdominal cramps and diarrhea if they ingest more than a small amount. Most people who are lactose intolerant can drink about 1 cup/250 milliliters of milk without symptoms, and eat larger quantities of fermented dairy products whose microbes consume lactose. Some milk brands include a lactose-digesting enzyme and can be drunk in larger amounts.

True milk allergy is much rarer and more serious than lactose intolerance. People who have a milk allergy develop an immune reaction to milk proteins, and may suffer a wide range of symptoms after consuming even trace amounts of any dairy product.

Goat and sheep milks are not reliable alternatives to cow milk for people with milk sensitivities. They contain similar lactose levels and their proteins are capable of causing similar allergic responses.

SHOPPING FOR MILK AND FRESH DAIRY PRODUCTS

Fresh dairy products vary widely in quality, flavor, and price. These can all be affected by animal breed and feed, collection and pasteurizing procedures, separation and blending processes, packaging materials, and distribution. Dairy producers also vary in the size and nature of their business—some are huge, some family farms—and their approach to such issues as animal welfare and sustainability. Try different brands, look into them, and choose the ones that taste, last, and feel best.

Fresh dairy products are perishable, and sensitive to temperature and to light. Fermented milks and creams keep longer than fresh because desirable microbes have already soured and thickened them, but they will still eventually spoil.

Check sell-by dates and don't buy anything about to expire.

Choose opaque containers to minimize off flavors caused by exposure to light.

Choose the coldest containers from the back of the display case, and speed them home to the refrigerator, ideally in a picnic cooler.

STORING DAIRY PRODUCTS

Keep most dairy products refrigerated below 40°F/5°C, in the cold rear of the refrigerator rather than the warmer door. Don't leave a milk container out at room temperature for more than a few minutes. Warmth greatly speeds staling and spoilage.

Many aged cheeses can be kept at cool room temperature for a few days, covered with a cheese dome or loosely wrapped.

Keep clear and translucent containers in the dark as much as possible. Bright light causes off flavors in dairy products.

Smell and taste dairy products before using them to judge freshness. Milks and creams smell like cardboard when stale, and are sour, bitter, or rancid when spoiled.

Don't freeze fresh or cultured milks or creams, which will separate and curdle.

To store butter and hard cheeses for months, freeze them after thorough wrapping in wax paper and then several layers of plastic wrap to exclude off flavors.

THE ESSENTIALS
OF COOKING WITH
DAIRY PRODUCTS

Milk and other dairy products are usually one component in a complex mixture of ingredients. They provide their own characteristic flavors, and they help deepen flavor by providing proteins and sugars for browning reactions.

Cooking with dairy products can thicken and enrich dishes. It can also make them curdled or greasy.

Milk is a mass of water with free-floating particles of protein and droplets of fat. If the protein particles begin to stick to each other in large, loose arrays, the milk thickens. If they stick too tightly to each other, they form compact solid curds that separate from the watery whey. And if the fat droplets begin to stick to each other and merge, they form greasy patches that eventually merge into clumps of butter.

Several kinds of ingredients thicken or curdle milk by causing milk proteins to stick to each other. The most common ones are the acids produced by bacteria. Acids, tannins, and solid particles are responsible for the thickening and curdling caused by fruits and vegetables, coffee, tea, and wine.

Heat speeds and increases the thickening and curdling caused by acids and other ingredients.

To control thickening and minimize curdling, cook with fresh dairy products and heat gradually and gently. Older dairy products have been made more acidic by the inevitable growth of bacteria, and are more likely to curdle.

To rescue a curdled dish, drain off the separated fluid, then whisk vigorously or blend to break up the curds and remix the proteins into the water.

Curdled dishes usually taste fine and can be delicious. The Eastern European cold soup chlodnik and Italian pork braised in milk are intentionally curdled.

Milk fat droplets stick to each other and separate mainly when they're crowded together in unhomogenized milks and creams.

To minimize dairy greasiness in cooking, avoid using milks or creams that have developed a thickened plug or surface layer of cream. Use these to make fresh butter, which is intentionally separated milk fat and delicious in its own way.

FRESH MILKS

Fresh milks come in several different forms.

Pasteurized milks have been heated to 140°F/60°C and above to kill bacteria and extend shelf life.

Homogenized milks have had their fat droplets broken down to a uniform small size that prevents them from rising in the container (fat is lighter than water) and collecting into a cream layer at the top. Their flavor is usually more bland than unhomogenized milk.

Pasteurized homogenized milk has been heated and homogenized. It has a slightly cooked flavor, and its fat remains evenly mixed throughout.

Raw milk has not been heated or homogenized. It has a distinctive flavor, and eventually develops a concentrated thick plug of cream at the top that is difficult to stir back in evenly. It has the shortest shelf life of any dairy product. Keep it in the coldest part of the refrigerator.

Pasteurized cream-top milk has been heated but not homogenized. It has a slightly cooked flavor, and develops a concentrated thick plug of cream at the top.

Low-fat, nonfat, and skim milks have been heated, and any fat has been homogenized. They contain 0 to 2 percent fat instead of regular milk's 3.5 to 4 percent. Because they look and feel thinner than regular-fat milk, low-fat milks are usually given more body with added milk proteins. These can impart a cardboard off flavor.

Low-lactose milks include a microbial enzyme that digests lactose (milk sugar), so that people who are intolerant of lactose can drink more of it without digestive disturbances.

Acidophilus milks include a potentially beneficial bacterium that can survive in the digestive system.

Goat's milk has a distinctive flavor and smaller fat globules than cow's milk, but is otherwise similar. Despite its reputation as a nonallergenic alternative to cow's milk, it can also cause reactions in people with cow's-milk allergies.

STABILIZED AND CONCENTRATED MILKS

Stabilized and concentrated milks have strong flavors, and are best suited to baking and as emergency supplies.

UHT milk has been homogenized and heated briefly above the boil, an "ultrahigh temperature" for milk, then packed in sterile conditions. It keeps for months unrefrigerated until the carton is opened. It has a strong cooked flavor, and can become bitter during storage.

Sterilized milk has been canned and severely cooked, tastes like it, and keeps unrefrigerated indefinitely.

Condensed or evaporated milk has been concentrated, homogenized, and sterilized. It has about double the fat, protein, and sugar of regular milk, a creamy consistency, tan color, and strong cooked milk-caramel flavor.

Sweetened condensed milk has been concentrated, homogenized, sweetened with enough table sugar to discourage microbes, and pasteurized. It is sweeter, lighter colored, and milder in flavor than condensed milk, and is used to make Southeast Asian coffees and teas, Latin American sweets and cakes, and key lime pie.

Powdered milk has been pasteurized and dried so that it is a solid mixture of protein, sugar, minerals, and some fat. It has a characteristic mild cardboard aroma, and is used in baking and to smooth the consistency of ice creams.

COOKING WITH MILKS

Milk is seldom cooked on its own, but can quickly create a mess when it is. Simply heating it in a pot can cause the proteins to scorch on the pan bottom, develop a skin at the surface, and foam up and boil over.

To avoid problems when cooking with milk, use very fresh milk and gentle heat, and check frequently. Even slight acidity can encourage curdling.

To avoid sticking and scorching, wet the pan with water before adding the milk, and use low direct heat. Or heat the pan in a pot of simmering water, or use the microwave oven.

To avoid surface skin formation, cover most of the pan with the lid, or stir the surface, to keep the proteins there from drying out.

To avoid boilovers, turn the heat down as you approach the boil, and keep the pan lid ajar to release steam.

To cook milk down to make **dulce de leche** *or* **cajeta,** combine milk and sugar and cook at a gentle simmer for an hour or more until the mixture thickens and browns. Include some alkaline baking soda to neutralize the acidity created by browning and produce a smoother result.

Be cautious when heating unopened cans of sweetened condensed milk. The contents expand with heat, and if allowed to boil they can cause the can to burst. Heat only in a simmering water bath (plain water boils at a lower temperature than the sweetened milk), and don't let the water bath run dry.

Milk foams atop coffee or chocolate drinks provide flavor and a visual contrast that an adept barista can work into a beautiful pattern. They also insulate and help keep drinks warm. Foams are made by creating steam or air bubbles in the milk, and heating so that the milk proteins will stick together and reinforce the bubble walls. Low-fat milks produce a firm, dry foam; full-fat milk a softer, richer-flavored one.

To make a milk foam with the steaming wand on an espresso machine, use a well-chilled metal pitcher filled halfway with very fresh, well-chilled milk, at least ²/₃ cup/150 milliliters. Immerse the steamer nozzle, turn on the steam, and move the pitcher down to maintain the nozzle just below the milk surface near the pitcher wall, where it will keep the milk circulating. Stop when the milk reaches about 150°F/65°C, to avoid a strong cooked flavor.

To make a quick milk foam without a steaming wand, put fresh cold milk into a jar with plenty of extra room, cover, and shake until it foams to fill double its original volume. Then remove the lid and microwave the jar on high heat until the foam rises to the top.

CREAMS

Creams are creamy because they contain more fat droplets than milk does. Exactly how much fat they contain determines what they're good for in the kitchen.

Read cream carton labels carefully. Fat content is important for many recipes. Most creams contain gummy stabilizing additives and have been ultrapasteurized at a high temperature to prolong shelf life. They're adequate to most tasks, but if it's available, fresh, plain pasteurized cream usually works and always tastes better.

Half-and-half is about 12 percent fat and is usually served with coffee and fresh fruits.

Light cream is about 20 percent fat, richer tasting than half-and-half but not capable of making stable whipped cream.

Light whipping cream is about 30 percent fat, enough that it can be whipped into a stable foam.

Whipping and heavy whipping creams are about 35 percent fat and at least 38 percent respectively, thick and quickly whipped into a foam.

Fresh pasteurized cream has been treated with moderate heat and is not homogenized. Its large fat droplets are desirable for whipping cream, but in the carton they can rise and separate into a thick surface layer that causes greasiness. Many fresh creams contain stabilizing gums that slow this separation.

Ultrapasteurized creams have been homogenized and pasteurized at a high temperature, but not sterile packed. They keep refrigerated for several weeks without separating. They have a cooked flavor and take longer to whip than fresh cream. Some ultrapasteurized creams also contain stabilizing gums.

Turn containers of unhomogenized cream gently a few times a day to slow the rising and separation of milk fat at the carton top.

COOKING WITH CREAM

The fat content of creams determines how they behave when cooked. The higher the fat content, the more stable the cream is to curdling.

Light creams, up to about 20 percent fat, can curdle when mixed with acid ingredients and heated. They're best used as an uncooked topping for fruits or pastries, to enrich coffee, tea, or hot chocolate, or to make intentionally curdled mascarpone.

To make mascarpone, a tart, thickened cream, heat light cream to 180 to 190°F/80 to 85°C, stir in cream of tartar or lemon juice, allow to cool and set, then refrigerate in a fine strainer or colander lined with cheese-cloth to drain watery whey overnight.

Heavy and whipping creams will not curdle when mixed with acid ingredients and heated, because they contain so little protein. They're excellent for enriching pan sauces. So is crème fraîche, a fresh fermented cream, when it's made from heavy cream.

To make a quick cream sauce for meats or fish cooked on the stove top, simply add heavy cream to the deglazed pan juices and simmer until the mixture is as thick as desired.

Whipped cream is dense, velvety cream lightened with air bubbles into a delicate foam. The bubbly liquid is held together by solid milk fat droplets that the whipping causes to stick to each other—but just barely. If the fat droplets get too warm and soft and sticky, they separate into masses of butter, and the delicate foam turns watery and greasy.

To make whipped cream:

- *Use whipping or heavy cream* with enough fat droplets to make a stable foam, 30 percent or more. For a sweet whipped cream, use superfine sugar that dissolves quickly. Thick crème fraîche can also be whipped into a dense foam.

- *Refrigerate the cream for at least 12 hours* to get the fat droplets to stick better.

- *Chill the cream, whisk or beaters, and bowl* in the freezer for 10 to 15 minutes, but not long enough for the cream to begin freezing.

- *To produce the lightest foam,* use a hand balloon whisk, which can work in more air than electric beaters. An immersion blender or food processor can make dense whipped cream more quickly than a whisk or beaters, but a few seconds too many will turn the foam into butter.

- *Whisk or beat without stopping* until the foam reaches the desired consistency, adding any sugar once it begins to thicken. Prolonged beating will warm the cream and churn it to butter.

- *If cream begins to look grainy or lumpy,* it has gotten too warm and is turning to butter. Start over with a fresh container of cream.

Refrigerate whipped cream if you're not going to use it right away, in a covered container to protect it from off odors. Make sure it's cold before piping or other manipulation that could warm it and begin to form grains of butter.

Once made, whipped cream will slowly drain a small amount of watery liquid that can be poured off or gently folded back into the foam.

To avoid watery drainage and make a stiffer foam, prepare some gelatin dissolved in a small amount of warm water and beat it in as the cream begins to thicken.

BUTTERS AND OTHER DAIRY SPREADS

Butter is a flavorful spread and versatile cooking fat, especially valuable in cakes and pastries. It's made by churning cream so that its fat droplets stick together in large masses. Butter is about 80 percent fat, the rest water, milk proteins, sugar, and emulsifiers that coat the fat droplets. When melted, butter separates into golden fat above, the milky water solution below.

Butter comes in several different forms. Read labels to make sure what you're buying.

Salted butter contains between 1 and 2 percent salt, which helps prevent spoilage by bacteria, amplifies butter aroma, and contributes saltiness when butter is used as a spread or in cooking. Butters are often sold in both salted and unsalted versions.

Sweet cream butter is made from pasteurized cream without any additional flavorings apart from salt, and has the simplest flavor.

Cultured cream butter is made from pasteurized cream and added bacterial cultures that give it a tartness and stronger butter aroma than sweet cream butter.

Sweet cream butter with added flavorings has been flavored with natural or artificial chemicals to resemble cultured butter.

"European-style" butter is sweet cream or cultured butter with a higher fat content, 82 to 85 percent, which is especially useful for making pastries.

Whipped butter is easier than ordinary butter to spread when cold, thanks to tiny bubbles of nitrogen gas that weaken the otherwise hard mass of chilled fat. A given volume measure contains less butter than the same volume of unwhipped butter.

"Clarified" butter is pure butterfat with all moisture and milk solids removed. It can be heated to higher frying temperatures without scorching than whole butter. **Ghee** is clarified butter made by heating the butter enough to brown the milk solids, and has a nutty aroma.

Margarines are butterlike spreads made with vegetable oils and added water and dairy flavorings. They have less saturated fat than butter, but some contain undesirable trans fats.

Stick margarines have the same consistency as butter and can be used similarly in baking.

Tub margarines are softer and easier to spread than stick margarines, and contain less saturated fat. They cannot substitute for butter in baking but can in frying.

Low-fat and nonfat spreads replace fat with water and various thickening agents, including proteins, starch, and gums. They cannot replace butter in frying or baking.

MAKING AND COOKING WITH BUTTER AND SPREADS

Butter is simple to make in the kitchen. It can take 15 minutes or more by hand, much less in a machine. The result is incomparably fresh flavor. One pint/500 milliliters of heavy cream will yield about ¾ cup/170 grams of butter.

To make sweet cream butter:

- *Place fresh unhomogenized cream in a deep bowl and beat it* with a whisk or electric beaters or a mixer blade until grains of butterfat form and clump together. Or process it in a food processor, or shake in a large jar with a tight lid. Partly cover open bowls with wrap or foil; separating cream really splatters.

- *Drain away the buttermilk* and refrigerate it for use in baking. This is sweet buttermilk and doesn't provide the acidity of commercial buttermilk, but contributes to fine texture and slows staling in baked goods.

- *Knead the fat clumps into a mass,* squeezing out moisture when you can, while keeping the mass cool and clean. Use a wood or silicone paddle or spoon, or your own well-washed or gloved hands, precooled in cold water. To amplify aroma, knead in ½ teaspoon/2.5 grams salt per initial pint/500 milliliters of cream.

To make cultured cream butter, find a brand of buttermilk with live bacterial cultures, add ¼ cup/60 milliliters to each quart/liter of unhomogenized cream, keep the mix at room temperature for 8 to 12 hours, then beat and knead as above. The buttermilk will be thin but tart with acidity.

Use freshly made butter promptly, when its flavor is at its best, and because it won't keep as well as commercial butter.

Store-bought butter surfaces often taste stale and rancid, especially if they look darker than a freshly cut piece. Many wrappings let enough air through to dry out and oxidize the fat.

For the best flavor, scrape away any dark surface areas before using stored butter.

Cold butter is too hard to spread without tearing breads and pastries.

To serve spreadable butter, let it warm to a cool room temperature, or speed its softening by pounding it a few times with a heavy utensil. Or keep it at room temperature, tightly wrapped from contact with air, for a day or two. Ceramic butter keepers work by immersing one surface in water. Change the water frequently.

To clarify butter, heat gently until the melted fat stops bubbling, an indication that the water has been cooked out. Lift off the protein skin at the surface and pour the yellow fat off the white protein residue at the pan bottom. To make ghee, or brown or black butters, continue the heating until the protein residue browns less or more deeply.

Beware of eruptions when clarifying or melting butter, and use low gentle heat. Because water is heavier than fat, it sinks to the container bottom as butter melts. If the heat is too high, either from a burner or in the microwave, the water can suddenly boil, turn to steam, and explode through the hot fat above it.

Use clarified butter or ghee for most sautéing, when the pan gets hot enough to brown or scorch milk residues.

Use whole unclarified butter for gentle frying of eggs and fish. At frying temperatures under 300°F/150°C, the emulsifiers in whole butter help prevent these delicate foods from sticking to the pan.

Mixing whole butter with cooking oil does not raise the temperature at which the milk solids brown or scorch. This is a very common misconception.

CULTURED YOGURT, BUTTERMILK, SOUR CREAM, AND CRÈME FRAÎCHE

Cultured dairy products are thick and creamy, pleasantly acidic and aromatic, thanks to the growth of helpful bacteria. Noncultured imitations are instantly acidified and flavored without bacteria. Low-fat, nonfat, and low-price versions are thickened with added milk protein, starches, and gums.

Check labels and choose products with "live cultures" and without additives. They're the most flavorful and delicately creamy. Don't buy products close to the sell-by date.

Cultured milks and creams slowly become more acid in the refrigerator, but resist spoilage and keep longer than fresh milk and cream.

Heat cultured milks and creams gently. Most cannot be cooked without curdling. If creaminess is important in the finished dish, add them just before serving.

Yogurts are milks cultured with particular bacteria that produce a very tart taste and fresh, applelike aroma.

"Natural" yogurts with no stabilizing additives tend to leak watery whey, but it's easily strained off or stirred back in.

Greek-style yogurts are made especially thick by draining away the watery whey, and sometimes by fortifying the milk with added protein, which can result in a harsh flavor.

Probiotic yogurts contain live cultures of bacteria that can survive in the digestive system and may have several beneficial influences.

Frozen yogurt is a low-fat ice cream with only about 20 percent added yogurt.

Yogurt cannot be cooked without curdling it and killing its bacteria. If creaminess or live bacteria are important, stir it into a cooked dish just before serving, when it's warm but not hot (lower than 120°F/50°C).

True buttermilk is the low-fat, sweet or tart, milky by-product of making sweet or cultured butter, full of emulsifiers and flavor, and excellent for baking. Sweet buttermilk can't combine with baking soda to leaven cakes and quick breads. To substitute it for commercial buttermilk, use baking powder instead of soda, or balance the soda with another acid ingredient.

Commercial buttermilk is low-fat milk, thickened and given a tart, buttery flavor by the bacteria used to make cultured butter, or by the simple addition of thickeners and flavors. It's not as helpful in baking as true buttermilk, but contributes to leavening when combined with baking soda.

Bulgarian buttermilk is a commercial cultured buttermilk made especially tart and thick with the bacteria used to make yogurt.

Cultured sour cream is cream with 20 percent fat, homogenized twice for extra body, thickened and given a tart, buttery flavor by the bacteria used to culture butter.

Acidified sour cream is an approximation of cultured sour cream, thickened and flavored by the direct addition of acid and flavorings.

Crème fraîche, the most versatile cultured dairy product, is cream thickened and given a tart, buttery flavor by the bacteria used to culture butter. It can be whisked into a dense whipped cream, and if made from heavy cream so that it contains about 38 percent fat, it can be boiled without curdling. Brands made with homogenized cream are less prone to leaking free butterfat when heated.

Use crème fraîche to flavor and thicken deglazed pan juices into a rich sauce. For the best results, use full-fat brands made from heavy cream, not "low-fat" versions.

MAKING YOGURT AND CRÈME FRAÎCHE

Yogurt and crème fraîche are easy to make in the kitchen using commercial products as starters, an instant-read thermometer, and jars or plastic storage containers. Start with a cultured brand of yogurt or plain buttermilk (not Bulgarian) whose flavor and consistency you like. Don't use a commercial crème fraîche; plain buttermilk contains a higher concentration of the same bacteria and works more reliably.

To make yogurt:

- *Heat milk to 180°F/80°C,* either on the stove or in the microwave oven, and let it cool slowly in the container to 115°F/46°C.

- *Stir in yogurt*, either commercial or some of your previous batch, 2 tablespoons/30 milliliters for each quart or liter of milk.
- *Wrap the covered container in kitchen towels and keep it undisturbed* for 2 to 4 hours, until the yogurt is set as you want it. Its consistency will firm as it chills in the refrigerator and then slowly continues to acidify.

Milk temperatures higher than 115°F/46°C thicken yogurt more quickly but will cause more separation of watery whey. Lower temperatures take longer and produce a softer consistency.

To make thick "yogurt cheese" or "Greek-style" yogurt, spoon the yogurt into a fine strainer or colander lined with cheesecloth, and let watery whey drain off for several hours in the refrigerator.

To make crème fraîche:

- *Heat heavy cream to 180°F/80°C,* either on the stove or in the microwave oven, and let it cool slowly in the container to 115°F/46°C.
- *Stir plain buttermilk* into the cream, 1 tablespoon per cup/15 milliliters per 250 milliliters.
- *Cover the container, wrap it in kitchen towels, and keep it undisturbed* for 2 to 4 hours, until the cream is set as you want it.
- *To make crème fraîche more casually but less predictably,* simply stir buttermilk and unheated cream together in the container, cover it, and let it stand at cool room temperature overnight, or until thick.
- *For a more even consistency* but a blander flavor, use homogenized cream. Unhomogenized creams will develop a thick upper layer during the fermentation. When this happens, gently mix the layers back together before refrigerating.

CHEESES

Cheeses are solid versions of milk, made by curdling the proteins with an enzyme and removing much of the water to concentrate the protein and fat. Most cheeses have also been salted and made more or less acid by helpful bacteria. Many are given additional flavor by bacteria or molds that "ripen" them over the course of weeks or months.

Fresh cheeses, including cottage cheese, quarg, cream cheese, mozzarella, and ricotta, are moist and perishable. Check expiration dates and keep them cold. Cheeses without stabilizing gums have a more delicate consistency.

Aged cheeses, including Brie and Camembert, cheddar, blue, and Parmesan, are salted, less moist, and less perishable. Quality versions may be several times the price of mass-market brands.

Process cheese and cheese spreads are made from a mixture of new and aged cheeses, blended together with emulsifying additives. They have a generic cheese flavor, are conveniently packaged, and melt well.

Low-fat and nonfat cheeses are imitations filled out with starch, gums, and proteins. Instead of melting, they just dry out.

Traditionally made cheeses are some of the most flavorful and diverse foods there are. Mass-market approximations with the same names have been made quickly and are not as good.

You get the cheese you pay for. The best cheeses are the most expensive. If you like cheese, be sure to try the imported French, Italian, and English originals, as well as artisanal American cheeses.

Buy cheese cut to order from a store where you can try a taste. Precut cheese quickly loses its flavor and develops off flavors. Avoid cheeses with brown discoloration, separating fluid, or mold growing on cut interior surfaces.

Scrape away the surface of precut cheese to remove off flavors.

Avoid grated cheese, which quickly loses its aroma. Buy Parmesan and other grating cheeses in whole pieces and grate just before using.

Keep perishable fresh cheeses tightly wrapped and very cold.

Keep unripe soft cheeses at 50 to 60°F/10 to 15°C, loosely wrapped in wax paper, so that they can finish ripening. Full refrigeration suspends the ripening action of microbes and enzymes.

Keep well-ripened cheeses cool to cold, loosely wrapped in wax paper or under a cheese dome or inverted bowl.

Serve cheeses at room temperature, not right out of the refrigerator. The texture of cold cheese is congealed and hard, the flavor muted.

COOKING WITH CHEESES

Heat affects different cheeses differently.

Melting cheeses soften into a thick liquid and spread. These include Camembert, Brie, Colby, blue cheeses, and process cheese products.

Stringy cheeses form cohesive, sticky strands when pulled. These include mozzarella, Emmental (Swiss with holes), and most cheddar cheeses.

Nonmelting cheeses soften and then dry out without spreading. These include most fresh goat cheeses, queso blanco, Indian paneer, feta and halloumi, ricotta, and dry grating cheeses such as Parmesan. Dry grated cheeses can be spread on a pan and heated to make thin, crisp wafers.

Make cheese sauces and soups with either dry grating cheeses or melting cheeses, which disperse easily in water.

To prevent cheese in sauces and soups from turning lumpy and oily:

- *Grate the cheese finely.*
- *Add the cheese to hot but not boiling liquid, at the end of the cooking.*
- *Stir as little as possible* to avoid developing stringiness.
- *Include flour and starches* to prevent protein clumping and fat puddling.

Cheese fondue is a cheese-based dip kept warm and molten over a low flame, thinned with wine and other liquids. It can become stringy or too thick.

Be sure to include tart white wine and/or lemon juice. Tartaric and citric acids prevent stringiness, as does the inclusion of some flour or cornstarch.

To remedy thickening as the fondue moisture evaporates, stir in splashes of white wine.

Eggs are as common a food as we've got

10

EGGS

ggs are as common a food as we've got, but that's because they're also one of the most extraordinary. What other food comes packaged by nature to keep for weeks, makes a satisfying and nutritious main course in minutes, and costs pennies? I'm happy to pay a premium for eggs from hens that are kept humanely; even at several times the supermarket price they're a bargain. But a high price and words on a carton don't guarantee humane production. If you want to be sure, check up on the farm that produces them.

Like milk, eggs contain all the ingredients needed to grow a new creature. Unlike milk, eggs package and concentrate those ingredients in handy amounts, and segregate them so that we can use them together or separately. And how we can use them! In the shell or out, intact or mixed, alone or enveloping other ingredients or weaving through and holding them together. The protein-rich white can lend either dense structure or foamy lightness to baked goods, the yolk fats and proteins a combination of richness and solidity to cakes and custards and creams and sauces. In Japanese cooking, raw egg yolk itself is served as a sauce.

Red beans led me to discover the insights of modern food science (p. 348), but eggs opened my eyes to the accumulated wisdom of traditional cooking. Early on I read in Julia Child's *Mastering the Art of French Cooking* that it's best to whip egg whites in a copper bowl, because copper makes an egg foam more acidic and so more stable. I knew that the chemical explanation was incorrect, so I assumed the whole idea was just an old cooks' tale. Months later I came across an annotated engraving of a French kitchen that showed a boy whipping egg whites in a copper bowl—in 1771. An old tale indeed! I immediately did a side-by-side test of copper and glass bowls, and the copper foam was much more stable and velvety. So I stopped assuming. Traditionally schooled cooks may not know chemistry, but they know cooking, and in the kitchen that's the knowledge that counts.

EGG SAFETY

Eggs are richly nourishing for chicks, for us, and also for microbes.

A variety of harmful bacteria readily grow in eggs and egg dishes. Careless handling at any stage can contaminate eggs and cause illness.

Intact, clean raw eggs can carry salmonella bacteria inside them. Salmonella cause illness that can be life threatening for the very young, the elderly, and people who are already ill.

The risk of exposure to salmonella is very small from one or two eggs cooked in a home kitchen and served right away. It's much greater when dozens of eggs are combined in food service and prepared, held, and served over a period of hours.

When preparing eggs for people who are especially vulnerable to illness, cook them thoroughly, to 160°F/70°C or above, or use pasteurized eggs.

To reduce the risk of illness from eggs and egg dishes:
- *Buy fresh, clean, refrigerated eggs.*
- *Keep raw eggs refrigerated* until just before cooking.
- *Discard raw eggs with cracked shells.*
- *Hold lightly cooked eggs for 30 minutes in water at 140°F/60°C* before serving. This effectively pasteurizes soft-boiled or poached eggs without hardening creamy yolks.
- *Serve egg dishes promptly.*

SHOPPING FOR EGGS

There's little practical difference among the various kinds of chicken eggs sold in supermarkets. Breed, shell color, fertilization, hens' living conditions and diet generally don't affect egg flavor or function significantly.

There are large differences among egg producers, in the scale of their operations, their approaches to animal welfare and sustainability, and the price of their eggs. Commodity eggs are among the cheapest of our major foods. Take an occasional look at the information on some pricier cartons, and consider whether it might be worth paying a premium to support other approaches to egg production.

Backyard and small-farm hens that forage and eat kitchen scraps have a more varied diet than commercial hens and produce deeper colored yolks.

Quail eggs and duck eggs are alternatives to chicken eggs and increasingly easy to find. Quail eggs have the appeal of their speckled shells and diminutive size, large duck eggs their deep orange yolks and rich flavor.

Egg grades indicate initial quality when the eggs were packed for shipping. Grade AA eggs start out with firmer yolks and whites than grade A or grade B eggs, qualities mainly important for eggs cooked whole (poached, fried, soft- or hard-cooked).

Packing or sell-by dates indicate the likely quality when you actually buy eggs. Packing dates are given as the numerical day of the year (1 to 365). In any given grade, the most recently packed eggs will have the firmest yolks and whites, and will keep longest. Newer grade A eggs may be firmer than older grade AA.

Egg sizes vary and are not always interchangeable. The common U.S. sizes and liquid weights per egg are medium (1.75 ounces/49 grams), large (2 ounces/56 grams), extra-large (2.25 ounces/63 grams), and jumbo (2.5 ounces/70 grams). Larger eggs take longer to cook. For baking, be sure to use the size specified in recipes, usually large, or to adjust proportions for different sizes.

When buying eggs, choose cartons with the latest sell-by date, and the size called for in your favorite recipes. Open the carton and check that all the eggs are intact.

Pasteurized eggs are available in the shell, in liquid form, and dried. These products eliminate worries about salmonella-infected eggs, but don't do quite as good a job as raw eggs at foaming or emulsifying sauces. They can have a pronounced cooked flavor.

STORING EGGS

Store eggs in the refrigerator, ideally in an airtight container to slow moisture loss and odor pickup. Eggs of good quality will keep for several weeks past their sell-by date.

Eggs seldom spoil, but their contents shrink and deteriorate. The normally thick white and yolk become runnier and the yolk membrane more likely to break.

To estimate the quality of stored eggs without cracking them open, place one in a bowl and add water. A fresh egg will lie flat, an older egg will lift its blunt end toward the surface, and a very old egg will float.

To tell whether an egg in the refrigerator is raw or cooked, spin it on its side. A raw egg will spin sluggishly, a cooked egg rapidly.

THE ESSENTIALS OF COOKING WITH EGGS

Eggs have two very different parts, the white and the yolk.

Egg white is a cloudy to clear, colorless, viscous fluid that's 90 percent water and 10 percent protein. The protein molecules are loosely tangled up with each other and give the white its thickness.

There are three zones of egg white with different consistencies: a runny outer layer, a thicker, cohesive inner layer, and two dense cords that anchor the yolk to the shell.

Heat solidifies egg white by coagulating its proteins. Heat causes the egg-white proteins to stick more and more tightly to each other and form a network throughout the fluid. This process turns the liquid white into a moist, opaque solid. The higher the heat, the tighter the proteins stick together, and the harder and more rubbery the solid white becomes.

Air bubbles also coagulate egg-white proteins. Whisking egg whites traps air bubbles in the fluid. Air bubbles pull egg proteins onto their surfaces and cause them to stick together and form a solid network. That network holds the bubbles together in a stable foam for making meringues and soufflés. The more the eggs are whisked, the tighter the proteins stick together. When overwhisked, the proteins separate into compact clumps, and the foam collapses into a curdled mix of solid clumps and runny fluid.

The egg yolk is a ball of creamy yellow liquid surrounded by a thin membrane. The yolk is 50 percent water, 30 percent fat and fatlike emulsifiers and pigments, and 20 percent protein. Its fatty materials provide much of the egg's color, flavor, and richness.

Heat solidifies egg yolk by coagulating its proteins. The yolk contains less water than the white, and its fat and much of its protein are contained in tiny spheres. When heat causes the yolk proteins to stick together, the network they form causes the yolk to thicken, then form a crumbly mass of solidified spheres. The higher the heat, the drier the crumbly yolk becomes.

The key to most good egg dishes is temperature control. Just the right level of heat and protein bonding produces a moist, tender white and a creamy yolk. Too much heat produces a hard, rubbery white and dry, crumbly yolk. In custards and creams, too much heat causes curdling and separation.

For a tender, even consistency, heat eggs and egg dishes just until they solidify. Eggs whites begin to solidify around 140°F/60°C, egg yolks around 145°F/63°C, and mixtures of eggs with other ingredients usually between 160 and 180°F/70 and 80°C.

Separated yolks and whites provide different qualities to cooked dishes. Both help thicken and set liquids with their proteins. Egg whites create a slick, slightly elastic firmness; egg yolks a tender, soft firmness combined with creaminess.

To separate yolks and whites, use two bowls. Crack the egg into two half-shells and let the white flow into one bowl while passing the yolk between the shell halves, using the shell edges to cut the clingy white from the yolk. Or crack the egg into your well-washed hand, and use your fingers to strain the white from the yolk. Put the yolk into the second bowl.

If the yolk breaks and some ends up in the white, scoop the yolk out with a spoon before proceeding to the next egg, especially if you'll be whipping the whites. Yolk interferes with foaming, though not fatally. Don't worry about a small residue.

SOFT- AND HARD-COOKING EGGS IN THE SHELL

Soft-cooked eggs have a soft or creamy yolk and a tender white. Hard-cooked eggs have a mostly solid yolk and a white firm enough to have the shell peeled from it cleanly. Both are usually cooked in a pot of hot water, fully immersed, but they can also be steamed. Steaming takes slightly longer.

Don't boil eggs. Boiling water is turbulent and too hot. It breaks shells and toughens proteins, intensifies cooked-egg flavor, and helps turn the yolk surface green. Soft-cook eggs in water or steam just below the boiling point. Hard-cook eggs well below the boiling point, at 180 to 190°F/80 to 85°C.

For consistent results, develop a consistent method. Exact cooking times depend on the desired doneness, the egg size and starting temperature, and the cooking method. Use the same egg size and start them fresh from the refrigerator. Use the same pot and volume of water. Cook at least one more egg than you need, and check its doneness early.

To make soft-cooked eggs, gently lower the eggs into copious water that has fallen just below the boil. Keep the heat on low and cook 2 to 4 minutes for mostly liquid oeufs à la coque, 3 to 6 minutes for soft-cooked eggs to eat from the shell, and 5 to 7 minutes for mollet eggs, soft-cooked eggs that can be removed whole from the shell.

To make very tender mollet eggs that slide out of the shell when they're cracked and have barely set whites, hold the eggs for 30 to 60 minutes at exactly 147°F/64°C. Check and adjust the water temperature frequently, or use an automatic immersion circulator or water oven.

For hard-cooked eggs that are reliably easy to shell, use eggs that are a week or two old. Very fresh egg whites stick to the inner shell and tear.

To make hard-cooked eggs simply, gently lower the eggs into copious water that has fallen just below the boil, or in cold water that is then raised quickly just to the boil. Cover the pot, turn off the heat, and let the eggs sit for 10 to 12 minutes.

To make hard-cooked eggs with reliably moist, just-set yolks, hold the eggs for 30 to 60 minutes at exactly 153°F/67°C. Check and adjust the water temperature frequently, or use an immersion circulator or water oven.

Chill hard-cooked eggs quickly in cold or ice water to prevent the yolk surface from turning green, and to firm the white for easier shelling.

To shell eggs cleanly, tap them all over to crack the shell into small fragments. Start with the air pocket at the wide end and carefully pull on the membrane to bring the shell fragments with it.

Use or refrigerate cooked eggs promptly.

POACHING AND FRYING EGGS

Poaching and frying are ways of cooking eggs free of their shells but otherwise intact, the yolk surrounded by the white and ready to become its sauce.

The challenge in making good poached and fried eggs is to produce an attractively compact shape, a tender white, and a creamy yolk.

To produce shapely poached and fried eggs, use very fresh eggs with a strong yolk membrane and a high proportion of thick white to thin.

Strain each egg before cooking in a large perforated spoon to drain away the runny thin white, or use rings or cups to contain the white.

To poach eggs:
- *Heat just below the boil a* shallow pan filled to a depth of at least 1½ inches/4 centimeters with salted water or another cooking liquid. Don't add vinegar to poaching water. It's ineffective at controlling the shape, and flavors the egg.
- *Gently slide the eggs into the liquid* from a shallow bowl or perforated spoon, and cook 3 to 5 minutes. Don't let the poaching water boil and become turbulent.
- *Remove the eggs* with a clean perforated spoon, drain the water, and blot the bottom dry with a clean towel.
- *Serve on a prewarmed plate* or on other warm ingredients.

To fry eggs:
- *Use a nonstick or a well-seasoned frying pan.*
- To minimize sticking, use whole butter rather than oil. Whole butter carries antisticking emulsifiers.
- *Heat the pan alone to 250 to 300°F/120 to 150°C,* when a flicked water droplet quickly evaporates but doesn't skate on the pan.

- *Add enough oil or fat to coat the surface,* and crack or slide the eggs into the pan.
- *Turn the eggs after a minute or so* with a thin-blade spatula and cook the upper surface for a few seconds (over easy); or baste the surface with hot fat, or add a spoonful of water to the pan and cover it to trap the steam.
- *Slide the spatula blade decisively* under the yolk and turn the egg onto a prewarmed plate.

MAKING SCRAMBLED EGGS, OMELETS, AND FRITTATAS

Scrambled eggs, omelets, and frittatas are all made by mixing raw yolks and whites together, then heating the mix into a more or less firm but moist and tender mass.

Scrambled eggs are cooked gently in a frying pan until moist and tender throughout. Additional liquid ingredients (cream, milk, stock, water) dilute the egg proteins and give a softer result, but also one more sensitive to overcooking and leaking watery juices.

To make scrambled eggs:
- *Precook any vegetables* to remove excess water.
- *Whisk together* eggs, any other liquids, and seasonings.
- *To avoid undercooked lumps,* strain slow-to-set yolk cords from the mixture.
- *Heat a nonstick or well-seasoned pan alone on medium heat to 200 to 225°F/93 to 107°C,* hot enough to make a water droplet steam and bubble. Add the oil or butter, and pour in the eggs and any other ingredients.

- *Stir and scrape* constantly to produce an even, creamy consistency, or occasionally to produce large, tender curds.
- *Remove promptly* when the eggs have barely set as desired.
- *Serve on prewarmed plates.*

Omelets are cooked briskly in a frying pan to make a thin mass of moist, tenderly coagulated egg that is folded onto itself and sometimes around a filling of other ingredients.

To make an omelet:

- *Choose a properly sized pan,* either well seasoned or nonstick, so that the eggs will form a medium-thin layer (an 8-inch-diameter/ 20-centimeter pan for 2 to 3 eggs).
- *Have any filling ingredients warm* and ready. Precook vegetables to remove excess water.
- *Whisk together* eggs, other liquids, and seasonings.
- *Heat the pan alone over moderately high heat to 275 to 300°F/135 to 150°C,* or hot enough to vaporize a water drop in 1 to 2 seconds. Coat the pan with oil or fat, and pour in the eggs.
- *Stir and scrape until the mass just begins to hold together.*
- *Place any filling on the top.*
- *Leave the eggs undisturbed* just long enough to set and, if desired, lightly brown the bottom surface.
- *Fold the omelet* in half or in thirds and slide onto a prewarmed plate.

Frittatas and flat omelets usually include vegetables, meats, or cheese, aren't folded onto themselves, and are made thicker to begin with.

To make a frittata or flat omelet:

- *Choose a properly sized pan,* either well seasoned or nonstick, so that the egg mixture will form a thick layer.
- *Precook meats and vegetables* to remove excess water.

- *Whisk together* eggs, other liquids, and seasonings. Mix in any other ingredients.
- *Heat the pan alone over moderately high heat to 275 to 300°F/135 to 150°C,* or hot enough to vaporize a water drop in 1 to 2 seconds. Coat the pan with oil or fat, and pour in the egg mixture.
- *Cook the mixture through until barely set,* when the center no longer jiggles with a shake of the pan. Brown the top if desired under a broiler, or by sliding the set mixture onto a plate and inverting it back into the pan.

EGG MIXTURES: CUSTARDS AND CREAMS

Custards and creams are cooked mixtures of eggs, milk, cream, and usually sugar. The egg proteins thicken and sometimes set the other liquids. Egg whites provide firm setting power and little flavor. Yolks provide a more delicate, creamy set along with eggy flavor and richness.

The egg proteins in custards and creams are greatly diluted by the other ingredients. A typical ratio is 1 egg per cup of liquid/250 milliliters.

Diluted egg proteins thicken and set at a high temperature compared to plain eggs, at 160 to 190°F/70 to 85°C instead of 140 to 150°F/60 to 65°C.

Diluted egg proteins form a fragile structure that is easily broken by overcooking.

Heat custard and cream mixes slowly and gently near their setting temperature to avoid shooting past it, overcooking and curdling the mix.

To ensure against curdling, include flour in the recipe (1 tablespoon per cup of mix/8 grams per 250 milliliters) or cornstarch (2 teaspoons per cup/5 grams per 250 milliliters). These starches protect the egg proteins, but produce a slightly puddinglike consistency and flavor.

The milk and cream are quickly preheated in most recipes, then combined with the eggs so that the mixture will cook faster.

Always add hot liquids to raw eggs, not the reverse. Adding eggs to the hot liquid will cook the eggs prematurely, coagulating their proteins and curdling them.

Lemon and other fruit curds are "creams" in which the milk and cream are replaced by fruit juice and butter. Fruit acidity reduces the danger of curdling but doesn't eliminate it.

CUSTARDS AND FLANS, CHEESECAKES AND QUICHES

Custards and flans are sweet or savory egg mixtures cooked in the oven without stirring, so that they set into a moist solid.

Custards meant to be sliced or turned out whole from their dishes need to be firmer than custards spooned from the dish they're baked in.

Whole eggs and egg whites contribute an elastic, cohesive firmness that's best for sliced or turned-out dishes. Yolks contribute a soft, creamy firmness better suited for custards spooned from the baking dish.

Custards are often baked in a water bath, partly immersed in a pan of water, which moderates the oven temperature to 190°F/85°C or lower, slows the cooking, and helps avoid overcooking.

Don't cover the water bath, which would prevent evaporative cooling and quickly raise the bath temperature to the boil. To protect the custard surface, cover its container only.

Fill the water bath with boiling water, and make sure that the water-bath temperature remains around 190°F/85°C. Water below the boil takes too long to heat up in the oven, and lower bath temperatures may not set the egg proteins. If the bath temperature drops below 190°F/85°C, turn up the oven heat.

To judge custard doneness, bump the dish to see how fluidly its contents move, or probe its center with the tip of a knife or a toothpick. For a creamy interior, remove the pan from the oven while the custard still jiggles slightly, or when some thickened mix clings to the probe. For a firm custard, wait until it no longer jiggles and the mix clings to itself instead of the probe, when the proteins have fully set.

Cheesecake is a rich, tender custard made with sugar and both low-fat and high-fat dairy products, usually some combination of ricotta cheese, cream cheese, sour cream, and cream.

To prevent curdling and to absorb moisture from the ricotta, include some flour or cornstarch.

Mix the custard ingredients gently to avoid creating bubbles, which cause oven rise and collapse, an uneven texture, and a cracked surface.

Avoid lumps by processing ricotta until smooth, and/or warming and softening cream cheese to blend it evenly with the other ingredients.

Bake slowly in a gentle oven. For more even heating, immerse the pan in a water bath.

To avoid overcooking, cracking, and a dry interior, turn off the oven when the custard is still slightly jiggly at the center.

To minimize shrinking and cracking, remove the pan from the oven, run a knife along the outside edge, then return to the oven and allow to cool gradually with the oven door ajar.

Chill for up to a day or two to set firmly before cutting. Allow to warm to a cool room temperature before serving.

Crème caramel is a custard with a soft caramel top that is turned out onto a serving plate. It requires a high proportion of whole eggs to be firm enough to stand on its own.

To make crème caramel:

- *Caramelize sugar* at the bottom of the empty custard dish with high heat, let the dish cool, and grease its inner wall.
- *Cook the custard mix* in the dish until firm, and chill for several hours to firm further.
- *Dip the dish briefly in hot water* to soften the caramel and the custard surface, and turn the custard out onto a plate.

Crème brûlée, "burnt cream," is a soft custard topped with a brittle, glossy sheet of caramelized sugar.

To make the brûlée sheet, chill the cooked custard to avoid overcooking, coat with a generous layer of coarse sugar, and heat the sugar as quickly as possible with a torch, broiler, or preheated salamander (a metal plate on a handle) until melted and brown.

Quiches are savory pie-shaped egg mixtures with relatively large proportions of egg to milk or cream, and therefore a dense, firm consistency that doesn't require a water bath. They're cooked in a prebaked pastry crust.

Precook meats and vegetables for quiches so they don't leak juices when the quiche mix cooks.

CREAMS

Creams are egg mixtures thickened on the stove top with frequent stirring, which prevents them from setting into a solid. Crème anglaise is a versatile pourable cream that's used as a sauce for fruits and pastries and as an ice cream base. Pastry cream is used to fill and decorate pastries and cakes. It and other cream fillings are stiffened with flour or starch to hold their shape and moisture.

Pourable and stiff creams are cooked very differently.

Gently heat pourable creams just until they begin to thicken to the consistency of heavy cream, around 180°F/80°C, to avoid curdling. They'll be thicker when cool.

Bring flour- and starch-stiffened creams to a full boil. Boiling inactivates egg-yolk enzymes that will otherwise digest the starch and thin the cream after it's been cooked. Starch protects the egg proteins from curdling at the boil.

To make crème anglaise:

- *Heat milk and cream near the boil* to extract flavor from any solid ingredients, including vanilla beans, and to speed the final cooking. Once extracted, strain out the solids.
- *Pour the hot liquid slowly into blended eggs and sugar* while whisking constantly. Return the mixture to the pan and stove.
- *Heat the mix with constant stirring* until it thickens to the desired consistency. To minimize minor curdling, heat creams in a double boiler over simmering water.
- *To prevent overcooking* from the pan's heat, immediately plunge the pan bottom into cold water while continuing to stir the thickened mix.

- *Pour the cream through a strainer* to remove any coagulated particles, and stir occasionally as it cools.
- *Add any fruit only after the sauce cools* to room temperature, to avoid curdling the cream with the fruit's particles and acidity.
- *To prevent the formation of a dry skin*, press plastic wrap into the cream surface, or dot the surface with small pieces of butter and let them melt to coat it.

To make crème anglaise without constant stirring, cook it in a water bath:

- *Blend the flavored cream, eggs, and sugar and seal the mix airtight in a zippered plastic bag.*
- *Immerse the bag in a water oven or large covered pot of hot water* at 185°F/85°C for 1 hour or until it has thickened. Maintain the pot temperature with an immersion circulator or by frequent checking and addition of boiling water.
- *Manipulate the bag gently and occasionally* to even out the cream consistency as it heats and cools.

To make pastry cream:

- *Combine the eggs with the sugar and with flour or starch*, usually 1 to 2 tablespoons per cup of liquid/8 to 16 grams per 250 milliliters.
- *Heat the milk to the boil and whisk it into the egg mixture.*
- *Heat the mixture with constant stirring to the boil.*
- *Stir the cream only occasionally* and gently as it cools, to avoid weakening the starch network and thinning the cream.

Beware of recipes for cream-pie fillings in which egg yolks are beaten off the heat into the other hot ingredients. This makes a lighter, smoother cream, but the egg enzymes will survive and liquefy the filling.

To make a stable cream-pie filling, heat it just to the boil after adding the yolks, if necessary thinning it out with milk.

FOAMING EGGS

Egg foams are light masses of egg and air bubbles. They're sometimes cooked and served on their own. More often they're folded into creams and batters to lighten them into airy soufflés and cakes.

Egg foams are usually made by beating air into the whites or yolks with a whisk or electric mixer. They can also be made with a siphon, a pressurized container mainly used to whip cream.

Egg foams are stable and delicious when the egg proteins bond to each other just enough to form a supporting network around each bubble. If the proteins bond too tightly, they clump together and curdle the foam.

Egg-yolk foams need gentle heat during the whipping to form the protein support. Too much heat causes protein clumping and curdling.

Egg-white foams don't need heat to form. Correct whipping alone forms the protein support. Too much whipping causes protein clumping and curdling.

Egg-white foams benefit from acid ingredients or copper bowls, which prevent curdling by limiting protein bonding.

To avoid overbeating egg-white foams, add ⅛ teaspoon/0.5 gram cream of tartar or ½ teaspoon/2 milliliters lemon juice per white. Or use a copper bowl (or a pinch of a copper dietary supplement).

To make egg-white foams:

- *Don't worry about egg age or temperature,* which are not major factors.

- *Separate the whites free of any yolk,* which interferes with foaming.
- *Clean the bowl thoroughly* of any oil or detergent, which also interfere with foaming.
- *Use a large balloon whisk or "planetary" stand mixer* (the spinning whisk moves around in the bowl) to incorporate air quickly and thoroughly.

Egg-white foams are whipped to different consistencies for different dishes.

Judge the consistency of egg foams by their behavior when drawn out into peaks in the bowl and on the whisk.

Soft peaks are droopy and form when the foam is glossy and semiliquid and slips along the bowl surface. The egg proteins are only partly bonded and can expand further to stabilize a larger volume of air bubbles.

Stiff peaks hold their shape and form when the foam is glossy and clings to the bowl. The proteins are mostly bonded and can only accommodate a slight additional expansion in air bubbles.

Dry peaks are matte rather than glossy, when the foam begins to leak some liquid and slip along the bowl again. The proteins have thoroughly bonded and no further expansion is possible.

FOAMED EGG YOLKS: ZABAGLIONE AND SABAYONS

Zabaglione and sabayons are thick, rich foams. They're made by heating a mixture of egg yolks and a flavorful liquid while whisking air into it. Zabaglione and sweet sabayons include sugar and a sweet wine or fruit juice; savory sabayons include meat or fish stocks. They can be pourable sauces or thick, spoonable desserts.

Heat the mix carefully as you whisk. The yolk proteins begin to gel and the mix to thicken and inflate far below the boil, as low as 140°F/60°C depending on the recipe.

To avoid forming curds at the pan bottom, cook the mix in a bowl over a moderately hot water bath, not over boiling water or direct heat.

As the yolk proteins begin to set in the heat, the liquid thickens and traps more and more air bubbles.

To make a pourable yolk foam, heat and whisk just until the mix thickens to the consistency of heavy cream. Pourable foams steadily lose their bubbles.

To make the lightest and most stable yolk foam, whisk and heat until the mix thickens enough to form streaks on the pan bottom.

Egg-yolk foams leak liquid if they stand for some time. Reincorporate the liquid with gentle stirring to avoid deflating the foam, or simply scoop the foam off the liquid.

FOAMED EGG WHITES: MERINGUES

Meringues are egg-white foams that can be soft, chewy, or brittle, depending on their sugar content and how they're cooked.

Added sugar reinforces the protein support network in a meringue. Heat sets the egg proteins and removes moisture, stiffening and eventually hardening the foam.

Meringue powders are a mixture of dried pasteurized egg whites, sugar, and stabilizing gums. They're useful for making uncooked meringues without the risk of potentially contaminated eggs.

Uncooked meringue is a creamy foam for a pastry topping or to fold into the ingredients for a mousse, chiffon, or soufflé. It can be light and soft or dense and firm enough to shape with a pastry pipe.

To make a soft uncooked meringue, whip whites and stabilizing acid alone to the stiff-peak stage, then gently fold in any sugar with a spatula.

To make a firm uncooked meringue, whip the whites, acid, and sugar all together.

Use superfine or powdered sugar to make uncooked meringues. Coarser granulated sugar dissolves slowly. Powdered sugar contains starch, which helps absorb egg moisture and prevent weeping and stickiness. Substitute weights, not volumes (there's about half as much powdered sugar in a cup as there is in a cup of table sugar).

Cooked, or "Swiss," meringue is a chewy meringue stiff enough to pipe into shapes and stable enough to keep at room temperature for days.

To make a cooked meringue, whip egg whites, sugar, and acid over a simmering water bath until they reach 170°F/75°C and form a stiff foam; then remove the mix from the heat and continue beating until it's cool.

Syrup-cooked, or Italian, meringue is a light, fluffy foam that's still firm enough to shape for decoration. The mix doesn't get as hot as a Swiss meringue does, and doesn't have as long a shelf life.

To make a syrup-cooked meringue, boil sugar and water on the stove top to 240 to 250°F / 116 to 121°C. Separately whip the egg whites and acid to stiff peaks, then continue while streaming the syrup in along the bowl surface, not onto the spinning beaters.

Meringues are often finished in the oven to harden and keep them, or to heighten their flavor and texture.

To make hard meringues that remain snowy white, dry them slowly in a low 200°F/93°C oven. Meringues brown very easily thanks to their high sugar content. Store them in an airtight container to prevent them from absorbing moisture.

To make a chewy browned meringue, heat it briefly in a medium oven, 350°F/175°C, to the desired color.

Meringues sometimes weep beads of sugar syrup and don't adhere properly when topping a pie. They can also shrink when cooked and break unevenly when cut.

To make meringues easier to work with, beat the egg whites with some dry tapioca starch or cornstarch cooked into a thick paste. Tapioca starch is precooked.

To prevent weeping from meringues, take care not to underwhip or overwhip the egg whites. Use powdered sugar and make sure that it dissolves completely. Try baking at a lower oven temperature. To prevent slippage on pies, make the meringue with powdered sugar and/or added starch. Apply the meringue to lukewarm filling, neither hot nor cold. Cover the filling with starchy crumbs before applying the meringue.

SOUFFLÉS

Soufflés are egg-white foams that are flavored and given body with various savory or sweet mixtures, and inflated and set by oven heat.

Soufflés have the reputation for being difficult, but they're straightforward and reliable. Even if they collapse, they can often be partly reinflated.

Soufflés rise in the oven when heat turns their liquid water into steam, and the steam inflates their air bubbles. Soufflés fall when they cool down and their steam condenses back into liquid water.

The soufflé base is the mixture of other ingredients into which the egg-white foam is folded.

Flavor soufflé bases strongly, even to the point that they taste overseasoned. Their flavor will be diluted by the egg whites and air.

Thin soufflé bases rise highest, collapse most dramatically, and re-inflate poorly. Their main ingredients are yolks and sugar.

Serve soufflés made with thin bases immediately, before they collapse.

Thick soufflé bases rise and fall modestly, and can be cooked in advance and reinflated. They're made with flour, starchy vegetables, pureed meat, chocolate, or cocoa, and should be fluid enough to blend easily with the whipped egg whites.

To mix the soufflé base and foam with minimal loss of air and lightness:

- *Cool a freshly cooked base briefly* to avoid setting the egg foam prematurely.
- *Allow at least one egg white per ½ cup/125 milliliters base.*
- *Whip egg whites to stiff but still glossy peaks,* still fluid enough to blend easily with the base.
- *Stir a quarter of the foam into the base* thoroughly to thin it. Scrape the remaining foam onto the base.
- *"Fold" the base and foam together with a spatula,* slowly and gently scooping up the base and trailing it along the foam, repeating until base and foam are just mixed evenly; or gently mix with a balloon whisk.

To prepare the soufflé mix for baking:

- *Butter or oil the soufflé dishes* to prevent the mix from sticking.

- *Sprinkle in bread crumbs or grated cheese or sugar* to provide crunch and/or flavor. They won't help the soufflé rise higher.
- *Fill the dish gently with the mix and tap it* to make sure the mix settles with no empty spaces.
- *Run a finger around the dish edge* to clean it of mix that would set quickly and restrain the rising.
- *Refrigerate or freeze uncooked soufflés in their dishes* if desired. Wrap tightly and refrigerate for several hours, or freeze for days.

To cook soufflés:
- *Preheat the oven to the desired cooking temperature.*
- *Choose a high temperature,* 400°F/200°C and up, to brown the soufflé surface while the interior remains moist and creamy. The soufflé will rise quickly and high, and will fall noticeably when served.
- *Choose a moderate temperature,* 325 to 350°F/160 to 175°C, to brown the surface while giving the interior time to cook through and firm. The soufflé will rise and fall less dramatically.
- *Avoid low oven temperatures,* which can cause the mix to expand and spill out of the dish before it sets.
- *Bake most soufflés on a rack or baking sheet low in the oven,* to speed bottom heating and rising. Bake small ramekins in a shallow water bath, to moderate the bottom heat and prevent the light mass from rising as a whole.
- *Judge soufflé doneness* by bumping the dish to see how fluidly its contents move, or by inserting the tip of a knife or toothpick into the center. For a creamy interior, remove from the oven

while the probe brings some mix with it. For a firmer interior, wait until the probe comes out clean.

- *Don't worry about opening the oven door* to check on doneness. The soufflé may shrink slightly as it cools briefly, but it will go on rising when the door is closed again.

To reinflate cooked soufflés, place them in a moderate oven until heated through.

Meats
are the
flesh
of land
animals
and birds

11

MEATS

Meats are the flesh of land animals and birds. They're especially satisfying foods: substantial, firm textured, mouthfillingly flavorful, rich in nourishing protein. Meaty. They're often the centerpiece of a meal.

Meats are challenging to cook well because their protein fabric is both fragile and stubborn. They become appealingly juicy in a very narrow range of internal temperatures, roughly 130 to 150°F/55 to 65°C. During cooking, they can pass through that range and go from juicy to dry in just a minute or two. But some tough cuts actually need prolonged high heat just to become tender enough to chew. So the essential key to cooking meat well is knowing what kind of heat a particular cut needs, and how to strike a good balance between juiciness and tenderness.

Given meat's special status, you'd think that any serious cook would make a point of knowing how to make the best of it. Alas, no. Many published recipes guarantee that meat will come out overcooked and dry. Less than diligent food authorities of all kinds, from TV personalities to trained chefs, offhandedly repeat old myths about meat that perpetuate misunderstanding and disappointing results.

There are also plenty of good meat recipes out there, and knowledgeable, reliable authorities on meat cooking. But in order to find them you have to be able to tell good from bad. So you need to become your own authority, at least for the basics.

It's not hard. No matter what you read in recipes or hear pronounced by people who should know, keep these simple truths in mind:

- **Searing meat does *not* seal in its juices, and moist cooking methods do *not* make meats moist.** Juiciness depends almost entirely on how hot you cook the center of the meat. If it gets much hotter than 150°F/65°C, it will be dry.
- **Meat overcooks quickly. Low heat slows cooking and gives you the greatest control over doneness.**
- **Most recipes can't predict correct cooking times.** There's no substitute for checking meat doneness yourself, early and often.

Cook by these truths and you'll be ready to make the best of any meats and meat recipes you choose.

MEAT SAFETY

Like dairy products and eggs, meats are a favorite haunt for microbes that cause spoilage and illness. Unlike dairy products and eggs, meats are almost sure to carry significant numbers of these microbes. Some contamination is inevitable when living animals are slaughtered and their bodies are butchered into meat.

Microbes are always present on raw meat surfaces, even the freshest and finest quality, and usually with no obvious smell or visible sign. They're normally not present in the meat interior, but may be if the meat has been cut into, and certainly will be if it has been ground up. Bacteria grow well on meat and can multiply quickly.

Meats carrying harmful bacteria cause many serious cases of illness every year.

Handle all meats with caution. Assume that any piece of raw meat may carry harmful bacteria.

Keep all raw and most prepared meats cold, as close as possible to the freezing point, 32°F/0°C. They won't actually begin to freeze themselves until several degrees below this. Dry-cured sausages and hams can be kept at cool room temperature.

Isolate raw meat and its juices from contact with other foods.

Wash hands, knives, and cutting boards with warm, soapy water before and after handling raw meat.

Use a reliable thermometer to measure cooking and internal meat temperatures, and wash it between measurements. Meat color is not a reliable indicator of doneness.

Avoid contaminating cooked meats with marinades or sauces that were applied to raw or partly cooked meats. Reserve a portion of the liquid for serving with the cooked meat, or reheat it to at least 160°F/70°C.

Meats made safe by cooking are usually not the most delicious meats. Temperatures high enough to kill harmful bacteria quickly also dry the meat out. Temperatures low enough to leave meat juicy don't necessarily kill harmful bacteria.

To prepare meat safely for people who are especially vulnerable, heat its surfaces to the boil or to temperatures high enough to brown, and its center to at least 155°F/68°C, a temperature that effectively eliminates harmful bacteria in 15 seconds. Prepared cold cuts and hot dogs are potential carriers of listeria bacteria; to be safest, heat them until they're steaming hot.

To prepare juicier meats and take the usual precautions and chances, keep meats cold, handle them with clean hands and utensils, and cook them to the doneness you prefer.

To prepare juicier meats and take more time and trouble to make them safer than usual, hold them at juicy temperatures long enough for the lower heat to kill most bacteria.

For a rare interior, cook until the center reaches 130°F/55°C, and hold that temperature for 90 minutes. For medium-rare, cook to 135°F/57°C and hold for 40 minutes. For medium, cook to 140°F/60°C and hold for 15 minutes.

To prepare safe raw meat dishes or quick-cooked ground meats— steak tartare, carpaccio, rare hamburgers—cut or grind your own low-microbe meat.

- *Start with a large, intact piece of meat,* whose interior is likely to be microbe-free.
- *Immerse the meat completely in rapidly boiling water* for 30 to 60 seconds to kill bacteria on its surfaces. Remove the meat with clean utensils.
- *Plunge the meat in an ice-water bath* for 1 minute to stop the cooking, then remove it and blot it dry.
- *Immediately prepare the meat with clean hands, knives, cutting boards, and grinders.*
- *Keep the meat very cold* until you're ready to cook or serve it.

To save leftover cooked meats, refrigerate them as soon as possible. Don't leave cooked meat out at room temperature for more than 4 hours, less if it's especially warm. Discard any meats or sauces inadvertently left out overnight. To keep cooked meat for more than a day or two, freeze it wrapped airtight.

To serve leftover cooked meats as safely as possible, reheat them quickly to an internal temperature of 160°F/70°C, and bring sauces and gravies to a boil. Reheat in covered containers to prevent evaporation from cooling the upper surfaces.

SHOPPING FOR MEAT

Fresh meats are available in a wide range of quality levels and prices, from a number of different production systems, and from convenience stores, supermarkets, gourmet markets, and butcher shops. If you want to know where your meats come from and how to get the best from them, shop around and find a butcher who's passionate about quality.

Commodity meats in supermarkets come from standardized animals bred for productivity rather than quality, raised in crowded factory operations on agricultural by-products, antibiotics, and growth-stimulating hormones. They're inexpensive, but generally have the least flavor and are most prone to becoming dry and tough when cooked.

Specialty meats, including organic, grass-fed, and heritage meats, often come from less common breeds that have been developed for the quality of their meat, and that have been raised in smaller operations with whole feeds and little or no manipulation of their growth rate. They're often older and more flavorful than commodity meats. Game meats—venison, buffalo, ostrich—come from undomesticated but farm-raised animals and usually have much less muscle fat. Because they're more expensive, specialty meats may sit longer in the display case and lose their quality advantage.

USDA beef grades provide an indication of potential flavor and tenderness, based on the general quality of a carcass and on the amount of fat dispersed within the meat tissue. "Prime" is the highest grade, scarce and expensive, "choice" the more common good-quality grade, and "select" the grade for ordinary quality.

Dry-aged beef is hung unprotected in a cold room for several weeks, a period that evaporates moisture, tenderizes, and intensifies flavor, and increases production costs and price. Wet-aged beef has been held in shrink-wrap for several weeks. It also becomes more tender and somewhat more flavorful, but doesn't develop the same intensity as dry-aged beef.

Judge and choose fresh meats by appearance. For a given cut of meat, the darker the color, the more flavorful it will be. Marbling, white streaks of fat in the red or pink meat, will make it moister and richer, as will abundant white fat particles in ground meats. For good hamburgers, look for ground beef with 20 percent fat.

For fresh meats with the best flavor, have them cut or ground to your order, and cook them promptly. Large and bone-in pieces will lose less moisture when cooked than small or boned pieces with more cut surfaces.

Precut meats, either exposed in the display case or packaged in a plastic tray, have a large surface area exposed to the air, light, and bacteria, and develop off flavors in a day or two. Avoid meats that are brown at the edges, or gray instead of pink, red, or purplish.

Among packaged and frozen meats, choose those with the latest sell-by date, and with no dark or off-color patches.

Vacuum-packed "primal" cuts—whole roasts, racks, legs—have been minimally handled and are enclosed in airtight plastic wrap. They keep for several weeks in the refrigerator. Their purple color will bloom to red when meat meets air.

Avoid vacuum-packed ground beef for hamburgers. Vacuum packing tightly compresses the beef particles, and this produces a dense, pasty-textured hamburger. Vacuum-packed ground meat is also more likely to come directly from a packer who combines scraps from many carcasses, a practice that raises the risk of contamination with E. coli. Grind your meat yourself, or have your butcher grind it for you fresh.

Prepared meats are often lower-quality cuts dressed up with added flavorings. Check ingredient lists.

Check the labels of "enhanced" fresh meats packaged in marinade and "self-basting" turkeys. You're likely to be paying meat prices for the substantial amount of injected salt water. Bacon with added water from brine-curing shrinks much more when cooked than dry-cured bacon.

To make chickens with crisp skin, choose dry-processed or kosher poultry, preferably not shrink-wrapped. Their skin is noticeably thinner and crisps faster because it hasn't been plumped with water.

Put fresh meats in your cart just before you check out. If it takes more than a few minutes to get back to the kitchen refrigerator, transport them in a cooler.

STORING MEATS

Most meats are at their best the moment we buy them, and gradually decline in quality until we cook them. Beef is an exception; its flavor and tenderness can benefit from a week or more of aging in the home refrigerator.

Age cuts of beef in the refrigerator sealed in their plastic vacuum pack, or exposed and loosely covered on a rack to allow evaporation of their moisture. Choose large cuts for exposed aging, to allow for the trimming and loss of dried and rancid surface patches.

The enemies of meat quality are oxygen and light, which turn fats rancid; microbes, which produce off flavors; and warm temperatures, which encourage the other two.

Keep meats in the coldest corner of the refrigerator. Store shrink-wrapped or freshly wrapped cuts unopened. For cuts sold in plastic trays, remove them and blot dry with paper towels before rewrapping tightly in fresh plastic wrap.

Use fresh meats promptly, within a few days, and ground meats within a day or two. Large cuts of meats with hard fats—beef, lamb—keep longest.

Freeze meats to keep them longer than a few days, but don't wait days before freezing them. Beef keeps for up to a year, pork for 6 months, poultry for 3 months.

Freezing does its own damage to meat quality. It forms ice crystals that puncture the meat cells and cause fluid loss. Dry freezer-temperature air causes "freezer burn," surface drying that toughens and creates off flavors.

To minimize freezing damage, freeze fast to minimize ice crystal size, and wrap meats tight with no air pockets. Set your freezer as cold as possible. If possible, divide the meat into small portions that freeze faster, and set in the freezer unwrapped. Once frozen, wrap the meats in several tight layers of plastic wrap and a final opaque layer of foil or paper.

PREPARING MEATS FOR COOKING

The first step in preparing raw meat is to bring it out of storage and refresh it.

Thaw frozen meat very gradually and gently in the refrigerator—large cuts can take several days—or much faster in a bowl of ice water. Don't thaw in hot water or at room temperature, which favors the growth of microbes. Meats can be cooked directly from the freezer, but it requires more time and a low cooking temperature to avoid overcooking the outside while the inside warms up.

Examine the meat, and clean and trim it as necessary. Remove it from the packaging and smell it. If there's an off smell, rinse the surface thoroughly, or briefly blanch it in boiling water. Scrape or cut away patches discolored by long exposure to air. Blot the surface dry.

Rinse poultry thoroughly, especially the body cavity of whole birds, and blot dry.

Once meat is cleaned, it's often pretreated before cooking to improve its flavor or texture.

Warming meat to room temperature and even higher reduces the cooking time and helps cook more evenly. Give steaks and chops an hour on the countertop, larger cuts more time.

Flavoring with spice rubs and pastes imbues the meat surface with intense flavors.

Leave only sparing amounts of rubs and pastes on meats during cooking, except in low-temperature, long-time cooking or Cajun-style blackening. Herbs and spices scorch at roasting and grilling temperatures. To prevent pastes from simply drying out on lean cuts, include some oil or fat.

Salting is the simple application of salt to meat surfaces. At first salt draws some moisture out, but then it diffuses into the meat interior, seasoning it and improving its ability to retain moisture and tenderness when cooked. Salt diffusion is very slow, and can take days to reach the center of a roast. Even when smaller cuts are salted many hours in advance of cooking, the surface portions will be saltier than the interior.

Brining is the immersion of meat in a weak solution of salt and water, with or without other flavorings, for hours to days before cooking. Injecting brine into the meat interior speeds the process. The salt penetrates the meat, seasons it, and improves its ability to retain moisture and tenderness.

Brines of a certain strength, 5 to 10 percent salt by weight, also cause the meat proteins to absorb extra water from the brine, making the meat seem exceptionally juicy when cooked. Very lean poultry and pork can benefit from this extra moisture, especially when they're overcooked.

Brine selectively. Brines have drawbacks: they dilute the meat's own flavorful juices with tap water, and usually make the pan juices too salty for deglazing into a sauce.

Marinading is the immersion of meat in acidic liquids, often wine based, to flavor and tenderize it. Marinades penetrate meat very slowly, so their effects are usually limited to the surface layers unless they're injected deeper into the meat. Acids do weaken meat proteins, but the result is often mealy rather than tender. More helpfully, they reduce the formation of carcinogenic substances on the meat surface during roasting and grilling.

To make a wine marinade, simmer the wine for a few minutes to reduce the alcohol, which has a drying effect on meat. Let the marinade cool before adding the meat.

Tenderizing is a method that weakens the protein structures of the meat and makes it easier to cut and chew when it's cooked. "Tenderizers" are protein-digesting enzymes from various plants, which break the long protein molecules into smaller pieces, and can weaken both muscle fibers and tough connective tissue. They're sold in powdered form, but are also present in fresh pineapple, ginger, kiwi fruit, and figs.

Don't rely on tenderizers to tenderize tough meat, especially before cooking. They don't penetrate meat on their own, so they work very unevenly, just at the surface or where they're injected. They're most active as the meat heats up during cooking, and stop working at temperatures above about 160°F/70°C.

To tenderize meat most effectively, break up its structure physically. Pound thin cuts gently with a mallet or pan bottom. Cut the fibers in a thicker cut with a Jaccard, a device with an array of small, sharp blades.

Grinding is a method that breaks the meat down into tiny pieces that can be pressed back together into a more tender mass.

To grind meats for sausages, hamburgers, and similar foods:

- *Use a meat grinder* or, if necessary, a food processor.
- *Prechill the meats, grinder or processor blade, and bowl in the freezer* to prevent the meat and fat from softening into a paste.
- *Process the meat in short pulses,* stopping every few to scrape down the sides of the bowl.
- *For a moist-cooked sausage or hamburger,* include pieces of fat to make a total of about 20 percent fat in the mix, about 3 to 4 ounces per pound/200 grams per kilogram.

TENDER MEAT AND TOUGH MEAT

To cook meat well, it helps to know why some meats start out tender and others tough, and what kind of cooking is best for each.

Standard roasts, steaks, and chops come from muscles that move the animal. "Variety meats," or offal, are its internal organs and skin.

Tenderness and toughness are textures created by the meat fibers and connective tissue.

Meat fibers are the long, threadlike bundles of meat cells whose proteins make the body move. They're about one-third protein and two-thirds water.

Raw meat fibers are chewy and mushy. Moderate heat firms their proteins, which makes them easier to chew and releases their water to make them juicy. High heat hardens the proteins and dries them.

Connective tissue is the physical harness that surrounds and connects individual cells, cell bundles, and whole muscles. Connective tissue is tough collagen protein, especially tough in beef, which comes from older, larger animals than veal or lamb or pork or chicken.

Raw connective tissue is chewy and tough. Moderate heat softens and partly dissolves it into gelatin over the course of many hours. High heat softens and dissolves it in an hour or two.

Fat tissue, the light patches interspersed among the meat fibers, contributes to their apparent tenderness and moistness.

There are two general categories of meats: tender and tough.

Tender meats have little connective tissue, and come from muscles that don't get used very much, along the back and sides. They include the loins of cattle, pigs, and lambs and the breasts of birds. Liver is a tender offal meat.

Tough meats have a lot of connective tissue and come from hard-working muscles, especially legs and shoulders. Tripe (stomach) and tongue are tough offal meats.

Tender meats are best cooked just to a moderate temperature at which they're juicy and tender.

Tough meats are best cooked long enough to dissolve their connective tissue and make them tender. This can take a few hours at high fiber-drying temperatures, a full day at moist-fiber temperatures.

MEAT DONENESS

Meat doneness is a set of qualities by which we define different stages of cooking. It's a combination of moistness and, in red meats, chewiness and color. Each of these qualities is caused by the meat's sensitive molecules, the fiber proteins. As the fibers heat up, their proteins stick to each other tighter and tighter, become firmer and firmer, and release more and more moisture until the moisture runs out.

In tough meats, chewiness also depends on the connective tissue proteins. The following descriptions apply most directly to tender steaks, chops, and roasts.

Raw meat is soft but chewy, and the moisture is trapped in the fibers and pasty.

Rare meat is firmer and easier to chew, and the moisture is free and juicy.

Medium meat is even firmer but still easy to chew, and the moisture is still free and juicy.

Well-done meat is very firm, becoming hard, and the moisture is gone.

It takes only a few degrees to go from firm and juicy to hard and dry, a transition that begins at around 150°F/65°C. When meat is cooking, its inner temperature may be rising several degrees every minute.

To get the meat doneness you want, check it early and often.

DONENESS AND COOKED QUALITIES OF TENDER MEAT CUTS

DONENESS	QUALITIES	TEMPERATURE, °F / °C	COLOR
Bleu, raw	Soft and chewy, slick, translucent	110–120/43–50	Pink to red
Rare	Slightly firm and tender, juicy	125–130/52–55	Pink to red
Medium-rare	More firm, very juicy	130–140/55–60	Paler pink to red
Medium	Firm, juicy	140–150/60–65	Pink
Medium-well	Becoming fibrous, less juicy	150–160/65–70	Pink-tan
Well	Fibrous, dry	160/70 and above	Tan-gray

These temperatures are 10 to 20°F lower than the USDA definitions for doneness, which include a large margin for error to reduce the chance that meat will be undercooked and potentially unsafe to eat.

Judge doneness by cutting into the meat to check the color; by inserting a thermometer into the meat to measure its temperature at the center; or by pressing on the meat to check its firmness, which increases with doneness. Judging by touch takes practice. A good model for rare, medium, and well done is the firmness of the muscle on the back of the hand between the thumb and the first finger when it's relaxed, extended, and clenched.

Don't judge doneness by color alone. Well-done birds are sometimes persistently pink-fleshed and red at the bone, underdone ground meats are sometimes brownish, and vacuum-packed meats slowly change color when they're cut and exposed to oxygen.

THE ESSENTIALS OF COOKING MEATS

The keys to cooking meats well are attentiveness and careful temperature control. Meats can overcook and dry out in minutes.

Don't rely on recipe cooking times or simple formulas to guarantee a good result. Recipes can't account for significant changes in cooking time caused by small variations in meat thickness, temperature, and the temperature of grills and ovens and pans.

Bring most meats to room temperature or even warmer before cooking. This reduces cooking times and the usual surface overcooking while the inside heats through. But cook thin cuts directly from the refrigerator, to give the surface time to brown.

Cook meats in large pieces and on the bone to retain the most moisture and flavor. The more meat is cut up, the more surfaces it has through which juices will get squeezed out.

Cook most meats in two stages. An initial dose of very high heat kills surface bacteria and browns and flavors the meat surface. A finishing period of low, carefully controlled heat cooks the meat through slowly and gently while preserving its moistness and tenderness. Keep the finishing cook-through as close as possible to the final inner temperature you want.

Check meat doneness early and often. If you're using a thermometer, check its accuracy beforehand.

When cooking at high temperatures, stop when meat is still slightly underdone, by 5 to 10°F / 3 to 5°C for steaks and chops, 15 to 20°F / 7 to 10°C for large roasts. The hot surface will continue to heat the interior for some time.

To cook tender cuts so that they're juicy, heat them to rare or medium rare, an inner temperature between 125 and 140°F / 52 and 60°C.

Loin roasts, most steaks and chops, poultry breasts, including duck and squab, and ground meats are tender cuts. Chicken and turkey breasts are less juicy but more pleasing at slightly higher temperatures, around 150°F/65°C.

To cook tough cuts relatively quickly, so that they're tender but dry and fibrous, heat them to an inner temperature of 180 to 200°F / 80 to 93°C. This common method will dissolve connective tissue into gelatin and produce tender meat in 2 to 12 hours, depending on the temperature and the cut. It works best with cuts rich in gelatin and fat, which can lend moistness to the dry meat fibers. These include pork shoulders, chuck roasts, and pork and beef cheeks.

To cook tough cuts so that they're tender and their fibers retain some juiciness, heat them to an internal temperature of 140 to 160°F / 60 to 70°C. This modern method will require cooking for 12 to 24 hours or more to dissolve connective tissue into gelatin and produce tender meat.

Cook ground meats, pâtés and terrines, and fresh sausages in the same manner as tender meats, briefly and moderately to retain juiciness. To make sure bacteria are killed throughout fresh sausages, poach them to an internal temperature of 140°F/60°C, hold that temperature for 30 minutes, then cool them briefly and flavor their surface quickly on the high heat of the grill or frying pan. Cooking isn't necessary for cured or precooked sausages, or for prepared pâtés or terrines.

See the pages listed below for cooking methods in which meats are treated like other foods.

SMOKING, p. 100

STIR-FRYING and DEEP-FRYING, pp. 92 and 93

STEAMING, p. 86

MICROWAVING, p. 102

GRILLING AND BROILING

Grilling and broiling expose meat to burning heat from flames or glowing coals or electrical elements. The high temperatures deeply brown or char the surface to create strong, distinctive flavors.

For maximum flexibility in grilling and broiling, divide the cooking into two stages. First cook the surface quickly with high heat, then cook the interior through more gently with low heat.

On the grill, arrange the coals or flames into two areas, one very hot and one moderately hot. Color the meat as desired over the very hot area, then finish cooking over the moderate area. Make the hot area too hot to hold your hand just above the grill for more than a second or two. The faster it can color the meat, the less time the meat interior spends being overcooked.

When broiling, use the oven to finish cooking meat through. First place the meat as close as possible to the broiler flame or electrical element and color the meat as desired on both sides. Then remove the pan from under the broiler and finish the cooking in a moderate oven.

Choose thick cuts for more flexibility in balancing flavor and juiciness. Thin cuts of ½ inch/1 centimeter or less cook through very quickly, often before the surface is browned.

Prewarm the meat so that it will cook more quickly and lose less moisture. Wrap steaks and chops watertight and immerse them in a pot of warm 100°F/40°C water for 30 minutes just before cooking.

Dry meat surfaces thoroughly before beginning to grill or broil so that they will start to brown immediately.

To prevent meat from sticking to the grill, keep the grill clean, preheat it well before cooking, oil the meat surface, and let the meat brown thoroughly before trying to turn it.

Flip steaks and chops frequently to cook them faster and more evenly. Turn the meat every minute or so, from the beginning if distinct grill marks aren't necessary, otherwise during the low-heat finishing.

Handle hamburgers gently to maximize their tenderness and prevent disintegration during cooking. Salt the ground meat to extract protein and help the particles stick together. Press the meat into a disk as gently as possible, and allow it to set and firm in the refrigerator for a few hours. Don't prewarm fragile patties, and don't flip frequently.

Go easy on the charring. Deep browning and charring produce chemicals on the meat surface that damage DNA and increase cancer risk. To reduce carcinogen production, soak meats beforehand in an acidic marinade.

BARBECUING

Barbecuing is a low-temperature method that heats foods for hours in an enclosed grill. The cooking is done mainly by hot, smoky air, not by direct strong heat from the coals or gas flames. It's essentially slow baking in an outdoor oven.

Barbecuing is usually applied to large, tough cuts of meat—shoulders, ribs, briskets—that benefit from many hours of heating at 170 to 200°F/75 to 90°C to dissolve their connective tissue into gelatin and produce smoky, flavorful, falling-apart tender meat.

Keep the food as far as possible from coals or heating elements, whose direct heat radiation can overcook it very quickly. Small backyard grills often don't have enough room to protect the food from excessive heat radiation. Use them briefly at the beginning or end to give smoky flavors to the food, but place it in an oven for the long hours of slow cooking.

Check the cooking temperature frequently. Have a reliable thermometer to check the air temperature inside the enclosure, and make sure that it doesn't rise much above 200°F/90°C for more than a few minutes (as when replenishing coals), or fall below 170 to 180°F/75 to 80°C (which will greatly slow cooking). Aim for 160 to 170°F/70 to 75°C inside the meat.

Frequent basting, or "mopping," with flavorful liquids slows the cooking significantly. Opening the grill interrupts the heating process, the basting liquid temporarily cools the food surface, and its moisture continues to cool the surface in the grill by evaporating.

Toward the end of cooking, baste with fresh liquid and utensils to avoid contaminating the cooked meat with bacteria from the raw meat.

ROTISSERIE COOKING

Rotisserie cooking is a method of cooking meats with repeated brief periods of heat radiation. The rotisserie is a rotating spit mechanism. The meat is impaled on the spit, a long metal rod, and the mechanism constantly turns the spit next to or above flames, coals, or an electric heating element.

Rotisserie cooking has two valuable features. It alternates a few seconds of exposure to high flavor-producing heat with longer periods of cooling down, so that the surface browns but the meat interior can heat through gently and gradually without overcooking. And it concentrates flavorful juices at the meat surface by causing them to cling and spread as the food turns, rather than dripping away.

Use a rotisserie in the open air or in an oven with the door left open. It's most effective when the meat can cool significantly as it turns away from the heat source. In a closed oven, the meat simply bakes and can quickly overcook. Outdoors it's best for the fire or coals to be alongside the rotisserie rather than directly below it, to avoid flare-ups and enveloping heat from rising hot air.

OVEN ROASTING

Oven roasting heats meats relatively slowly, by means of hot air and radiation from the oven walls, at temperatures ranging from 200 to 500°F / 90 to 260°C. It's used mainly for large cuts that take 30 minutes or more to heat through. The prolonged dry heat produces brown, flavorful surfaces on the meat and juices in the pan.

Choose oven temperatures according to the cut of meat and your cooking and eating preferences. In general the larger the roast, the lower you should set the oven temperature, so that the outside doesn't overcook while the inside cooks through.

Low oven temperatures, below 300°F/150°C, cook roasts through slowly and evenly, but also are slow to brown the surface and crisp poultry skin.

Use low temperatures for large or tough roasts that will cook for hours, or to cook any roast through after an initial period of high heat to brown the surface.

High oven temperatures, above 400°F/200°C, brown and cook through quickly, but overcook the outer portions while the center gets to the proper temperature, can quickly overcook the center, and can scorch pan drippings. They require close monitoring.

Use high oven temperatures for chickens and other small roasts that cook through in less than an hour, or for an initial browning followed by low-temperature roasting to finish.

To stop valuable pan drippings from scorching in a hot oven, carefully pour enough water into the pan to cover the bottom and remoisten the drippings. Repeat as necessary.

Use moderate oven temperatures, around 350°F/175°C, to brown and cook moderately quickly and evenly, and without the close attention required by high temperatures.

Convection fans speed surface drying, browning, and cooking through by blowing the hot oven air onto the meat surface, and can cause scorching at ordinary oven temperatures. To avoid scorching, reduce nonconvection roasting temperatures by 25 to 50°F / 15 to 30°C, and check browning often.

Don't trust the timings in recipes. There are too many unpredictable variables for them to be reliable. Among them are these useful adjustments:

Basting with a water-based liquid will slow browning and cooking through, because it interrupts the heating and cools the roast surface by evaporation.

Prerubbing a roast with oil or butter will speed browning and cooking through. Fat limits evaporation and the cooling it causes.

Roasting pans and tents of foil slow cooking by blocking heat radiation from oven surfaces. If the roast sits directly on the pan, not raised up on a rack, the roast bottom will fry, and brown faster than the other surfaces. A deep pan will slow the heating of the roast sides unless the rack raises the roast above the pan walls.

Remove the roast from the oven several degrees early, 5 to 10°F/3 to 5°C for a small roast, 15 to 20°F/7 to 10°C for a large one, if you're cooking at moderate to high oven temperatures. Residual heat near the surface will continue to raise the temperature of the center.

Let the roast rest for at least 30 minutes before carving, and preferably until the center temperature has cooled to 120 to 130°F/50 to 55°C. The meat will retain more of its juices when cut. Cover the roast loosely with foil to prevent the surface from getting too cool.

Whole birds are a challenge to roast well. Their breast meat is low in connective tissue and best cooked to 150°F/65°C for chickens and turkeys, 135°F/57°C for ducks and squab, but their leg meat is high in connective tissue and best cooked to 160°F/70°C, and their skin is best cooked to 350°F/175°C to make it crisp and brown.

To obtain moist breast and tender leg meats:

- *Don't stuff the body cavity or rely on a pop-up thermometer.* Stuffing must be heated to 160°F/70°C to kill bacteria, so the breast meat will be overcooked and dry. Pop-up indicators pop only when the breast meat is already overcooked.

- *Don't truss the legs.* Trussed legs look neater but take longer to cook through, and longer cooking makes it even more likely that the breast will be overcooked.
- *Prewarm the legs.* Let the bird and legs sit at room temperature for an hour with a bag of crushed ice keeping the breast cold.
- *Start the bird breast down* in the roasting pan to slow its cooking. Turn it and cook breast up just long enough to brown the breast skin.
- *Baste the breast with stock* or another water-based liquid, or put a foil tent loosely over the breast, to slow its cooking.

To obtain a crisp skin:

- *Start with a kosher or halal bird* or one labeled "air-chilled," which is not soaked in water during processing.
- *Predry the skin* by cleaning the bird the day before and leaving uncovered on a rack in the refrigerator.
- *Oil the skin,* and don't baste with a water-based liquid.
- *Cook in a hot oven.* Prebrown quail, squab, and other small birds in a frying pan, and then cook through in the oven.
- *Cut the skin from the bird as soon as it's done,* to separate it from the steaming meat underneath.

To salvage overdone breast meat, pull it into shreds and bathe in pan juices.

FRYING, PAN ROASTING, AND SAUTÉING

Frying and sautéing are methods that transmit heat from a metal pan through a thin layer of fat or oil. They can brown and flavor meat surfaces very quickly, in a minute or less.

Frying is the general method of pan cooking steaks, chops, and other large pieces of meat. It's best suited to flat tender cuts, or to browning tough cuts that will go on to be slowly braised.

Pan roasting is a convenient and effective hybrid of frying and oven roasting. It quickly browns the meat on the stove top in a frying pan, then transfers the pan to the oven, which heats the meat through from all sides more gradually and evenly.

Sautéing and stir-frying are methods for frying small pieces of meat that move the pieces frequently to color all surfaces and cook them through evenly.

The key to effective frying and sautéing is to keep the pan hot enough to sizzle constantly. Sizzling is the sound of the meat's moisture vaporizing as it hits the pan. If the pan temperature is too low, the moisture will accumulate, sizzling and browning will stop, and the meat will boil. By the time the moisture cooks away and browning resumes, the meat will be overcooked.

To keep the pan hot enough to fry:

- *Dry the meat* of excess surface moisture.
- *Preheat the pan alone to* 400 to 450°F / 200 to 230°C, then add the fat or oil. Oil heated up along with the pan is more likely to get gummy and cause sticking.

- *Cook the meat in small, uncrowded batches.* Too much meat will cool the pan down.
- *Adjust the heat* to maintain a constant sizzle of rapid water vaporizing.
- *Leave the pan uncovered,* or use a perforated spatter guard, so the water vapor won't condense back into the pan.

If sizzling and browning do stop, remove the meat from the pan, raise the heat, and add the meat back when the liquid has evaporated.

To brown faster and more evenly, press meat with a spatula or weigh it down with a heavy pan or foil-wrapped brick, to force contact with the pan surface. Don't worry, pressing won't make the meat less juicy. When you turn the meat, start the second side on a part of the pan that had been unoccupied. Move the meat occasionally to make full use of the pan surface.

To avoid overcooking, check the pan side of the meat often. As soon as it has browned, turn the meat. Then check the meat interior often. As soon as it's done, remove the meat from the pan.

- *For thick cuts, lower the burner heat* after the second side browns and then turn frequently, every minute or two, or move the pan into a moderate oven, where less efficient heat transfer will cook gently.

POACHING, CONFITS, AND LOW-TEMPERATURE COOKING

Poaching is a method that cooks tender meats by immersing them in a hot liquid below the boiling point, usually between 130 and 180°F/55 and 80°C.

To produce moist poached meats, cook at low temperatures. Start with the poaching liquid near the boil for a few seconds to kill bacteria on the meat surface, then quickly lower the liquid temperature and finish cooking tender cuts at 130°F/55°C for rare, 140°F/60°C for medium, 150°F/65°C for well done.

A meat confit is made by presalting and seasoning a tough cut of meat overnight, then poaching it for hours in that meat's fat, and storing the meat covered with the fat. Duck legs and gizzards are an example. Traditional confits often call for temperatures close to the boil, 190 to 200°F/85 to 93°C, produce tender but fibrous meat, and would be kept for months at cool temperatures while their flavor developed.

To produce moister, less fibrous confits, poach them at 160 to 180°F/70 to 80°C until a fork easily penetrates them. Low heat is slower to tenderize, so cooking times will be longer.

To keep a confit for weeks, remove the meat from its juices to a fresh pot, pour off the fat onto the meat and bring it to 160°F/70°C, then cool and refrigerate.

Low-temperature cooking heats meat at the temperature that corresponds to the particular doneness you want in the meat. It's carried out in a water oven or a pot of water whose temperature is maintained either manually by the cook, or automatically by an immersion circulator. It produces meat that is evenly and perfectly cooked throughout, and that remains that way for hours without any risk of drying out or toughening.

Low-temperature heating also makes it possible to cook shoulder meat, brisket, short ribs, and other tough cuts as if they were tender cuts, to a juicy medium rare instead of well done. Medium-rare temperatures will dissolve the tough connective tissue if they're held steadily for a full day or two.

The disadvantage of low-temperature cooking is that it doesn't create the rich, savory surface flavors that high-temperature frying and grilling do.

To get the best of both low- and high-temperature cooking, heat meats in the water bath until they're done, allow them to cool somewhat, and then quickly sear them over very high heat just long enough to flavor the surfaces and reheat the interior.

Tender meats are typically cooked in a water bath at 130 to 140°F/ 55 to 60°C for an hour or so before searing.

Tough meats can be cooked in a water bath at 135 to 150°F/58 to 65°C for 48 hours or more.

Understand and avoid the potential hazards of low-temperature cooking. Low cooking temperatures are slower to kill the bacteria that cause foodborne illness, and tight wrapping makes it possible for botulism bacteria to grow. Use recipes that explain the hazards, and follow their instructions exactly. In general, it's simplest and safest to serve foods cooked at low temperatures immediately.

To cook meats at low temperatures:

* *Heat the water oven or a large pot of water* up to the temperature that corresponds to the desired doneness: 130°F/55°C for rare, 140°F/60°C for medium, and so on.

* *Seal the meat in a plastic Ziplock storage bag,* pressing out as much air as possible by immersing it in the water just up to the zipper and then zipping it; or vacuum-pack using a home vacuum-packing machine.

* *Immerse the bag in the water* and heat until the meat is cooked through to the desired texture. Low temperatures heat slowly, so allow more time than usual: an hour or so for steaks and chops, for example.

- *Make sure that the bag remains fully immersed in the cooking water and surrounded by it.* Air and vapor pockets in a bag can cause it to float, and water flow or crowding can push bags against each other or the pot sides.

- *If you're not using a water oven or circulator,* stir the water regularly, monitor the temperature frequently with an accurate digital thermometer, and heat or add hot water as necessary to maintain it. Be very careful not to let the water fall below 130°F/55°C and into the microbe growth zone. For long unattended cooking, especially tough cuts that cook for many hours, experiment with your oven to find a thermostat setting that will keep the covered pot at the correct temperature.

Sous-vide cooking is a restaurant version of low-temperature cooking in which the meats are vacuum-packed in plastic bags. Vacuum packing in a professional chamber machine can speed the infusion of marinades and other flavors into meat, and removes all air from the package, so that the meat heats more evenly and can be kept longer after cooking. Household vacuum-packaging machines don't create a strong enough vacuum to infuse foods, can't be used with liquid ingredients, and leave some air in the package.

BRAISING AND STEWING

Braising and stewing are methods that cook meat in a water-based liquid that will become its sauce. An initial frying browns the meat and deepens the overall flavor.

Many braise and stew recipes call for temperatures near the boiling point, which will badly dry out all but the fattiest or most gelatinous cuts of meat.

Beware of recipes that call for an oven temperature over 180°F/80°C. Never let a braise or stew get hot enough to bubble when the meat is cooking. A closed pot in an oven at any temperature above the boiling point will come to the boil. At oven temperatures above 180°F/80°C, leave the pot open to allow evaporative cooling and produce a lower cooking temperature.

To braise or stew tough cuts of meat in a few hours, heat them at 180°F/80°C. They will develop the fibrous tenderness of standard braises and stews.

To braise or stew tender cuts quickly, or tough cuts over a day or more to keep them more moist and less fibrous, heat them at 140 to 150°F/60 to 65°C.

Braise tender pieces of meat, including poultry breasts, gently and briefly. A piece of meat 1 inch/2.5 centimeters thick will be done in about 15 minutes of cooking, *including* browning time. If cooking breasts and legs, remove the breasts when done and keep warm while the legs finish.

To braise or stew:

- *Keep the meat in large pieces* to minimize cut surfaces.
- *Brown the chilled meat quickly* in a very hot pan to flavor the surfaces without cooking through. Dust the meat in flour first to provide a browned thickener for the sauce if desired.
- *Add the cooking liquid and other ingredients and heat slowly* to the cooking temperature. Presimmer any wine for 10 minutes to boil off some of its alcohol.
- *Braise and stew in the oven* whenever possible, not over a burner. Oven heat is more even.

- *Keep the liquid at the cooking temperature and check meat doneness often.*
- *Once the meat is done, stop the cooking.* If the liquid needs to be boiled down or thickened, or the vegetables softened, remove the meat first.
- *Cool and store the meat in the liquid,* some of which it will reabsorb.

When reheating a braise or stew, take care not to overcook it. Remove the meat, bring the liquid to a boil and toss the meat briefly in it, then remove from the heat and let the liquid temperature fall to 140°F/60°C. Hold it at that temperature until the meat is heated through.

SERVING MEATS

Serving meats at their best calls for just as much care as the cooking.

Rest most meats, from steaks to large roasts, before cutting and serving. Just-cooked meats are soft and prone to lose more juices when cut immediately. Rest steaks for a few minutes, roasts for 30 minutes or more. Meats that have been cooked slowly at low temperatures can be served without resting.

Preheat plates to serve hot meat dishes, especially beef, veal, and lamb. As they cool below body temperature, meat fats congeal and the gelatin in connective tissue becomes solid and rubbery.

Cut meats with a sharp knife to avoid pressing down and squeezing out juices.

Carve meats across the direction of the fibers, or grain. This minimizes the length of the fibers in the mouth and makes the meat easier to chew. The grain changes direction in many steaks and roasts, so adjust the carving angle accordingly. Slice chewier cuts very thin.

Shred dry, overcooked meat instead of cutting it, and moisten the fibers with a sauce made intentionally thin and juicelike.

Hold cooked meats at 130°F/55°C to prevent the growth of bacteria, especially if the meal will last for more than an hour or two.

LEFTOVERS

Refrigerate or freeze leftovers as soon as possible after the meat is removed from the heat. Divide large quantities into smaller portions that will cool faster.

The quality of most cooked meat deteriorates in the refrigerator, even in a stew or other dish whose overall flavor may improve for a day or two. Freeze leftovers to keep them in good condition for more than a few days.

Duck and pork confits may be refrigerated for weeks because the flavor changes during storage and rewarming helps define them. To keep them that long without spoiling, be sure to free the meat of all cooking juices and immerse it completely in hot fat before chilling.

Minimize the meat's exposure to air. Wrap separate pieces tightly in plastic wrap, and cover braised and stewed meats with their cooking liquid.

Reheating meat causes the development of stale "warmed-over" flavors, especially in poultry. Reheating above 140°F/60°C dries meat out.

Consider serving leftover meats cold. Chicken and turkey especially benefit from not being reheated.

Rewarm leftover meat as little as possible consistent with safety. Turn it briefly in a pan of boiling liquid—the liquid portion of a stew, for example, or some meat stock—to kill any bacteria on the surface, then heat the meat through gently.

12

FISH AND SHELLFISH

ish and shellfish are strange, diverse, delicious creatures from the earth's waters. We eat dozens of different species that may come from halfway around the world, finger-length smelts and tunas that weigh half a ton, rock-bound oysters and crawling crayfish and rocketing squid.

Having grown up in the Midwest in the 1950s and knowing only the same frozen swordfish that we fed to my pet turtles, I fell in love with seafood late and indiscriminately, when I moved first to New England and then to northern California. I enjoyed the local bounty of the coasts, and, as the fishing industry got more sophisticated, not-so-local pleasures from Asian and South American waters.

Today the first obligation of all cooks who love seafood is to discriminate: to find out which species are being harvested or farmed sustainably, choose them, and help give all the rest a chance to recover from our ravenous appreciation.

The flesh of fish and shellfish is very different from animal and bird meats because it was shaped by their home, the earth's cold waters. Fish and shellfish are cold-blooded, live their lives at the equivalent of refrigerator temperatures, and spoil quickly unless they're kept alive or ice-cold. And ocean waters can carry and taint its inhabitants with a variety of toxins and microbes that aren't found on land or in meats.

Fish and many shellfish are even trickier to cook than meats because their cold-working muscle proteins firm and then dry out at lower temperatures than meat proteins. Fish flesh remains moist and tender in a lower and narrower range of internal temperatures, roughly 120 to 130°F/50 to 55°C. The slow, gentle heat that works well with meat doesn't with many fish, whose muscle enzymes can turn it unpleasantly soft.

So the simple truths of meat cooking also apply to fish. Fish (and most shellfish) overcook quickly. Recipes and the "10-minute rule" for each inch of fish thickness can't predict correct cooking times. To make the best of fish, check its doneness yourself, early and often.

FISH AND SHELLFISH SAFETY

Many people enjoy eating raw and lightly cooked fish and shellfish. Yet like meats and other protein-rich foods, raw fish and shellfish often carry microbes that could cause illness. They also commonly carry other health hazards that meats seldom or never do: viruses, parasites, toxins from algae and from certain fish themselves, and mercury, a toxic metal.

Parasites are small worms that a number of common fish and some shellfish can carry and transmit to humans. They may require surgery to remove.

Toxins are chemicals that damage our bodies. Shellfish and some fish can carry a number of different toxins, most of them made by ocean algae in warm weather. They can't be destroyed by cooking.

Mercury is a toxic metal that accumulates in large fish, notably shark, swordfish, king mackerel, tilefish, and albacore tuna. It's especially harmful to the unborn and to young children.

If you prepare fish or shellfish for people who are especially vulnerable, the ill, the very young, the elderly, or pregnant women, then take special care to minimize their risk of illness.

- *Use only the freshest tuna, mackerel, bluefish, sardines, and mahimahi,* all of which can accumulate a toxin when stored improperly.
- *Avoid serving any oysters, clams, mussels,* or lobster or crab organs (lobster tomalley and coral, crab butter), which can carry toxins and/or viruses even when well cooked.
- *Heat all fish and shellfish through to at least 160°F/70°C,* a temperature that effectively eliminates harmful bacteria and parasites in a few seconds.
- *Check for current guidance on low-mercury seafood* at the U.S. Food and Drug Administration site, www.fda.gov, if you're cooking for pregnant or nursing women or young children.

When you prepare raw or lightly cooked fish or shellfish for people in good health, be aware of the potential hazards and try to minimize them.

Bacteria are always present on and in raw fish and shellfish, even of the best quality, with no obvious smell or visible sign.

Human stomach and hepatitis viruses may also be present in shellfish harvested near cities, and can survive thorough cooking. Raw shellfish are among the most common causes of foodborne illness.

Handle all fish and shellfish with caution. Assume that any raw piece may carry harmful bacteria and viruses.

Keep raw fish and shellfish cold, as close as possible to the freezing point (32°F/0°C).

Isolate fish and shellfish and their juices from contact with other foods.

Wash hands, knives, and cutting boards with warm, soapy water before and after handling.

Use a reliable thermometer to measure cooking and internal temperatures.

Avoid contaminating cooked fish with marinades or sauces that were applied to the raw or partly cooked fish. Reserve a portion of the liquid for serving with the cooked fish, or reheat it to at least 160°F/70°C.

To make raw fish and shellfish as safe as possible, buy the highest-quality, freshest products from a reliable seafood specialist, and keep them ice-cold until you prepare and serve them.

To eliminate parasites in fish, freeze the fish for 7 days at −4°F/−20°C, or cook it through to 140°F/60°C. Home freezers don't usually get cold enough to kill parasites reliably. Most fish sold as "sushi grade" is hard-frozen to eliminate parasites and extend shelf life for shipping.

Avoid toxins by buying shellfish from large seafood markets that can offer products from the safest waters in a given season. If you have wild-harvested shellfish, check with local marine authorities for any restrictions, including warnings against the use of toxin-accumulating soft organs (lobster tomalley and coral, crab butter).

To prepare moist fish and shellfish and take the usual chances, cook fish to the doneness you prefer, even if the temperature is far below 160°F/70°C, and serve it immediately.

Refrigerate leftover fish and shellfish as soon as possible after serving. Don't leave cooked fish out at room temperature for more than 4 hours, less in hot weather. Cook raw leftovers thoroughly before eating them.

SHOPPING FOR FISH

Fish and shellfish call for especially careful shopping. They're highly perishable and often sold in poor condition. They can come from anywhere in the world, be wild or farmed, harvested sustainably or not, treated with chemicals to control disease or to look misleadingly fresh. They may have been frozen and then thawed for sale.

Buy fish and shellfish from a seafood specialist with high turnover. Ask where the fish comes from. Check government (www.nmfs.noaa .gov/fishwatch) and aquarium (www.montereybayaquarium.org) Web sites for current information about endangered species and sustainable fisheries.

Take along a cooler and ice packs when you go shopping, to keep fish as cold as possible.

Inspect fish carefully before buying.

Avoid fish that smell strongly fishy, an early sign of deterioration and spoilage. All fish should have an odor of the seashore. Slight fishiness is common and washes away.

Choose whole fish instead of precut pieces, which develop off flavors more quickly. Have the market clean the fish or do it yourself.

Choose whole fish with a glossy, taut-looking skin; bright, full eyes; and red inner gills. Avoid fish with dull, wrinkled skin; sunken or clouded eyes; or brown gills.

Choose live fish that are active and come from clean, well-aerated tanks.

Choose precut pieces that look moist and shiny, with no gaps between muscle layers and no dry or brown edges.

Be wary of cherry-red colors in tuna or tilapia, which may come from treatment with spoilage-disguising carbon monoxide.

Have your purchase packaged in ice, and refrigerate it as soon as possible. Fish quality deteriorates quickly.

Frozen fish and shellfish may offer better quality than fresh. Some frozen products are prepared at sea within hours after the harvest. Choose packages from the coldest depths of the freezer compartment.

Check the labels of canned, bottled, and other prepared seafood. The best-tasting products will usually be more expensive and packed without preservatives, which cause off flavors.

SHOPPING FOR SHELLFISH

Crabs, lobsters, and shrimp have very perishable flesh and are usually sold frozen, frozen-thawed, cooked, or alive. Truly fresh raw crustaceans are rare and expensive. Inexpensive shrimp are often farmed in Asia and treated with plumping and antibrowning chemicals.

Examine crustaceans carefully and avoid any that have an off smell, black spots or other discoloration, or slime. Choose whole lobsters and crabs that are heavy for their size. Whole head-on shrimp spoil faster than shrimp tails, but have more flavor.

Choose live lobsters and crabs that look lively and come from a clean tank.

Bivalve molluscs are hardy when kept cold and moist, and are often sold live in the shell.

Choose live clams, mussels, and oysters that are kept on ice or in a shallow tank, not submerged in water or in a plastic bag.

Choose preshucked oysters whose surrounding liquid is clear. Cloudy liquid indicates disintegration and possible spoilage.

Choose scallops that are off-white to slightly orange and not too glossy. Very white, glossy pieces have been treated with moisture-retaining chemicals, weep copious fluid when heated, and are hard to brown on the stove.

Squid and octopus are often sold frozen-thawed or cooked. Small sizes are relatively tender and cook quickly; large sizes are tougher and need long cooking.

Choose raw squid that have sharply defined pigment spots on their surfaces. Blurring indicates deterioration.

STORING FISH AND SHELLFISH

Fish and shellfish are at their best the moment we buy them, and deteriorate in quality until we eat or cook them.

The enemies of fish quality are oxygen and light, which turn fats rancid; microbes, which produce off flavors; the fish's own enzymes, which soften the muscle fibers; and temperatures above the freezing point, 32°F/0°C, which speed the effects of all the others.

Store fresh fish in the refrigerator or freezer, and as briefly as possible. If you can, buy it the same day that you'll prepare it. Lean warm-water fish—snapper, catfish, tilapia—keep longest; fatty cold-water fish—salmon, mackerel—the shortest.

Rewrap fish tightly in plastic wrap, covered with an opaque layer of foil or paper.

Keep fish surrounded by fresh crushed ice, or in the coldest corner of the refrigerator. Icing fish can increase its usable life by several days over ordinary refrigeration.

Freeze fish to keep it for more than a day or two.

Freezing takes its own toll on fish quality. It forms ice crystals that puncture the fish cells and cause fluid loss. It can also denature and toughen fish fibers. Dry freezer-temperature air causes "freezer burn," surface drying that toughens and creates off flavors.

To minimize freezing damage, freeze fish fast to minimize ice crystal size, and protect it from air. Set your freezer to its coldest setting. Divide the fish into small portions that freeze quickly, and freeze them unwrapped. Once they're frozen, wrap them tightly in plastic wrap and an opaque layer of paper or foil. Or dip them repeatedly in ice water and refreeze to glaze the surface with a layer of ice.

Refrigerate live lobsters, crayfish, and crabs wrapped in a moist loose cloth for 1 to 2 days.

Store live clams, mussels, and oysters loosely wrapped in a wet cloth in the refrigerator, or on ice, for as much as a week. Keep oysters cupped-shell down. Don't let live molluscs become covered in melted ice, which has no salt and will kill them.

Store preshucked bivalves, as well as fresh squid and octopus, wrapped and buried in ice for up to several days.

Refrigerate raw and fresh-cooked crustaceans as briefly as possible, tightly wrapped and buried in crushed ice. Cleaned shrimp in the shell can keep for a week or more. Whole shrimp with the head are more perishable.

Use frozen shrimp, crab and lobster, and squid and octopus within a few weeks. They deteriorate more rapidly in home freezers, which are not as cold as commercial freezers.

PREPARING FISH FOR COOKING

The first step in preparing fish is to bring it out of storage and clean it. If you prepare fish often, keep a fish scaler and needle-nose pliers on hand.

Thaw frozen fish gradually and gently in the refrigerator, or faster wrapped watertight in a bowl of ice water. Don't thaw at room temperature, which favors the growth of bacteria. Don't thaw frozen breaded fish products; cook these directly from the freezer.

Prepare whole fish by scraping away scales and removing inner organs from the belly. To prevent scales from scattering, immerse the fish in water for scaling. Take care to avoid popping the greenish bile sac, and cut away any flesh discolored with its bitter contents.

Prepare fillets and steaks by pulling out small bones with needle-nose pliers.

Rinse cleaned whole fish and precut pieces thoroughly in cold running water, scraping any residual blood or organs from the belly cavity, then blot dry. Strong fishy smells come mainly from surface deterioration, and should wash away.

To purge surfaces and firm outer layers, presalt fish for 5 minutes after cleaning. Rinse or brush salt off and dry thoroughly before cooking.

To reduce fishy flavors and toxin formation during grilling, marinate fish briefly in wine or other acidic liquids. Rinse and dry thoroughly before cooking.

For neat individual servings, cut pieces to size before cooking. Once cooked, fish flesh flakes and doesn't cut neatly.

To speed heat penetration in a large whole fish and cook it more evenly, make spaced shallow cuts in the thick areas.

To obtain a crisp skin, scrape the skin repeatedly with a knife to remove moisture, then cover with salt and refrigerate for 1 hour or more. Brush off salt and dry thoroughly before cooking. The skins of some fish— catfish, halibut, shark, swordfish—are too tough to be enjoyed.

PREPARING SHELLFISH FOR SERVING OR COOKING

Thaw frozen crustaceans, squid, and octopus gradually and gently in the refrigerator, or faster in a bowl of ice water. Don't thaw them at room temperature, which favors the growth of bacteria.

Wash raw and live shellfish thoroughly in cold water. Scrub shells with a brush to remove any grit and slime.

Remove the "vein" in shrimp and lobster tails, actually the digestive tract, to eliminate its grittiness.

Purge sand from clams by immersing them for several hours in cold water with ⅓ cup granulated salt per gallon/20 grams per liter.

To help shrimp retain more moisture when cooked, brine them briefly.

To speed and even out the cooking of shrimp and lobster, "butterfly" by cutting through lengthwise and spreading two halves flat. Reserve lobster roe, liver, and shells for making sauces.

To reduce the reactive movements of live lobsters when they're boiled or steamed, prechill them for 15 minutes in the freezer or in crushed ice.

To serve more tender oysters and scallops, cut away the tough round plug of muscle in oysters, or the tough side muscle in scallops.

RAW FISH AND SHELLFISH: SUSHI, SASHIMI, CRUDO, AND CEVICHE

Sushi, sashimi, and crudo are raw preparations. Ceviche is raw fish marinated briefly in acidic citrus juice, a treatment that doesn't eliminate microbes or parasites.

Uncooked fish and shellfish carry a significant risk of food poisoning or infection with parasites.

Buy only the highest-quality, freshest fish and shellfish for serving raw. Sushi-grade fish is relatively expensive, usually prefrozen and thawed, and more likely to be free of parasites.

Keep the fish and shellfish ice-cold.

Clean and handle the fish and shellfish carefully to minimize contamination. Clean hands, knives, and cutting boards frequently with hot, soapy water or a diluted solution of vinegar or chlorine bleach.

Serve raw fish and shellfish immediately after preparing them, or chill them quickly in the refrigerator.

THE ESSENTIALS OF COOKING FISH AND SHELLFISH

The key to cooking fish and shellfish well is attentiveness. Thin cuts of fish and small shellfish cook very quickly and can go from raw to dry and fibrous in as little as 3 or 4 minutes. The center of thicker cuts and whole large creatures can go from moist to overdone just as quickly.

Don't rely on recipe cooking times or simple formulas to guarantee a good result. Recipes can't account for significant changes in cooking time caused by small variations in food thickness, temperature, and the temperature of grills and ovens and pans.

Check doneness early and often. If you're using a thermometer, check its accuracy beforehand.

Judge doneness in fish by measuring the temperature with a thermometer, or by prying two layers of flesh apart and looking. Underdone or barely done fish will still be mainly translucent and cohesive. Cooked but moist fish has a small translucent area at the center and more easily breaks apart. Overcooked fish is fully opaque, dry, and fibrous.

To maintain moistness in fish and shellfish, aim to keep the inner temperature between 120 and 135°F / 50 and 57°C, the range in which the flesh turns from translucent to opaque. At higher temperatures the fibers lose their moisture and become progressively drier. Tuna is moister at 110 to 120°F / 43 to 50°C.

If safety is paramount, cook fish to an inner temperature of 160°F/70°C. It will be dry and fibrous.

Adjust cooking heat to the thickness of the fish. Cook thin fillets at high temperatures briefly, for just a minute or two per side. Start thick steaks or whole fish or lobsters at high temperatures to flavor the outside and kill microbes, then moderate the heat to minimize overcooking of the outside while the inside cooks through.

Arrange tapering fillets to even out the heating in a steamer or microwave. Fold over the thin ends or interleave them so they don't overcook while the thick ends heat through.

To keep fish pieces intact, minimize handling during and after cooking. Fish flesh has little connective tissue and becomes fragile as it cooks. Cut neat portions before cooking; support whole pieces on a broad spatula when moving them. Grill fish pieces held snugly in a grilling basket. Broil thin pieces without turning by placing them on a preheated plate.

To produce crisp skin on a piece of fish, scrape and presalt the skin to remove moisture. Fry the piece over moderate to high heat, skin side first to make sure it has enough time to brown and crisp. Serve the fish skin side up to avoid steaming the skin between its hot flesh and the plate.

Crustaceans in the shell are among the few animals foods that are commonly cooked by boiling. Boiling cooks shrimp, crabs, and lobsters very quickly, and prevents their enzymes from turning the flesh mushy, but leaves them somewhat dry and fibrous.

To boil shellfish, keep the water temperature as high as possible throughout cooking. Use a large pot of salted water, get it to a rolling boil, add the crustaceans, and cover the pot until the water resumes boiling.

Check doneness often to minimize overcooking and fibrousness, no matter what cooking method you use.

For more moistly tender crustacean meat, poach it far below the boil.

Molluscs are a varied group of creatures and call for several different cooking methods.

Cook trimmed scallops briefly on high heat until just warmed through or barely opaque at the center. They are pure and tender muscle tissue, at their best when barely cooked.

Cook squid, octopus, abalone, and geoduck clams either very briefly or long and slowly. Their muscles contain abundant connective tissue, which makes them crunchy when barely cooked, moistly soft when long cooked, and tough in between. Tenderize the meats beforehand if desired by gentle pounding to break and separate muscle fibers and connective tissue.

Cook live oysters, clams, and mussels in the shell quickly with high heat, just until the shells open to keep the muscle as tender as possible, or for several minutes afterward to eliminate more microbes from the digestive and reproductive organs. Discard any shells that don't open.

To minimize fishy cooking smells in the kitchen, cook fish and shellfish in a covered pan or in a wrapper, and allow them to cool somewhat before uncovering.

See the pages listed below for cooking methods in which fish and shellfish are treated like other foods:

GRILLING, p. 98

SMOKING, p. 100

FRYING and DEEP-FRYING, pp. 89 and 93

STEAMING, p. 86

MICROWAVING, p. 102

COOKING IN A WRAPPER

Cooking fish in a wrapper with flavorful herbs and vegetables is a neat and versatile cooking method. It can be done on the grill or in a frying pan, an oven, a steamer, or a microwave.

The wrapper may be a sheet of parchment paper, foil, plastic wrap, or pastry, or a large plant leaf, from edible cabbage to aromatic banana. It protects the contents from direct heat, heats them more gently, and traps aromas to be enjoyed when the package is opened.

Wrappers don't trap moisture in fish or prevent overcooking. Once the sheath puffs up or emits vapor, the fish is essentially steaming.

Use thin pieces of fish that cook through quickly, and cut the other ingredients finely so that they will too. Check the doneness of one packet a minute or two after the wrapper puffs up.

OVEN ROASTING

Oven roasting heats fish relatively slowly, by means of hot air and radiation from the oven surfaces, at temperatures ranging from 200 to 500°F / 93 to 260°C. Moderate and low temperatures are good for cooking through thick pieces of fish that have been quickly browned on the stove top or broiler.

Choose oven temperatures according to the fish and your cooking and eating preferences. In general, the thicker the piece, the lower you should set the oven temperature, so that the outside doesn't overcook while the inside cooks through. High heat requires close monitoring, but produces browned, flavorful surfaces.

Low oven temperatures, 200 to 250°F / 93 to 120°C, cook fish through slowly and evenly and can produce a wonderful soft, custardlike texture, notably in salmon. But they're too low to brown the surface or crisp skin.

To avoid white globs of coagulated fluid on the surface during low-temperature roasting, presalt or brine the fish for 5 to 10 minutes, then wipe away the salt and dry thoroughly before cooking.

High oven temperatures, above 400°F/200°C, can overcook the outer portions while the center gets to the proper temperature, and can quickly overcook the center. They require close monitoring.

Convection fans speed browning and cooking through by blowing the hot oven air onto the fish surface, and can cause scorching at ordinary oven temperatures. To avoid scorching, reduce nonconvection roasting temperatures by 25 to 50°F/15 to 30°C, and check browning often.

Check doneness early and often, especially if you're using a hot oven.

POACHING, STEWING, AND LOW-TEMPERATURE COOKING

Poaching and stewing are methods that heat fish in flavored liquids, usually water-based broth or stock but sometimes oil or melted butter. The liquid can become a sauce or soup.

The keys to good poached or stewed fish are to start with a flavorful cooking liquid and control its temperature to avoid overcooking the fish.

Prepare flavorful broths or stocks in advance, by making a fish stock or a court bouillon. The short cooking times and low temperatures that fish need don't extract flavor well from vegetables and herbs.

To make a court bouillon, add the acidic wine or vinegar only after the vegetables have softened, and the pepper in the last few minutes to avoid bitterness.

Cook fish and shellfish stocks (fumets) for less than an hour to avoid extracting cloudy calcium from bones or shells. Don't include gills, which often carry or cause off flavors.

To keep fish pieces intact when cooked, cut neat portions before cooking, cook just until done, and support them when serving on a large spoon or spatula. Don't leave fragile fillets to cool in the cooking liquid; they'll fall apart with the continued heat.

To produce the moistest fish and most tender shellfish, add them to the stock or bouillon at 180°F/80°C, to kill surface microbes. Then remove from the heat to let them cook through as the temperature falls to 120 to 140°F/50 to 60°C. Check doneness frequently. Thin fillets may take less than a minute to cook through. Poach shrimp as is, crab and lobster meat after a brief initial boil to remove it from its thick shell.

If the liquid needs to be cooked down or thickened, remove the fish and shellfish first.

To tenderize tough squid, octopus, or abalone, simmer in liquid at 180°F/80°C until tender. Don't bother including wine corks, which have no effect.

Bouillabaisse is a southern French seafood stew in which a mixture of fish parts, some bony and gelatinous to provide body, is boiled in an aromatic broth with olive oil to disperse the oil in tiny droplets.

To make bouillabaisse so that the fish pieces are moist rather than dry, reserve the fleshy fish parts to cook through off the heat after the liquid has boiled.

Low-temperature cooking heats fish and shellfish at the temperature that corresponds to the particular doneness you want in the flesh. It's carried out in a water oven or a pot of water whose temperature is maintained either manually by the cook or automatically by an immersion circulator. It produces fish and shellfish that are evenly and perfectly cooked throughout.

Fish and shellfish are typically cooked at 120 to 140°F/50 to 60°C just until done. Unlike meats, seafood flesh tends to deteriorate in quality if held at low temperatures.

Some fish should not be cooked at low temperatures because their muscle enzymes turn them mushy when heated slowly. These include flatfish, tuna, mackerel, sardines, and tilapia.

Understand and avoid the potential hazards of low-temperature cooking. Low cooking temperatures are slow to kill the bacteria that cause foodborne illness, and temperatures below 130°F/55°C don't kill them at all. Tight wrapping makes it possible for botulism bacteria to grow. Use recipes that explain the hazards, and follow their instructions exactly. In general, it's simplest and safest to serve fish and shellfish cooked at low temperatures immediately.

To cook fish or shellfish at low temperatures:

- *Heat the water oven or a large pot of water* up to the temperature that corresponds to the desired doneness.
- *Seal the fish in a plastic ziplock storage bag,* pressing out as much air as possible by immersing it in the water just up to the zipper and then sealing it; or vacuum-pack using a home vacuum-packing machine.
- *Immerse the bag in the water* and heat until the food is cooked through to the desired texture, typically 20 to 30 minutes for single-serving portions.
- *Make sure that the bag remains fully immersed in the cooking water and surrounded by it.* Air and vapor pockets in a bag can cause

it to float, and water flow or crowding can push bags against each other or the pot sides.

- *If you're not using a water oven or circulator,* stir the water regularly, monitor the temperature frequently with an accurate digital thermometer, and heat or add hot water as necessary to maintain it.

Sous-vide cooking is a restaurant version of low-temperature cooking in which the fish are vacuum-packed in plastic bags. Vacuum packing in a professional chamber machine can speed the infusion of marinades and other flavors into fish, and removes all air from the package, so that the meat heats more evenly and can be kept longer after cooking. Household vacuum-packaging machines don't create a strong enough vacuum to infuse foods, can't be used with liquid ingredients, and leave some air in the package.

SERVING FISH

It's worth taking some trouble to serve fish and shellfish at their best.

Prechill plates to serve raw fish and shellfish.

Preheat plates to serve hot fish dishes.

- *Keep any reserves of raw fish or shellfish well chilled* during a meal.
- *Keep any reserves of cooked fish or shellfish at 130°F/55°C or hotter,* immersed in liquid or covered to prevent drying. This is especially important if the meal will last for more than an hour or two; it prevents the growth of bacteria.
- *To balance and tone down strong-flavored seafood,* provide acidic lemon wedges, a tart mayonnaise-based sauce, or a tart white wine.

LEFTOVERS

Seafood leftovers are more fragile than most because fish and shellfish flavors quickly deteriorate and become more strongly fishy.

Minimize the exposure of cooked fish or shellfish to air. Wrap separate pieces tightly in plastic wrap, and cover braised and stewed fish with their cooking liquid.

Refrigerate or freeze leftovers as soon as possible after the fish is removed from the heat. Divide large quantities into smaller portions that will chill faster.

Freeze leftovers to keep them in better condition for more than a few days.

Reheating fish and shellfish accentuates their fishiness.

Consider serving quickly refrigerated leftover fish and shellfish cold, right from the refrigerator.

Reheat leftover fish as little as possible consistent with safety. Turn it briefly in a pan of boiling liquid—the liquid portion of a stew, for example, or some fish stock or salted water—to kill any surface bacteria. Then turn the heat down, cool the liquid to 140°F/60°C, cover, and heat the fish through gently.

13

SAUCES, STOCKS, AND SOUPS

S auces are pourable pleasure. Sauces and dressings and dips bring heightened flavor and lingering moistness to our basic and often mild foods, to meats and fish and grains, and make them more delicious. Soups are flavorful liquids served as foods themselves, often thinner and less intense versions of sauces. And stocks are handy water extracts of meats, fish, and vegetables that can provide the base liquid for sauces or soups.

These days you can buy almost any sauce premade, and give a dish an instant accent in whatever dialect of deliciousness you want, Italian or Chinese or Mexican or Indian. But many sauces take only minutes to make, and others are usually less challenging or time-consuming to prepare than their reputations suggest. Homemade sauces can be more flavorful than store-bought because they're fresher, and you can use them to discover and satisfy your own tastes. My daughter took over our mayonnaise making when she was about twelve years old so that she could get as garlicky an aioli as she wanted—and because she had fun making it and serving it.

Sauces that do take time and trouble offer their own satisfactions. I don't make a big batch of veal or beef stock very often, but when I do I still marvel at how I can slowly coax a pot of meat scraps and bones and water into a golden, clear, intense, refined essence of meatiness. And maybe because a fraction of me comes from India, I really love the opposite, all-in approach to sauce making, the gathering of a dozen or more vegetables and spices and herbs and nuts, and crushing and toasting and simmering and melding them into an Asian curry or Mexican mole.

Cookbooks are awash with countless recipes for sauces and their relatives. This chapter covers the more common kinds, beginning with simple oils and dips and working up to the meat stocks and sauces that are the foundation of classic French cooking. For chocolate and caramel sauces, see pages 491 and 504.

SAUCE AND SOUP SAFETY

Many sauces and soups offer ideal conditions for the growth of bacteria and molds. Meat and fish stocks are very similar to the jellies used for growing microbes in laboratory petri dishes! They're highly perishable, and can cause foodborne illness if they're mishandled.

Minimize the opportunities for bacteria to grow when making and serving sauces and soups.

Wash hands, utensils, and ingredients thoroughly, especially when preparing raw dips and salsas.

To avoid the very slight risk of salmonella when making mayonnaise, use pasteurized eggs instead of the usual raw eggs.

Don't let sauces, dips, or soups sit out at room temperature for more than 4 hours. For more extended serving, hold hot sauces and soups at 130°F/55°C or above. Keep dips on ice, or reserve a portion in the refrigerator to set out later. Thanks to their antimicrobial vinegar, vinaigrettes can be held safely at room temperature.

Reheat leftover cooked sauces and soups to 165°F/73°C. If this causes the sauce to break, or separate, then use the broken sauce to make a new one, or discard it. Egg and butter sauces don't reheat well.

Reboil refrigerated meat or fish stocks every few days. They're so perishable that they can spoil even in the refrigerator. For extended keeping, freeze them.

SHOPPING FOR PREPARED SAUCES AND SOUPS

Prepared sauces, dips, broths, and soups are sold in countless varieties and forms, both fresh and sterilized to keep indefinitely.

Manufactured meat stocks, usually called broths or bouillons, are especially convenient because they take many hours to prepare. They're available canned, concentrated into a hard jelly (meat glacé or demiglace) or viscous dark syrup (meat extract), and dehydrated to a solid powder (bouillon grains and cubes). Their quality varies widely.

Check labels and choose products with few ingredients that aren't recognizable foods. Many manufacturers substitute special industrial ingredients for more complex and expensive meats, vegetables, and herbs. They produce approximations of the original product that are generally not as good.

Improve prepared products by supplementing them with fresh ingredients, including herbs, good olive oil, or vinegar.

STORING SAUCES AND SOUPS

Most sauces, dips, and soups are highly perishable. The major exception is vinaigrette, but its flavor also deteriorates with time.

Refrigerate or freeze all sauces, dips, and soups made with any kind of stock or puree, dairy products, or eggs.

When refrigerating a large batch of stock or soup, chill the pot quickly in ice, or divide the contents into smaller batches that will cool quickly.

To keep sauces, dips, and soups for more than a few days, freeze them, with a layer of plastic wrap pressed into the surface to minimize off flavors from freezer burn.

Sauces thickened with butter or egg often break after chilling or freezing. Try to reconstitute them by separating the water and fat portions and remaking them with the help of a fresh egg yolk or initial portion of water.

THE ESSENTIALS OF COOKING SAUCES: FLAVOR

Sauces provide flavor, the sensations of taste on the tongue and aroma in the nose. There are thousands of different aromas, but only a handful of tastes: saltiness, sourness, sweetness, bitterness, and savoriness. Taste serves as the foundation of flavor, aroma its superstructure.

Be sure that a sauce's taste base is solid and balanced, especially in salt and acid. Many cooks neglect acidity. To boost it quickly, keep a shaker of sour salt, or citric acid.

Salt doesn't just provide saltiness. It helps amplify aromas, even in sweet sauces, and masks bitterness. Use fine-grained salts in uncooked sauce making so that they dissolve quickly, especially in mayonnaise and other emulsified sauces.

Flavor sauces intensely. Sauces are always eaten with something less flavorful, so they need to be highly flavored for the combination to work.

Taste sauces critically as you make them, and adjust the flavor to make them both balanced and intense. Take enough to spread the sauce all around your mouth, not just in the front; it should taste full and make your mouth water.

Have someone else double-check the seasoning. People have different sets of taste and smell receptors and experience foods differently. Find out whether you are especially sensitive or insensitive to the basic tastes, and adjust your seasoning accordingly when you're cooking for other people.

Don't overthicken sauces. Starch, proteins, fat, and other thickening ingredients tend to mute flavor. Remember that sauces will get thicker when they're served and begin to cool.

THE ESSENTIALS OF COOKING SAUCES: CONSISTENCY

The appealing consistency of sauces comes from the way they move on the food and feel in the mouth. Most sauces are thicker than water, so they cling to the foods they dress and provide lingering pleasure in the mouth.

Some foods are natural sauces because they're already thick liquids. They include purees, oils, egg yolks, cream, sour cream and crème fraîche, strained yogurt, and butter.

We can thicken thin but flavorful liquids by adding ingredients that obstruct the liquid from moving easily.

The main sauce thickeners are flour and various starches; proteins in eggs, meats, fish, and shellfish, and dairy products; and fats and oils, which we can *emulsify,* or beat into microscopic droplets that obstruct the flow of the sauce's water.

When adjusting the consistency of hot sauces, keep them thinner than you want them to be when served. Sauces get thicker as they cool, and if overthickened will congeal on the plate.

Sauces usually fail by separating, or not thickening in the first place, so that they become an uneven mixture of watery, oily, and/or lumpy parts.

To avoid starch lumps, never mix dry flour or starch with a hot sauce. Premix the powdery ingredient with cold water or with fat or oil, then add this slurry to the hot sauce.

To avoid protein lumps, heat the sensitive protein thickeners just enough to develop the thickness, but not enough to coagulate them. "Temper" the egg yolk or other ingredient by adding a small amount of moderately hot sauce to it to disperse and begin to heat it, then combine sauce and thickener and heat gently just until thickened.

To avoid separation of oils or fats from water, whisk them into sauces gradually. Add enough water to provide room for the droplets as they form. Keep the sauce warm enough for fats to remain liquid.

To smooth out separated sauces, pass lumpy ones through a fine-mesh sieve or pulse briefly in a blender. Strain emulsified sauces, skim off the separated oil or fat, and reemulsify it.

FLAVORED OILS

Flavored oils are versatile ingredients for instantly adding aromas and richness to a dish, often as a finishing touch. They're made simply by steeping various herbs, spices, citrus peels, or other aromatics in the oil and then straining the oil off.

Covering raw foods with oil can allow the growth of botulism bacteria. Botulism bacteria are common in soils, can be present on produce surfaces, and thrive when protected from the air. They cause serious and sometimes fatal illness.

Add salt and/or sour salt (citric acid) to moist flavoring ingredients for steeping, to limit bacterial growth. Dry spices and dried citrus peels don't have enough water for microbes to grow.

Steep and store flavored oils in the refrigerator, not at room temperature. Cold limits bacterial growth, and slows the staling of the oils themselves.

Use flavored oils within a week or two.

DIPS

Dips are simple sauces that cling to pieces of food touched to them just before eating. They include mayonnaise and sour-cream sauces, guacamole and salsas, pureed beans and nuts, and quickly made Asian dipping sauces based on soy or fish sauce.

Serve dips in ways that minimize the growth of bacteria in them and the possibility of causing illness.

Don't leave dips out at room temperature for more than 4 hours. If the party or meal will last longer than that, divide the dip into two or more refrigerated containers and set out one at a time, replacing as needed.

Discourage double-dipping, the redipping of a piece of food that has been partly eaten, which passes mouth microbes from one person to everyone else. Serve dips with small one-bite chips and vegetable pieces.

SALAD DRESSINGS AND VINAIGRETTES

Most salad dressings combine the richness of oil with the tartness of vinegar or citrus juices, buttermilk or sour cream. The simplest, a mixture of oil, vinegar, salt, and herbs, suspends vinegar droplets in oil. Dressings based on mayonnaise or cream suspend oil droplets in a water base.

Manufactured dressings are often thickened with xanthan gum and contain less oil than freshly made dressings.

Dress raw salads just before serving. Dressings wilt salad greens.

To keep a green salad fresh-looking longer, choose a water-based cream or mayonnaise dressing, which darkens leaves more slowly than a vinaigrette.

"Boiled dressing" is an oil-free dressing for coleslaw and other raw-vegetable salads. It's made with seasoned and diluted vinegar thickened with flour and eggs.

To make boiled dressing, cook the ingredients gently and stop heating as soon as it thickens to avoid curdling.

Vinaigrettes are versatile oil-and-vinegar sauces, usually flavored with herbs. They're the simplest dressing for salads. Italian salsa verde, Caribbean mojos, and Argentine chimichurri are vinaigrettes served with meats.

Adjust vinaigrette proportions and ingredients to your own taste. The traditional proportions are 1 volume of vinegar to 3 volumes of oil, but many modern recipes are closer to a ratio of 1 to 2. The balance depends in part on vinegar strength, which can run from 4 to 8 percent acetic acid. Try different ingredients: nut oils and animals fats, unusual vinegars or tart fruit juices.

Vinaigrettes can be made by different methods. All of them break up the vinegar into tiny droplets and disperse them in the oil. You can slowly whisk the vinegar into the oil, or do the reverse, or shake the two liquids in a closed container, or blend them in a blender.

Make simple vinaigrettes just before dressing the food with them. Whisked and shaken vinaigrettes begin separating into oily and vinegary patches within a few minutes. Or sprinkle oil and vinegar directly onto the food and combine them casually by tossing the pieces.

To make more stable vinaigrettes, include crushed herbs or mustard (powdered or prepared), which coat the vinegar droplets and slow their coalescence, or emulsify them with a blender, which breaks up the vinegar into very small droplets that coalesce slowly.

MAYONNAISE

Mayonnaise is an oil-and-acid sauce that can be made thick enough to spread on a sandwich. It's essentially a small amount of water, usually diluted lemon juice, crowded until stiff with many millions of oil droplets. The key ingredient is egg yolk, whose proteins and emulsifiers coat the oil droplets as we form and crowd them, and prevent them from merging and puddling together.

Like vinaigrettes, mayonnaise can be made with many different oils and fats, tart liquids, and flavorings. Aioli is a popular mayonnaise flavored with garlic. Mayonnaise can be made by hand with a whisk, with a stick blender, or in a blender or food processor.

To eliminate the very slight risk of salmonella contamination from raw egg yolk, use pasteurized eggs, or pasteurize the yolk yourself. Combine 1 yolk in a small bowl with 1 tablespoon/15 milliliters each of lemon juice and water, and microwave the mix on high power until it heaves close to the boil. Remove the bowl, stir briskly with a clean fork, and repeat the heating. Remove and stir again with a clean fork until lukewarm. Then start whisking in oil to make the sauce.

Don't worry about the proportions of egg yolk and oil. One yolk can coat the droplets from many cups of oil.

Do be careful about the proportions of liquid and oil. As you incorporate oil into the egg base, be sure to add 1 teaspoon/5 milliliters of lemon juice or water whenever the sauce gets stiff, a sign that the oil droplets are very crowded and need more room.

Do be careful when you make a mayonnaise with olive oil. Olive-oil mayonnaise often separates after a few hours, because this unrefined oil contains substances that slowly push the stabilizing coats off the oil droplets. For a more stable sauce, make it mostly with a refined vegetable oil, and finish with olive oil to taste.

Start the sauce making slowly to be sure that the oil gets broken up into the yolk base, and not the other way around. Mix the yolk in a bowl with salt and 1 to 2 teaspoons/5 to 10 milliliters water, then add the oil just a few drops at a time, whisking until the drops disappear, until the mix stiffens. Thin it with a few drops of lemon juice or water, and continue, adding the oil in larger doses as the volume of sauce increases.

If the sauce thins while you're adding oil, it has probably separated. Stop and let drops of water and oil fall onto the surface. If the oil drops quickly, disappears, and the water doesn't, the sauce has separated. Start again with a fresh yolk, and slowly whisk the separated sauce into it.

If you use a blender or food processor, be careful not to overwork the sauce, which will break it. Stop the motor as soon as the last oil has been added. Recipes for machine mayonnaise usually include the egg white and mustard to provide more droplet-coating material.

To rescue a broken mayonnaise, start with a fresh egg yolk and carefully work the broken sauce into it.

FRESH SALSAS, PESTOS, AND PUREES

Many popular sauces are made simply by breaking up solid vegetable and fruit tissues and mixing the broken-up solids and juices together. When the solids are coarsely chopped, we often call the sauce a salsa. Coarsely crushed herbs make a pesto. Smoothly integrated mixes are called purees.

Different tools for breaking up foods produce different textures and

flavors. The more thoroughly they pulverize, the finer the sauce texture, and the more its flavor is affected by the food's active enzymes and exposure to the air.

To retain more fresh flavor of the ingredients in pestos and other fresh herb sauces, chop coarsely or grind the ingredients coarsely in a mortar rather than a blender, so that some of the tissue remains intact.

For tomato salsas and sauces, be sure to include the seeds, or strain out the seeds while pressing the thick jelly that surrounds them into the sauce. The jelly is the most flavorful part of the tomato.

Rinse chopped onions or garlic in copious water to remove harsh flavors from the cut surfaces.

Uncooked salsas, pestos, and purees are more fragile in flavor and consistency than cooked sauces.

Make fresh sauces just before serving. Oxygen and uncontrolled enzymes begin to change flavor and cause brown discoloration as soon as the plant tissues are damaged.

If you make fresh sauces ahead, store them in the refrigerator with waxed paper pressed onto the surface. Most plastic wraps allow some air to pass through; they're less effective air barriers. If the sauce discolors, scrape the surface layer off before serving.

To prevent the weeping of watery fluid from a fresh puree or juice, supplement with a small quantity of xanthan gum, an ingredient used in gluten-free baking. Lightly dust the puree surface with xanthan gum powder, allow to absorb moisture until surface looks like a jelly, then whisk or blend vigorously and allow to stand.

COOKED PUREES, APPLESAUCE AND TOMATO SAUCE, AND CURRIES AND MOLES

Cooked purees are made by heating the ingredients before they're pureed, or as part of the pureeing process. Heat softens firm fruits and vegetables, releases their juices, develops flavor, and thickens the puree consistency by cooking off excess moisture.

To make carrot, cauliflower, sweet pepper, and other solid vegetable purees:

- *Precook the cleaned vegetable until soft.* Boiling, steaming, and microwaving are fast and change the flavor least; sweating in butter or oil adds flavor and richness; oven roasting adds browned flavors.
- *Puree the vegetable, and strain if necessary.* Stand blenders produce silkier purees than the food processor or food mill.
- *Blend hot liquids with care to avoid eruptions* of scalding-hot liquid. Blend in small batches, filling the blender jar no more than halfway, leaving the lid slightly ajar to allow steam to escape at the beginning, and pulsing briefly to start.
- *To thicken the consistency further,* heat gently, in a broad pan to evaporate from a large surface area, with frequent stirring and scraping to avoid scorching on the pan bottom.

Apples and tomatoes are soft enough to break down into a puree as they cook.

To make purees from soft-textured apples or tomatoes:

- *Cook both with their skin and seeds,* which contribute significantly to the flavor.

- *Cut them up* to speed the softening and ease stirring.
- *Put tomatoes in a wide skillet or pot* with a large area for evaporation.
- *Add a thin layer of water to the pot and heat carefully* to avoid scorching on the pan bottom.
- *When the water reaches the boil, cover the pot and cook on gentle heat* until the food has softened enough to crush. Mash apple pieces into a coarse mass, and continue to cook gently until it's uniformly soft.
- *Pass the puree through a food mill* to strain out the skins and seeds.
- *Continue cooking tomatoes* to remove excess moisture.
- *Stir often to prevent settling and scorching* on the bottom and to cook the entire mass evenly, or place the pot in a moderate oven and stir occasionally.
- *To shorten or eliminate the cooking-down,* predry the cut tomatoes in a moderate oven.

Indian and Thai curries and Mexican moles owe their complex flavors to wet purees that are cooked down enough to fry in their own oil. Common curry ingredients are onions, fresh herbs and spices, and fresh coconut. Many moles include rehydrated dried chillis.

To develop the full flavor of curries and moles, carefully reduce the purees until you see oil separating and rising to the top. Continue on moderate heat with constant stirring and scraping until the color darkens and the taste is rich and full.

Do the cooking-down and frying on an outdoor grill or burner if possible, so that pungent vapors and spatter won't be a deterrent to thorough flavor development.

CREAM AND MILK SAUCES

Cream is a sauce in its own right thanks to the rich flavor and full body provided by its tiny butterfat droplets. When added in significant amounts to purees or starch thickened liquids, it makes a cream sauce. It can also be a last-minute, minor but valuable enrichment to many other sauces. Fresh cream and its acid-thickened products, sour cream and crème fraîche, go well with many seasonings and foods, both savory and sweet.

When cooked in sauces, cream can form curdled particles or leak butterfat.

To avoid curdling, either use high-fat creams, 38 to 40 percent butterfat, or avoid exposing the cream to high heat. Add sour cream and other lower-fat types at the last minute, after the rest of the sauce has been cooked.

To avoid fat separation and greasiness, use very fresh cream, or homogenized cream or crème fraîche. If a plug of butterfat has risen to the top of the carton, use only the remaining liquid; the plug will behave more like butter.

Milk is too thin to be a sauce, so it's thickened with starch to make béchamel sauce (Italian balsamella), used mainly to provide moistness and a readily browned surface in casserolelike mixtures. It's also a binding for soufflés and croquettes, and a leaner thickening alternative to cream, velvety rather than creamy.

To make béchamel sauce, cook flour in butter very gently until bubbling stops and mixture gives a pleasant aroma. Slowly add milk to the pan and simmer for 15 minutes, longer for a thinner, finer consistency.

CHEESE SAUCES AND FONDUE

Cheese sauces are made by melting and dispersing solid cheese into hot liquid. The cheese adds both flavor and body thanks to its concentrated proteins and fats, but these can also cause stringiness, lumping, and greasiness.

To make cheese sauces and soups, use either dry grating cheeses or moist cheeses, which disperse more easily in water than cheddar or Swiss cheeses.

To prevent cheese in sauces and soups from turning lumpy and greasy, grate the cheese finely. Add the cheese to hot but not boiling liquid. Stir as little as possible to avoid forming protein strings. Include some flour or starch to prevent protein clumping and fat puddling.

Cheese fondue is a cheese-based dip kept warm and molten over a low flame, thinned with wine and other liquids. It can become stringy or too thick.

Be sure to include tart white wine and/or lemon juice. Acidity prevents stringiness, as does the inclusion of some flour or starch.

To remedy thickening as the fondue loses moisture, stir in splashes of white wine.

BUTTER SAUCES

Butter makes a rich, flavorful spread or sauce on its own, or mixed simply with other ingredients into compound and whipped butters, or emulsified with egg yolk.

Butter and butter sauce consistencies are sensitive to temperature.

Butterfat is hard enough at refrigerator temperatures to tear bread and break crackers, but soft and spreadable at room temperature, and liquid at body temperature and above. Liquid butter sauces congeal and break unless they're kept warm.

To keep melted butter sauces from congealing quickly, preheat plates and serve food piping hot.

Beurre blanc is a sauce of butterfat droplets emulsified in a mixture of wine and vinegar or lemon juice, the equivalent of a tart-flavored cream with double the butterfat of heavy cream.

To make beurre blanc, start with a small amount of the liquid ingredients, hold over low heat, and slowly melt chunks of cold butter into it while stirring constantly.

Don't worry about proportions. You can add butter chunks indefinitely because they release enough moisture to keep the butterfat droplets separated.

Keep finished beurre blanc stable by holding it at 110 to 120°F / 45 to 50°C, either covered or with occasional spoonfuls of added cream or water to compensate for evaporation.

Beurre monté, or emulsified butter, is beurre blanc without the acidity, a prepared cream with double the butterfat of heavy cream, made in the same way as beurre blanc but starting with plain water.

Emulsified butter is a useful alternative form for butter in which to poach delicate foods or toss cooked vegetables. It provides butter's flavor in a creamy consistency instead of an oily one.

Hollandaise, béarnaise, and their variations are also sauces of butterfat droplets emulsified in water, but the water base is thickened with egg-yolk proteins. The tricky thing about these sauces is that they need to be cooked carefully, enough to thicken the proteins but not enough to harden and curdle them.

To make a hollandaise or béarnaise sauce:

- *Heat the egg-yolk base only to the point that it begins to thicken,* around 140 to 150°F / 60 to 65°C depending on the recipe.

- *Be very careful with recipes that heat the yolks* before adding clarified butter. The yolks are easily curdled. Either work over indirect heat, in a pot set over a pan of simmering water, or work on a very low burner, and move the pan on and off the burner to prevent overcooking.

- *For a simpler, nearly foolproof hollandaise or béarnaise,* precook the flavorful liquid portion if necessary, then place it and all other ingredients together in a cold saucepan, the butter cold and cut into small chunks. Set the pan on low heat and start stirring. The mixture will become thin as the butter melts. Keep heating and stirring until the sauce thickens and reaches the desired consistency.

Keep finished egg-butter sauces stable by holding them at 130°F/55°C, either covered or with occasional spoonfuls of cream or water added to compensate for evaporation.

To rescue a curdled egg-butter sauce, strain the solid protein particles from the sauce, then whisk slowly into a fresh egg yolk over low heat. Or place in a prewarmed blender with a small amount of warm water or egg yolk, pulse briefly, then strain back into a warmed bowl.

EGG-YOLK SAUCES:
ZABAGLIONE AND SABAYONS

Egg yolks have a saucelike creamy consistency on their own, and are used alone as a dipping sauce in some Japanese dishes.

Zabaglione and sabayons are foamy but rich sauces. They're made by heating a mixture of egg yolks and a flavorful liquid while whisking air into it. Zabaglione and sweet sabayons include sugar and a sweet wine or fruit juice, savory sabayons meat or fish stocks.

Heat the mix carefully as you whisk. The yolk proteins begin to gel and the mix to thicken and inflate far below the boil, as low as 140°F/60°C depending on the recipe.

To avoid forming curds at the pan bottom, cook the mix in a bowl over a moderately hot water bath, not over boiling water or direct heat.

To make a pourable sauce, heat and whisk just until the mix thickens to the consistency of heavy cream. Pourable sabayons steadily lose their bubbles and are best served immediately.

To make the most stable yolk foam, whisk and heat until the mix thickens enough to form streaks on the pan bottom.

Egg-yolk foams leak liquid if they stand for some time. Reincorporate the liquid with gentle stirring to avoid deflating the foam, or simply scoop the foam off the liquid.

PAN SAUCES

Pan sauces are made in the frying or roasting pan immediately after meats and fish have been cooked, using the juices that they've released and that have been dried and browned by the pan heat. Added liquid dissolves, or deglazes, the browned juices and contributes flavor. Pan sauces can be served as thin as the original juices, or thickened with added fat, or with gelatin from added stock.

To make a pan sauce:

- *Pour off juices and fat* from the pan. Remove the fat from the juices by letting fat rise to the top of the container, then scooping it off.
- *If thickening with flour or other starch,* add the thickener to the pan and cook gently in residual fat until it smells toasty. For deeper color and flavor, cook until the thickener browns.
- *Deglaze with such liquids as wine or beer, stock, water,* and the defatted cooking juices to dissolve flavorful browned solids from the pan bottom. Wine brings tartness and savoriness, stocks savoriness and the body created by gelatin. Intensify these qualities by repeatedly adding liquid and boiling it down.
- *Adjust the amount and consistency of the sauce* by boiling it down, or by adding other ingredients to make a larger quantity of thickened, enriched sauce.
- *Use butter or creams to augment, enrich, and thicken pan sauces.* Take the pan off the heat to cool somewhat, then swirl and melt in chunks of butter to make a pan version of beurre blanc, or stir in sour cream. High-fat heavy cream and crème fraîche made from it can tolerate boiling heat without separating.
- *Salt pan sauces at the very end,* after all the other ingredients have been incorporated.

Keep butter-thickened sauces warm to prevent them from congealing and separating.

GRAVIES AND STARCH-THICKENED SAUCES

Gravies are pan sauces that are thickened not with butter or cream, but with some kind of starch, either pure or in the form of flour.

Many other sauces, including classic sauces made from meat stocks, are also thickened with starch.

When heated in a liquid, starch granules soak up water, swell, and release long, tangly starch molecules, all factors that cause the liquid to thicken.

Different starches give the finished sauce different qualities. Flours make a sauce opaque, purified cornstarch somewhat milky, arrowroot and other root starches more translucent. Potato and tapioca flours and starches produce a slightly stringy consistency.

Different starches have different thickening powers. Root starches and flours (potato, arrowroot, tapioca) thicken at lower temperatures than wheat flour and cornstarch and have a milder flavor, and are especially good for last-minute thickening. But sauces made with them thin out more when reheated or frozen.

To substitute among flours and starches, replace 3 parts of wheat or potato flour with 2 parts of most pure starches, 1½ parts of potato or tapioca starch.

Never add dry flour or starch directly to a hot sauce. The thickener will clump and become almost impossible to disperse evenly. Instead, premix the thickener with a fat or with some lukewarm sauce or water to separate the particles.

To give flour an appealing flavor before adding it to a sauce, preheat it in a moderate oven until it turns a golden color, or cook it in fat or oil to make a roux.

To make a roux, heat flour or starch on the stove top with a similar volume of butter, oil, or fat from the roast until it develops the flavor and color you want, from delicate and pale yellow to strong and dark brown. Dark roux can be bitter, and has about half the thickening power of a light roux.

To thicken a sauce with a roux, stir it directly into the sauce. Prewetting with some of the sauce isn't necessary.

Quick or last-minute adjustments to sauce consistency are made with flour in the form of a butter-flour paste called beurre manié, or starch in the form of a water-starch slurry, or manufactured "instant" flour whose starch is precooked and thickens faster.

For quick thickening with plain flour, rub together flour and butter to make beurre manié, and then melt pieces of this paste directly into the sauce.

For quick thickening with starch or instant flour, mix it with enough lukewarm sauce or water to form a thick liquid suspension, or slurry, then stir the slurry directly into the sauce.

To adjust the consistency of a sauce, bring it to the simmer, add the roux, beurre manié, or slurry, continue to heat until it thickens, and add more thickener if necessary. Prolonged cooking will begin to break down the starch and thin the sauce again.

For the best flavor and serving consistency, add a minimal amount of thickener and keep sauces thin in the saucepan. Thickeners dull flavor. Starch-thickened sauces get thicker as they cool, and if overthickened will congeal on the plate. Test a sauce's serving consistency by spreading a spoonful on a warm plate.

MEAT STOCKS, REDUCTIONS, AND SAUCES

Meat stocks are basic preparations from which meat sauces and soups are made. They are water extracts of the flavorful substances in meat, together with gelatin. Gelatin is a protein thickener that dissolves out of the connective tissue in meat, bone, and skin, and that gives body to sauces and soups.

Meat reductions, including glace and demi-glace, or "glaze" and "half-glaze," are stocks that have been boiled down to concentrate them to sauce consistency and even thicker. They're intensely flavored, contain enough gelatin to solidify into a stiff, glasslike jelly when cooled, and are used as meat essence, to reinforce and finish sauces, soups, and other dishes.

Meat sauces are made from stocks or reductions by combining them with aromatic vegetables and herbs, wine, often additional meats, and often a starch thickener. The possibilities and recipes are endless, from the quick to the long and elaborate.

For a quick meat sauce to go with a roast, fry scraps from the roast together with aromatic vegetables (onions, carrots, celery) until well browned, then add some wine and/or water, herbs and pepper; simmer to dissolve and extract flavors; then remove the solids, boil down the liquid, and thicken it with some butter or a roux.

Flavorful, full-bodied meat stocks are made by cooking a mixture of meat and bones for hours.

Meat contributes flavor but relatively little gelatin. Veal produces a mild, generically meaty flavor; other meats are more distinctive. Mature stewing hens are more flavorful than adolescent fryers.

Bones contribute abundant gelatin, but little flavor. Especially gelatinous are cartilage-rich joints of young animals (veal knuckles and pigs' feet), as well as pig and bird skins.

To prepare ingredients for making stock:

- *Soak bones in cold water* to remove blood.
- *Wash raw meat, bones, and skin* to remove surface off flavors. Cut meat into thin pieces, and crack bones, to increase surface area for water penetration and extraction.
- *For a neutral white stock,* blanch raw meat, bones, and skin to remove off flavors and reduce clouding. Start in a pot of cold water, heat quickly to the boil, then pour off the water and rinse.
- *For a brown stock with roasted flavors and colors,* brown raw meat, bones, skin, and vegetables in a hot oven. Deglaze the roasting pan with water and add the liquid to the stockpot.

To make meat stock:

- *Start the prepared meats and bones in just enough cold water to cover,* usually between 1 and 2 quarts or liters per 2 pounds/ 1 kilogram. Excess water will produce a weak-flavored stock.
- *Heat uncovered to reach and maintain a simmer that never breaks into a boil.* Bubbling clouds the stock with tiny particles of protein and fat; gently moving water allows the particles to cluster and either rise to the surface or fall to the bottom. The open pot cools the stock surface, dries the protein scum, and begins the concentration process.
- *Skim scum and particles from the surface.*
- *Add aromatic vegetables, herbs, and wine* in the last hour of cooking. Carrots and onions contribute sweet sugars as well as aroma.

- *Adjust cooking times to the meat.* Cook poultry stocks for 1 to 4 hours, veal, lamb, and pork for 4 to 8 hours, beef for 6 to 12 hours. Meats and bone from older animals take longer to release their gelatin. If necessary, add water to keep solids barely covered.

- *To make a few quarts of stock in about half the time,* use a pressure cooker. Cool the cooker thoroughly before venting and opening, to avoid boiling and clouding the contents.

- *When the extraction is done, strain the stock* through cheesecloth without pressing on the solids, which would cloud it. Ladling the stock makes it easier to leave most of the solids in the pot.

- *Defat the stock* by chilling it, then scraping congealed fat from the surface. If time is short, let the stock sit for a while, then spoon off liquid fat from the surface, or blot with paper towels.

Reductions are made by simmering stocks for hours until their volumes are reduced by half or more, often with starch thickeners to supplement the gelatin, and other ingredients that contribute flavor and color.

Store stocks and their reductions in the refrigerator or freezer, with plastic wrap pressed into the surface. Stocks are highly perishable. To keep them for a week or more, freeze them, or reboil every few days. When freezing, leave room for the stock to expand by about 10 percent. Freeze in ice cube trays to make convenient portions for deglazing sauté pans.

When thawing frozen stocks and reductions, first rinse the exposed surfaces in cold water to wash away off flavors.

To freshen the flavor of manufactured stocks and reductions, cook them briefly with fresh aromatic vegetables (carrots, onion, celery) and/or herbs.

FISH STOCKS AND SAUCES

Fish stocks are water extracts of the flavorful substances in these creatures together with their gelatin, the protein thickener that dissolves out of the connective tissue in flesh, bones, and skins.

Fish stocks are best when cooked briefly; they're lighter in flavor and consistency than meat stocks.

Fish sauces may be made ahead from stocks, or from the liquid in which fish has just been poached or steamed.

To make fish stock, or fumet:

- *Choose very fresh fish, scraps, and gelatin-rich heads* with a pleasant oceanic smell. Remove the gills and scrape the spine clean of any blood, both of which carry and cause off flavors.
- *Soak and then rinse* coarsely chopped raw flesh, bones, and skin in cold water to remove discoloring blood and surface off flavors.
- *Sauté aromatic vegetables in fat or oil until soft,* so that they can release their flavors during the short simmer. Then add fish parts and cook until opaque.
- *Add just enough cold water and wine to cover.* More liquid will produce a weak-flavored stock.
- *Heat uncovered to reach and maintain a simmer* that never breaks into a boil.
- *Simmer for about 30 minutes.* Longer cooking will produce a cloudy stock with a coarser flavor. Skim scum and particles from the surface.
- *When the extraction is done,* carefully pour off the stock and strain through a fine strainer or cheesecloth.

Store stocks in the refrigerator for a few days, or freeze, with plastic wrap pressed into the surface.

To use frozen stock, rinse exposed surfaces in cold water before thawing, to wash away off flavors.

To make fish sauces, supplement the flavor with fresh herbs, then thicken with a pale roux, cream, or with the proteins in a variety of ingredients, stirred in when the stock is at serving temperature to avoid curdling: egg yolk, or sieved lobster eggs or liver, or crab liver, or sea urchins.

Dashi is a conveniently quick, savory Japanese fish broth made from dried kombu seaweed and fine shavings of katsuobushi, bonito fish that has been dried, smoked, and fermented. Both ingredients are steeped carefully for the best flavor, neither too vegetal nor fishy.

To make dashi, combine kombu and cold water in a saucepan and bring just to a boil. Or for more flavor, presoak the kombu in the water overnight and then bring to a boil, or cook the kombu at 150°F/65°C for an hour. Remove the kombu and add the katsuobushi. Steep the katsuobushi just until the shavings fall to the bottom. Immediately pour the finished broth from the shavings.

VEGETABLE STOCKS AND COURT BOUILLON

Vegetable stocks make a flavorful base liquid for soups and sauces, and for cooking fish, grains, and pastas.

To make vegetable stocks:

- *Include a range of vegetables, herbs, and spices* to provide both aroma and a balanced taste base. Carrots, onions, and leeks contribute sweetness, celery saltiness, mushrooms savoriness; tomatoes are sweet, savory, and tart. Wine and wine vinegar contribute tartness and another layer of aromas.

- *Avoid strong-flavored vegetables,* especially sulfurous cabbage and its relatives (brussels sprouts, cauliflower, kale). Potatoes and other starchy vegetables will cloud and thicken the stock.
- *Cut vegetables into small pieces* or thin peelings, or chop coarsely in the food processor, to speed flavor extraction.
- *For added flavor,* sauté the vegetables briefly in butter or oil before adding water.
- *Add cold water to the pan, and bring to a gentle simmer.*
- *Avoid using too much water,* which would make a watery stock. Aim for between 1 and 3 parts water to 1 part vegetables, measuring by weight. One cup/250 milliliters of water weighs 250 grams, a little more than ½ pound/225 grams.
- *Add any wine or vinegar after 10 to 15 minutes of simmering.* Acids interfere with vegetable softening and flavor extraction.
- *Simmer the stock gently* for another 30 to 40 minutes, or pressure-cook for 10 to 15 minutes, longer if the vegetable pieces are larger, until the flavor is good. Prolonged cooking can develop an unpleasant overcooked-vegetable aroma.
- *Strain the stock without pressing* on vegetable solids, which would cloud the stock.

Court bouillon, or "quick-boiled liquid," is a vegetable stock made freshly and quickly as a poaching liquid for fish and other delicate foods.

To make court bouillon, chop aromatic vegetables, soften if desired in oil or butter on low heat, add cold water and herbs, and bring the water to the simmer. Simmer for about 10 minutes, then add some combination of wine, vinegar, and lemon juice, and return to the simmer for about 20 minutes. Then strain the liquid and use immediately.

Store vegetable stocks in the refrigerator for a few days, or freeze, with plastic wrap pressed into the surface, or in ice cube trays.

To use frozen stocks, rinse exposed surfaces in cold water before thawing, to wash away off flavors.

WINE AND VINEGAR SAUCES

Wine sauces include wine as a dominant ingredient, not a minor contributor to flavor complexity.

Simmer wine or the wine-sauce mixture long enough to evaporate away much of the alcohol. Alcohol has a harsh taste when hot. Gentle simmering preserves more of the wine's flavor than a rolling boil.

Choose red wines with low astringency. Concentration and heat unpleasantly intensify mouth-drying astringency.

To moderate astringency, cook red wines along with some meat or gelatinous stock. Astringent wine tannins bind to the proteins and can no longer affect our mouth proteins. This binding may cause the sauce to pale and cloud with microscopic tannin-protein particles.

Gastrique is a sweet-sour sauce quickly made by heating a mixture of vinegar and either sugar or honey, sometimes with a fruit ingredient. It's usually served with rich meats.

SOUPS

Soups are probably the least definable, widest-open category of foods there is. They can contain pretty much any ingredient there is, be clear or murky, smooth or chunky, thick or thin, hot or cold. As long as it's fluid enough to eat with a spoon, it can be a soup.

That understood, there are a few general principles worth describing.

Flavor balance in soups is important and infinitely adjustable. When seasoning, aim for a strong taste foundation, with a balance among saltiness, tartness, and savoriness. Rich soups can benefit from a counterpoint of acidity. Vegetable purees can benefit from the background savoriness of a little bacon or tomato or Parmesan cheese, or soy sauce or Vietnamese fish sauce or Japanese miso.

Many hot soups are thickened and enriched by sensitive ingredients, as are many sauces, and they need to be made with similar care.

To thicken with egg yolk or other uncooked animal protein (crustacean livers, sea urchin, pureed liver, blood), take care not to overheat and curdle the protein. Start with the soup well below the boiling point. Add small amounts of hot soup gradually to the thickener to dilute and warm it gradually, then mix all together and heat slowly, just to the point that the soup begins to thicken. Reheat leftovers to 160°F/70°C, not to the boil.

To thicken or enrich with cream, use heavy whipping cream or high-fat crème fraîche, which contain too little milk protein to form noticeable curds even at the boil. If you use light cream, sour cream, yogurt, or butter, or a swirl of flavored or olive oil, add at the last minute and keep temperature well below the boil. Reheat leftovers to 160°F/70°C, not to the boil.

To reduce the risk of curdling, choose recipes that include starch or flour, which help protect proteins from coagulating and creams from leaking fat.

To thicken soups with flour or starch, always predisperse the thickener in a roux, beurre manié, or slurry to prevent lumpiness. Add the thickener and then simmer just until the soup develops the right consistency.

Add uncooked ingredients in stages to a simmering soup to avoid over- or undercooking them. First add whole grains, or firm carrots or celery, then more tender onions or cauliflower, pieces of chicken breast, or white rice or pasta; at the last minute, delicate spinach leaves, fish or shellfish. Alternatively, cook each ingredient separately in the soup liquid, and then combine them just before serving.

While serving soup, keep the pot covered and warm, around 140°F/60°C. Refrigerate leftovers within 4 hours of turning off the heat.

To serve leftovers, reheat to at least 160°F/70°C, being especially careful with protein-thickened soups to avoid curdling.

CONSOMMÉS AND ASPICS

Consommé is a crystal-clear soup prepared from meat stock. It's made unusually clear by one of two methods, the traditional one quick but laborious, the modern one longer but simpler.

To clarify consommé in the traditional way, use egg whites to trap impurities, and add lean meat and vegetables to replace the flavors and gelatin lost with impurities.

- *Finely chop meat and vegetables* to maximize extractable surface area.
- *Mix with egg whites,* lightly whisked to break up thick white.

- *Stir the mix into cold stock, heat gently,* and gently simmer without boiling for an hour.
- *Push aside the raft of egg white* that has formed and ladle out the stock.
- *Strain* through a fine strainer or cheesecloth.

To clarify consommé in the modern way, use the stock's own gelatin to trap impurities. The result is a relatively small yield of sparkling-clear and gelatin-free consommé.

- *Freeze stock solid overnight.* Remove the frozen mass from the container.
- *Place it in a colander* suspended over a pot or bowl, and leave in the refrigerator for 24 hours.
- *Collect the stock liquid* that melted and dripped out of the intact gelatin network, leaving fat and protein particles behind.
- *To restore some body,* add a small amount of gelatin or xanthan gum, a starchlike thickener used in gluten-free baking.

Aspics are solid meat or fish consommés, or other flavorful fluids that contain enough gelatin to solidify and hold their shape until eaten, when they literally melt in the mouth.

The key to an ideal aspic is the right concentration of gelatin to produce a serving consistency that's solid but not rubbery.

Stocks contain varying amounts of gelatin, and clarification removes some gelatin. Fish gelatins form weak gels, and often need to be supplemented with prepared gelatin.

To make sure that a consommé for aspic will set, test it: cool a spoonful quickly in the refrigerator.

Supplement the consommé with prepared gelatin if necessary. The gelatin concentration required for a delicate aspic is around 2 tablespoons/20 grams per quart or liter of liquid; if a stock won't set, add 1 teaspoon/

5 grams per liter or quart, retest, and repeat if necessary. The concentration necessary to coat a terrine, pieces of meat, or to bind chopped meat together is 10 to 15 tablespoons/100 to 150 grams per quart or liter of liquid.

Always moisten manufactured gelatins in cold water before mixing with hot liquids. Hot liquid alone will cause clumping and delay the dissolving process.

Avoid boiling or prolonged heating of the consommé, which breaks down gelatin and can prevent the aspic from setting.

Rice, wheat, and corn fueled the birth of civilization

14

DRY GRAINS, PASTAS, NOODLES, AND PUDDINGS

R ice, wheat, and corn fueled the birth of civilization, and they continue to nourish more people in the world than any other foods. These and the other grains are seeds, concentrated packages of nourishment for the embryonic plant they contain, dormant while dry and easily stored for months. Grains are inexpensive and satisfyingly substantial, and their mild flavors make them an ideal partner for more assertive ingredients. We can make them into fine main or side dishes and dessert puddings with little more than heat and some flavorful liquid, often just salted water. And we can prepare them much faster than many recipes say, simply by soaking them first. They can't cook themselves, but they know how to absorb the right amount of water without our supervision.

Pastas and noodles are grains that have been ground up, moistened into a dough, and re-formed into a host of different shapes that cook through quickly in hot water. Manufactured pastas and noodles can be excellent, but it's also enjoyable and not that much trouble to make them by hand.

In my pantry, only the spice shelves are more crowded than my grain gallery. It wasn't so many years ago that farro from Italy and red rice from Bhutan were exotic discoveries, but now you can find them easily, along with spelt and millet and purple barley and black rice and teff and many other grains. Be sure to branch out from pastas and white rice and polenta, wonderful as they are. The world has cast up many other seeds for tasty and nourishing dishes.

GRAIN SAFETY

Most grains and grain products start out dry and are cooked thoroughly in boiling water, so they present little health hazard in themselves.

Discard discolored or musty-smelling batches of grains or grain products. These are signs of mold contamination.

Don't keep cooked grain dishes at room temperature for more than 4 hours. Either hold them at 130°F/55°C or above, or refrigerate or freeze them promptly. Reheat leftovers to 165°F/73°C or above.

If you leave a grain dish out overnight or longer, discard it. Grains commonly carry bacterial spores that can survive cooking, germinate in the warm cooked food, and produce toxins that reheating won't destroy.

To serve cooked rice safely over several hours, keep it hot, at 130°F/55°C or higher; or chill batches and reheat them before serving; or acidify the freshly cooked rice while it's still hot. Sushi rice can be held and served at room temperature because it's sprinkled with rice vinegar, which suppresses bacterial growth.

Celiac disease is a serious illness provoked by particular grain proteins in people who have an extreme sensitivity to them.

Don't serve celiacs wheat, barley, rye, oats, or any ancestors or close relatives of modern wheat, including einkorn, emmer, kamut, or spelt.

SHOPPING FOR GRAINS AND GRAIN PRODUCTS

Supermarkets now sell more different kinds of grains and grain products than ever, from a wide range of producers and from all over the world, often in small packages ideal for trying something new. Many health-food stores and organic groceries sell grain products in bulk, and may take the care to refrigerate them. And there are now farmers and millers who sell heirloom grains online, mill them to order, and ship them frozen for unparalleled freshness.

Most grains are sold and made into grain products in several forms: whole, refined to remove their seed coat and germ (embryo), and as coarse- or fine-milled pieces.

Whole intact grains—wheat berries, brown rice—are more flavorful and nutritious than refined grains, and take longer to cook. The outer bran coat and the germ are rich in vitamins, oil, fiber, and valuable phytochemicals, but the bran coat slows water absorption, and their oil makes them more vulnerable to staling. They cook in 40 to 60 minutes.

Refined or polished grains—pearled barley, white rice—contain fewer nutrients than whole grains, stale more slowly, and cook in 15 to 30 minutes.

Milled grains—flours, rolled oats, flaked barley, cornmeal—may be more or less refined. Stone-ground grains include more of the bran and germ and are more flavorful and nutritious than conventionally milled grains, but stale faster.

"Instant" and "minute" grain products have been precooked and dried or freeze-dried, and reconstitute quickly in hot water. They often have off flavors.

Check sell-by dates, and look for sturdy plastic packages. All grain products develop stale flavors with time, and paper and cardboard packaging offer little protection. But some Asian and Italian rices are intentionally aged to develop distinctive flavors.

Buy whole and less refined products in small quantities, since they quickly go stale in storage.

For the freshest-tasting whole-grain flours, buy whole grains and grind them yourself as needed. Use the grain mill attachment for stand mixers, or an electric or hand-cranked mill.

Breakfast cereals and grain snacks, including whole-grain granolas, are often loaded with sugars and fats. Check labels.

Pastas and noodles are available in broad quality and price ranges. Inexpensive ones are made from lesser flours, and dried eggs rather than fresh. They won't be as flavorful as they could be, and when cooked are more likely to be soft and sticky and break up easily.

When buying non-egg pastas, check the label to make sure they're made from durum wheat, a high-protein type that is standard for good Italian pastas and makes firm noodles.

STORING GRAINS

Grains and their products can be kept in the pantry for years without spoiling, but their flavor can deteriorate in just days if they're not taken good care of.

Store grains and grain products tightly sealed in a dry, cool, dark place. If they're packaged in air-permeable paper or cardboard, overwrap them in heavy plastic or place them in hard containers.

Store grains and flours from bulk market bins in separate sealed containers of glass or plastic. Flimsy storage encourages infestation by the Indian meal moth, whose small larvae eat through paper and thin plastic bags and spoil the contents.

Freeze grains or flours that may have been exposed to infested products, to kill any insect eggs or larvae.

Before using an opened package of grain or flour, examine and smell the contents. Off odors or clumping are signs of staleness and/or infestation.

Store whole grains and their meals and flours in the refrigerator or freezer, tightly wrapped to exclude moisture and other odors. These products, as well as refined but stone-ground products, contain polyunsaturated oils that quickly go rancid and cause stale aromas and bitterness. Warm the closed package to room temperature before opening, to prevent moisture from condensing on the cold grain.

Store cooked grain products in the refrigerator or freezer, tightly wrapped to exclude other odors. They will get less firm in the freezer; refrigerator temperatures speed the hardening of their starch.

THE ESSENTIALS OF COOKING GRAINS

Most grain cooking consists of two different processes: getting moisture into the dry grain for its cells and starch to absorb, and heating the moist grain to soften the starch and cell walls. Cooks can save some time and trouble by handling them separately. They can save the trouble of monitoring the cooking by using electric rice cookers, which do a good job of cooking all grains automatically.

Whole grains are harvested and processed in huge numbers, and require a final sorting and cleaning in the kitchen.

Remove dust, chaff, defective grains, and tooth-breaking pebbles by swirling grains in a pot of water.

To add a toasted flavor to grains before softening them, spread washed grains on a baking sheet and heat in a 350°F/175°C oven until they emit a pleasant aroma. Or toast small amounts in a stove-top skillet.

Grains are hard, dry seeds, and usually need both water and heat to make them soft enough to eat with pleasure. Most grains will become pleasantly soft when they absorb about 1.7 times their weight in water, or about 1.4 times their volume. Many recipes call for more water than this, to allow for water lost to evaporation, or to provide a saucelike liquid for the finished grains. Their weight and volume more than double when cooked.

Whole grains take longer to cook than grains with their seed coat removed, or than flattened or milled grains.

Cut cooking times by half or more by presoaking grains for up to 8 hours. Water penetrates grains much more slowly than heat does, especially whole grains with an intact protective seed coat. Grains also cook much faster in a pressure cooker.

Cook grains in liquid in three stages: high heat to bring the water to the simmer; low heat to maintain the simmer until the grains are almost tender; dying heat to allow the grain moisture to distribute evenly from outside to center.

- *To avoid boilovers and stuck or burned grains* on the pan bottom, include a small amount of foam-killing fat or oil with the grain and cold water, and control the heat carefully.
- *Start the heat on high with the lid off,* and check regularly.
- *Turn down the burner to low* when water is near the boil, leave the lid barely ajar to moderate the heat, and check every few minutes.
- *When the water level has fallen below the grain surface,* cover fully with the lid and turn the heat to the lowest setting.
- *When the grains are almost tender,* turn off the heat and allow to sit for 10 minutes or until fully tender.

Cook grains in flavorful liquids. As the grains absorb water into themselves, the remaining liquid becomes more concentrated with everything else. Milk becomes creamy; a meat or fish stock becomes gelatinous. Don't add tomatoes or other acid liquids until the grains are almost done; acids greatly slow softening.

To produce more intact individual grains and fewer that are broken or crushed, cook them in excess water, drain, and allow to dry by evaporation in a wide pot to avoid excessive weight on the grains at the bottom. Or cook as usual without stirring; when the grains are done, leave the lid ajar and allow them to cool for 15 to 30 minutes before gently lifting and turning them with a spatula. Freshly cooked grains are soft and fragile and easily broken, but firm up as they cool.

Some cooked grains harden unpleasantly in the refrigerator when their starch reorganizes itself. This is especially true of long-grain rice.

To soften hardened grain leftovers, reheat them to starch-disorganizing temperatures. Sprinkle them with water and heat covered on high power in microwave, or rewarm on medium heat with added water, or fry them.

BREAKFAST CEREALS

Dry breakfast cereals commonly prepared at home are made from rolled or flaked grains, which have been flattened and sometimes flash-steamed so they're easy to chew when dry, and quickly absorb moisture from cold milk or yogurt.

To make muesli, combine raw rolled oats with dried fruit and sliced nuts.

To make granola, lightly oil and honey rolled oats and sliced nuts, bake them in a medium oven until lightly browned and crisped, and add dried fruits.

Hot breakfast cereals are grains heated in water or milk until very soft and moist. Whole grains can take an hour to cook. For quicker-cooking cereals, use fragmented steel-cut oats, rolled oats and other grains, or "instant" cereals, some of which are precooked and then dried.

Precooked cereals often have flavors and antioxidant preservatives added. Check labels.

To speed the cooking of whole- or coarse-grain cereals, presoak them in the refrigerator overnight in milk or water.

Cook hot cereals quickly in the microwave oven or pressure cooker. Include a small amount of butter or oil to prevent boilovers.

KINDS OF GRAINS

A dozen or so different grains are readily available for cooking. Here are a few words about the ones less commonly cooked every day, followed by longer descriptions of rice, corn, and pastas and noodles.

Wheat comes in a handful of species and varieties.

Hard wheat is the usual type sold as whole wheat berries. It's a bread wheat, high in elastic protein, develops a springy, chewy texture, and is better for cooking whole than more starchy soft wheat.

Farro, the Italian name for ancient emmer wheat, is added to soups and cooked in excess liquid to make a dish similar to risotto. Its whole berries are often sold slightly abraded to help them absorb liquid and cook faster.

Spelt and **kamut** are two other wheat species, and triticale is a wheat-rye hybrid. Kamut berries are especially large and cream colored.

Cracked wheat has been milled into bran-free pieces that have less flavor than whole berries, but cook much faster. Cook coarse cracked wheat in water to make ricelike dishes or porridges; use fine to add texture to doughs and batters.

Bulgur or burgul is cracked wheat without bran or germ that has been precooked and dried. It keeps indefinitely, recooks quickly, and has a persistent chewiness. Coarse bulgur is most familiar from the Lebanese parsley salad tabbouleh.

Barley has a distinctive flavor and springy texture, and is sold in three different forms: whole (hulled), with seed coat intact, sometimes rolled into flakes; pot or Scotch, retaining a dark line of seed coat and some germ; and pearled, with nothing but the tender inner grain remaining.

Rye has an earthy flavor. Rye grains are softer than wheat and absorb more moisture thanks to a high soluble-fiber content. It's also rolled.

Oats are more fragile seeds than wheat, easily rolled and chewed. They have a distinctive flavor and a moist, slippery consistency that suits them well for hot breakfast cereal. They're especially rich in soluble fiber.

Thin flakes of rolled oats have been presteamed and dried, and can be eaten without further cooking in granola and muesli. Quick-cooking and "instant" oats have simply been rolled extremely thin so that they absorb hot water rapidly. Coarsely chopped steel-cut oats take longer to cook and are chewier.

Buckwheat is a small and distinctively flavorful seed, somewhat astringent, unrelated to true wheat, with no gluten and safe for people with celiac disease. It's sold both whole and as hull-less groats, and sometimes as pretoasted kasha. Groats stale more quickly than intact seeds; refrigerate or freeze them.

Small grains—some of them the size of the period at the end of this sentence—include amaranth, quinoa, millets, sorghum, and teff. They have a high proportion of seed coat to starchy interior, and are especially nutritious. They're unrelated to wheat and safe for people with celiac disease. They can be popped in oil, and cook very quickly in liquid.

RICE

Rice feeds more people directly than any other grain in the world. There are a number of different kinds of rice, each calling for its own treatment to bring out its finest qualities.

White or polished rice has been milled to remove the outer bran and part or all of the germ, and keeps well for months.

Brown rice retains the bran and germ, and is best stored in the refrigerator. It takes two to three times longer to cook than the milled version of the same variety, and has a more chewy texture and distinctive aroma. It leaks less starch during cooking, so the grains get less sticky. Brown rice includes more vitamins, minerals, and healthful phytochemicals than white rice.

Long-grain rice is standard in most Chinese and Indian cooking and has been the standard rice in the United States. It requires more water and time to cook than other types, and ends up firmer and less sticky. It gets firm as it cools, and hard when refrigerated. Reheating restores its softness.

Aromatic rices, often called basmati and jasmine, are mainly long-grain rices that carry a distinctive aroma also found in popcorn. They're originally from India, Pakistan, and Thailand, and the best still come from Asia. Brands grown in North America often have little or none of the special aroma. Indian and Pakistani basmatis are often aged for months to develop flavor and a firm cooked texture.

Medium-grain rices are standard in Italian and Spanish cooking. They require less cooking water than long-grain rice, and become more tender and clingy. They don't harden as much when refrigerated, and can often be eaten without thorough reheating.

Short-grain rice is standard in Japanese cooking, including sushi. It remains both clingy and tender at cool room temperature. The Japanese prize freshly harvested "new crop" rice.

Sticky rice is standard in northern Thai and Laotian cooking, and in certain Japanese dishes. It's also known as waxy, glutinous, or sweet rice. It requires the least cooking water, and is so tender that it's soaked and steamed, not boiled.

Red rice and black rice are varieties with pigmented outer bran coats, which slow their cooking. The bran coats on some brands are slightly abraded to speed cooking.

Converted rice has been partly precooked and dried. It takes longer to cook than raw rice, has a distinctive aroma, a very firm, sometimes coarse texture, and little stickiness. Its great advantage, and disadvantage, is that its grains remain firm and slippery no matter how long they're cooked or held. It's a traditional form of rice in south India, and today is often used in food service and catering.

Quick-cooking rice has been thoroughly precooked and dried, and also fractured to speed water penetration during the final cooking. Its grains easily break into pieces, and often carry off flavors.

Wild rice is a distant North American relative of true Asian rice, with unusually long, thin grains, a dark seed coat, and distinctive earthy or tealike flavor from brief fermentation and then heat-drying just after harvest. It has an especially water-resistant seed coat, so it can take a long time to cook. Some producers abrade the seed coat to shorten cooking.

To be sure to get a taste of the wild, read labels carefully. Most wild rice is now cultivated in California rather than gathered in the upper Great Lakes and Canada. Unevenly colored grains are more likely to have been gathered than uniformly black ones.

Cooking Rice

There are two basic ways to cook rice, and countless refinements on them.

Boiling in excess water produces intact separate grains but leaches out nutrients. It works well for most long- and medium-grain rices.

Boiling in measured water retains nutrients but produces a stickier mass and can result in a browned or scorched bottom.

Salt in the water is optional.

To prepare rice for cooking, rinse it thoroughly to remove surface residues. This washes away added vitamins on U.S. rices; to retain these, don't rinse the rice. To speed and even the cooking, soak rice in water, or allow to rest rinsed and wet. This is traditional for basmati and Japanese rices. Soak basmati rices for 30 minutes and brown rices for an hour or two. Rest rinsed Japanese rices for 30 to 60 minutes.

To cook rice in excess water:

- *Add rice to rapidly boiling water.*
- *Cook at the boil* for 10 minutes or until the grains are not quite tender.
- *Drain off all the water.*
- *Cover the pot over very low heat* for a few minutes until the grains are properly done, shaking every minute or two to prevent sticking.

To cook rice in measured water:

- *Use a broad, heavy-bottom pot* so that the rice forms a layer 1 to 2 inches/2.5 to 5 centimeters thick, for evenest heating.
- *Measure water* according to the recipe or machine instructions, or allow twice the volume of rice for long-grain American and Indian rices, 1.25 times the volume of rice for medium-grain Italian and Spanish rices, and the same volume for wetted Japanese sushi rice. Double these quantities for brown rices unless they've been presoaked.
- *Bring water and rice to a boil* over high heat, with the lid off to permit observation and prevent boiling over.

- *Lower the heat,* cover, and simmer gently for 10 minutes for white rices, 30 minutes or until tender for brown rices.
- *Turn the heat off* and allow the rice to steam until done.

As alternatives to stove-top cooking, use an electric rice cooker or microwave oven.

Allow plain rice cooked in any manner to rest with the lid slightly ajar for 15 to 30 minutes after it has finished steaming. The grains will firm as they cool and stay more intact when served.

If the rice at the pan bottom browns, serve it separately as the special treat that it is in many cultures.

Risotto is a popular Italian rice dish in which starch released from the rice thickens its cooking liquid into a sauce. The traditional preparation demands frequent attention.

To make risotto:

- *Use Italian medium-grain rices.* The arborio variety tends to have a chalky texture, vialone nano and carnaroli a finer-grained chewiness.
- *Sauté the dry rice* briefly in oil or butter to prevent the grains from sticking, to firm them, and to contribute a toasty flavor.
- *Add wine* before other liquids to provide tart and savory elements to the taste base while boiling off most of the alcohol.
- *Add small amounts at a time of simmering cooking liquid,* usually a broth, stirring the rice until the liquid is absorbed, then repeating. This causes extra evaporation of water from the cooking liquid, so that more cooking liquid is required and the flavor becomes more concentrated; and it abrades softened surface starch from the rice grains to help thicken the liquid. If you add the liquid in one or two doses and stir less, the

grains will release less thickening starch and will break when stirred because they've softened throughout.

- *Stop adding liquid* when the rice is al dente, or still slightly chewy, and add butter, cheese, or other final enriching ingredients.
- *To approximate a risotto with less constant attention,* incorporate the first portion of the cooking liquid into the rice, then spread it out on a baking sheet to cool quickly, and store it refrigerated, which hardens the cooked exterior. Finish the rice just before serving with simmering cooking liquid and final enrichments. A little rice starch can supplement the thickening.

Pilafs are dishes made by briefly sautéing firm long-grain rice in butter or oil to keep the grains separate, often along with onions or other aromatics, then adding a full volume of liquid and other ingredients—vegetables, meats, fruits, spices—and cooking the mixture through. Stir occasionally toward the end of cooking to mix the ingredients evenly.

To make rice salads for serving cold, use short- or medium-grain rices that don't harden badly on cooling. Dress the grains with a vinaigrette or other acidic sauce to inhibit bacterial growth.

To make rice for room-temperature sushi, use short-grain sushi rice and season it with the traditional vinegar-sugar mixture.

CORN

Corn, or maize, is the most important grain from the New World. It's much larger than the other grains and has a distinctive flavor. Its seed coat is so tough that dry popcorn is the only common whole-grain corn we eat. Corn comes in a number of different colors, from white and yellow to blue and deepest purple, and in varieties with particular cooking qualities. Colored corns are richer in valuable phytochemicals than white corn.

Popcorn is made from a high-protein corn with a seed coat that's strong enough to contain the pressure of steam building up inside it, which partly cooks the kernel and bursts and expands it.

Keep popcorn sealed in an airtight container. Popcorn kernels can absorb or release moisture depending on air humidity, and they require a narrow range of moisture contents to pop well.

To pop popcorn, heat the kernels rapidly to around 400°F/200°C, either in a thin film of oil on a preheated pan bottom, or in an air popper, or in the microwave on high power. Leave the pan lid ajar or replace it with an oil-spatter screen to avoid trapping moisture, which will make the popcorn tough and chewy.

Cornmeal, grits, and polenta are milled corn kernels that are cooked into a porridge with several times their volume of water or other liquid (broth, milk). They're sold in both coarse and fine grinds, and precooked.

Choose stone-ground corn for the most flavorful grits and polenta. It includes fragments of the germ and seed coat. Most ground corn is refined and relatively bland. Stone-ground corn stales quickly; store airtight in the freezer, and put your nose in leftover bags to make sure it still smells fresh.

To make polenta, grits, and cornmeal mush in the traditional, time-consuming way, slowly stream the meal into boiling liquid while stirring constantly, to avoid forming clumps of meal. Continue to stir constantly for up to an hour as the corn absorbs water and the mix develops flavor, to prevent sticking and burning on the pan bottom and small, messy eruptions of hot porridge.

To make these dishes more easily, stream the meal into the boiling water while stirring, then: place the uncovered pot in the oven at 250°F/120°C, which heats the pot gently and evenly from all directions and prevents eruptions. Check occasionally to stir and scrape the pan sides and bottom, adding water if necessary.

To make grits, mush, and polenta very easily in the microwave, start the meal in a bowl of cold water, leave it uncovered, and heat on high, stirring every 5 to 10 minutes until fully thickened.

To make mush or polenta to be cooled into solid pieces and fried or baked, use less water and make a firmer mush. This will produce pieces that are easier to cut and can develop a thicker crust.

Hominy is the term for whole corn kernels cooked in mineral lime to soften and remove the tough seed coat. It has a dense, meaty texture. Lime is alkaline and has a slippery, soapy feel in the mouth. If necessary, soak hominy in water to remove residual lime before using it in soups and stews.

Masa is a dense dough of corn kernels made by grinding hominy, and masa harina is masa dried and powdered into a flour so that it can be reconstituted conveniently. Fresh masa is available in ethnic groceries, and masa harina in many supermarkets. They're used to make tortillas, corn chips, and tamales.

Fresh masa is more cohesive than a dough reconstituted from masa harina. The flour develops a toasty aroma when the masa is dried and ground.

Tamales are corn cakes stuffed with meats and/or other ingredients, wrapped in corn husks, and steamed.

To make light-textured tamales, leaven them with lard. Whip lard until it's aerated, loosen masa with a meat broth, then whip all together until the mix is fluffy.

PASTAS, NOODLES, AND COUSCOUS

Pastas and noodles are thin pieces of dough (paste) made from grain flours, cooked quickly in hot water, and flavored with a variety of sauces or served in soups. Pastas are the Italian version, always made from wheat. Noodles are similar foods made in other parts of the world from wheat, rice, or purified starch. Pastas and noodles can be dried and kept for months before cooking.

Western pastas and noodles are made in countless types and shapes.

Dried pastas, spaghetti and fettuccine and fusilli and their many relatives, are usually made from strong-protein durum wheat, whose cohesive dough can be fancifully shaped and produces firm, robust strands when cooked.

Dried noodles are usually made from all-purpose wheat flour and egg. They're more delicate than durum pasta and have a mild egg flavor.

Fresh pasta is usually made from all-purpose flour and eggs. Soft Italian flour and high-protein semolina flour also work. Whole eggs produce cohesive, slightly elastic light-colored pasta. Yolks only produce a richer, yellower, but more fragile pasta.

To make fresh pasta:

- *Clear plenty of work space* for rolling the dough into very thin sheets.
- *Mix eggs, flour, salt,* and other ingredients and knead into a homogeneous mass. Recipes often include oil, which makes the dough easier to roll out.

- *Rest the dough in the refrigerator* to allow the flour particles to absorb the egg moisture fully.
- *Divide the dough into several pieces.* Small batches are easier to roll and cut.
- *Roll the dough into very thin sheets* using a flat rolling pin or the rollers on a pasta maker. Sprinkle the sheets with flour to prevent sticking and tearing.
- *Cut the dough sheets into the desired shapes* with a knife or the cutting attachments on a pasta maker. Toss the noodles immediately with flour to prevent the cut edges from sticking to each other.

Use or dry fresh pasta immediately, or refrigerate or freeze it. It's highly perishable.

Dry fresh pasta only in dry weather, or in a dehydrator or an oven at 140 to 150°F / 60 to 65°C. Slow drying will allow microbes to spoil it.

Cook fresh pasta attentively. Its surface flour provokes sudden boilovers, and it cooks quickly, in just a few minutes.

There are several different ways to cook pasta and noodles.

To cook pasta in the traditional way:
- *Use a large pot of water,* 4 to 8 quarts or liters per pound/500 grams of pasta, salted for flavor.
- *Heat the water to a rolling boil.* Cover the pot to speed heating.
- *To help prevent boilovers and the sticking* of flat fettuccine or fine spaghettini, add 1 tablespoon/15 milliliters of oil to the boiling water and swish the pasta through the oil as you immerse it. Or prewet the pasta in tap water before adding to the pot. Purists object to these methods, but they work.

- *Add the pasta while stirring* to prevent the pieces from sticking to each other.
- *When the water returns to the boil, lower the heat* to maintain a moderate boil, and cook until done. Leave the lid ajar to prevent the pot from boiling over.

To cook dried pasta more efficiently, with less time, water, energy, and sticking, rehydrate the pasta first.

- *Presoak the pasta* in salted water for an hour before cooking.
- *Add it to a pot of boiling salted water,* 1 to 2 quarts or liters per pound/500 grams pasta. Lower the heat when the water returns to the boil.
- *Stir gently and occasionally until done.*

To cook either fresh or dried pasta more efficiently without presoaking:

- *Immerse it in a pan of cold water,* 1.5 quarts or liters per pound/ 500 grams pasta.
- *Turn on the heat, bring to a boil* with occasional stirring, and cook until done.
- *Use the starch-thickened pasta water* to make a simple sauce by tossing it with the pasta, some olive oil, and flavorings.

To cook compact pasta shapes while imbuing them with flavor, cook them in the manner of risotto, adding small amounts of broth and wine and stirring until done.

To avoid overcooking pasta and noodles, stop cooking when they're still slightly hard at the center. They will continue to soften as they're sauced and served.

Drain cooked pasta and noodles of excess cooking water in a colander. Don't rinse them with tap water, which would cool them down and prevent them from taking up the sauce.

Serve cooked pasta immediately, or moisten it slightly with a little sauce to prevent sticking.

Couscous is a very fine form of pasta invented in North Africa, usually less than the diameter of wheat or rice grains. It's made by sprinkling water onto durum semolina, then stirring, rubbing, and sieving it to make small 1- to 2-millimeter granules. They're dried, and then are steamed and moistened with water in several stages, the last above a simmering stew, to make an unusually light, fluffy mass.

Most manufactured couscous has been precooked and dried.

To make prepared couscous quickly, moisten it with water and heat for a few minutes on high in the microwave, stirring every minute or two to even out the moisture and heat.

Pearl (Israeli) couscous and Sardinian fregola are larger round pastas, the first extruded and the second formed as couscous is. Cook them in excess water as other pastas.

ASIAN NOODLES AND WRAPPERS

Asian noodles and wrappers are made from various grain flours (wheat, buckwheat, rice) and extracted starches (rice, mung beans, sweet potatoes). A slippery surface is prized in Asian noodles.

To make cooked noodles slippery and not sticky, immerse the cooked noodles in ice-cold water to rinse away excess surface starch and congeal the rest.

Rice and starch noodles and rice paper are attractively translucent, and convenient because they're precooked and need only to be remoistened.

To prepare rice noodles and paper, soak them briefly in hot water (noodles) or lukewarm water (paper) until they become pliable.

Serve noodles with sauce or in soup. Use rice papers to make refreshing cool wraps for vegetables, meats, and fish.

DUMPLINGS, GNOCCHI, AND SPAETZLE

Dumplings are small portions of grain dough or batter that are dropped into hot liquid, boiling water, or a stew and cooked through.

Gnocchi are made from cooked and riced potatoes or other starchy roots, or from ricotta cheese, kneaded into a dough with flour and sometimes egg.

Spaetzle are small irregular shapes made by drops of a thin flour batter.

To make tender dough dumplings, knead the dough as little as possible.

To make the most delicate gnocchi, use as little flour as possible, and omit eggs, which give them a springy cohesiveness.

To cook dumplings, gnocchi, and spaetzle:

- *Keep the cooking liquid at a gentle simmer.* Vigorous boiling can break the delicate morsels apart.
- *Remove them from the cooking liquid* after they've risen to the surface and cooked there for a minute or two.
- *Check one for doneness* before straining out the remainder. Floating is usually a sign that they've filled with hot steam, but some dough pieces or batter drops may float before they've cooked through.

PUDDINGS

Puddings are dense, moist dishes thickened with grains (rice), grain flours, or starch (cornstarch, tapioca). They're usually sweetened, sometimes enriched with eggs and/or fats, and then baked, steamed, or boiled.

The key to a good pudding is a good recipe, with enough liquid to hydrate the dry grain ingredients fully, and enough sugar and fat to make it moist and tender. The ingredients are combined and cooked very simply.

Heat puddings covered and with low to moderate heat to avoid drying them out.

Beans and their legume-family relatives

15

SEED LEGUMES

Beans, Peas, Lentils, and Soy Products

Beans and their legume-family relatives are main-course seeds, even more so than the grains. They can't make raised breads or chewy pastas the way grains do, but they're the heart of the meal in many parts of the world for people who don't have access to meat or choose not to eat it. They make a more nutritionally balanced side dish than rice or bread or potatoes, and small legumes like the lentils cook just as quickly as rice.

Seed legumes have double the protein of the grains, a stronger savory-sweet flavor, and a range of striking colors that signal the presence of valuable phytochemicals. They're simple to cook, but it takes some care to get them to come out intact and with the best beany consistency, neither crunchy nor mushy, but creamily firm. The soybean has its own kind of versatility, giving us a range of fresh and fermented foods, from blank-canvas soy milk and tofu to mushroomy tempeh and intensely aromatic miso.

Beans will always be close to my heart because they were too close to a friend's and provoked him to provoke me into writing about food. At a potluck dinner sometime around 1975, not long after the release of Mel Brooks's *Blazing Saddles,* a displaced Louisianan and fellow literature student wondered out loud why it is that beans give people gas, an effect that compromised his full enjoyment of red beans and rice. The question was good and funny enough to send me to the library in search of an answer. Even better than the answer, I discovered that much of the relevant research had been funded by NASA, which was concerned about anything that might compromise air quality in space capsules. With that, and the intriguing window that science gave on everyday life, I was hooked.

SEED LEGUME SAFETY AND COMFORT

Like the grains, the seed legumes are stored dry and generally prepared by boiling, so they pose little risk of foodborne illness in the cooking or immediate eating. Once cooked, they can be contaminated as any other food, and should be handled with the usual care.

Don't keep cooked bean dishes at room temperature for more than 4 hours. Either hold them at 130°F/55°C or above, or refrigerate or freeze them promptly. If you want to serve a cool salad over a longer time, finish it with an acidic dressing that inhibits bacterial growth. If you leave a dish out overnight, which is long enough to develop heat-resistant toxins, discard it. Reheat properly handled leftovers to 165°F/73°C or above.

Raw sprouts of various beans do pose a risk of foodborne illness. The warm, moist conditions that sprout seeds also encourage bacteria to grow without obvious signs. Don't serve uncooked sprouts to vulnerable people.

Fava beans can make some people ill. Favism is a hereditary sensitivity to substances in fava beans that can cause serious anemia.

Raw and undercooked legume seeds can cause discomfort. Many legumes contain chemical defenses that can interfere with the digestive system. Thorough cooking destroys most of them.

Fully cooked seed legumes often do cause gassy discomfort. They contain indigestible carbohydrates that don't nourish us, but do nourish microbes in our digestive system. When those microbes feast, they produce copious gas.

Commercial antigas enzyme preparations can reduce the discomfort from eating beans for some people, according to clinical trials.

To minimize the discomfort of intestinal gas from legumes, choose them carefully and cook them thoroughly. Chickpeas, black beans, and lentils contain fewer indigestibles than soy or navy or lima beans. Prolonged cooking breaks some indigestibles down into more digestible sugars.

To reduce the gassy potential of any kind of legume, leach out some of the indigestible carbohydrates before you cook them. Bring the seeds slowly to the boil in excess water, turn off the heat and let them soak for an hour, then discard the soaking water and proceed with cooking. Or soak them overnight in excess water, then discard the water and proceed with cooking.

Tolerate some gassiness to get the fullest nutritional benefit from seed legumes. Leaching out indigestible carbohydrates also removes color, flavor, and nutrients, including the indigestibles themselves. The microbes they feed in us are beneficial ones.

BUYING AND STORING LEGUMES

Dried seed legumes can be stored for years without spoiling, so they sometimes are.

Old seeds take longer to cook. If stored in hot and humid conditions, they develop the "hard-to-cook defect" and become impossible to soften.

Try to identify and buy legumes from the most recent crop. Examine packages or bins, and avoid buying if there are many broken seeds, damaged seed coats, or discolorations.

Store dry seed legumes in a cool, dry, dark place. Heat and moisture can cause the hard-to-cook defect and encourage spoilage.

Try specialty beans and peas, which are more expensive than the bulk versions, but are often higher in quality and still a good buy compared with many other foods.

To save preparation time, choose quick-cooking small lentils, or hulled legumes—split peas, many Indian dals—that soften in 10 minutes.

Precooked canned and "instant" legumes are convenient but rarely taste as good as when freshly prepared. Canned legumes have been heated to very high temperatures, and instant versions lose aroma when they're freeze-dried.

To get the best flavor in canned beans and peas, check labels and choose brands with the fewest added flavors and lowest sodium content. Rinse them thoroughly, taste, and if they're oversalted, soak them in warm water for 1 to 2 hours.

SPROUTS

Sprouts are fresh, tenderly crunchy, mild vegetables. Many different seeds are germinated to produce these very young plants, 3 to 6 days old. Among the most common are mung beans, soybeans, and alfalfa.

Keep sprouts cold, and use them promptly. Buy them only if very fresh-looking. Avoid if there is wilting, browning, off smells, or more obvious spoilage.

To store sprouts, blot and air-dry to the touch, wrap loosely in a towel, and enclose in a plastic bag before refrigerating.

When in doubt about raw sprout quality, cook thoroughly at or close to the boil, or discard.

To sprout seeds in the kitchen:

- *Buy seeds intended for sprouting and eating,* not planting. Garden seeds may be treated with chemicals.
- *Soak the seeds in water for several hours,* then rinse and drain.
- *Keep the seeds in a sprouting jar, cool and shielded from light,* until they're ready in several days. Rinse and drain the seeds several times a day to prevent the accumulation of microbes.

THE ESSENTIALS OF COOKING SEED LEGUMES

Beans and other legumes can be cooked very simply, by washing the seeds, putting them in a pot with flavor ingredients and copious water, heating the water to the boil, and simmering until they're soft. But this process often takes hours, leaches color from the bean skins, and leaves many of them broken. There are ways to shorten times and get more reliably good results.

Cooking dry seeds includes two different processes: getting water into the seeds to moisten their cell walls and starch, and heating them through to soften their interior. Seeds take much longer to absorb water than they do to heat through, especially if they have intact seed coats.

To shorten cooking times by half or more, presoak legumes in salted water, 2 teaspoons/10 grams per quart or liter, for several hours or overnight. To cook whole legumes exceptionally fast, presoak them and then pressure-cook them for just 10 to 15 minutes. For the fastest cooking, choose split peas and lentils.

Salt does not harden beans or other legumes or prevent them from softening, though it can slow their cooking. Added to the presoak water, it actually speeds later cooking. Added to the cooking water without presoaking, salt does slow water absorption.

If legumes seem to cook slowly, check your water hardness. Hard water high in calcium can keep seeds firm. Try cooking with distilled water.

Sometimes dried legumes never fully soften no matter how they're cooked. This hard-to-cook defect develops when they've been grown in unusually hot and dry conditions, or stored for months in warm and humid conditions. There's no remedy except to find a more reliable brand.

To cook beans and other seed legumes:

- *Rinse and pick them over in a pot of water,* to remove stray chaff, soil, pebbles, and any beans that are much smaller than average, which often fail to soften.
- *Choose a pot wide enough to hold the seeds in a thin layer,* to heat evenly and avoid crushing seeds at the bottom.

- *Add just enough water for them to absorb and remain barely immersed in liquid.* For unsoaked legumes, this is about 2 parts water for every 1 of seeds, by weight or volume. For fully soaked legumes, reduce this to 1 part water. Include a little more to compensate for evaporation during cooking, and check the water level occasionally during cooking.
- *For the most even heating,* bring the pot to a simmer on the stove top, then cover tightly and move it to a 200°F/93°C oven.

To preserve depth of color in black and red beans, minimize the amount of cooking liquid that draws pigments out of the seed coats. Start the beans in barely enough cold water to cover, and add hot water from the kettle to maintain that level as they absorb water.

To preserve intact seed coats as much as possible, heat as gently as possible. Presoak with salted water to expand tissues gradually. Heat the pot slowly to 180 to 190°F / 80 to 85°C, but not high enough to cause boiling and turbulence. Cook the beans until tender, then allow to cool and firm in the cooking liquid before handling them.

To prevent legumes from softening too much, add a firming ingredient when they've softened correctly. These ingredients include acids of all kinds (vinegar, tomatoes, wine, fruit juices), sugar, and calcium. The molasses used in Boston baked beans is acidic and provides both sugar and calcium.

Serve cooked legumes whole or pureed more or less smoothly. Because most contain starch, a small portion can be removed, pureed, and stirred into the cooking liquid to thicken it into a sauce.

COMMON SEED LEGUMES: ADZUKIS TO TEPARIES

The legume family is large and diverse. Most of these can be readily found in stores or online.

Asian beans include a number of relatively small, quick-cooking beans that are low in gas-producing carbohydrates. They include adzuki or azuki (Japan), black gram (India), mung or green gram (China, India), and rice beans (Thailand).

Broad or fava beans have a tough seed coat and benefit from brief precooking in water with a little baking soda, which makes the skins easy to slip off. Fava beans can induce a serious anemia in some people of Mediterranean background.

Chickpeas or garbanzos have a distinctive flavor, bumpy shape, and often granular texture. They come in two general types: the familiar large cream-colored type from Europe and the Middle East; and smaller varieties available in Indian markets that are a darker brown or even dark green.

Common beans, including white, navy, kidney, red, black, pinto, and cannellini, are descendants of Mexican originals that have spread all over the world. They vary in coloration, size, seed coat thickness, cooking times, and textures.

Lentils come in two general types: flat, broad, and light-colored; and round, small, and dark green to black. They're the quickest-cooking legumes, taking less than an hour without presoaking, and are low in gas-producing carbohydrates.

Small lentils can be cooked like rice, in minimal water to produce separate grains.

Hulled red Indian lentils cook into a golden mush in just a few minutes.

Lima beans are popular as a fresh vegetable, but are rarely cooked when mature and dry due to their thick seed coat.

Lupini are seeds from lupins, relatives of the true beans that contain no starch, abundant soluble fiber, and often bitter alkaloids that must be leached out by presoaking in several changes of water.

Peas, both green and yellow, are generally sold hulled and split because their seed coat is tough. They quickly cook into a mush.

Black-eyed peas are an African relative of the Asian mung bean, with a distinctive aroma and a dark pigment ring that survives cooking.

Soybeans are a Chinese native that contain more oil than starch and are especially rich in protein. They're seldom simply cooked and served as is. They develop a strong beany aroma, don't get as soft and creamy as starchier beans do, and tend to cause strong, gassy discomfort.

Tepary beans are a little-known native of the American Southwest, small and quick-cooking and especially sweet, with the aroma of molasses.

SOY MILK, TOFU, TEMPEH, AND MISO

These traditional processed soy products are less beany-flavored and gassy than plain soybeans, and more versatile.

Check labels and choose the latest sell-by dates. Soy milk, tofu, and tempeh are perishable.

Soy milk is a bland, milklike fluid made by grinding the boiled soaked beans with water, then cooking this mix and sieving off the solids. It has about the same protein and fat content as cow's milk, but without the high proportion of saturated fat, or the lactose and cow proteins to which some people are sensitive.

Check ingredient lists. Many soy milks are heavily sweetened and include vanilla and other flavorings.

Bean curd, or tofu, is soy milk coagulated into a bland, solid mass with calcium salts (Chinese style, using the mineral gypsum), a mixture of slightly bitter magnesium and calcium salts (Japanese style, using nigari, the seawater minerals left after extracting sodium chloride), or Epsom salts (magnesium sulfate). Different types span a range of textures, from firm and chewy to silken, delicate, and custardy.

Store fresh, unpackaged bean curd covered in water in a cold corner of the refrigerator. Change the water every day.

Check the edibility of fresh or packaged bean curd by smelling and touching it. Discard it if it has an off aroma or a slimy surface.

Freezing bean curd changes its texture and causes separation of water from the solid curd.

To give firm bean curd a meatier texture and help it absorb flavors better, freeze it before using, then thaw and cut it, and press the thaw water out. Freezing forms ice crystals that force the curd proteins into a fibrous network, and leave behind voids that can fill with flavorful cooking liquids.

Tempeh is a thin cake made from whole cooked soybeans pressed together and fermented with a special mold. It's drier than bean curd and has a pleasant mushroomy aroma. Frying gives it a meaty flavor.

Freeze tempeh to store it indefinitely without much change in texture.

Check the edibility of tempeh by smelling and touching it. Discard it if it has an off aroma or a slimy surface. Ignore normal white or black spots of its own mold.

Miso is a flavorful paste made from fermented soybeans and a grain, usually rice or barley. It comes in a wide range of colors and flavors, with dark-colored types aged longer and stronger flavored. Miso provides salt, savoriness, an aroma of soy sauce and often pineapple, and acts as a coarse thickener.

Check package labels and avoid inferior industrial versions of miso made with corn syrup and alcohol.

Store miso paste indefinitely in the refrigerator. Refrigerate packages of dry miso powder after they're opened, but seal them airtight.

Use miso as an instant soup base, a flavor supplement in soups and sauces, and part of a seasoning paste or marinade for fish, meats, and vegetables.

Nuts are oil-rich seeds that give us an important reference

16

NUTS AND
OIL SEEDS

Nuts are oil-rich seeds that give us an important reference point for flavor. *Nutty* names the characteristic aroma of toasted nuts, which develops when their proteins and sugars are essentially fried in place by their own oil.

Unlike the grains and seed legumes, most nuts are tender enough to be eaten raw or quickly crisped by high heat. They and the oil seeds are filled with oil instead of starch, so they release a moist richness in the mouth, and become so creamy and smooth when finely ground that the results are called butters. Ground with added liquid, they make "milks" and "creams" that can be turned into dairy-free sauces and ice creams.

Most nuts are borne on trees and are contained inside a hard shell. Their papery seed coats are often removed to refine appearance and flavor, because the seed coats are brown and astringent. But they're also rich in valuable antioxidants, and are probably part of the reason that nuts have been found to be associated with good cardiovascular health. A few walnuts in particular can help balance the fats in a dish or a meal; they happen to be high in essential and uncommon omega-3 fatty acids.

The same oils that make nuts delicious also make them vulnerable to going stale, when they start to taste a little like cardboard or paint. Really fresh-tasting nuts, raw or roasted, can be hard to find. When I do manage to get some good raw hazelnuts or walnuts or almonds, I'll toast a handful in the morning while I make my coffee. The aroma in the kitchen is wonderful, and I've even come to anticipate the sounds, usually the faint whistle of escaping water vapor that evolves into a sizzle as the oil heats up to frying temperatures. Have you ever listened to shelled pumpkin seeds, not while they're toasting but as they cool down? They'll crackle away for a minute or two as the air inside them contracts and shatters the thin walls, but so delicately that it's like a whispered secret.

NUT AND SEED SAFETY

Nuts and seeds are among our driest foods and not normally hospitable for bacteria to grow on, so they generally present little risk of common foodborne illness. The exceptions to this rule have involved unusual contamination during processing.

Nuts are a common cause of serious food allergies.

Inform people if you're serving foods made with nuts and the nuts aren't obvious.

Some nuts are susceptible to molds that produce aflatoxin, a carcinogen that may increase the long-term risk of developing cancer.

Discard shriveled, discolored, or off-tasting kernels, which may have been infected with mold.

BUYING AND STORING NUTS AND SEEDS, NUT BUTTERS AND OILS

Nuts and seeds keep for months without spoiling. But they gradually develop stale and rancid flavors from their polyunsaturated oils, which are easily attacked by oxygen in the air.

For the best quality and longest shelf life, buy nuts in the shell and freshly harvested, in late summer and fall. Choose nuts that feel heavy for their size; old nut meats shrink. Store them in a cool, dry place.

Keep shelled nuts and seeds in an air- and lighttight container in the refrigerator or freezer. Before removing them from the container, allow them to warm up to room temperature.

When buying nuts and seeds from open bins or in transparent packages, look for mostly intact pieces, and for opaque, cream-colored interiors. Avoid batches with translucent or yellow interiors, which indicate rancidity, as well as any with signs of mold infection. If possible, smell the container or taste a sample. Don't buy if you detect cardboard staleness or paintlike rancidity.

When buying preroasted nuts and seeds, avoid batches with dark brown edges, which have off flavors. Most nuts and seeds have enough oil that they can be dry-roasted without added oil. Cooking oils increase oiliness and can be a source of off flavors.

When buying nut butters and pastes, check labels for the presence of added sugars, flavorings, and fats. Avoid products that include hydrogenated oils, which may contain unhealthful trans-fatty acids.

Nut and seed oils carry characteristic flavors, and make an excellent alternative to standard cooking oils when dressing salads and vegetables.

For flavorful nut and seed oils, choose oils extracted from toasted nuts by the expeller-press or cold-press method. Solvent-extracted oils usually have less flavor, but also fewer traces of allergy-inducing compounds.

Store nut and seed oils in opaque containers in the refrigerator. Their valuable but fragile polyunsaturated fatty acids cause them to go rancid faster than other oils.

THE ESSENTIALS OF COOKING NUTS AND SEEDS

Dry heat removes moisture from nuts and seeds, crisps them, and creates characteristic nutty flavors as they cook in their own or added oil.

For the best flavor, heat nuts and seeds until the interior turns golden brown, and just before serving. Dark brown color often signals the development of harsh, bitter flavors. Cooked nuts lose flavor within a day or two and then become stale and rancid.

Nut skins are a thin layer between shell and seed. Some skins are tough and adhere tightly to the nut, others are more brittle and easily rubbed off. They're the source of mouth-drying tannins that can also create bluish purple off colors in baked goods. But they're also rich in healthful antioxidants.

Don't remove nut skins if they won't detract from the appearance or flavor of a dish.

To remove thin skins (peanuts, hazelnuts), toast nuts briefly and then rub them in a rough kitchen towel.

To remove thicker almond skins, blanch the nuts for 30 to 60 seconds in boiling water, then remove into cold water and peel the skins off.

To reduce the astringency and discoloring power of walnut and pecan skins, which are hard to remove completely, blanch the nuts for 30 to 60 seconds in boiling water to extract some of the tannins, then dry and toast immediately.

To remove tough chestnut skins, make the skins softer by boiling or roasting in the shell, then peel. Or pare the skin off like an apple skin.

To crisp and brown nuts and seeds, toast them on a baking sheet in a medium oven, 350°F/175°C, for 10 to 15 minutes, or fry with constant stirring in oil over medium heat until light golden. In a toaster oven, place the rack at its lowest position and shield the nuts and seeds from the upper heating element with foil.

To toast nuts and seeds in the microwave oven, heat on medium or low power, checking every 1 to 2 minutes, and more often when they're close to being done. A few seconds too many can cause irregular scorching.

To coat nuts with salt, sugar, or other seasonings, coat a bowl with oil or melted butter, or briefly beaten egg white or sugar syrup. Toss the cooked nuts in the oil or melted butter, remove them and blot the excess, then toss in a fresh bowl with seasonings. Or toss with egg white or syrup, toss again with seasonings, then spread out on a plate or baking sheet and dry in a low oven. To add salt only, dissolve some in just enough water to coat the nuts, toss with the nuts and then toast or dry them.

To slice nuts neatly, heat them in the oven or microwave just until soft, then cut them with a very sharp knife before they cool and become brittle.

Fresh nut pastes and butters are made by grinding raw or more flavorful roasted nuts or seeds in a food processor, heavy-duty blender, or auger-fed juicer. Home-ground pastes and butters are seldom as fine and silken as manufactured versions.

To make a paste, process the nuts or seeds until the particles are small but still stick to each other and form a solid mass.

To make a fine-textured almond paste, include powdered confectioners' sugar, which soaks up oil during extended grinding. To make a fine-textured nonsweetened paste, replace the sugar with cornstarch.

To make butter, process the paste for several minutes longer, until freed oil lubricates the particles into a slowly flowing mass. Fragile high-oil nuts—walnut, pecan, pine—go from paste to butter very quickly. Other harder nuts break down slowly, and remain somewhat coarse.

Nut milks are suspensions of nut oil and protein in water that make flavorful and healthful substitutes for cow's milk in drinks, ice creams, and other dishes. They're more milklike if discoloring skins are removed first, and more flavorful if the nuts are lightly toasted.

To make nut milk:

- *Grind skinned, toasted nuts* in a blender or food processor, adding just enough hot water to keep the mass of particles lubricated and moving.
- *When the particles become very small,* add enough water to create a thinner, milklike liquid.
- *Strain everything through cheesecloth,* squeezing the solids dry.
- *Dry the leftover solids* in a warm oven, and use them to replace some flour in cookies or pastries.

COMMON NUTS AND SEEDS: ALMONDS TO WALNUTS

Almonds are easily blanched, or freed from their skins, and are unusually rich in vitamin E. Most U.S. almonds are now pasteurized due to the possibility of salmonella contamination during harvest and processing. Standard "sweet" almonds have a mild flavor.

Almond extracts safely concentrate the aroma of bitter almonds, which contain enough cyanide to be hazardous if eaten in any quantity. Apricot, peach, and cherry pits carry the same aroma and risk.

Brazil nuts are large and so rich in selenium, an essential mineral, that one nut contains more than the recommended daily allowance.

Cashews contain more starch than most nuts and so make a good thickener for soups, stews, and puddinglike desserts.

Chestnuts store energy in starch, not oil. They're moist and perishable when fresh, mealy rather than crisp when roasted, and are dried and ground into flour for making cakes and other starchy foods.

Choose chestnuts that feel heavy and hard. Hold very fresh chestnuts for a day or two at room temperature to convert some of their starch to sugar, then store tightly wrapped in the refrigerator and use quickly.

To roast chestnuts, cut a small notch in the bottom of the nut to allow steam to escape, and heat in a medium oven or in coals until the shell is brittle enough to break off.

Coconuts are tropical seeds that weigh several pounds, with a woody shell and an interior that starts out as a sweet liquid, becomes milkily gelatinous, and ends up as a firm, moist, fatty "meat" when mature.

Choose coconuts that feel heavy for their size and make a sloshing sound. To open, use a hammer and screwdriver to poke in two of the three "eyes" at one end. Pour out the liquid, then hammer the nut into a few large pieces. Pull or cut the meat away from the shell, peel the brown skin from the meat, and rinse before using.

To make coconut milk, grind, pound, or process mature coconut meat or dried shredded coconut together with hot water. Knead the resulting paste, then strain the liquid off the solids through cheesecloth, and let the milk stand to separate into a rich cream layer on top and leaner milk beneath. Add more water to the solids and repeat.

Canned coconut milk is often stabilized with flour or starch and lacks the creamy consistency and full flavor of fresh coconut milk.

Flaxseeds are small, flat, tough, and useful mainly as a nutritional and flavor adjunct to other foods. They're the richest plant source of essential omega-3 fatty acids, and also a rich source of soluble fiber, which gels in water and can help stabilize vinaigrettelike emulsions and foams. To get the most nutritional value from flaxseeds, crush or grind them.

Hazelnuts, or filberts, are rich in vitamin E. Intensify their characteristic aroma by roasting, frying, or even boiling. They are hollow and scorch easily at the inner surface; roast at low temperatures and check frequently.

Macadamia nuts have very hard shells that are almost always removed before they're packaged and sold. Choose nuts that have been packed airtight, and avoid any with brown discoloration, which indicates rancidity.

Peanuts are mainly a snack and children's food in the United States, but an important thickening and enriching ingredient in Asian and African sauces, soups, and stews. There are several common varieties, Virginia among the most prized for its flavor. Boiling peanuts in the shell, a traditional preparation in the U.S. South, gives them a vanilla flavor. Discard in-shell peanuts with any appearance or smell of mold, to which they're vulnerable because they develop underground. Peanuts are a common cause of serious food allergies. When cooking for other people, make sure that their presence in a dish is clear.

Pine nuts come from several different continents and tree species. Asian types are more than three-quarters oil, American and European types much leaner. All are fragile and prone to rancidity. Store them in the dark and cold and use quickly. Toast pine nuts very attentively at low temperatures. They're very easy to scorch.

Pistachios are unusual for being green with chlorophyll, and especially so when grown at high altitude and harvested young. To retain the green, heat pistachios gently and briefly, just enough to dry and crisp them.

Poppy seeds come from the same plant that produces opium, and can carry traces that will show up on a drug test: check with competitive athletes before serving them. Taste poppy seeds before using. They often have a bitter or peppery taste due to damage to the tiny seeds and their oil during processing.

Pumpkin seeds, like pistachios, are green with chlorophyll, which stays more vivid with the lightest possible toasting. They have a distinctive, somewhat animal flavor. Some varieties come in a tough seed coat; more convenient ones come naked and don't need to be hulled. Naked seeds scorch easily during toasting. Pumpkin-seed oil is visually striking: dark brown in a bowl, but deep green clinging to a piece of bread.

Sesame seeds come in shades from white to black, and are usually toasted to develop their characteristic flavor. They're the main ingredient in the Middle Eastern paste called tahini. Sesame-seed oil is usually made from toasted seeds, and is unusually stable and resistant to rancidity. Toast with care; they're so small that they quickly scorch.

Sunflower seeds are especially rich in antioxidants and vitamin E.

Walnuts and pecans are distant relatives with similar lobed, wrinkled shapes. They're high in essential fatty acids but also fragile and prone to rancidity. Store them in the cold and dark. For less mouth-drying astringency, choose kernels with a light or red seed coat, or blanch them. To reduce the purplish discoloration of baked goods that include them, use toasted nuts. While they're still hot, rub off as much seed coat as possible with a coarse kitchen towel.

17

BREADS

reads are dry seeds turned into a soft and fragrant and nourishing clay, shaped by the cook's hand, crusted outside and steamed inside by high heat. They can be dense and flat or light and lofty, moist or dry, tart or sweet. The lightest breads are leavened, inflated from within by microscopic bubbling yeasts or simple chemical reactions.

When I learned to make yeasted breads in the 1970s, it was standard procedure to knead a stiff dough for 10 or 15 minutes to develop its elasticity and help it rise into a lofty loaf. Today you can still make bread by working this hard, but you don't have to. Bakers have come to realize that a soft dough and little or no kneading can also yield loftiness. So bread making still takes hours, but now the yeasts do most of the work.

One key to good bread is knowing when the shaped loaf of dough has risen just enough to go into the oven, where the heat will cause it to spring higher and lighter. I found that the best way to know was to bake often and learn what too little, too much, and just enough rising feel like.

I did this in the 1990s, when I was impressed by breads from Berkeley's Acme Bread Company and wanted to figure out its secrets. I ended up baking almost every day for a year, in part because I kept following up on little details, but mainly because I loved it. I couldn't wait to get out of bed in the morning to see how an overnight rise had turned out, or to hear a well-sprung loaf crackle as its interior cooled and shrank and broke the crust, or to cut across the loaf and see the stop-action frame of the dough's exuberant rise.

For all their pleasures, raised breads do take planning and time. But you can also turn out wonderful flatbreads in minutes, start to finish. Just make plenty of dough so you'll be sure to have some bread that actually gets to the table.

BREAD SAFETY

Bread itself is thoroughly cooked and poses no general safety problem unless it's stored long enough to get moldy.

Never eat moldy bread. If only a portion is moldy, cut deeply and smell the remainder before eating. Mold filaments can spread extensively and invisibly into the interior of a loaf.

Burns are the most common hazard in making bread. To avoid burns to the hands and arms as you move bread into and out of a very hot oven, wear a long-sleeved shirt and use dry towels or oven mitts.

SHOPPING FOR BREADS
AND BAKING INGREDIENTS

There are two basic kinds of plain bread.

Presliced or whole loaves sold in plastic bags are generally mass-produced, flavored quickly with yeast rather than gradually raised by them, have a dense, cakelike interior and soft, chewy crust, are already several days old, and are made with shelf-life-lengthening additives.

Whole loaves sold in paper bags are generally not mass-produced, are yeast raised and have a more open, irregular interior and crisp crust, are baked within a day of sale, and are made with few if any preservatives.

Mass-produced breads offer convenience and uniformity. Small-production breads offer fresh-baked textures and flavors.

For fresh bread that will keep for a few days, choose sourdough or levain breads, whose acidity slows staling.

When making bread, read recipes carefully to make sure you shop for the correct ingredients. Flours and yeasts come in different forms that are not always interchangeable.

Choose the freshest flours and yeasts you can find by checking sell-by dates. If you're buying whole-grain flours, try to find packages that have been refrigerated.

STORING BREAD
AND RESTORING IT

Freshly baked bread has been heated very hot, and it's not moist enough for bacteria to thrive on. So bread isn't perishable the way many foods are. But there are still some challenges to storing it well.

Once baked, fresh bread can suffer two kinds of damage. It can be spoiled by the growth of molds, and it can stale, or develop a firm, hard texture.

Bread gets moldy when its surface is moist and warm enough for mold to grow. This happens when bread is stored at room temperature in a plastic bag.

Bread gets stale when its starch molecules settle back into a more solid structure after the disturbances of baking. This happens gradually at room temperature, much faster at refrigerator temperature, and very slowly in the freezer. Staling is not the same process as drying, though both make the bread hard.

To keep fresh bread for a day or two, keep it in a bread box or porous paper bag or on the countertop, cut-side down on a board to slow drying. Sourdough breads keep for several days. To avoid picking up odors from a wooden board, protect the cut side with foil.

To keep fresh bread for more than a day or two, wrap it airtight and freeze it. Its texture would harden much more in the refrigerator.

To thaw frozen bread, unwrap and set it on a rack at room temperature, or in an oven at 250°F/120°C.

Staling is easily reversed by reheating the bread to at least 160°F/70°C and redistributing the starch. Because reheating also drives moisture out of bread, it leaves the bread somewhat drier afterward.

To restore a partial or whole loaf of stale bread, moisten its crust to prevent scorching, and bake in a medium oven for 15 minutes or until hot and soft inside.

To restore a few slices of stale bread, toast or grill them. The surfaces will be dry but the center soft.

Take advantage of stale bread firmness to make croutons, bread salads, puddings, and French toast (pain perdu), dishes in which fresh bread will disintegrate.

BREAD INGREDIENTS: FLOURS

Most breads are made from wheat flour, whose uniquely stretchy, elastic gluten proteins can trap gas bubbles and create a light, airy texture.

A dough with "strong" gluten is very elastic and rises well; a dough with "weak" gluten is more easily torn when stretched, and doesn't rise well.

Gluten-free breads usually replace wheat flour with a combination of rice flour and xanthan gum, with the gum providing some gas-trapping power.

Different wheat flours have very different bread-making properties, and absorb different amounts of water.

Try to use the exact flour type called for in a given recipe. Substitutions will require adjustments in the proportion of water, and may not work well.

Refined wheat flours include all-purpose and bread flours. They have had the grain's fiber-rich outer bran coat and oil-rich inner germ (embryo) removed, so they're nearly all protein and starch.

Bleached flours have been chemically treated to lighten the off-white color and strengthen the gluten, and have lost some minor nutrients and flavor. Most artisan bakers prefer unbleached flour.

All-purpose flour is the most common flour sold and used in bread making. Its gluten protein content varies among regions and brands, so proportion adjustments are sometimes necessary when switching.

Bread flour contains more gluten protein than all-purpose flour. It requires more water, and makes a stretchier, more elastic dough that rises higher. The resulting bread has a chewy texture and a distinctive, slightly eggy flavor.

Whole-wheat flours include the wheat grain's bran and germ. They add a brownish color, a stronger grain flavor, and more nourishment (vitamins, minerals, antioxidants) to a dough, but make a weaker gluten and a denser, moister loaf. White wheat varieties make milder flavored whole-wheat flours and breads.

Commercial whole-wheat flours often suffer from staleness and a bitter taste, and should be bought and kept as fresh as possible.

To give a fresh whole-wheat flavor to a refined-flour bread, grind a few spoonfuls of whole-wheat kernels to add to a refined-flour dough.

Self-rising flours are not suitable for making yeast-leavened breads. They contain baking powder for leavening quick breads and griddle cakes.

Nonwheat flours—rye, barley, rice—add flavor to breads but produce a weaker dough and a denser texture. To maintain some lightness, make them a small fraction of the total amount of flour, a quarter or less.

Vital gluten is a purified form of the wheat gluten proteins. Add a few spoonfuls to doughs made with weaker flours or with gluten-weakening fats or sugars, to improve their elasticity and the lightness of the final breads.

Store all flours in closed containers, protected from air and light. Roll down the tops of partly empty flour bags and press out as much air as possible. Keep especially sensitive whole-grain flours wrapped airtight in the refrigerator or freezer, and allow them to warm to room temperature before opening them.

BREAD INGREDIENTS: WATER AND SALT

Water makes up nearly half the weight of bread dough. Water-to-flour ratios vary significantly among recipes, and directly affect dough handling and bread texture.

Dry doughs are firm, easy to handle, and produce a relatively dense loaf with small, regular air cells.

Wet doughs are soft and sticky but rise and inflate easily and can produce a light loaf with large, irregular air cells.

Water chemistry can affect doughs and breads. The minerals in hard water make a more elastic dough, as does somewhat alkaline water. Acidic water weakens the dough gluten. Heavily chlorinated water may slow the growth of yeast and sourdough bacteria.

Salt contributes to a balanced taste and intensifies aroma in bread, but it also affects structure and texture. Salt makes a dough less sticky, the gluten more stretchy, and the finished loaf lighter. In sourdoughs, salt helps control the growth of acid-producing, gluten-weakening bacteria.

Double-check the kind of salt specified in your recipe. Adjust the amount if you're using a different kind. One teaspoon of compact granulated table salt can contain up to twice as much salt as a teaspoon of flaky kosher salt. A good amount of salt is a weight equivalent to 2 percent of the weight of the flour: or, in volume measures, ½ teaspoon of granulated salt for every cup of flour.

BREAD INGREDIENTS: YEASTS

Yeasts are living microscopic creatures that generate carbon dioxide gas, and fill bread dough with bubbles and flavor. They're sold in three different forms for baking. Yeasts sold as nutritional supplements are no longer alive and can't leaven bread.

Fresh yeast is sold as moist foil-wrapped cakes. It's perishable and must be kept refrigerated. To revive it, mix it with warm 70 to 80°F/20 to 27°C water.

Active dry yeast is sold as loose granules in sealed envelopes or jars, which can be kept at cool room temperature until they're opened when leftovers should be refrigerated or frozen. To revive it, mix it in warm water (105 to 110°F/40 to 43°C) before adding it to the flour. Water hotter than 140°F/60°C will kill yeasts and produce a dough that doesn't rise.

Instant yeast is a version of active dry yeast that can be mixed directly into the other ingredients without an initial revival.

The proportion of yeast helps determine how fast a dough rises and what the bread will taste like. It can vary tenfold from one recipe to another. A high dose will raise dough in 2 hours, while a low dose may take 10 hours or more.

Choose low-yeast recipes for a slow rise and delicate grain flavor, high-yeast recipes for a quick rise and strong yeasty flavor. The flavor of packaged yeast can be harsh and mask the flavor of the grains.

BREAD INGREDIENTS: PRE-FERMENTS AND STARTERS

Pre-ferments and starters are yeast preparations that have been actively growing for a few hours or more before they're incorporated into a dough. Various versions are called sponge, levain, biga, and poolish.

Pre-ferments and starters produce a complex bread flavor and slow staling. They reduce or eliminate the harsh flavor of packaged yeast, and include flavor-producing bacteria whose tart acids slow staling and spoilage.

Pre-ferments are made by mixing a small amount of commercial yeast with some flour and water hours before making the dough. Liquid and unsalted pre-ferments develop more quickly than firm and salted ones.

Sourdough starters are made without commercial yeast. Flour is mixed with water and various other ingredients, often including fruits, milk, or honey, to encourage yeast growth. Desirable bacteria also grow and produce the acids that make sourdough sour.

Sourdough starters can be tricky to develop and maintain. They may take several days to develop enough leavening yeasts to make bread. If not fed often enough they become too acid, which inhibits yeasts and weakens gluten, and produce dense loaves rather than light ones.

If a starter becomes too acid, dilute a small amount in several times its volume of water and flour, and feed it regularly. Use the acid leftovers to make sourdough pancakes, with baking soda to moderate the acidity.

To keep starter yeasts happy and bubbly, refresh semiliquid starters twice a day with fresh water and flour and a good aerating whisking. To make room for the new ingredients, remove some of the starter and use or discard it. If that schedule isn't feasible, add more flour to make a stiff dough and refrigerate it; divide and refresh this slower-growing starter every few days.

Use a starter to make dough only when it's actively growing and bubbly. If it's been in refrigerator hibernation, bring it out a day or two ahead of time and get it growing again.

Be sure to add a full measure of salt to the dough, to help control bacterial gluten-weakening enzymes.

Raise doughs from starters at moderate room temperature, around 70°F/20°C, which favors yeast growth.

Adapt fermenting and baking schedules to your pre-ferment or starter. Each one is different.

OTHER COMMON BREAD INGREDIENTS

Bakers use a number of other ingredients to adjust the qualities of doughs and breads, and to flavor and enrich them.

Vitamin C or ascorbic acid helps strengthen gluten structure.

Lecithin helps slow staling and the firming of bread texture.

Most other bread ingredients interrupt gluten structure and make a denser, more tender loaf. Nuts, coarse grains, and dried fruit are examples. In addition:

Sugars and honey sweeten bread and help it retain moisture, and slow staling. They speed yeast growth in small quantities, but slow it in very sweet doughs.

Oils and fats slow moisture loss and provide their own sensation of moistness.

Milk and other dairy products contribute their own flavor and speed browning and more flavor development with their protein and lactose sugar.

Whole eggs and egg yolks contribute flavor and fatty moistness, deepen color, and slow staling.

THE ESSENTIALS OF MAKING YEAST BREADS

The ingredients for a good yeast bread arc good flour, the right proportion of water, an active yeast culture, time, and flexibility.

Try to work with recipes that specify weights, and use an accurate scale to reproduce them. The volume occupied by a fixed weight of flour varies depending on how loosely or firmly packed the flour is, so a cup of flour measured in your kitchen may contain significantly more or less flour than a cup measured by the recipe writer.

The ratio of water to flour in a recipe helps determine the dough's consistency and the bread's texture. The flour type also matters because different flours absorb different amounts of water, bread flour more than all-purpose flour, whole-grain flour more than refined flour.

A bagel ratio of about 50 parts water to 100 parts flour by weight, or 50 percent hydration, produces a vcry firm dough and a very dense, chewy texture.

A standard sandwich-bread ratio of about 65 percent hydration produces a firm, easily kneaded dough and a dense, even texture.

A baguette ratio of about 70 percent hydration produces a more easily stretched dough and a more open interior.

A ciabatta ratio of about 75 percent hydration produces a sticky dough that's messy to knead, and an open, irregular interior. A similar ratio using absorbent bread flour makes pizza dough, easily kneaded and stretched.

A wet ratio of 80 to 90 percent hydration produces a dough that can be lifted and folded but not kneaded, and that can fall when put in the oven and then rise into a moist, irregular loaf.

In a typical home bread recipe for a couple of loaves, it takes only a few spoonfuls more or less of flour or water to make the difference between a loose ciabatta dough and a firm sandwich-bread dough.

The bread-making process has five steps:

- mixing the wet and dry ingredients into a dough,
- kneading the dough to develop its elasticity,
- letting the dough expand, or rise, and further develop its elasticity,
- shaping the dough for baking, and
- baking.

There are several general approaches to the bread-making process, each with its own advantages and drawbacks.

Mixing and kneading by hand takes 30 to 45 minutes of hands-on work and cleanup.

Mixing and kneading in a stand mixer or food processor saves 10 to 15 minutes of hands-on time but little or no cleanup time.

No-knead methods save much of the hands-on work time and cleanup, and can produce just as good a loaf as hand or machine kneading does.

Quick-rise methods give you fresh-baked bread from scratch in a few hours, but with a strong processed-yeast flavor from the large dose of yeast and warm rising temperature.

Long-rise methods produce more flavorful loaves by giving a small amount of yeast or starter a long time to grow and produce flavor. They offer more flexibility in the timing of the various steps, but require more advance planning because they take all day or overnight.

Bread machines automate the mixing, kneading, rising, and baking, and save time and cleanup, but don't produce the best texture or flavor.

Develop your own personal method for making bread. Experiment with different recipes and adopt the details that work best in your kitchen and your life.

MIXING AND KNEADING DOUGH

Mixing the flour, water, leavening, and other ingredients forms the bread dough. It creates an inner network of gluten proteins that will trap gas bubbles and make possible a light, airy interior.

To make dough by hand with minimal cleanup, use a large, shallow bowl for both mixing and kneading. Transfer the finished dough to a narrower bowl for rising, and simply scrape the mixing bowl clean with a flexible plastic scraper.

Don't leave a stand mixer unattended when it's mixing or kneading dough. The dough can climb up the dough hook and cause the machine to vibrate its way off the countertop.

To mix dough in less than a minute, use a food processor. Be careful not to overheat or overwork the dough. Start with cool to cold water, briefly pulse just often enough to form the dough, and allow the dough to cool down to 70 to 75°F / 20 to 25°C before covering for fermentation.

Kneading the new dough strengthens the gluten network and its gas-trapping ability by repeatedly stretching it, and adds tiny air pockets to inflate during fermentation and baking.

Kneading is an optional and flexible step. The dough's gluten network will also be stretched and strengthened from within as the gas bubbles expand during the rising.

Knead the dough if you enjoy seeing and feeling it develop its responsive elasticity, and especially if it will rise quickly, in a couple of hours. The less time it has to stretch and develop itself, the more it can benefit from kneading.

Shorten or skip the kneading in most recipes if you're short on time, and especially if the dough will ferment overnight or longer.

"Lift and fold" doughs that are too wet to knead. Use hands, a spatula, or a scraper to lift one edge of the dough, stretch it straight up, then fold it onto the rest of the dough. Work all the way around the dough mass, then let it rest, and repeat as desired or directed.

FERMENTING DOUGH

During the fermentation, or rising, the yeasts grow and fill the dough with bubbles of carbon dioxide gas. Fermentation may last just 1 to 2 hours, or 12 hours or more, depending on the yeast dose or starter activity and the temperature.

Put the dough to rise in a narrow, steep-sided bowl about three times its volume, to help the dough retain gas from the fermentation and stretch its gluten network fully. Cover the bowl to prevent drying out.

The dough temperature strongly affects rising time and bread flavor. Yeasts are living cells, and are much more active when they're warm. At cool room temperatures they grow and raise dough slowly and produce a delicate, complex flavor. Higher temperatures speed their production of gas and stronger flavors. An increase of 10°F/6°C can shorten the fermentation time by a third.

To raise bread as quickly as possible, put the dough in a warm place, 80 to 85°F/27 to 30°C. The dough will develop a strong, yeasty flavor.

To make bread with a more delicate and complex flavor, raise the dough at cool room temperature, 70 to 75°F/20 to 25°C or below.

Allow fermenting dough to rise until it has expanded significantly and feels light and soft rather than dense and elastic when poked.

Scrape the dough down along edges and knead gently to deflate it and reorient the gluten network. If you have time, repeat the rising and scraping down for more gluten and flavor development.

Retarding fermentation in the refrigerator is a very useful technique. Refrigerator temperatures slow yeast metabolism and dough rising to a crawl. They also firm the dough and make it easier to handle.

Refrigerate the dough to delay baking for a day or more. Mix a batch of dough ahead of time, refrigerate it, and use portions to bake fresh bread on several different days.

For an open, rustic interior structure, refrigerate fermented dough for 12 to 24 hours after the final rise, or after forming loaves. This redistributes the inner gases to form fewer and larger bubbles.

FORMING AND RAISING LOAVES

Give the dough time to rest when you divide it and form loaves. Pause regularly to allow each piece to sit for a few minutes. Handling stretches the dough and causes it to pull back and resist shaping, but it relaxes when rested.

For a fine-textured, dense bread to be used for sandwiches or over several days, form the dough into large, round loaves.

For a more open, irregular interior and maximum crustiness, form elongated or small, divided loaves such as baguettes, ciabattas, and rolls. Thin or small loaves expand faster in the oven and have more surface area for forming the crust.

To encourage a well-aerated interior, support shaped loaves for rising in bread pans, bowls, or baskets. Choose dark metal or glass pans for faster baking and a darker, thicker crust.

To prevent the sticking of loaves that will be turned out from bowls or baskets, line containers with floured cloth sprinkled with wheat bran or with cornmeal, finely ground to avoid grittiness.

Allow formed loaves to rise until they've expanded but are still springy to the touch.

To encourage expansion during baking and to decorate the loaf, slash shallow-angled cuts into the top of loaves with a razor blade or very sharp knife. Cut just before baking. This will allow the expanding moist interior to push the hardening crust aside and rise through it.

BAKING

Baking cooks a soft, fragile mass of dough into a stable, solid loaf of bread. Oven heat causes the gas bubbles to expand and the loaf to rise, and then sets the starch and gluten into a rigid structure. Several initial minutes of steam heat will boost the dough's rise significantly and create a glossy crust.

Bake bread in an electric oven if you have a choice. Electric ovens are usually sealed more tightly than gas ovens and retain steam better.

To approximate the even, high heat of a traditional bread oven, place heat-retaining ceramic inserts or common bricks in the oven, and preheat it long enough to bring them up to 450°F/230°C. Modern oven heating elements cycle on and off and can quickly scorch loaf surfaces.

Bake loaves on a baking stone or ceramic tiles instead of a baking sheet to get the best initial rise and a thick, crunchy bottom crust. Preheat the oven for at least 30 minutes to get the stone or tiles hot.

To fill an oven with steam, fill a large cast-iron pan with clean pebbles or small rocks, a heavy steel chain, or large ball bearings. Place it in the oven below or to the side of where you'll place the loaves. Preheat the oven and pan to the oven's highest temperature for at least 30 minutes. When you slide the loaves into the oven, toss a dozen ice cubes into the pan and quickly close the oven door. Be careful: misdirected ice can crack baking stones and warp oven floors, and steam burns skin instantly. Lower the temperature to 450°F/230°C.

To use the dough's own moisture to create steam, bake in a clay baking cloche or in a pot and lid, which make an intimate oven within the oven. Preheat the pot and lid along with the oven, remove them and carefully roll the dough into the pot, cover, and return it to the oven.

Minimize bumps and shocks to the dough loaves as you transfer them to the oven; these pop gas bubbles and deflate the dough. Wet doughs can tolerate some deflation since they're loose and quickly reinflate in the oven. Turn the loaves out onto a rimless pan or baker's peel, a flat paddle designed for sliding breads in and out of the oven. Coat the loaf bottoms and/or the pan or peel with wheat bran, or line the surface with parchment paper, to help the loaves slide without sticking.

Leave the paper under the bread until it's fully baked, or baked enough that the paper easily pulls free.

Turn down the oven heat after 10 to 15 minutes to 400°F/200°C to prevent scorching by the heating elements. If loaves are browning unevenly, turn and move them.

Check the loaves for doneness when the crust turns an even brown. Tapping on the bottom of a fully cooked loaf should make a resonant, hollow sound. An instant-read thermometer inserted into the loaf will register above 200°F/93°C.

For a thicker crust, or if you're in doubt about doneness, keep baking, turning down the heat to 250 to 300°F / 120 to 150°C if the crust is getting dark.

Cool finished loaves on a stove-top grate or a rack, not a solid surface that will trap moisture and soften the bottom crust.

Resist the temptation to cut the bread while it's still hot. Even a sharp knife will tear and compact the soft interior.

Cool the loaves completely before wrapping them for storage.

UNUSUAL RAISED BREADS: BAGELS AND SWEET BREADS

Some popular raised breads call for special handling.

Bagels are small, chewy bread rings with a shiny crust and dense interior. Use high-gluten bread flour to make a dry, stiff dough. After making the dough and forming rings, retard them in the refrigerator overnight. Briefly immerse the warmed rings in simmering water flavored with malt syrup to develop the crust, then bake them.

Brioche, panettone, and other sweet and enriched breads require several adjustments to the standard methods due to their added sugar, eggs, and/or butter. Large amounts of sugar slow yeast growth and cause rapid browning in the oven. Eggs and butter weaken gluten. Good recipes call for extra yeast, longer rising times, and lower baking temperatures, and often direct that eggs and butter be added after the other ingredients are mixed and kneaded to make the gluten. Chilling firms enriched doughs so they're easier to handle and shape.

FLATBREADS: PITA, TORTILLAS, ROTI, NAAN, INJERA, CRACKERS, AND OTHERS

Flatbreads are traditional convenience foods, the quickest way to enjoy the deliciousness of fresh-baked bread. It takes just a few minutes to make the dough, roll it out thin, and cook it on a hot surface.

To make flatbreads even more convenient, keep the dough in the refrigerator for up to a week, and pull off pieces to cook immediately whenever you want them.

Flatbreads can be made from any grain that will form a doughlike paste, and even from chickpeas, a seed legume. Whole-grain flours make especially flavorful and nourishing flatbreads. Leavened wheat doughs make especially puffy, light ones.

To make tender unleavened flatbreads, roll or press the dough out to ⅛ to ¼ inch/3 to 6 millimeters thick, and cook briefly on high heat. Thicker sheets and lower heat slow cooking and produce tougher breads. Leavened doughs are tenderized by their bubbles and can be made in a range of thicknesses.

Cook most flatbreads on a very hot stove-top griddle or a pan with a low rim, or on a ceramic baking stone in an oven preheated to 500°F/260°C. Avoid nonstick surfaces that can't tolerate high heat. Check cooking temperatures with an infrared thermometer or by flicking flour onto the hot surface; it should start to brown in a few seconds. Turn the dough occasionally until the surfaces blister and darken. Stack the breads together to keep them warm and moist until they're served.

To make pocket breads whose two sides puff apart, roll out or press the dough to a thickness of ⅛ inch/3 millimeters. Thicker sheets are often too dense to split evenly during cooking.

To restore the softness of leftover flatbreads, reheat them directly over a low stove-top flame, on a medium-hot griddle, or between two plates in the microwave.

To make dry crackers, roll the dough very thin, dock it by gently pressing fork tines into the surface to limit blistering, cut it into pieces, and bake them in a moderate oven until dry and crisp.

PIZZAS

Pizzas are leavened flatbreads that are decorated with a variety of toppings. They're made in many different styles and may be thin or thick, brittle or chewy or soft, baked on a metal pan, ceramic stone, or even on an outdoor grill.

Pizzas in the original style of Naples, Italy, are thin-crusted disks baked on stone in very hot ovens for just 2 to 3 minutes until slightly charred. Pizzas baked on oiled metal pans partly fry and must cook longer to get crisp. Grilled pizzas are made by grilling the dough alone until stiff, then adding toppings and finishing.

The main challenges in pizza making are stretching the dough into a thin sheet, sliding a Naples-style disk intact onto a baking stone, and getting the top bubbling and the crust well browned.

To ease the handling of pizza dough:

- *Mix a relatively wet dough* that will spread easily.
- *Once the dough has risen, punch it down thoroughly* to eliminate gas pockets that would blister in the oven.
- *Divide the dough into relatively small pieces* that will form manageable plate-size disks rather than pizzeria diameters. If there's time, chill them to make them less elastic.
- *Pull or roll out the pieces, resting the dough regularly* to relax its gluten and lower its resistance to stretching. For thin-crust pizzas, aim for a thickness of ⅛ to ³/₁₆ inch/3 to 5 millimeters.
- *For the crispest, most flavorful crust,* prepare dough disks so that you can slide them onto a preheated baking stone in the oven. Form or place them on a rimless pan or baking peel lined for easier sliding with a piece of parchment paper cut to size, or generously sprinkled with wheat bran.
- *Apply toppings sparingly, sparsely, and with a light touch,* to avoid weighing the dough down, causing it to stick to the peel, or producing a soggy result. Precook vegetable toppings that won't soften in a few minutes of high heat, and squeeze out any surplus moisture.

Preheat the oven to its maximum temperature. If using a baking stone, place it just above or below a heating element. If the stone is just below the broiler, place a second stone or baking sheet on a lower rack to finish pizzas whose tops cook faster than the crust.

Slide the pizza briskly onto the baking stone, or place the baking sheet in the oven. Make sure that no ignitable parchment edges end up close to the broiler. For a crisper baking-sheet crust, place the sheet on the oven floor or just above the lower heating element. Remove the pizza when the top is sizzling and the bottom well colored.

To keep pizza crusts as crisp as possible, transfer them from the oven to a cooling rack, and cut them using kitchen shears. Crusts quickly soften when placed hot against a cutting board or plate that traps steam.

QUICK BREADS

Quick breads include scones, soda bread, and cornbread. They are made and raised in minutes with baking powder and/or baking soda, rather than with slow-growing yeasts. They're tender rather than chewy, relatives of cakes and muffins that usually contain less sugar and fat. They stale quickly.

Chemical leavenings are handy but quirky. Baking soda requires an acid partner, often buttermilk, to generate carbon dioxide. Baking powder is a complete leavener that contains both baking soda and one or more acid partners.

Use fresh baking soda and baking powder. Old batches lose their leavening power and have an off flavor.

Make sure that there's a partner acid in recipes calling for baking soda. If not, the result will be dense and taste soapy.

Blend baking soda or baking powder thoroughly with other dry ingredients. This can take a full 60 seconds of whisking. Unevenly distributed leavening can cause an uneven texture and brown spots and other odd colors, including green carrot shreds and blue walnuts.

Mix wet and dry ingredients briefly and bake immediately. Chemical leavenings begin to release some carbon dioxide as soon as they get wet.

Manipulation of the dough or batter toughens the gluten and the texture.

For quick breads that stale less quickly, use recipes that include whole grains, some oil, fat, egg yolk, and/or sugar, or that call for both baking powder and an acidic ingredient. A tart loaf stales more slowly.

Restore stale quick breads by reheating them.

Biscuits American style are made from doughs rich with butter, lard, or shortening and raised with baking powder or soda and steam. They're either stiff enough to roll to ½ inch/13 millimeters thick and cut out into disks, or they're very tender free-form morsels. Biscuits are small and bake quickly, and require a hot oven to puff them up.

Make biscuit dough with a low-protein flour, and handle the dough as little as possible, to minimize gluten formation and chewiness. Use a soft flour from the southeastern United States, or pastry flour, or a mixture of 2 parts all-purpose flour with 1 part cornstarch.

Make sure the cutter has a sharp edge. Pressed edges inhibit expansion and rise during baking.

Bake biscuits in a very hot oven to maximize steam production inside the dough.

FRIED BREADS: DOUGHNUTS AND FRITTERS

Doughnuts and fritters are deep-fried pieces of dough. Some are also made from more liquid batters. Doughnuts are usually sweet, while fritters may be sweet or savory.

Fry most doughnuts and fritters in a fresh neutral oil. Avoid strongly flavored corn and olive oils.

For doughnuts or fritters to be served cool, fry in shortening or another fat that is solid at room temperature. This leaves the doughnut surface dry and waxy rather than greasy.

Keep the oil temperature around 350°F/175°C. Lower temperatures increase oil absorption; higher temperatures will brown the dough surfaces excessively before the interior cooks through. The sweeter the dough, the faster it will brown. Don't crowd the pot with too many pieces of dough, which will drop the oil temperature too far and slow its recovery.

Shake off excess oil immediately and vigorously as you remove the doughnuts or fritters, while the oil on their surfaces is still hot and runny.

18

PASTRIES
AND PIES

P astries offer the pleasures of dryness, the crisp and crumbly and flaky and browned. Like breads, pastries are mixtures of ground grains and water and air, cooked into a solid mass. But they contain very little water and include a tenderizing measure of fat, which breaks up their structure and prevents them from being simply hard. Some pastries stand on their own, while others serve as contrasting containers for moist fruits, rich custards, and savory stews and pâtés.

Pastry making can be a challenge because some recipes work right at the edge of failure. There may be barely enough moisture to hold things together, or just a few degrees separating workable butter consistency from either dough-ripping hardness or dough-weakening softness. The dough layers in strudel and phyllo and puff pastry end up thinner than a human hair, and on a dry day can harden and crack in moments.

The methods for making these very fine pastry layers involve very specific manipulations of the dough, long and tedious to describe in words, but quickly and effectively demonstrated. Here I'll stick to basic descriptions of the methods and how they work. For the turn-by-turn details and tricks, watch some of the many good video demonstrations on the Web.

I've found that, as is true of baking, the best way to make good pastry is to make it often, ideally every day or two, so you can experience failure and learn to recognize landmarks on the way to success. If you make pastry only occasionally, then relax and enjoy your exploration of this unique branch of baking. Most failed crusts still taste good. And you'll appreciate the artistry of an excellent pastry more than ever.

PASTRY SAFETY

Most pastries pose no hazard to health. They're thoroughly cooked and inhospitably dry for microbes.

Filled pastries, especially those containing eggs, dairy products, or meats, may be moist and rich enough to harbor harmful bacteria, though they're commonly kept at room temperature for many hours.

To minimize the risk of foodborne illness from filled pastries, eat them promptly, or store them in the refrigerator or freezer and reheat to a minimum of 160°F/70°C before serving.

SHOPPING FOR PASTRY INGREDIENTS AND STORING PASTRIES

Most pastry ingredients are standard pantry items: flours and sugars, fats and oils. Of course it's best for them to be as fresh as possible so you don't start out with stale flavors.

Read recipes carefully to make sure you have or buy the correct ingredients. There are many different flours and sugars and fats, and they're often not interchangeable.

Store uncooked pie crusts, puff pastry, and other pastry doughs in the freezer, well wrapped to protect against off odors and freezer burn. Some can be baked directly from the freezer. Thaw others in the refrigerator before using them.

Store finished pastries without dairy or meat fillings in a bread box or paper bag for a day or two in a dry climate, wrapped tightly in a humid climate. Wrap them tightly and refrigerate or freeze them for longer keeping.

Store finished pastries with dairy or meat fillings wrapped tightly in the refrigerator for a few days or freeze.

SPECIAL TOOLS FOR PASTRY MAKING

A number of special utensils are good to have on hand when making pastries.

A marble or granite slab has a high heat capacity and helps keep the fat from warming and softening excessively as pastry doughs are made and shaped.

A rolling pin makes it possible to form pastry doughs into evenly thin sheets. Rolling pins are made from wood, metal, and plastic, in different shapes and sizes, with and without handles. Plastic and nonstick surfaces usually do stick less and are easier to clean.

Rolling pin spacers are bands that fit over the ends of a rolling pin to lift it a certain height from the rolling surface. They make it easier to roll pastry evenly to a specific thickness.

Pastry tubes and bags are tools for extruding or piping choux pastry dough and other soft ingredients (whipped cream, pastry cream, decorative icings) into neat shapes or patterns.

Tart and pie pans determine how oven heat penetrates pastry doughs during baking. They come in many finishes, shapes, and dimensions, all of which affect heating and may require adjustments in baking time or temperature. Heavy metal pans with a dull surface are a good general-purpose choice.

PASTRY INGREDIENTS: FLOURS AND STARCHES

Several different kinds of flours and starches are used to make the cohesive, solid part of pastries. They're very different and can't be directly substituted for each other. Low-protein pastry and cake flours form a more tender gluten than moderate-protein all-purpose flours, and absorb less water. So the same amount of water that produces a firm dough with all-purpose flour may produce a wet sticky one with pastry or cake flour.

Use the flour specified in a recipe, or be ready to adjust proportions and handling to compensate for not doing so. Raise the protein content of a flour by adding some vital gluten, or lower it by adding cornstarch.

All-purpose flours have a versatile medium protein content, but it varies significantly among brands and regions of the country. Try to use the brands specified in recipes, or be aware of the possible need to make adjustments. Southern U.S. brands tend to be lower in protein and better for tender pastries, northeastern and northwestern brands higher in protein and better for flaky pastries. National brands are most balanced and versatile.

Pastry flour is low in protein for making tender crusts and cookies. It's often hard to find in supermarkets. To approximate it, mix 2 parts all-purpose flour with 1 part cake flour (measuring by either weight or volume).

Cake flour is low in protein and chemically treated to make tender cakes that can handle large proportions of sugar and fat. To approximate it, mix 6 parts all-purpose flour with 1 part cornstarch.

Bread flour is high in strong gluten protein and sometimes called for in crisp choux and puff pastries.

Whole-wheat flour is sometimes used for its richer flavor, color, and nutritional value. It quickly goes stale and becomes bitter and rancid. Check sell-by dates on packages, and store them tightly wrapped in the refrigerator or freezer. Let them warm again to room temperature before opening.

Precooked or instant flours, often packaged as a quick gravy ingredient, are sometimes used to make pastry doughs easier to handle. They behave more like starch than flour, and have a characteristic cooked flavor.

Cornstarch is a protein-free pure starch often used to thicken fruit pie fillings, and to lower the effective protein content of all-purpose flour for tender pastries.

Tapioca and tapioca starch are protein-free starches that are also used to thicken fruit pie fillings. They produce a clearer filling than cornstarch.

PASTRY INGREDIENTS: FATS AND OILS

Fats give flavor, moistness, and richness to pastries, but their main job is to break up the dough's structure and make it flaky or crumbly. Solid butter, lard, and shortening can make flaky or crumbly pastries. Semi-solid poultry fats and liquid oils make tender crumbly pastries. Low-fat spreads don't work in pastry making.

Fats develop stale, rancid flavors when exposed to air and light, and these can spoil otherwise well-made pastries.

Check fats for off flavors before using. Scrape away any discolored surface areas from butter, lard, or shortening. If measuring from a stick of fat, be sure to compensate for any you've scraped off.

Butter is delicious and can make excellent pastries, but is trickier to work with than shortening when making flaky pastries. It's brittle and unworkable when very cold, pliable over a range of a few degrees, and then unworkably soft at warm room temperature and above.

Butter is also about 15 percent water, and may be salted. "European-style" butters generally contain more fat and less water than standard American butters. Most pastry recipes specify unsalted butter. Substitutions will require adjustments in added water and/or salt.

Lard, fat rendered from the pig, is soft but melts at a higher temperature than butter, and makes good flaky pastries. It readily develops off flavors and may already be stale when bought. Most commercial lard contains antioxidants and is also hydrogenated to slow this deterioration, and therefore may contain unhealthful trans fats. Choose lard with a sell-by date well in the future, and look for freshly rendered lard in butcher shops and ethnic markets.

Vegetable shortenings are made by chemical manipulation of vegetable oils to be an ideal solid fat for pastry and cakes, workable over a broad temperature range, and prefilled with tiny leavening bubbles of nitrogen gas. They're either flavorless or artificially flavored to resemble butter. Most no longer have any trans fats.

Vegetable oils are liquid at room temperature and can't form the separate sheets that butter and shortening do to make a flaky structure in doughs. They tenderize and moisten throughout the dough.

OTHER PASTRY INGREDIENTS

Pastry doughs often include a number of other ingredients that can affect both flavor and texture.

Salt contributes to a balanced taste in all pastries, savory or sweet.

Sugar makes pastries more tender as well as sweetening them, by absorbing moisture and limiting gluten development. In low-moisture doughs, powdered confectioners' sugar dissolves most quickly and reliably.

Liquid ingredients are usually added to pastry doughs last, to minimize gluten development that makes the dough tough and pastries chewy. The ratio of water to flour is critical for determining the consistency of a dough and the texture of the pastry it makes.

Vinegar or some other acid is often included to limit gluten development and make pastry doughs more pliable.

Eggs provide cohesiveness; yolks also contribute color, richness, and flavor.

Check and use the egg size specified in recipes. A different size will throw off the critical balance between liquid and flour.

Dairy products, from simple milk and cream to cream cheese and aged cheeses, contribute tenderizing fat, add their own flavor, and promote faster and deeper browning.

THE ESSENTIALS OF PASTRY MAKING

Most pastries are made from a stiff dough of flour and just enough water to hold the flour particles together, along with fat or oil that interrupts the dough structure and makes the baked pastry fragile and tender instead of hard.

Pastry structure and texture are created by the cook's choice of fat or oil, and the technique used to combine it with the flour.

- **A pastry will crumble into small bits** in the mouth if you work any fat or oil thoroughly into the flour.
- **A pastry will come apart in thin, broad flakes** if you break a solid fat into chunks and roll it out into thin sheets that separate the mass of flour into layers. Those layers become separate dough layers, and bake into separate flakes of pastry.

Making pastry requires greater precision than other kinds of cooking. Small differences in ingredients, proportions, pan materials, and handling can make big differences in the finished pastry. Pastry recipes are often very precise for that reason. Even so:

No recipe can tell you precisely what to do with your particular set of ingredients and pans and oven.

If you can, make pastries often to develop eyes and fingertips that know when a dough needs a little more water or a little more time to warm up.

MIXING AND FORMING PASTRY DOUGHS

The three basic rules for making pastry doughs are:

- *Measure the ingredients precisely.*
- *Keep the ingredients cool or cold.*
- *Handle the dough as little as possible,* just long enough to distribute all the ingredients.

Each rule helps minimize the development of stretchy gluten in the flour, which would result in a tough pastry that shrinks during the baking.

Measure ingredients by weight whenever possible. If a recipe specifies only volumes, be sure to measure them as directed. Sifting, leveling, and other details can change ingredient volumes significantly.

Sift dry ingredients after measuring to make them easier to mix evenly with the water.

Crumbly pastry doughs are relatively forgiving because the tenderizing fat is worked evenly into the flour. The fat can begin to melt without affecting the dough structure, and it gives added insurance against gluten development during the mixing and handling.

Flaky and layered doughs require careful temperature control and handling, to keep the pieces of solid fat pliable but not soft and limit gluten development in the dough between the fat pieces.

Work in a cool part of the kitchen, in the cool part of the day.

Start with prechilled ingredients and bowls.

Minimize heat from hands and high-energy machines. Pulse mixers and processors briefly on and off. Stop and chill the dough if the fat begins to get too soft.

Keep the dough temperature cool, around 58 to 68°F / 15 to 20°C when working with butter, 58 to 75°F / 15 to 25°C with lard. Shortenings remain firm enough at temperatures up to 85°F/30°C.

To mix most pastry doughs, combine fat and flour first, then just enough cool liquid to hold the dough together. Knead just long enough to wet the flour evenly.

Be ready to adjust the liquid amount. The correct proportion depends on many unpredictable details of flour composition and fineness of fat mixing.

To disperse a small volume of water evenly into a flour-fat mixture with minimal handling, use a water mister. First measure how many sprays add up to a given volume or weight, then spread the mixture out and spray across its entire surface.

Roll out the finished dough immediately, or refrigerate for an hour or more to distribute the moisture evenly, relax the gluten, and make the dough easier to handle. Flatten dough into a disk before refrigerating to speed cooling and reduce later rolling out. Store fresh pastry doughs for several days in the refrigerator or weeks in the freezer.

To roll out a dough that has been refrigerated, let it warm up until its fat softens and it can be worked without cracking.

Roll dough out on a cold surface or cloth, rotating the dough to prevent sticking. If the dough resists or contracts, chill it for 5 to 10 minutes to relax the elastic gluten.

Chill rolled-out dough briefly just before baking, to avoid shrinking or slumping when it heats up.

BAKING AND COOLING

Pastry doughs usually cook quickly because they're so thin and dry. They can also overcook quickly. So it's good to know your oven well and watch the baking closely.

Study your oven while it heats up and during cooking. Use an infrared thermometer to check actual floor, roof, and wall temperatures at a given thermostat setting. Get to know where heat comes from, and how to control it to suit particular pastries.

Oven heating elements switch on during baking—which you can hear as a hiss or click—to maintain the thermostat temperature. They're hot enough to scorch pastries if they switch on often.

To avoid overbrowning pastries at the correct thermostat setting, keep the heating elements off as much as possible.

- *Place a baking stone on the oven floor* to retain heat and shield the heating element. Or shield with a sheet of kitchen foil, shiny side facing down.
- *Preheat the oven 25 to 50°F/15 to 30°C hotter* than the baking temperature so that loading the oven will bring it down to the baking temperature. Then reset the thermostat to the baking temperature.
- *Open the oven door as seldom and briefly as possible.*

To bake most pastries evenly, place them in a single layer on the middle rack. Correct uneven heating by moving pans to different positions during baking.

Different baking pans and molds heat pastries differently. If you switch to a different kind, or don't use the kind specified in a recipe, you may need to adjust baking temperatures or times. These differences are less important in a convection oven.

Thick, heavy metal pans heat more evenly and quickly than flimsy ones. Shiny metal pans reflect heat away and heat slowly. Dull pans absorb more heat and heat up faster. Dark-finish pans heat the fastest. Glass pans transmit some heat radiation directly to the pastry and cook more quickly than opaque ceramic pans.

To prevent edges and surfaces from overbrowning while pastries cook through, shield them with pieces of foil or pastry guards once they begin to color.

Cool pastries on a rack, not on a solid surface. A rack provides constant air cooling and, for pastries removed from the pan, an escape route for any remaining moisture that would otherwise get trapped and compromise crispness.

CRUSTS

Crusts are thin layers of dry pastry designed to support or contain something moist, often fruits, a custard or cream, or a pâté. They should be moisture-resistant to prevent sogginess, and easily cut for serving and eating.

The simplest crusts are sweet pressed crusts. They're formed from the crumbs of already prepared baked goods or ground nuts, which are mixed with some combination of butter, sugar, corn syrup, and water, then pressed into a pan, and baked. The moist ingredients dissolve sugar into a syrup that glues the crumbs together as it bakes and dries, while the fat keeps some crumbs unglued and the structure easily fractured.

To avoid hardness in a pressed crust, include some sugar-free ground nuts or bread crumbs, and some corn syrup to weaken the sugar glue.

If a pressed crust slumps during baking, next time reduce the amount of fat and bake at a higher temperature.

Crusts made from rolled-out pastry dough are named inconsistently and prepared in many different ways from one cookbook to another. Their texture depends mainly on how the flour and fat are mixed, no matter how a recipe is named or described.

There are two basic styles of crust made from doughs: crumbly and flaky.

Crumbly crusts are crumbly because the fat and flour are thoroughly mixed before the liquid wets the flour into a dough.

For the most tender and crumbly crust, choose a recipe that mixes softened fat with flour and then adds liquid. The more fat and/or sugar in a recipe, the more tender the crust. If the dough is difficult to roll out, press it into the pan instead.

For a more cohesive crumbly crust, replace the water with egg, or mix fat and liquid first and add the flour last.

Flaky crusts break apart in crisp flakes because the fat and flour are layered in separate thin sheets before the liquid wets the flour into a dough.

To make a flaky crust, cut chilled fat into small pea-size pieces in the flour, by hand or in a mixer or processor, then add liquid, form the dough, and roll out once as a single mass.

For the flakiest crust, choose a recipe that first repeatedly rolls out chilled fat chunks in flour to form hundreds of thin sheets, then adds water to form the dough.

For a tender flaky crust, work the dough as little as possible, with frequent rests in the refrigerator, to avoid toughening the gluten.

Some rules apply to all rolled-out crusts.

To make any crumbly or flaky crust more tender, use pastry flour instead of all-purpose flour, or approximate pastry flour by replacing a third of the all-purpose flour with cake flour, or a quarter with instant flour or cornstarch.

To roll out any pastry dough evenly to the correct thickness for a crust, use specialty or improvised guides at each end of the rolling pin. Roll from the dough center outward. It you don't have guides, lift the rolling pin as you reach the edge to avoid overthinning it.

When placing pastry dough in a pan or mold, avoid letting it stretch, which thins it and can encourage it to contract when baked.

Refrigerate the dough in the pan before baking to relax the gluten and prevent it from shrinking when baked.

FILLED CRUSTS:
PIES AND TARTS

The challenge in making pies and tarts is to cook two very different materials—a barely moist dough and a wet filling—so that the dough ends up very dry and crisp and the filling thick and moist.

For a crust that best resists sogginess from wet fillings, choose a crumbly crust made with egg. Flaky crusts more readily soak up liquid.

To make sure that the crust won't be undercooked and to minimize sogginess, prebake the crust in the pan "blind," without filling. Line the crust with parchment paper and weigh it down with dry beans or ceramic pie weights for part of the prebaking. When weights are removed, "dock" the dough by pressing down with fork tines to prevent blistering. Protect exposed edges from excess heat with strips of kitchen foil or pie guards.

Give the prebaked crust a moisture-resistant coating of beaten egg, chocolate, melted butter, concentrated fruit preserves, or pastry cream, or a layer of moisture-absorbent crumbs. For an egg wash, return the crust to the oven for a few minutes until the coating is dry, then let it cool before filling and baking.

Fresh fruit fillings often release copious liquid and fail to thicken well, especially if the fruit has been sliced.

To control the consistency of a fresh fruit filling, concentrate and thicken the juices before baking. Cut the fruit, toss it with sugar in a colander, and let the juices drain into a bowl. Cook down the juices until thick, recombine them with the fruit and thickener, and fill the crust.

For a translucent fruit filling, thicken the fruit juices with tapioca instead of flour or cornstarch.

Bake fruit pies or tarts near the oven floor, or directly on a baking stone on the floor, to ensure rapid heating of the bottom crust.

Cream and custard pie fillings may fail to thicken in the oven, or may thicken well but then reliquefy.

For cream and custard fillings thickened with eggs and flour or starch, be sure to heat the flour-egg mixture to 180 to 190°F / 80 to 85°C, either before or during baking. Undercooked egg yolks contain an enzyme that breaks down starch and liquefies fillings.

Quiche fillings are easily overcooked and dried out.

Check quiches frequently during baking and remove from the oven as soon as a toothpick or knife tip inserted in the center comes out clean. Allow quiches to cool until the custard is firm enough to cut without slumping.

Lemon meringue pies often weep liquid from the meringue surface or the bottom, where it floats the meringue from the filling.

Make a stable meringue topping by using powdered sugar that includes cornstarch and placing the meringue on a lemon filling that's still hot. Or make a precooked meringue on the stove top, then place on the pie and finish it in the oven to warm it through and brown the edges.

Ensure a stable lemon filling by cooking the cornstarch-sugar-egg mixture to 180 to 190°F/80 to 85°C, and adding the lemon juice afterward off the heat.

PUFF PASTRY FOR TARTS AND NAPOLEONS, CROISSANTS, AND DANISH PASTRIES

Puff pastry is the ultimate flaky pastry. Where pie pastry is flaky but dense, puff pastry is a light and airy mass of crisp, paper-thin pastry sheets.

Puff pastry requires considerable care and several hours to make. You enclose a mass of butter in a flour dough, and then repeatedly roll out in one direction, fold up, quarter-turn, and roll again, until you've made hundreds of alternating butter-dough layers. When it's baked, moisture in the dough and butter vaporizes and puffs the greased dough layers apart.

The key to puff pastry is managing the temperature of the butter and the elasticity of the dough, so that the two materials can be rolled out together evenly and finely. The dough is refrigerated repeatedly so that the butter can cool down and the dough gluten can relax between rollings.

There are many different ways to make good puff pastry. Recipes often run five pages or more and can be intimidatingly precise, but they differ on many basic points, some even calling for precooked instant flour.

Find a recipe with clear and encouraging directions, and watch videos of the technique on the Web.

Pay special attention to the quality and consistency of the butter. Trim good butter of any surface discoloration and rancidity. Keep its temperature around 60°F/15°C. If much colder, it will tear the dough; if warmer it will melt into it and damage the layering.

Make a quick, less formal version of puff dough in about 2 hours. Cut butter into small pieces with flour, add cool water, and gather into a stiff dough; then roll out, fold, give a quarter-turn, and repeat; and rest the dough in the refrigerator. Repeat this sequence once or twice.

Cut any puff-pastry dough with a very sharp knife and by pressing down, not back and forth. For the best rise, the dough edges should be compressed or smeared as little as possible.

Chill and relax the dough after the final rolling and cutting to prevent shrinking in the oven.

Bake at a high initial oven temperature to maximize steam production and puffing up.

To use frozen manufactured dough, thaw it in the refrigerator and bring it to cool room temperature before cutting.

Croissants and Danish pastries are made from puff-pastry doughs that include yeast. Once the doughs are formed, they're allowed to rise before baking.

Danish dough mixes eggs and sugar with the flour. Croissant dough includes milk and is allowed to rise before being folded and rolled out with butter.

Croissant and Danish doughs require especially careful handling. They're softer and more fragile than standard puff-pastry dough.

PHYLLO AND STRUDEL

Phyllo and strudel are astoundingly delicate pastries, made from a single sheet of dough stretched to the thickness of a human hair. They're wrapped or rolled around a fruit or vegetable or meat filling, or stacked, then baked until golden and crisp.

Phyllo and strudel doughs are especially tricky to make. It's necessary to stretch out and handle a gossamer-thin sheet of dough 3 or 4 feet in diameter without having it tear, and to work quickly to prevent the sheet from drying out and cracking. Watch videos of the technique on the Web.

Use a high-protein flour that develops a strong gluten, and include oil to help make the dough less elastic.

Approximate strudel by overlapping manufactured phyllo sheets to make the desired dimensions.

To use frozen manufactured phyllo sheets, thaw them in the refrigerator. Keep the sheets covered or brush with oil or butter to protect them from drying out and cracking.

CHOUX PASTRIES: CREAM PUFFS AND GOUGÈRES

Choux or cream-puff pastry is unlike all other pastries. It bakes into a thin, crisp crust, but it starts out as a solid ball of moist precooked dough. High heat from an oven or frying oil sets the outside, vaporizes the moisture on the inside, and inflates the ball into a crisp, hollow shell (*choux*, pronounced "shoo," is French for "cabbage".) The shells are served as is or filled with whipped cream, pastry cream, or ice cream.

To make choux pastry dough:

- *Boil water or milk* in a saucepan together with butter, fat, or oil.
- *Remove the pan from the heat and beat in flour* to form a thick paste.
- *Heat and beat the paste for a few minutes* to cook it through and remove some moisture.
- *Remove from the heat and beat in the eggs one by one,* to blend them more evenly. If using a food processor for this step, beat the eggs together in a bowl and then pour slowly onto the dough.

To prepare choux dough that will bake into the lightest, crispest shells, use water instead of milk or cream, bread flour instead of all-purpose flour, more egg whites than yolks, and enough liquid to make the dough as fluid as possible while still able to hold its shape when spooned or squeezed from the tip of a pastry pipe. Milk fat and yolks produce a richer, softer pastry.

To make especially light versions of cheese-flavored gougères, replace the usual Gruyère with a drier grating cheese such as Parmesan.

Use the dough immediately or refrigerate it for up to a day.

Space the spooned or piped dough with room to expand on the baking sheet. Use a nonstick or greased surface that will readily release the sticky dough.

For crisper shells, shape the dough into small balls that will make thinner walls. Large shells may end up soft and heavy enough to collapse.

Bake in a hot 400 to 450°F / 200 to 230°C oven to generate a good burst of leavening steam. Watch puffs and turn down the heat when they begin to color, to dry them out. When they're fully colored, turn the oven off, cut knife slits in the crust bottoms to let steam escape, and leave to continue crisping in the cooling oven.

To keep and use finished choux pastries, freeze them wrapped airtight, and recrisp them directly from the freezer in a medium oven.

To bake an approximation of deep-fried choux pastry, prepare the shaped dough as above and brush the surfaces with oil before baking.

19

CAKES, MUFFINS, AND COOKIES

akes indulge our primal love of the sweet and rich, and make the ideal food for celebrations of all kinds. Like breads and pastries, cakes are mixtures of ground grains and water and air. But they flesh out these bare structural bones with sugar, fat, and eggs, and form tender masses that fall apart deliciously in the mouth. And we decorate them with even sweeter, richer glazes and icings, pleasure piled on pleasure.

Where pastries challenge the cook with scantness, by working with barely enough water to hold the flour and fat together, cakes challenge with plenitude, by loading the flour with as much sugar and fat as it can support. Food manufacturers have even gone to the trouble of developing special flours, shortenings, and mixes to maximize sweetness and richness. These ingredients accomplish that task well, but may not produce the most delicious cake. I wasn't reading ingredient lists during my early cake-eating years. But I did stick a finger—once—into a can of shortening, and can still remember how waxy and dead it seemed in my mouth. I really didn't care for cake until I was in my twenties and tasted one made by a local baker who used butter for both cake and icing. That was the moment when I understood what cakes are all about.

Whether you choose traditional or "improved" ingredients for making cakes, you'll want to use a good electric mixer, which can aerate a cake batter in minutes instead of the hour or two called for in nineteenth-century recipes, where the recommended appliance is a manservant. And you'll want to pay special attention to cake pans. The right size is important, so before you start mixing the batter, be sure to check what the recipe calls for and what you've got.

Cookies are miniature sweet baked goods of all sorts, from little pastries to little cakes. Because they're small and cook so quickly, they bake by their own rules.

CAKE AND COOKIE SAFETY

Cakes and cookies seldom pose any health hazard apart from their concentrated calories. They're thoroughly cooked and inhospitably dry and sweet for most microbes.

Uncooked or lightly cooked icings made with eggs can pose a slight risk of salmonella contamination.

To ensure that icings are safe, use pasteurized eggs or a technique that cooks the eggs to a minimum of 160°F/70°C, and store leftovers in the refrigerator.

SHOPPING FOR CAKE AND COOKIE INGREDIENTS AND STORING CAKES

Most baking ingredients are pantry staples and don't require special selection, except to choose the materials specified in recipes. There are many different flours, fats, leavenings, and egg sizes, and they're often not interchangeable.

Keep leftover cake covered at cool room temperature for a day or two, refrigerated for several days, or frozen for months.

Cover cut surfaces closely with wrap or foil to prevent drying out.

To freeze cake, place in the freezer long enough to firm the frosting, then wrap it tightly in plastic wrap, and then in a thicker plastic bag or foil to block off odors.

To thaw a cake with frosting, unwrap the cake and thaw it in the refrigerator, ideally covered with a cake dome or inverted bowl, to prevent moisture from condensing on the frosting. Then bring it out to room temperature.

To thaw a cake without frosting, leave it wrapped and warm it on the kitchen counter.

SPECIAL TOOLS FOR MAKING CAKES AND COOKIES

A number of specialized utensils and appliances make cake and cookie preparation easier.

A scale is especially valuable in cake making, where accurate flour measurements are essential for good results.

A flour sifter or fine-mesh strainer helps aerate dry flour, cocoa, and leavenings, so that they'll mix more readily and evenly with fat and wet ingredients. Sifting does not do a good job of blending dry ingredients; do this with a hand or electric whisk instead.

A countertop stand electric mixer with a "planetary" motion that moves the whisk around the bowl does the best job of beating batters and coatings for the 5 to 15 minutes often required.

A handheld electric mixer can mix cake batters well, provided you move it all around the bowl. It's not powerful enough for beating some stiff icings.

Mixing bowls hold the batter while it's beaten. Thin metal has the advantage of quick heat transfer in case the batter needs cooling or warming. Invest in several 2- to 4-quart bowls, since many recipes call for separate mixing of groups of ingredients.

Cake pans determine how oven heat penetrates the batter to raise and set it. They come in many finishes, shapes, and dimensions, all of which affect heating and may require adjustments in baking time or temperature. Most important is that the batter fill the pan between two-thirds and three-quarters full. Too large a pan will shield the cake bottom from oven heat; too small a pan will let the expanding batter overflow.

Sheet pans and baking sheets for making sheet cakes and cookies are best made of heavy-gauge metal that won't warp as it heats up or cools down.

Parchment paper can line pan bottoms and ease removal of cakes.

Nonstick sprays that contain oil, lecithin, and sometimes flour help grease pan interiors to ease removal of the finished cake. Butter and shortening do the same thing.

Silicone liners for baking sheets provide a nonstick surface for baking cookies.

Cake pan strips cool the pan sides during baking, slow the setting of the batter at the sides, and help produce a high and even oven rise.

A cake tester is a stiff wire for probing doneness at the cake's center. It's longer than a toothpick and leaves a smaller hole, but is so thin that underdone batter doesn't always stick to it. Many bakers test with a small knife.

A wire rack allows air to flow underneath and around the pan to cool evenly.

A turntable makes it easier to coat cakes evenly with icings and glazes.

A pastry bag and set of tips are versatile tools for piping icings into decorative designs.

A cake dome covers and protects the cake without touching and marring its surface.

CAKE AND COOKIE INGREDIENTS: FLOURS

Flour provides much of the solid structure of cakes and cookies with its protein and starch.

All-purpose wheat flour is the most versatile flour for making cakes and most commonly specified in recipes. Its high content of toughening gluten protein is not ideal but is balanced by added tenderizing ingredients, sugar and fat. Some recipes mix all-purpose flour with potato or other starches to increase tenderness.

Cake flour is a low-protein flour, very finely ground and treated with chlorine to carry far more sugar and fat than usual and produce "high-ratio" cakes. Commercial cake mixes include it. Many cake recipes call for it. Some bakers avoid it due to its somewhat harsh taste and the extremely fine texture it produces.

Self-rising cake flour includes chemical leavening.

Double-check recipes and labels to make sure you're using the specified flour. All-purpose and cake flours can't really be doctored to repalce each other.

CAKE AND COOKIE INGREDIENTS: FATS AND OILS

Fats and oils moisten and tenderize cakes and cookies by interrupting and weakening the protein-starch structure.

In cakes and cookies leavened by the creaming method, solid fats trap and accumulate tiny air bubbles that will expand during baking to raise and tenderize the cake.

Fats develop a rancid-tasting surface when exposed to air. Many wrappers allow air to reach butter and shortening.

Scrape away the surface of butter or shortening if it has become dark or translucent.

Oils become stale and then rancid when opened and kept for months. Taste old oil before baking with it.

Butter is the traditional cake fat and is still used to make the finest cakes. Butters vary in their butterfat content and in their flavor, but these differences are not as important in cakes as they are in pastries.

Butter is more sensitive to temperature than shortening during creaming, and often doesn't produce as light a cake, but its flavor is better.

Shortening is made from vegetable oils modified to optimize their cake-making qualities. It can be creamed over a wider temperature range than butter, and contains emulsifiers and tiny gas bubbles that aid in leavening.

Shortening makes cakes that rise higher and often keep better. Used with cake flour, it makes possible high-ratio cakes with more sugar and fat than a traditional cake, and a simple method of mixing all ingredients together in one bowl.

The main disadvantage of shortening is its artificial flavor.

Taste shortening and butter side by side, consider how they're made, and how important flavor, lightness, and ease of preparation are to you. Choose your fat and recipes accordingly.

Margarines are not useful in cake baking. They're designed for good spreading and to imitate the feeling of butter, not its aerating powers.

CAKE AND COOKIE INGREDIENTS: SUGARS

Sugars sweeten and soften the starch-protein structure of cakes and some cookies, and help retain moisture. They contribute to the crunch of low-moisture cookies. There are several kinds of sugar that can't always be substituted for each other.

Granulated table sugar consists of relatively coarse crystals, good for creating air bubbles during creaming, but slow to dissolve when liquid ingredients are added. In low-moisture cookies it may not dissolve at all, and contributes to crunchiness.

Superfine, or baker's, sugar consists of fine crystals, and is preferred by some bakers for creaming. It dissolves faster than table sugar. To make fine-grained sugar, grind table sugar in the food processor.

Powdered, or confectioners', sugar consists of sugar particles too fine to feel on the tongue and too fine for creaming. It's useful in making quick icings and other smooth-textured coatings. It contains a small amount of cornstarch.

Brown sugars, honey, and molasses contribute distinctive flavors, and retain moisture better than white sugar. All are somewhat acid, and can react with baking soda or other alkaline ingredients to produce leavening bubbles.

Corn syrup is a mild-flavored combination of glucose and long glucose chains in water. It speeds browning, retains moisture, and slows the hardening of texture in cookies.

Noncaloric sweeteners can't substitute for sugar's many roles in cakes.

CAKE AND COOKIE INGREDIENTS: EGGS AND LEAVENERS

Eggs contribute several different materials to cakes and cookies: moisture, air-trapping and structure-building proteins, and tenderizing yolk fats and emulsifiers. Separated whites produce a drier, lighter texture; yolks a moister and denser one.

Eggs of different sizes contain different amounts and proportions of these components.

Check recipes to make sure you're using the egg size specified. If you're not, adjust the quantity of egg you use.

Chemical leaveners, baking powder and baking soda, are concentrated alkalis and acids that create carbon dioxide gas when they dissolve. They're used to help raise quick- and high-ratio cakes.

Baking powder and baking soda are not interchangeable.

Baking soda is an alkaline salt that produces carbon dioxide gas the moment that it comes into contact with a dissolved acid. That acid can be in one of the major ingredients—such as buttermilk or honey—or it can be added in pure form as cream of tartar.

Baking powders are combinations of baking soda and acid in proportions that maximize their gas production. Single-acting baking powder is made with cream of tartar or acid phosphates that react immediately when the dough is mixed.

Double-acting powders are the most effective chemical leaveners. They contain special acids that produce some gas only during the cooking process, when the cookie or cake can better trap it and rise. Despite some popular suspicion, there's no evidence that a common one, SAS (sodium aluminum sulfate), is unhealthful.

Store leavenings airtight. Baking soda absorbs odors, and baking powder slowly reacts with moisture and loses power.

To test baking powder, pour hot water onto a spoonful in a bowl; it should bubble vigorously. If it doesn't, discard it.

To make an emergency single-acting baking powder, combine 1 tablespoon/15 grams baking soda with 2 tablespoons/18 grams cream of tartar and 1½ tablespoons/11 grams cornstarch.

Hartshorn, or baker's ammonia, is a chemical leavener used only with thin, dry cookies. In other baked goods it can leave an unpleasant ammonia residue.

Beware of overleavening cakes and cookies. Too much leavening causes batters to rise too quickly and then collapse. A general rule of thumb is 1 teaspoon/5 grams of baking powder or ¼ teaspoon/1 gram of baking soda per cup/120 grams of flour. Adjust recipes that call for significantly more.

CAKE AND COOKIE INGREDIENTS: CHOCOLATE AND COCOA

Chocolate and cocoa contribute to the structure of chocolate cakes and cookies as well as their flavor. They contain solid particles of the cacao bean, which behave like starch and absorb moisture.

Chocolate and cocoa are sold with many different proportions of cocoa solids, cocoa fat, and added ingredients.

Chocolate always contains cocoa particles and cocoa fat, and may include sugar and milk solids. It is sometimes labeled with the percentage of cocoa solids and cocoa fat. Baking chocolate is 100 percent cocoa solids and cocoa fat, dark chocolates usually 50 to 80 percent, milk chocolates less than 50 percent. "White" chocolate contains no cocoa particles, just cocoa fat, sugar, and milk solids.

Try to use the chocolate specified in your recipe. If you have to replace dark chocolate with baking chocolate, use less chocolate and more sugar; to replace baking chocolate with dark, use more chocolate and less sugar.

Cocoas are mainly the solid particles of the cacao bean. They're intense and sometimes harsh in flavor. They may be sweetened or unsweetened, and are made in two different styles.

"Natural" cocoas, the usual American style, are acidic.

"Dutch process" cocoas, usually European, have been chemically treated and are alkaline, with a milder flavor.

Make sure which style of cocoa your recipe calls for. If you use Dutch process cocoa in a recipe designed for natural, the cake may not rise or set and may have a soapy taste due to excess alkalinity.

Flourless chocolate cakes replace flour with chocolate and/or cocoa, often nut flours or meals, and rely on eggs as the setting agent. They set best with natural cocoas. To use Dutch process cocoa and prevent it from interfering with egg setting, balance its alkalinity with acid cream of tartar, and reduce the amount of baking powder.

It's possible but tricky to substitute chocolate and cocoa for each other in baking. Chocolate contains fat and sugar as well as cocoa particles, so substitution means adjusting fat and sugar quantities as well.

THE ESSENTIALS OF CAKE MAKING

There are three important stages in cake making: measuring, mixing, and baking.

Measure out all the ingredients first, by weight whenever possible, using a reliable digital scale. If you measure by volume, follow the recipe's instructions for exactly how to do so.

Mix the ingredients in the correct order and mix thoroughly to maximize aeration and lightness.

Bake in a pan of the correct size, and in an oven whose temperature you have checked, so that the batter gets hot enough to set it when it has risen to its maximum height. Before you make a new recipe, check to make sure you have the pan it was written for or a pan that holds a similar volume.

Cakes are built from two opposing pairs of main ingredients. One pair, flour and eggs, provides the bland but solid structure. The other pair, sugar and fat, fills that structure with sweetness and richness, and weakens it so it will be moist and soft. A fifth ingredient, bubbles of air or gas, spreads the other four into tiny thin sheets that create lightness and delicacy.

Ingredient proportions and types are finely balanced in good recipes. Too much flour or egg makes a dry and dull cake; too much sugar or fat makes it dense and soggy. Cake flour can carry a higher proportion of sugar and fat than all-purpose flour. Shortening weakens batter structure less than butter.

Don't substitute for the ingredient type specified in a recipe without being ready to experiment and adjust proportions.

Mixing combines the batter ingredients evenly, and captures air to leaven the batter and lighten the cake texture. Mixing is done in several stages. In each, be sure to stop and scrape clinging ingredients from the beaters, whisks, and bowls into the main mass, so that the mixing is as even as possible.

- *Whisk the flour thoroughly with other dry ingredients,* any chemical leavenings, or cocoa powder to avoid the local pockets of excess concentration that simple stirring leaves.
- *Sift the dry ingredients* to separate and aerate the particles so that they'll mix more quickly and evenly with the wet ingredients. Use a flour sifter or a fine-mesh sieve.
- *Beat air bubbles into softened fat, or liquid eggs,* or into a combination of ingredients with an electric mixer.
- *Combine the separately aerated fat or eggs* with the other ingredients.

Creaming and folding are special mixing techniques that are often used in making cakes and cookies.

Creaming is the prolonged beating of softened, semisolid butter or shortening with sugar crystals, which gradually aerate the fat with countless tiny air bubbles. It can take 10 minutes or more, and requires careful control of the butter temperature.

Folding is the gentle mixing by hand of two batter components, one light and one dense, to minimize the loss of aeration. Using a flexible spatula, repeatedly scoop the light material onto the spatula surface, then cut down vertically through the second material and lift some of it from beneath onto the first.

Folding is the standard method for combining whipped egg whites with the other cake ingredients. Some cooks find that quickly blending with a balloon whisk works just as well.

There are two basic families of cakes, defined by how their batters are filled with gas bubbles.

Butter cakes include basic white, yellow, pound, and chocolate cakes. They're aerated by beating air into butter or shortening, or into the batter as a whole.

Foam cakes include angel, chiffon, and sponge cakes. They're aerated by beating air into egg whites or whole eggs, and folding the egg foam into the other ingredients.

MIXING BUTTER-CAKE BATTERS

Batters for standard butter cakes are mixed in several ways. Here are three common ones.

Creaming, the traditional method, is time-consuming but best for producing well-aerated, light cakes. It mixes semisolid fat—butter, shortening, or a combination—with granulated or superfine sugar, to trap air bubbles for leavening.

- *If you'll be creaming butter in a warm kitchen, 65°F/18°C or above,* prepare a wide container of ice or cold water in case you need to cool the butter quickly.

- *Beat the cool fat and sugar for 5 to 10 minutes,* until the mixture is light and fluffy. Use medium speed in an electric stand mixer, or high speed with a less efficient handheld mixer.
- *Don't let butter get warmer than 68°F/20°C, or shortening warmer than 85°F/30°C.* The friction of mixing generates heat, and if the fat melts, it loses its air bubbles. If the bowl bottom gets noticeably warm, stop creaming and cool the bowl.
- *Mix in the remaining ingredients in stages and at low speed,* to avoid coarsely foaming the eggs or toughening the flour gluten. Add the eggs one at a time to incorporate them evenly, then part of the flour, then part of the liquid ingredients, then the rest of the flour, and finally the remaining liquid.

Two-stage mixing is easier and faster than creaming, and produces a tender but denser cake.

- *Whisk all the dry ingredients* together very thoroughly.
- *Whisk all the wet ingredients* together in a second bowl.
- *Add the softened butter or shortening to the dry ingredients* and briefly mix on medium speed.
- *Add the wet ingredients in several doses* until evenly incorporated.

One-bowl, or "dump," mixing is easiest of all, but doesn't produce the tenderness and lightness of the other methods, and works best with cake flour and shortening. It's the method for most supermarket cake mixes.

- *Whisk and sift together all dry ingredients but the leavening.*
- *Add the shortening and wet ingredients* and mix for several min-

utes at low and then moderate speed, then add the baking powder for the last minute.

- *Or mix the dry ingredients and fat with most of the milk,* then add the rest of the milk and the eggs and mix at low and then moderate speed for several minutes.

MIXING EGG-FOAM BATTERS

Batters for sponge, chiffon, and angel cakes are leavened by beating air bubbles into eggs instead of fat. Egg-leavened cakes are usually lighter and less rich than butter cakes. The egg white and yolk can be beaten separately or together. Angel cake is made with the whites only.

Separated-egg mixing produces the lightest batter.

- *Always whip egg whites with acid* cream of tartar or lemon juice. Acid stabilizes egg foams, and also whitens the interior of angel food cake.
- *Beat the yolks with some sugar* until they turn light with air bubbles.
- *Beat the whites in a separate bowl* with cream of tartar until they form soft peaks. Then add the rest of the sugar and beat until they form stiff peaks.
- *Sift flour onto the yolks,* add a third of the whites and stir together, then fold in the remaining whites. Butter can be barely melted and folded in at the end.

Whole-egg mixing is simpler.

- *Beat the whole eggs with sugar,* starting on low speed and increasing to medium, until the mix is cream-colored and thickened from the air bubbles. Add the liquid ingredients and beat them in.

- *Sift the flour* onto the top of the batter, and fold in until well mixed.
- *To add butter,* beat it separately until soft and creamy, then soften further with a small amount of batter, and fold the butter mixture gently into the batter.

Génoise batter produces a dry, firm cake meant to be moistened with syrup.

- *Stir and warm whole eggs and sugar* to around 100°F/40°C.
- *Whip the mixture* on high speed and then medium to low speed for a total of 10 to 15 minutes until thick and risen to about triple its original volume. Remove a portion to mix with melted butter.
- *Fold in the flour and then the butter mixture.*

PREPARING AND FILLING THE PAN

Pan materials and shapes have a strong influence on how well the oven transforms batters into cakes.

Choose dull metal pans and molds for the most even heating. Shiny pans will reflect radiant heat and slow cooking; black pans can over-brown the sides while the center cooks through. Tube pans create more batter surface and speed cooking. Springform pans with removable sides, and flexible silicone pans, ease unmolding of the finished cake.

Don't overfill or underfill pans, which will result in spilling over or an underdone top. The batter should fill the pan to between two-thirds and three-fourths of its height. To determine a pan's volume, fill it with water using a measuring cup.

To prevent sticking of most cakes, grease the pan with melted but thick butter or spray with nonstick spray. Coat fluted molds especially well. Line the greased pan bottom with greased parchment paper.

Dust greased surfaces with flour to help the batter wet the pan evenly.

Don't grease pans for chiffon and angel cakes, which are fragile and need to cling to the pan sides while cooling.

After filling, knock the pan on a hard surface or run a sharp knife through the batter to settle and fill any void areas.

BAKING AND COOLING

Oven heat causes the air bubbles in cake batter to expand and raise the batter. It also causes the batter proteins and starch to set and solidify. When a cake is well baked, the batter sets just as it reaches its maximum expansion and lightness.

Bake cakes in an electric oven if you have a choice. Gas ovens don't retain rise-enhancing steam as well.

The oven temperature and placement of the pan determine how fast the batter heats up and what kind of texture it develops.

Low baking temperatures and a long baking time favor a higher rise and open texture.

Higher temperatures and quicker baking favor a denser but finer structure.

Bake most cakes at moderate oven temperatures, 325 to 375°F / 160 to

190°C. Below this range most cakes set too slowly; above it they brown before they're cooked through.

For even heating, place the pan on the middle oven rack.

To prevent the top from browning too fast, place a sheet of foil on the top rack or loosely over the pan to shield it from radiant heat.

For rapid bottom heating and expansion, place the pan on a preheated baking stone resting on the oven floor, or on the lowest rack.

Don't open the oven until the cake is nearly done, to retain steam that promotes heating and rising.

Check the cake's doneness early, before the sides begin to shrink from the pan.

To judge doneness, probe the center with a cake tester, skewer, or knife. Most properly done cakes will not leave a residue clinging to the probe, unless they're intentionally underbaked to have puddinglike or liquid centers.

Freshly baked cakes are soft and fragile. They become firmer as they cool.

Cool delicate chiffon and angel cakes to room temperature in the pan. Suspend the tube pan upside down over a standing wine bottle, to let gravity keep the cake stretched to its full volume as it firms.

Remove other cakes from pans after a brief cooling to firm their edges. Rest the pan on a rack for a few minutes. Run a knife along the cake edge to loosen it from the pan, remove the cake by inverting the pan onto a plate then invert it again onto a rack and allow it to finish cooling there.

Cool cakes completely before decorating, to avoid tearing the cake or melting the icing or glaze.

TROUBLESHOOTING CAKES

If a new cake recipe doesn't turn out well, there may be something wrong with the recipe.

If a familiar or reliable cake recipe doesn't turn out well, there was probably something wrong with your ingredients or procedure.

Take some time to think through what might have been wrong, and make a note to adjust your ingredients or procedure the next time.

Many cake failures are caused by a batter that rises either too little or too much before it sets.

Make sure to mix the batter long and carefully enough to aerate it fully.

Check the amount and quality of leavening. Too much produces coarse, fallen cakes; too little produces dense, humped cakes. A standard amount is ¼ teaspoon/1 gram soda or 1 teaspoon/5 grams powder per cup/120 grams flour. Test old baking powder (page 421) and replace if it's not active.

Coarse-grained or sunken cakes also result from undermixing or too low an oven temperature, so the center doesn't rise enough or sets after it falls again. Try a higher temperature and/or longer mixing.

Cracked or peaked cakes result from overmixing batter or too high an oven temperature, so the center continues to expand after the surface has set. Try a lower temperature and/or shorter mixing.

Dry, tough cakes result from baking too long. Check for doneness earlier.

High-altitude baking requires major adjustments to ingredient proportions and methods. Batters expand and dry out much faster at elevations above about 3,000 feet/900 meters.

Adjust proportions in high-altitude batters to give them more moisture and help them set faster. Reduce sugar and leavening, increase egg and other liquids and flour, and replace milk with buttermilk to speed protein setting.

- *Beat egg whites less,* to soft peaks instead of firm, to allow greater expansion.
- *Use a tube pan and increase the baking temperature* to speed heating and setting.

CUPCAKES, SHEET CAKES, AND FRUITCAKES

Cupcakes are standard cake batters that are baked quickly in the cups of muffin pans, greased or lined with paper to prevent sticking.

To make cupcakes, fill cups two-thirds full with batter and bake at 350°F/175°C for about 20 minutes.

Check doneness early to avoid dryness, and remove cupcakes from the oven when a toothpick or other probe comes out clean from the center. Allow them to cool and firm for a few minutes before removing from the pan.

Sheet cakes and roll cakes are made from standard cake batters that are spread out onto a sheet pan and baked in a thin layer for 10 to 15 minutes.

Prevent sheet cakes from sticking to the pan with a piece of parchment paper or waxed paper.

Shape the batter to be as evenly thick as possible. Thin edges scorch and crack.

To avoid cracks, watch carefully and don't overbake. If the cake becomes too dry to roll, brush it lightly with syrup.

Fruitcakes are butter cakes with a high proportion of nuts and candied fruits, often soaked with spirits after baking and aged for weeks to mellow in flavor.

For a moister fruitcake, presoak dried fruits in spirits or syrup so they won't absorb moisture from the batter.

Allow fruitcakes to cool and firm before unmolding. They're especially fragile because the nuts and fruits interrupt the batter structure.

Keep spirits-soaked fruitcakes for weeks at room temperature, months in the refrigerator. Store tightly wrapped to avoid drying out.

MUFFINS AND QUICK CAKES

Muffins and quick cakes are sweet, rich versions of quick breads, leavened with baking powder or soda and without the laborious aeration of standard cakes.

Mix muffins and quick cakes as rapidly as possible to minimize toughening gluten and losing leavening gas. One standard method is to beat the liquid ingredients with sugar to dissolve it, then to combine this mix with flour and leavening.

To obtain a shapely peak on the muffin tops, make sure the batter isn't overleavened, fill the pan cups almost full, and use a relatively high baking temperature, 400 to 425°F / 200 to 220°C.

Start checking doneness early. The cups in muffin pans have varying capacities, and quick cakes can be baked in cake or loaf pans, so cooking times will vary. Remove from the oven when a toothpick or other probe comes out clean from the center.

Allow muffins and quick cakes to cool and firm for a few minutes before removing them from the pan.

Muffins and quick cakes keep better than quick breads due to their sugar and fat. Keep them for a day or two at room temperature, a week or more in the refrigerator, or months in the freezer.

To restore stale muffins and quick cakes, reheat them until steaming hot and soft inside.

GLAZES, ICINGS, FROSTINGS, AND FILLINGS

Cake coatings are decorative and often delicious, but also help the cake retain its moisture and eating quality longer. Coatings with fat are especially good moisture barriers. Royal icing, fondant, and other all-sugar coatings absorb moisture and become sticky in humid weather.

Cake fillings are usually a creamy contrast to the cake's own texture. They're commonly made from sweetened whipped cream, an egg-based custard, fruit curd or starch-stabilized pastry cream, or a chocolate-cream mixture, ganache.

For a more stable whipped cream filling, choose a recipe that stabilizes the cream with gelatin. Underwhip the cream to soft peaks, so that the final manipulation of spreading or piping doesn't cause it to break.

There are many ways to coat cakes. They range from glazes of warmed fruit preserves, to icings of confectioners' sugar mixed with enough liquid to make it flow, to sweetened cream cheese or whipped cream, various versions of meringue, and more elaborate preparations. Here are guidelines for a handful of common ones.

When adding hot syrup to eggs, avoid pouring onto spinning beaters, which will throw the syrup onto the bowl walls and make hard sugar lumps.

To make poured glazes and icings as smooth as possible, apply in two coats, the first touched up to cover the cake surface completely, the second not touched at all.

Chocolate glazes are made by melting chocolate into warm water, cream, sugar syrup, or clarified butter, so that the mixture is thin enough to pour onto a cake and solidifies into a tender coating rather than a hard one. Store refrigerated or frozen; reheat gently.

Make chocolate glazes shinier by including some butter, oil, or corn syrup. To retain the shine, don't refrigerate or wrap tightly.

Royal icing is a matte material for fine decorations, made by beating egg whites with about five times their weight in confectioners' sugar into a dense, thick meringue.

Boiled icing is a firm, glossy cooked meringue. Heat sugar and water to 234 to 240°F / 112 to 116°C, then pour this syrup onto egg whites as they're being beaten in a mixer. Continue mixing until the meringue has cooled.

Fondant is a firm, dense, creamy glaze, a smooth mass of tiny sugar crystals held together with sugar syrup that can be flavored or colored. Poured fondant is cooked and forms thin coatings. Rolled fondant is kneaded and makes thicker coatings. Both can be bought premade.

Make poured fondant by heating sugar and water, plus cream of tartar or corn syrup to keep crystals fine. Once the mix reaches the soft-ball stage, 234 to 240°F / 112 to 116°C, pour onto a moistened countertop or work surface, allow to cool to 150°F/65°C, and stir and scrape until it becomes a dry, white mass. Knead portions by hand until they become smooth. Cover and rest for a day or more at room temperature, or refrigerate for weeks.

To use poured fondant, knead in flavorings and colorings, then warm to 100 to 105°F / 38 to 41°C. If it's not thin enough to pour, add a little sugar syrup.

Make rolled fondant by dissolving gelatin in hot water, adding corn syrup, glycerin, and shortening, and kneading in powdered sugar until smooth. Cover and rest for a few hours, or refrigerate for days.

To use rolled fondant, grease surfaces to avoid sticking. Roll no thinner than ¼ inch/0.5 centimeter to make the smoothest cake surface. Always roll rather than pull, which will tear the sheet. If the fondant begins to crack, cover it with plastic wrap to prevent further drying.

Buttercreams are stiff, dense mixtures of sugar and fat that can be flavored and formed into decorative shapes by piping through pastry tips. Traditional buttercream is made laboriously from sugar, butter, and eggs. Quick buttercream is made in minutes with confectioners' sugar and a mixture of butter and shortening.

To make traditional French buttercream, beat egg yolks or whole eggs until light, then drizzle in a sugar syrup cooked to 234 to 240°F / 112 to 116°C, and beat until the aerated but dense mixture cools to a warm room temperature. Then gradually beat in softened butter and any flavoring. Refrigerate for days or freeze tightly wrapped for months, though butter tends to absorb off flavors.

To pasteurize eggs for the safest possible buttercream, heat beaten eggs and most of the sugar with constant stirring to 160°F/70°C over a pot of simmering water. Then whip on high speed for 10 to 15 minutes until stiff and cool, add remaining sugar, and beat in softened butter and flavorings.

Keep buttercream in the refrigerator or freezer. After thawing in the refrigerator, rewhip it to restore its consistency.

To make quick buttercream, beat together butter, shortening, or a mixture with confectioners' sugar, which is too fine to feel grainy, and whose cornstarch absorbs moisture and prevents separation. A high proportion of fat makes a soft cream, a high proportion of sugar a stiff one.

To use buttercream, let it warm up to room temperature, rebeat, and then heat it gently until it's soft enough to spread easily.

COOKIES AND BROWNIES

Cookies are miniature versions of moist cakes, dry pastries, and often something in between. Many cookie doughs are made like cake batters, but with more flour and less liquid. Cookie doughs and batters refrigerate well and take only a few minutes to cook, so they're easy to bake fresh.

Cookie doughs often have very little moisture, and small changes in proportions can cause big differences in consistency and how much the dough pieces spread when baked.

The flour for cookie doughs and batters is usually a low-protein pastry, cake, or southern all-purpose flour, to produce the tenderest result. National all-purpose flours make more gluten and absorb more moisture, so substituting with them will produce less tender, drier cookies that spread less when baked.

To make more tender cookies with all-purpose flour, replace a quarter of the flour weight with cornstarch.

Cocoa powder, chocolate, and ground nuts, including nut butters and meals, can replace some or all of the flour in cookies while also tenderizing and intensifying flavor. They contain starch or starchlike particles and fat, but no toughening protein.

Real butter is essential for a good texture in cookies whose recipes call for it. Don't substitute margarine or low-fat spreads.

To make most cookie doughs, beat butter or shortening with sugar to develop leavening air bubbles. If the recipe includes leavening, whisk it thoroughly with the flour to disperse it evenly and avoid uneven texture and unpleasant taste. Mix in the flour and then the eggs, adding them one at a time to blend them evenly. Minimize the final mixing to avoid developing gluten or causing the egg proteins to foam.

Rest cookie doughs in the refrigerator for hours to even out moisture and relax gluten, and to firm the fat and produce neater edges.

To develop more flavor, refrigerate doughs for days wrapped airtight. Refrigerated doughs slowly break down some starch and protein, and make progressively darker and more flavorful cookies.

Freeze doughs to keep them for more than a few days, presliced to avoid thawing and refreezing.

Size dough pieces according to the cookie qualities you want, small for uniformly crisp or soft, large for crisp edge and moist center.

Bake cookies on a heavy-gauge sheet pan for the most consistent results. Line the pan with a silicone sheet, parchment, or other nonstick surface. Space the dough pieces to leave room for spreading. In a standard oven without convection to circulate the hot air, bake one pan at a time on the middle rack, rotating the pan if necessary for even heating.

Monitor cookie doneness closely. Cooking times are short.

Allow cookies to cool and firm somewhat before removing them from the pan. If they cool enough to stick, return the pan to the oven for a minute or two to release them.

Before storing cookies, cool them thoroughly on a rack to release free moisture and prevent spoilage. Store in an airtight container to prevent moisture loss or gain.

To soften hardened cookies, warm them in a medium oven for a few minutes, or microwave on medium power for a few seconds.

Cookie recipes often need adjustment to produce a specific texture or shape. Adjustment of one ingredient often requires rebalancing of others.

- *To make cookies less crumbly,* add more egg.
- *To make cookies more tender,* add more fat or egg yolk and less white sugar.
- *To make cookies crisp,* add more white sugar.
- *To make cookies more moist,* replace some white sugar with brown sugar, corn or agave syrup, or honey.
- *To get darker brown color and flavor,* replace some sugar with corn or agave syrup, brown sugar, or honey, or add some baking soda.
- *To make cookies spread more,* replace shortening with butter and granulated white sugar with superfine sugar.
- *To make cookies spread less,* replace butter with shortening, and Dutch process cocoa with natural cocoa.

Brownies are a cookie-cake hybrid, the result of reducing the flour in a cookie recipe to make a dough into a batter. They can be cakelike or fudgelike, crusty or crustless.

Make brownies cakelike by using a large proportion of flour to liquid, cocoa rather than chocolate, and baking until an inserted toothpick or knife tip comes out clean.

Make brownies fudgelike by using less flour, chocolate rather than cocoa, and baking until barely set, when an inserted toothpick or knife tip still brings a slight trace of batter.

To avoid a thin surface crust, mix eggs into the batter gently. To make a crust, beat the batter vigorously after adding the eggs.

To get a crisp crust and moist interior, bake at a relatively high temperature, 350°F/175°C rather than 300°F/150°C.

To cut brownies cleanly, allow them to cool completely first.

20

GRIDDLE CAKES, CREPES, POPOVERS, AND FRYING BATTERS

G riddle cakes and their ilk are made from batters, flour-thickened fluids that spread into a thin layer and cook through very quickly into sheets. The basic batter ingredients are simple—flour, milk, eggs, butter or another fat—but the cook can use different kinds of heat and a touch of leavening to create very different textures and flavors.

Give a basic batter a minute on a hot pan to make pale, moist, flat crepes. Thirty minutes in a hot oven inflates a muffin cup of the same batter into a crisply brown popover, or a pan of it into browned but custardy Yorkshire pudding. Bring a little yeast or chemical leavening into the mix and you get blini or American-style pancakes on an open pan, waffles in a waffle iron. Leave out the fat and milk, use plain water, and you get a crisp binder or coating for fritters and deep-fried foods. Pour something like that frying batter onto vegetables as they fry in a pan, and you get Korean or Vietnamese pancakes.

I've cooked most of these batter foods many times over many years, but it took me quite a while to realize that they're so closely related, and that the basic formula is so flexible. If there's enough flour in the mix to give the liquid some weight, so that it flows more like thin cream than like water, then it will set when you heat it. That proportion is around 1 part flour to every 2 of liquid by weight, 1 to 1 by volume. How you flavor the mix, how you enrich it, whether or not you use more flour for more density, whether you leaven it for more lightness, how you cook it—the rest of the design is up to you.

It's safest to follow a recipe when you want to try a popover or waffle for the first time, but it's liberating—and fun—to start with the basic formula for a griddle cake and invent your own.

GRIDDLE CAKE AND BATTER SAFETY

Batter foods are thoroughly cooked and don't present a health hazard when prepared fresh.

Many recipes suggest letting batters sit for several hours to allow dry ingredients to absorb moisture fully.

Refrigerate batters for aging periods longer than 2 hours, especially if they contain eggs.

Refrigerate leftover griddle cakes to keep them for more than a few hours.

GRIDDLE CAKE INGREDIENTS AND STORAGE

Batter ingredients are mainly familiar kitchen staples and require no special attention.

Buy fresh flour and leaveners if yours are a few months old. Baking soda and powders slowly absorb off odors, flours go stale, whole-grain flours go rancid.

Premade pancake and waffle mixes are available in various degrees of completeness. Some are mainly flours and leavening and require milk and eggs; others require only water or are ready to pour. Mixes often suffer from stale and off flavors, and are only slightly more convenient than starting from scratch.

Store batters for a day or two in the refrigerator. Before using them, restore depleted chemical leavening with baking powder; give yeast-leavened batters 1 to 2 hours to warm up and bubble.

Refrigerate or freeze leftover griddle cakes and popovers. Reheat griddle cakes in a medium oven; briefly recrisp popovers in a hot oven.

THE ESSENTIALS OF MAKING FRIED AND BAKED BATTERS

The keys to success with batters are creating the right batter consistency and cooking them at the right temperature. Both are easily adjusted as you cook.

Batter consistency determines the finished texture. A thick batter will make a dense, cakelike texture; a runny batter a lighter, moister texture. Adjust the batter as you cook with small additions of liquid, flour, or leavening to produce the texture you want.

Most batter foods should be tender, not chewy.

Use low-gluten flours or flour mixtures that won't produce a chewy, tough texture. These include pastry and cake flours, or all-purpose flour combined with cornstarch or buckwheat, rice, or corn flours.

Melt any butter or other solid fats in milk and whisk well to disperse the fat evenly into the batter and help tenderize.

Stir the flour with the liquid ingredients just enough to mix, to minimize gluten development and toughening.

Griddle cakes may be either unleavened or leavened with yeast, baking powder, baking soda and an acidic ingredient, or whipped egg whites.

Don't overdo chemical leavening. Too much will cause batters to collapse into a coarse, dense structure and produce a harsh flavor. Typical proportions are 1 teaspoon/5 grams baking powder per cup/120 grams flour, or ½ teaspoon/2 grams baking soda per cup/250 milliliters buttermilk.

To avoid strange green and gray colors from blueberries and nuts, pay special attention to the alkaline baking soda that causes them. Blend soda thoroughly with flour to avoid local excesses, and replace some soda with baking powder to reduce overall alkalinity.

Replace some baking soda with baking powder in recipes that neutralize acid ingredients with soda. A slight excess of acidity can improve both flavor and texture.

To leaven without powders or yeasts, or to supplement them with extra lightness, beat egg whites separately and fold into the rest of the mix just before cooking.

Prepare most unyeasted griddle cake batters an hour or more before cooking, to give the flour time to absorb moisture and produce a velvety cooked texture. (Don't do this with the batter for waffles, which should be crisp and not velvety.) Refrigerate for rests longer than 2 hours. Withhold baking soda or powder and/or beaten egg whites, and add just before cooking to maximize their leavening power. Whisk powders with a little flour first to help incorporate them evenly.

Check the batter consistency often, after resting and during the cooking of several batches. Gently stir in more liquid as needed to keep the batter fluid and the texture light.

Cook griddle cakes on a nonstick or well-seasoned griddle or pan. Flat griddles may span more than one burner or extend past the burner edge. Watch for uneven heating as you cook and adjust accordingly.

Apply fats and oils sparingly to the pan to avoid greasiness.

Cook gently over moderate heat, so that the surface browns pleasantly in the few minutes it takes for the cake to cook through. An infrared thermometer will read 325 to 350°F/160 to 175°C; a drop of water flicked onto the surface will sizzle and evaporate in a few seconds.

Preheat plates and toppings, including butter and syrups. Thin griddle cakes cool fast.

PANCAKES AND BLINI

Pancakes are moist and tender disks made from a relatively thin batter that spreads easily in the pan.

Blini are yeast-raised pancakes, often especially rich and delicate from the inclusion of cream and buckwheat flour.

Yeast-raised batters will rise before and during preparation for the griddle. Gently stir to deflate large bubbles before pouring them onto the pan.

To make especially delicate pancakes, replace milk or water with yogurt or buttermilk. These thick liquids need less flour to make a batter with the right consistency. Neutralize part or all of their acidity by replacing baking powder with baking soda. Some tartness can be delicious in pancakes.

Leave room for spoonfuls of batter to spread when pouring them onto the pan.

Turn pancakes when the upper batter surface has set around the edges, and when bubbles are rising near the center. Don't wait for the batter edge to look dry and the bubbles to break; this will give a coarse, dry result.

To make the first batch less irregularly colored than usual, wipe excess oil firmly from the pan surface, so that all batter comes into direct contact with metal.

If some inner batter remains uncooked after the surfaces have browned on a moderately hot pan, the batter is too thick. Thin the batter with milk or water so it will spread into a thinner layer.

Don't stack cooked pancakes onto each other if you're not going to serve them right away. To avoid flattening and steaming them, spread them out on a rack or plate in a low oven.

German and Austrian baked pancakes are really sweet soufflés stabilized with flour or starch, started in a hot frying pan and finished in the oven. Egg whites are beaten into a foam for leavening, and mixed with sweetened yolks and flour.

For the lightest texture in baked pancakes, beat the egg whites with cream of tartar until firm but still moist, to allow expansion during cooking. Fold or whisk the other ingredients in gently to minimize loss of air bubbles, and add the batter immediately to the preheated pan.

CREPES AND BLINTZES

Crepes are delicate griddle cakes, about 1 millimeter thick, usually cooked one at a time on a small, shallow pan, moist and flexible enough to be folded into quarters or rolled around a filling.

Blintzes are essentially crepes barely cooked on one side only, the upper side being the surface on which fillings are placed before folding and finishing on a buttered pan.

Make crepe batter 2 hours or more ahead of cooking to allow flour particles time to absorb moisture fully, and soften more during the brief 1 to 2 minutes of cooking.

Make crepe batter very thin, between the consistencies of milk and cream, so that when poured onto the hot pan it spreads quickly without setting into thick and thin areas. Adjust the thickness with water just before cooking, and during extended cooking.

Oil or butter the pan only lightly. Unlike pancakes, crepes cannot absorb excess oil and will become greasy.

Preheat the pan only to 250 to 275°F/120 to 135°C, so that a drop of water gently sputters, before wiping with oil or fat and pouring on the batter. Higher temperatures will set the batter before it spreads, cook unevenly, and cause bubbling and holes in the crepe.

Turn or flip the crepe as soon as it releases from the pan, around 1 minute. Cook the second side just long enough to set and release. Don't overcook, or it will turn out dry.

Brittany-style crepes, or galettes, made with buckwheat flour may be too fragile to flip. If so, gently stir a few spoonfuls of cohesion-creating wheat flour into the remaining batter, and then enough water to produce the correct thin consistency.

Store crepes wrapped airtight for a few days refrigerated, a few weeks frozen.

CLAFOUTIS

Clafoutis are crustless fruit tarts made by surrounding pieces of fruit with a batter similar to crepe batter.

Make the batter an hour or more ahead of time to allow full hydration and a more even cooked texture.

Don't use a tart pan with a removable bottom. The thin batter is likely to leak out before it sets.

To make clafoutis easier to cut and serve in neat wedges, bake a portion of the batter in the pan until just set to form a solid sheet for the fruit pieces to rest on. Then place fruit on this sheet, pour in the rest of the batter, and finish baking.

To ensure a moist interior, bake clafoutis just until set.

Allow clafoutis to cool fully before cutting.

WAFFLES

Waffles are meant to be mostly crisp and crunchy crust, and their batter should be handled more as a frying batter than a pancake batter. The indented waffle iron provides extra surface area to maximize the amount of crust.

For crisp waffles that release well from the pan:
  * *Include plenty of fat.* Recipes often call for as much as

¼ pound/115 grams of butter for every cup/120 grams of flour, or about equal weights.

- *Make the batter thin.* Thin batter expands well for good crisping and coating of the iron, especially Belgian waffle irons that are flipped during the cooking.
- *Mix the waffle batter briefly and cook it immediately,* before the flour has a chance to soak up much moisture.

Reduced-fat waffle recipes, including pancake recipes, produce a denser, harder crust that becomes leathery if it reabsorbs moisture.

Give the batter room to rise and become light in the iron. Don't overfill the iron, which produces a dense, pancakelike result.

To avoid having waffles stick to the iron, be sure metal surfaces are well seasoned, or nonstick surfaces clean, not sticky with old fat. Allow the iron to preheat fully before spooning on batter. Keep the iron closed until the flow of steam is greatly reduced.

If waffles won't release from the iron, let them cook for another minute or two to further dry their surfaces.

To keep waffles crisp until they're served, hold them in a single layer on a rack in a low oven.

Store leftover waffles wrapped airtight in the refrigerator for a few days, or the freezer indefinitely. Recrisp in a medium oven or in a toaster on the lowest setting.

POPOVERS

Popovers are irregular, muffin-shaped, hollow pastries made from a batter like crepe batter, but cooked in metal cups in a hot oven. The bottom, top, and sides set while the inner batter forms steam and expands, pushing the top up.

For a higher rise and crisper texture, use a recipe that calls for some separated egg whites as well as whole eggs. Mix the batter just before baking.

Use a metal pan with deep, well-separated cups, to encourage even heating and rising. Grease the cups, preheated in the oven if desired, and fill them halfway with batter.

Start popovers in a hot oven, 450°F/230°C, until the batter rises fully after 15 to 20 minutes. Then turn the heat down to cook through and crisp their surfaces without excessive browning.

To save time and energy, start popovers in a cold pan and cold oven. Many recipes call for preheating the oven and pan to maximize the batter's rise, but it will rise surprisingly well without tricky handling of hot metal and fat.

Cut slits in the side of finished popovers so that the inner steam will escape and the popovers won't collapse.

Store popovers wrapped airtight in the refrigerator for days, or the freezer for weeks.

To refresh leftover popovers, reheat them for 5 minutes in a hot oven.

FRYING AND FRITTER BATTERS

Frying and fritter batters are thin mixtures of flour and liquid that coat a solid piece of food, or coat and hold several small pieces together, and then fry in oil to a crisp but tender crust.

A good frying batter has just enough protein from flour and/or eggs to hold the batter together and to the food. Too much flour gluten or egg yolk fries into a dense, tough, oily crust.

To make tender, crisp crusts, mix batters that dilute wheat flour gluten with cornstarch or rice flour, and that contain more egg whites than yolks.

For a more crumbly crispness, replace up to half of the liquid with vodka, whose alcohol limits gluten formation and reduces water absorption by starch. It boils off quickly during frying.

For a lighter, crunchier crust, break the batter up into fragile little chambers by leavening it. Include some baking powder, fold in whipped egg whites at the last minute, or use very cold beer or carbonated water for the liquid.

Mix the batter with as little stirring as possible, and just before frying, so the flour has little time to absorb moisture and the batter will crisp quickly. If you'll be frying over a period of an hour or more, prepare the solid and liquid ingredients separately ahead of time, then mix together in batches just before frying.

Japanese tempura batter produces an especially delicate, irregularly lacy crust. Mix ice-cold water with the flour and egg briefly and incompletely just before frying, to minimize the formation of tough gluten and the time required to crisp the crust.

To help batters adhere to foods, dredge foods in dry flour or starch just before dipping in batter.

Use fresh, neutral-flavored oil for frying. Fresh oil is thinner than old oil and clings less to fried foods.

Check the oil temperature often during frying and adjust the heat as needed to maintain the desired temperature, usually 325 to 375°F/160 to 190°C. The first minute or two of cooking require more heat to maintain the temperature than later stages, when heat should be turned down.

Discard batters for meat or fish after 4 hours. The repeated exposure to raw foods may result in hazardous numbers of disease bacteria.

21

ICE CREAMS, ICES, MOUSSES, AND JELLIES

C hilled and frozen desserts really do melt in the mouth, the classic description for something luscious. They cool and refresh, and provide that intriguing sensation of a solid mass disappearing into elusive, flavorful fluid. Chilling and freezing are methods that give structure and firmness to foods just as heating does, but they have the unusual virtue of being reversible. We can firm many ices and jellies and then melt them, adjust them, and firm them again. Cold dishes make a good introduction to cooking for children, safe and easy and tasty even when the texture isn't quite right. The best reasonably priced ice cream maker is still the entertaining bucket-style freezer that uses ice and salt. It's also easy to improvise an ice cream freezer from three plastic bags and some water and salt.

Most ice cream making puts a premium on smoothness, which comes from freezing the mix very quickly and preventing its ice crystals from growing big enough to feel on the tongue. It's difficult to match the smoothness of commercial ice creams using a home machine. When I found that out the hard way, it occurred to me to ask: why does all ice cream have to be smooth?

Of course it doesn't have to be! I found that one of the first printed recipes for ice cream was named ice cream "with pins" for its intentionally large ice crystals. I made it and found that the crystals did indeed prickle at first, but then they melted away into smooth creaminess, so that I had two contrasting textures in each bite. I liked it and still make it. Then there's the salep ice cream of Turkey and neighboring countries, which is made intentionally and delightfully chewy by thickening the mix with the powdered bulb of a particular orchid and then kneading the frozen mix like bread dough. You can get a similar effect by using locust bean gum or guar gum, more readily available thickeners.

By all means enjoy home-style smoothness and vanilla and chocolate, but then think about other possibilities. If you're going to make your own ice cream, why not really make it your own?

COLD AND FROZEN FOOD SAFETY

Cold and frozen foods are less hazardous than many foods because they're prepared and served at temperatures that slow the growth of microbes.

Cold and frozen foods can still cause illness if they're prepared with contaminated ingredients or handled carelessly.

Observe the usual food safety precautions when making cold and frozen foods. Wash hands, utensils, and raw ingredients. Thoroughly cook meats, fish, and stocks made from them. Avoid putting these foods in contact with other uncooked foods.

Raw and barely cooked eggs are sometimes used to make cold mousses and soufflés. There's a very slight possibility that they may carry salmonella and cause illness.

To eliminate the risk of salmonella illness from eggs, use pasteurized eggs or meringue powder instead of fresh eggs.

To pasteurize fresh eggs in the kitchen, carefully heat either yolks plus sugar, or whites plus cream of tartar, over a water bath with constant stirring until they reach 160°F/70°C. Take off the heat and continue stirring until they're no longer hot.

SHOPPING FOR AND STORING COLD FOODS

The best cold and frozen foods, with the best flavor and most melting consistency, are made with good-quality fruits and juices, fresh milk and cream and eggs, and genuine flavorings. Use these to make your own jellies, ices, and ice creams.

Many manufactured foods are imitations of the fresh-made original, made with cheaper dried dairy and egg ingredients, extracted or artificial flavorings, excessive sugar in the form of corn syrups, stabilizing starches and gums, and preservatives.

Read labels to find out what you're buying. For fresh-made quality, choose brands with the fewest and most familiar ingredients.

When choosing ice cream, heft cartons and compare prices. A container of commercial ice cream can be as much as half air bubbles, so a smaller but denser container may contain just as much solid pleasure.

Partial warming and rechilling damages the texture of frozen foods, even when they remain frozen. Partial warming melts small ice crystals; rechilling adds their water to the surviving big crystals and makes them bigger. This temperature cycling turns a fine, smooth consistency into a coarse, grainy one.

Bring along an insulated cooler when shopping, to keep cold foods cold.

Pick up chilled and frozen foods last, just before checking out.

Choose the coldest containers, usually from the back of the compartment.

Choose small containers of frozen desserts that you will finish quickly. Their temperature changes frequently in your freezer as the chilling unit cycles on and off and when the door is opened and closed. Every time a container is warmed up for serving and then refrozen, its texture gets grainier.

Keep the freezer as cold as possible, ideally 0°F/−18°C or lower.

Wrap leftover foods airtight to minimize freezer burn and the pickup of off odors. Press plastic wrap directly into the surface of ice creams and ices.

Warm stored ice creams and ices before serving to about 20°F/−7°C, so that they're firm but not hard.

Serve cold foods promptly on prechilled dishes, so that they stay cold at the table.

THE ESSENTIALS OF FREEZING ICES AND ICE CREAMS

Freezing is the process of chilling a liquid mix cold enough to turn most of its water into a mass of solid ice crystals, with the rest of the mix forming a syrup that coats and lubricates the crystals.

The consistency of an ice or ice cream is set by the size of its ice crystals and the proportion of syrup coating them. The smaller the crystals, the finer the texture. The more liquid syrup and other ingredients there are to keep the crystals apart, the softer the texture.

Crystal size and syrup proportions depend on the mix ingredients, how you freeze the mix, and the serving temperature.

Small crystals and fine texture are favored by sweeter mixes, and rapid freezing with constant agitation.

Soft texture is favored by sweeter mixes and warmer serving temperatures. Mixes with too much sugar make sticky, syrupy ices and ice creams.

Other mix ingredients that help produce fine, soft consistencies are corn syrup, honey, alcohols, egg yolks, dried milk solids, gelatin, fats, fruit pectins, and air. They all interfere with the formation of large ice crystals.

There are two basic methods for freezing ices and ice creams: still-freezing and churning.

- **Still-freezing** chills the mix in a pan or mold in the freezer with little or no agitation. It produces a coarse, hard texture unless the mix contains plenty of ingredients that interfere with ice crystal growth.
- **Churning** chills the mix in an appliance that allows frequent or constant agitation. It will produce smaller ice crystals from a given mix, and a smoother texture. Churning also works air into the mix, which makes it lighter and easier to scoop.

Ice cream makers come in three types: electric makers, freezer canisters, and brine bucket makers.

- **Electric ice cream makers** are miniature freezers that move the mix as they chill it and continuously extrude it. Most have limited chilling power and produce a fairly soft result that is good when eaten immediately, but gets grainy when hardened in the freezer.

- **Freezer canisters** contain a coolant substance within their hollow wall and bottom, and must be chilled in the freezer overnight before they're cold enough to freeze a batch of mix.
- *To be sure that the mix will freeze fully* in a canister maker, pre-chill the mix in the freezer until it begins to crystallize.
- *To make the smoothest ice cream in a canister,* and to avoid a stuck dasher, crank the dasher continuously.
- **Brine machines** are modern versions of the original ice cream machine, and work very well. They surround the mix with a slush of ice and salt. The higher the proportion of salt in the slush, the lower the slush temperature.
- *To freeze a mix efficiently,* keep the slush significantly colder than the freezing point of the mix, 20°F/−7°C or lower.

There are four steps in making frozen dishes: mixing the ingredients, prechilling the mix, freezing the mix, and hardening the freshly frozen mix.

Combine the mix ingredients, cooking them if necessary. Don't bother cooking a sugar syrup to add to the other ingredients unless you're making several different mixes quickly. The sugar will dissolve without heating.

Season and flavor cold foods boldly. Our perception of flavor is muted when foods are cold, so they need more flavor to make an impression.

Prechill the mix in the refrigerator freezer, stirring occasionally, until it begins to freeze at the edges. This will speed the churning process and produce a finer texture.

To freeze the mix in a canister or machine, fill the container up to two-thirds full, to leave room for the mix to expand with air and rise over the dasher edge. Leave more room if you're going to add nuts, fruits, or other ingredients near the end of freezing. Churn until the mix is too stiff to continue. For the lightest result, churn the fastest as the mix stiffens, when it can trap texture-softening air bubbles.

To freeze a mix slowly without a canister or machine, use a broad, shallow pan, which provides more surface from which heat can escape. If possible, stir and scrape occasionally to prevent the mix from freezing solid. Slow freezing can take a few hours depending on the mix volume, and produces a relatively grainy consistency.

To freeze a small amount of mix quickly without a canister or machine, use a plastic bag to spread it into a thin layer. This method takes about 30 minutes and produces a finer texture than slow freezing.

- *Prechill a pint/500 milliliters of mix in a 1-gallon/4-liter freezer bag.*
- *Immerse the bag in a large bowl of brine,* with 2 to 3 pounds/1 to 1.3 kilograms of crushed ice tossed with ½ cup/150 grams of granulated salt. Massage the bag occasionally to mix the contents, until they're stiff.
- *To thin-freeze mixes regularly and less wastefully, keep the brine in bags too.* Dissolve 1 pound/0.5 kilogram salt in 3 quarts or liters water, divide this brine between two 1-gallon/4-liter bags, and prefreeze them for at least 5 hours. Then place the prechilled mix bag between the brine bags to freeze.

Harden the newly frozen mix in the refrigerator freezer for several hours to reach its full firmness and keep its ice crystals small. Divide the mix into two or three prechilled containers to harden quickly, and cover them to protect from off odors.

Foods direct from the freezer are too cold to enjoy. They're icy hard and make teeth and heads hurt.

Warm ice creams and ices for serving to 10 to 20°F/−12 to −7°C. If you're going to refreeze the container, remove the food as soon as you can scoop it and refreeze the leftovers immediately to minimize ice crystal growth and graininess.

To warm ices and ice creams quickly, microwave the container for 5 to 10 seconds, then check the consistency and repeat if necessary. Microwaves penetrate deep into icy foods, and slight thawing causes large changes in softness.

ICE CREAMS

Ice creams are frozen mixtures of sweetened milk and cream.

A good ice cream is smooth textured, firm, almost chewy, and cold but not icy. It melts slowly and evenly.

The keys to making a good ice cream are a balanced mix of ingredients and quick freezing, which produce small ice crystals surrounded by a sweet, thick, concentrated cream.

A basic mix for a smooth consistency is equal parts whole milk and heavy cream, and about 20 percent of the total liquid weight in sugar (about 7 tablespoons/100 grams per pint/500 milliliters). This mix is high in milk fat and sugar.

Other ingredients can contribute smoothness and replace some butterfat or sugar. They include egg yolks, evaporated and powdered milks, and corn syrups, starches, pectins and gums, and gelatin.

There are three basic styles of ice cream: fresh, or Philadelphia; custard; and gelato.

- **Fresh or Philadelphia-style ice cream** is made by freezing a mix of fresh milk and cream, sugar, and flavorings. It's the simplest, with the pure flavor of cream, and is at its best freshly made. It becomes hard and grainy when stored. It has a relatively high butterfat content.
- **Custard-style ice cream** is made from a cooked mix of milk, egg yolks, sugar, flavorings, and sometimes cream. The ingredients are heated together to thicken them into a cooked stirred custard, which then freezes to an especially smooth consistency. It's often made with little or no added cream, and has a relatively low butterfat content. The technique can also be applied with heavy cream to make a very rich mix.
- **Gelato custard-style ice cream** is made from a cooked mix of milk, sometimes cream, and a large number of egg yolks, 5 or more per pint/500 milliliters, and is churned gently to minimize aeration and maximize density. Thanks to the abundant yolk emulsifiers and protein, gelato has a very smooth consistency and gloss.

Reduced-fat, low-fat, and nonfat ice creams, and ice milks and frozen yogurt have less milk fat than the 10 percent commercial minimum for ice cream. They replace texture-smoothing milk fat with powdered nonfat milk, corn syrup, and various gums.

Soft-serve ice creams can be made with less sugar and fat than standard ice creams because they're served partly thawed at higher temperatures.

Frozen yogurt is also low in fat, and refreshingly tart. Commercial versions contain very little yogurt and few of its healthful bacteria. To make frozen yogurt with fresh flavor and bacteria, add sugar or fruit preserves to taste to plain yogurt, prechill the mix, and freeze.

To make ice cream, start with the freshest milk and cream. Ultrapasteurized cream has a bland flavor compared to less widely sold pasteurized cream, but helps keep ice crystals small and resists being accidentally churned into butter. Delicious but tart ice creams can be made using crème fraîche.

Handle high-cream mixes carefully to avoid churning their fat into butter. Prechill them thoroughly and churn as briefly as possible.

If using whole vanilla beans or other flavorings, infuse them in hot milk or cream before making the mix. If using flavor extracts, add them after the mix has cooled. Include a small pinch of salt to enhance other flavors.

To make a custard-style mix, whisk together the eggs and sugar, heat the milk and/or cream separately to 180°F/80°C, and whisk the hot liquid into the eggs. Don't add eggs to hot liquid. Heat and stir the mix just until it thickens, around 180°F/80°C. Quickly take the mix off the heat and stir until it cools. Pour it through a fine-mesh strainer and chill.

Don't bother to age ice cream mixes for hours. Aging is important in commercial mixes that include gelatin and stabilizing gums, but in homemade ice cream it encourages cream to separate and churn into butter.

Prechill the mix in the freezer, occasionally stirring and scraping down ice crystals from the edge. To speed this process, divide the mix among several small containers. When the mix reaches 30°F/−1°C or the crystals re-form in a few minutes, the mix is ready to freeze.

Freeze quickly in the ice cream maker with frequent or constant churning to produce the finest ice crystals and texture, and to avoid churning cream into butter. If still-freezing the mix in a pan, stir and scrape every few minutes.

To lighten the mix with air, churn vigorously once the mix has become semisolid and can retain it.

To make a dense, gelato-style ice cream, stir the semisolid mix with as little aeration as possible.

Fold in solid ingredients including nuts, pieces of fruit, or chocolate at the end of churning.

Harden the mix in the freezer once it has become too stiff to churn. Divide the batch into several smaller prechilled containers.

Store ice creams as cold as possible in the back of the freezer. Press plastic wrap directly onto the ice cream to protect it from off odors and freezer burn. Massage out any air pockets.

To scoop a light, delicate ball of ice cream while it's still hard, use the scoop edge to cut a thin, continuous ribbon from the surface and roll it into a ball.

Serve ice creams in chilled bowls.

ICES, GRANITAS, SORBETS, AND SHERBETS

Ices are simple frozen dishes made with just fruit or a flavored water (coffee, tea, cocoa, wine), sugar, and sometimes milk. They melt in the mouth to a refreshing sweet-tart moistness.

Granitas and granités are still-frozen ices, usually less sweet than sorbets and intentionally coarse and grainy.

Sorbets are churned ices, relatively sweet and fine textured.

Sherbets are churned ices made with some milk.

Most ices are robust and even reversible. They can be pulverized and softened for serving in a food processor, or thawed, modified, and refrozen.

Ice consistency depends on the sugar content of the mix and the consistency of the fruit ingredient.

The higher the sugar content, the smaller the ice crystals and the finer the consistency.

Thick purees make finer-grained ices than thin purees and juices. Apricot, raspberry, and pineapple purees make especially fine-grained ices.

To make unusually creamy ices, include some avocado, which is high in oil, at 1 part for every 3 parts of the main fruit. In larger amounts it becomes less anonymous.

Mixes produce a smooth ice when they contain 25 to 30 percent sugar by weight, including the fruit's own sugar. This ranges between 3 and 6 tablespoons/45 and 90 grams added sugar per pint/500 milliliters. Less sugar makes a grainier ice, more sugar a sticky-sweet, syrupy ice.

To make a lower-sugar smooth ice, replace a quarter of the sugar with corn syrup or a few spoons of high-alcohol spirits or liqueur.

To make an intentionally coarse granita, add as little sugar as you like.

Balance the sweetness of added sugar with acid from lemon or lime juice or sour salt (citric acid).

Some fruit juices and purees benefit from dilution with water to make them taste more delicate, less like simple frozen fruit. Melons and pears are examples. Sour lemon and lime juices require dilution just to be palatable. Dilution also makes a larger volume of ice from the same volume of fruit.

To make simple granitas, freeze the mix without stirring in a pan. To serve, scrape crystals from the surface with a spoon or fork and collect them in a prechilled container. Or thaw the ice just until soft enough to break up with a fork, then crush by hand or in a food processor.

To make granitas ready to serve directly from the freezer, stir the mix occasionally during freezing so that it forms loose crystal masses.

To make sorbets and sherbets, prechill the mix in the freezer, stirring occasionally, until it begins to crystallize around the edges, then churn in an ice cream maker until stiff.

Store ices airtight, pressing plastic wrap directly onto the surface to protect them from off odors.

Warm ices before serving to make them easier to scoop and eat. To warm quickly, heat the container in a microwave oven for 10 seconds, check the consistency, and repeat if necessary.

Serve ices in chilled bowls.

COLD AND FROZEN MOUSSES AND SOUFFLÉS

Mousses are flavorful liquids, purees, or pastes given both structure and lightness by being combined with whipped egg whites and/or whipped cream, and then chilled or frozen until set.

Frozen mousses are a good alternative to homemade ice creams. They're frozen without stirring, their texture is usually smoother, and they're easier to serve.

To make mousses with full flavor, minimize the proportion of flavor-diluting egg or cream foams.

To retain as much of the foam's volume as possible, gently fold the ingredients together or stir with a balloon whisk. To fold, mix a quarter of the foam thoroughly with the rest of the mix to loosen it, pour the mix onto the foam or vice versa, and stroke down into and up out of the foam, repeating until the two are evenly combined.

Gelatin is included in the base mix for Bavarian creams and some other mousses. It provides extra firmness for unmolding and an attractive gloss. Before adding it, warm the base mix to at least 100°F/38°C, to make sure that the gelatin is evenly dispersed before it cools and gels.

Refrigerate cold mousses until chilled and firm throughout, at least 2 hours for individual servings and 4 hours for larger dishes.

Frozen mousses and soufflés are essentially lightened versions of ices and ice creams. The mixes are frozen without stirring in a mold or individual serving dishes.

Semifreddos are chilled or frozen combinations of cake and a custard-style ice cream mix made light and fluffy by the addition of whipped cream.

Freezing without stirring can produce an icy, grainy consistency.

To minimize graininess in frozen mousses and soufflés, choose a mix that includes egg yolks, corn syrup, or gelatin, which interfere with ice crystal growth, and whip the cream and/or egg whites to their maximum volume.

Cover mousses and soufflés loosely with plastic wrap to minimize the pickup of off odors during chilling, freezing, and frozen storage.

COLD JELLIES

Cold jellies (not the fruit preserves) are flavorful, glossy, slick, often transparent masses that melt in the mouth. They're made from many different liquids, including meat stocks (aspics, p. 320), wines, spirits (jelly shots), fresh fruit and vegetable juices and purees, and milks and cream (panna cotta). Pieces of meat or fish, eggs, vegetables, and fruits can be embedded in jelly.

Gelatin turns liquids into solid jellies. Gelatin is a protein extracted from animal skins and bones. It dissolves invisibly into warm or hot liquids, sets them into moist solids when chilled, and melts again when warmed to body temperature, in the mouth or in a warm room.

To make jellies without animal gelatin, use vegetarian substitutes made from seaweed carbohydrates. Supermarkets carry versions made from carrageenan that come with detailed instructions. Agar, also called kanten, is a seaweed carbohydrate available in Asian markets. Agar jellies aren't the same as gelatin jellies. They need to be cooked near the boil to dissolve the agar. When cooled, they set to a brittle texture, and melt again only at 185°F/85°C, not in a warm room or in the mouth. To be eaten, they need to be chewed.

Manufactured gelatin is sold in two forms, as a powder and in sheets.

Powdered gelatin is measured out by packet, volume, and weight. Packets usually contain about 2 ¼ teaspoons/7 grams of gelatin.

Sheet gelatin is measured by the sheet or by weight. Sheets come in different weights, sizes, and strengths. There's no general way to convert proportions between sheet and powdered gelatins.

Premoisten all gelatins in cold water to prevent clumping when added to the warm or hot liquid. If clumping occurs, stir constantly until the clumps eventually dissolve. This can take some time.

To prepare powdered gelatin for use, pour a small amount of cold water into a shallow bowl, sprinkle gelatin evenly over the surface, and let it absorb water for 5 to 10 minutes. Then mix the moistened gelatin with other ingredients.

To prepare sheet gelatin for use, place it in a bowl, cover with cold water, and let it absorb water for 5 to 10 minutes. Then remove it, squeeze out excess water, and dissolve it into other ingredients.

Add gelatin to liquids only after they're cooked and ready to set. Gelatin breaks down and loses setting power when it's exposed to high or prolonged heat.

Jelly firmness depends on the concentration of gelatin in the liquid, and on the other ingredients. Too much gelatin makes a rubbery, chewy jelly, while too little won't set the liquid at all.

The standard firm dessert jelly made from packaged mixes is about 3 percent gelatin, or 1 packet in 1 cup/250 milliliters water.

To make a tender jelly that can still be unmolded, use 1 packet to 2 cups/500 milliliters liquid. For a tremblingly delicate jelly, use 1 packet in 3 cups/750 milliliters water.

Ingredients that firm jellies include moderate amounts of sugar, milk, and alcohol.

Ingredients that soften jellies include salt and acids. Fruit juices and wines are acid and require more gelatin for a given firmness than other liquids.

Don't try to make jellies with fresh fruits and spices that contain protein-digesting enzymes, which break down gelatin and jellies. These include figs, kiwis, mangoes, melons, papayas, peaches, and pineapples, and fresh ginger. Thoroughly cook these ingredients first, or use canned fruits instead of fresh.

To make the clearest jellies from fruit juice, strain or clarify it, and dilute with some water if necessary.

Tea and red wine make cloudy jellies because their tannins cluster with the gelatin proteins.

To prevent food pieces from sinking or floating instead of being dispersed evenly in a jelly, allow the gelatin solution to thicken somewhat before adding the pieces.

Chill gelatin mixtures to set in the refrigerator. Jellies will set in a few hours, but they will continue to firm slowly for several days. Large volumes take longer to set than individual portions.

To rescue a jelly that fails to set, warm it gently to 105°F/40°C, sprinkle additional powdered gelatin on a small portion to moisten and dissolve, then stir into the rest of the mix, and chill a spoonful quickly in the freezer. If it doesn't set when cold, then repeat.

Store jellies in the refrigerator. Don't freeze them, which causes them to leak liquid when thawed.

Unmold and serve jellies by gently warming the mold and knife.

When cutting jelly into decorative shapes, chill the cutting surface and knife to avoid melting.

Serve jellies on chilled dishes.

Chocolate is one of the most mouth-fillingly delicious

22

CHOCOLATE AND COCOA

Chocolate is one of the most mouthfillingly delicious foods we have and one of the most elaborately processed. It starts with a fatty tropical seed, the cacao bean, which gets fermented, dried, roasted, ground, and sweetened with sugar. The result is deeply nutty, fruity, bitter and astringent, and sweet, with a brittle snappiness that melts in the mouth to rich velvet.

Chocolate is also the one triumphant creation of the food industry. None of today's velvety chocolates could exist until manufacturers figured out how to separate cacao beans into their cocoa fats and solids, and grind the solids down to nearly undetectable fineness.

Many chocolate foods are easy to prepare. Not so easy is making chocolate coatings and candies that are as glossy, as snappy to bite into, and as luscious in the mouth as the ones we can buy.

The key to much of chocolate's magic is its cocoa fat, which is what allows us to melt it and shape it. If we melt it and cool chocolate casually, then its cocoa fat forms a casual, disorganized structure. The chocolate surface becomes uneven and mottled, and it feels soft and greasy on the fingers and in the mouth.

But if we *temper* the chocolate, or melt and shape it at just the right temperatures, then its cocoa fat sets in a highly organized structure. That's what gives chocolate a beautifully matte or mirrorlike surface, and a dry solidity that snaps between the teeth and melts juicily and coolingly in the mouth.

Tempering takes time and trouble, but it's a fascinating process even when it goes wrong, and it's easy to start over again and get it right. I've been captivated enough by chocolate to have spirited fresh cacao pods from South America to California, fermented the beans for days in my kitchen, then dried and roasted and pounded them, just to get some feeling for how a bitter, astringent, and aromaless raw seed could possibly become an epitome of deliciousness. I can't do that every day! But I can always melt some chocolate, temper it, and mix it with toasted nuts to make after-dinner chocolates as fresh and snappy as anything I can buy—and enjoy the inscrutable serendipity of a tropical seed whose fat is so well designed to please.

SHOPPING FOR CHOCOLATES AND COCOA

Cacao beans are grown and fermented in many tropical and subtropical countries, and most are shipped to consuming countries to be processed into chocolate and cocoa. "Fair-trade" products are meant to have been made from beans for which a higher price is paid to farmers in developing countries. Chocolate and cocoa are highly variable ingredients. They're sold in many different formulations that may include milk solids, other flavorings, and anything from no sugar to a lot of sugar. A recipe that works well with one kind or brand of chocolate can be a disaster with a different one.

Double-check what kind of chocolate or cocoa a recipe calls for and try to buy that kind, especially if a percentage of cacao bean solids is specified. If you can't, try to adjust the recipe for the kind you have.

Taste different brands of chocolate and cocoa to know what choices you have.

Inexpensive mass-market chocolates are made with inexpensive cacao beans, the minimum allowed proportion of cacao solids and the maximum allowed sugar, and have a simple, mild flavor.

Expensive "fine" and "artisan" chocolates are usually made with a higher proportion of higher-quality cacao solids. They have a relatively strong, complex flavor.

Milk chocolates contain less cacao solids than dark chocolates and include dried milk powder. They have the mildest chocolate flavor.

"White chocolate" contains no cacao solids at all, just cocoa fat, sugar, dried milk powder, and flavorings. It has a very mild flavor, mainly from vanilla and milk.

CHOCOLATE SAFETY AND STORAGE

Chocolate itself, and foods made primarily of chocolate, present little hazard. They're too dry and sweet for most microbes to survive on them.

Don't discard chocolate that develops a white surface film or mottling, which is fat or sugar particles created by temperature changes or high humidity. Use the chocolate in cooking, or melt and temper it.

Keep chocolate confections for a few weeks at room temperature. In humid climates, wrap airtight to avoid development of white, gritty sugar "bloom" on surface. Eat nut confections quickly; nut oils stale faster than chocolate does.

Store chocolate confections for weeks or months wrapped airtight in the refrigerator or freezer. Before freezing, refrigerate them for a day or more; and to thaw, leave them for 24 hours in the refrigerator before bringing them to room temperature. Large temperature changes can cause cracking when chocolate and fillings expand or shrink. Allow chilled candies to warm up fully to room temperature before opening the package. Air moisture will condense on cold chocolates and make them sticky and mottled.

Store plain dark and milk chocolate for months wrapped airtight at cool room temperature. The cocoa solids prevent oxidation, but don't prevent gradual flavor loss and the development of crumbliness. Choose a place where the temperature doesn't change much, to avoid development of a waxy-looking fat "bloom" on the surface.

Store white chocolate for a few weeks wrapped airtight at cool room temperature, somewhat longer in the refrigerator. White chocolate has no antioxidant cacao bean solids and stales faster than dark chocolate.

TOOLS FOR WORKING
WITH CHOCOLATE

Successful chocolate work is made much easier by tools that provide precise control over proportions and temperatures.

A kitchen scale is essential for measuring out chocolate, and useful for measuring everything else with greater precision than cups and spoons can.

An accurate thermometer is essential for tempering chocolate reliably. Inexpensive instant-read thermometers are not accurate enough. Digital cooking thermometers are better. Special chocolate thermometers measure between 40 and 130°F / 4 and 55°C. Infrared thermometers are ideal for tempering because they give instant readings without immersion or the need for cleaning. But don't use them in making ganache to measure cream temperatures, whose water content makes hot surface readings inaccurate.

Spoons made of wood or silicone don't conduct heat out of molten chocolate as they stir, which gives better control of the chocolate temperature.

A water bath or double boiler heats chocolate indirectly and gently. It's a nested set of two saucepans, the bottom one containing water heated by the stove top, the top one containing the chocolate and heated by water or steam from the bottom. Improvise a double boiler by placing a bowl on top of a slightly narrower saucepan of hot water.

Be careful not to wet the chocolate with stray drops or vapor when warming chocolate with water or steam. Small amounts of water cause chocolate particles to clump up and form a hard paste.

A marble or granite slab helps cool melted chocolate for tempering, and isn't damaged by vigorous scraping. A greased baking sheet or a silicone liner can be used instead.

Pastry tubes and bags are tools for extruding or piping ganache into neat, even portions.

Dipping forks and tools ease the handling and draining of food pieces to be coated in melted chocolate.

Chocolate molds hold and set melted chocolate into a variety of decorative shapes.

WORKING WITH COCOA POWDER

Cocoa powders consist mainly of the dried particles of the cacao beans, which carry nearly all the flavor. They also include varying amounts of cocoa fat, from 5 to 25 percent. Higher-fat cocoas make richer dishes. To compare the fat contents of different brands, check their nutrition labels.

"Instant" cocoas contain sugar and milk solids as a mix for making hot chocolate. They're convenience foods, not ingredients for baking.

There are two types of unsweetened cocoa powder: "natural" and "Dutch process." They have different flavors, and can't always be substituted for each other.

"Natural" cocoa is untreated cocoa powder, reddish-brown, very bitter and astringent, and acidic. Its acidity can react with baking soda to help leaven baked goods, and it speeds the setting of flour and egg proteins.

"Dutch process," "alkalized," or "alkali process" cocoa has been treated with a chemical relative of baking soda to make its taste milder. Its color ranges from light brown to nearly black. The darker the color, the milder the taste. It is neutral or slightly basic rather than acidic, doesn't react with baking soda, and slows the setting of proteins.

Make sure you have the type of cocoa called for in a recipe. If you don't, then adjust the recipe to balance the acidity of natural cocoa with baking soda, or the alkalinity of Dutch process cocoa with some acid.

The main challenge in cooking with cocoa is mixing the very dry particles with the other ingredients.

The fat-coated particles can be hard to mix evenly with wet ingredients, and will soak up hot liquid and clump.

To mix cocoa with liquids, whisk in small amounts of cold or warm liquid until you develop a paste. Don't use hot liquid, which causes clumping. Then add the remaining liquid, which may be cold or hot.

KINDS OF CHOCOLATE

The four main types of chocolate are defined by their relative proportions of cacao-bean materials, sugar, and milk solids. Almost all chocolates contain added cocoa fat, natural or artificial vanilla flavor, and lecithin, an emulsifier that helps blend particles and fat together.

Unsweetened chocolate is all cocoa powder and cocoa fat, with no sugar. It's bitter and astringent, an intense source of chocolate flavor and liquid-absorbing power, designed for cooking with other ingredients, not for eating as is.

Bittersweet or semisweet chocolates contain a minimum of about a third cacao-bean materials, powder plus cocoa fat, but can be as much as 90 percent. They're usually between 10 and 50 percent sugar.

Bittersweet chocolates are often sold with a percentage indication. "Seventy-percent" chocolate is 70 percent cocoa particles plus cocoa fat, and 30 percent sugar. Percentages indicate the balance between chocolate flavor and sweetness, not quality.

Sweet chocolate is a minimum of 15 percent cacao-bean materials, and seldom more than 50 percent. It's usually 50 to 60 percent sugar.

Milk chocolate is a minimum of 10 percent cacao-bean materials, and includes as much as 15 percent dried milk solids. It's about 50 percent sugar.

Couverture chocolate is any kind of chocolate formulated with enough additional cocoa fat that when melted it flows well to make thin, even coatings.

"White chocolate" is not really a chocolate. It contains no cocoa particles or chocolate flavor, just mild or deodorized cocoa fat, sugar, and dried milk powder.

Compound coatings or nontempering chocolates are versions of chocolate in which some or all of the cocoa fat has been replaced with other tropical seed fats. They resist softening at warm temperatures and stay shiny and break with a snap without special handling.

WORKING WITH CHOCOLATE

Chocolate has two primary roles in the kitchen. It's melted and rehardened on its own as a coating or candy. And it's mixed with other ingredients to flavor and thicken them.

For shapes or coatings that are evenly matte or glossy, hard, and break with a snap, chocolate must be melted and held in a specific temperature range. This process is called *tempering* and is described below.

Tempering is not essential for many chocolate coatings or shapes, especially if they'll be eaten freshly made and without close attention to their texture. Untempered chocolate tastes just as good. Temper chocolate when you want to savor its appearance and texture, and have the time to do it.

Chocolate work is difficult in hot weather or hot kitchens. Cocoa fat melts around body temperature, and begins to get soft and sticky at warm room temperature.

To melt chocolate without tempering, grate or chop it into small pieces, then heat it with frequent stirring in a water bath or held above a low burner. Or heat it in a bowl in the microwave oven, stopping to stir every 30 seconds.

Don't heat chocolate on its own to more than 120°F/50°C. Plain dark chocolate can tolerate somewhat higher temperatures, but they're best avoided to prevent emulsifier damage and separation of the solids and fat.

When chocolate is mixed with liquid ingredients such as milk and cream, their water dissolves the chocolate's sugar particles into a sugar syrup, and gets absorbed by the flourlike cocoa particles.

Successful chocolate mixtures depend on the correct balance of cocoa fat, syrup-making sugar, and moisture-absorbing cocoa particles. Because different chocolates have different proportions of fat and particles and sugar, be sure to use the kind called for in the recipe, or make adjustments for the chocolate you have.

To substitute a high-percentage artisan chocolate for standard bittersweet, add less chocolate and more sugar. For example, to use 70 percent instead of standard bittersweet at about 50 percent, decrease the amount of chocolate by a third, then add double that subtracted weight in sugar.

When mixing chocolate and liquids, always add at least a quarter to half of the chocolate's weight in water. Too little water will cause the sugar and cocoa particles to stick to each other, and the chocolate will seize up into a hard paste. Chocolates with a higher percentage of cocoa solids require the higher proportion of liquid. When working with cream, remember that it's only 60 to 80 percent water, depending on its fat content.

To rescue chocolate that has seized up, add more liquid so that the sugar particles will dissolve and the cocoa particles will unstick.

To mix chocolate evenly with liquid ingredients, chop the chocolate finely, heat the liquid to at least 120°F/50°C, combine, and stir until the chocolate has completely melted and mixed into the liquid. This can be done in a bowl, mixer, or food processor. Make sure the liquid stays warm enough to keep the cocoa fat melted, at least 90°F/32°C. If necessary, gently reheat the mixture.

The consistency of a chocolate mixture changes with temperature and time. When a chocolate mixture is heated, the cocoa particles continue to absorb moisture, swell, and thicken the mixture. When a chocolate mixture cools to room temperature or below, the cocoa fat solidifies and stiffens the mixture even more.

To lighten or soften the consistency of a chocolate mixture, add cream and/or butter, whose fat is softer than cocoa fat.

TEMPERING CHOCOLATE

Tempering is the process of carefully melting and cooling chocolate so that it sets into a matte or glossy solid that breaks with a snap and melts juicily and coolingly in the mouth. Without tempering, solid chocolate can develop a streaky surface, break softly, and feel either fatty or powdery in the mouth.

Effective tempering methods heat and melt the solid cocoa fat in chocolate into a liquid, then slightly cool it to maintain some of the cocoa fat in the form of specific kinds of solid crystals. These crystals then guide the proper crystallization of the rest of the cocoa fat as it cools all the way to room temperature and hardens.

Tempering methods either add the guiding crystals to the melted chocolate from an already tempered piece of chocolate, or form them from scratch in the melted chocolate.

There are several effective methods for tempering chocolate, and countless minor variations. Some call for measuring precise temperatures; others rely on the sense of touch.

For precision and ease of measuring, use a point-and-shoot infrared thermometer. Check any thermometer for accuracy, because just a degree or two makes a difference.

If you don't have a thermometer, then judge temperatures by placing a toothpick with some chocolate between your lips. The correct end temperature for tempering dark chocolate should feel neither warm nor cool.

Target temperatures are different for dark, milk, and white chocolates. For milk and white chocolate, subtract 4°F/2°C from the temperatures given below.

For quick stove-top temperature adjustments, use a thin metal bowl that can transfer heat rapidly from water bath to chocolate. Use a flexible spatula to scrape chocolate down the sides of the bowl efficiently.

Chop or shave the chocolate into small pieces, to speed warming and ease mixing.

Melt the chocolate in a bowl held over a low burner or partly immersed in hot water at 140 to 160°F/60 to 70°C, or in an oven set on low, around 150°F/65°C. Or melt in a bowl in the microwave oven, heating in 30-second pulses and stirring in between.

FOUR METHODS FOR TEMPERING CHOCOLATE

Here are four different ways to obtain a mass of liquid tempered chocolate. It's easiest if some or all of the solid chocolate is newly bought and snappy, a sign that it's in good temper. A simple but expensive alternative is to use a chocolate tempering machine, which automates the process.

To convert a new batch of shiny and snappy dark chocolate into liquid tempered chocolate, melt it very carefully until its temperature reaches 90°F/32°C (feels neither cool nor warm on the lips), and never gets any higher. The liquid chocolate is now in temper. If you overshoot that temperature, continue with one of the other methods.

To use a piece of tempered dark chocolate to temper a larger batch, melt the batch thoroughly by heating it to 120°F/50°C (hot to the lips), allow it to cool to 93°F/34°C (slightly warm to the lips), then stir the tempered piece gently around the bowl to cool it gradually and release guide crystals. Remove any remaining solid chocolate when the batch reaches 90°F/32°C. This chocolate is now in temper.

To temper dark chocolate from scratch, melt the chocolate to 110 to 120°F / 43 to 50°C (hot to the lips), allow it to cool to around 105°F/41°C (still somewhat hot), then stir continuously until it cools down and thickens noticeably with guide crystals. Then carefully heat it back up to 88 to 90°F / 31 to 32°C (neither warm nor cool). The chocolate is now in temper.

To temper chocolate from scratch more quickly, melt chocolate to 110 to 120°F / 43 to 50°C (hot to the lips), pour half to two-thirds onto a clean, dry stone slab or countertop or sheet pan, and work it with a scraper until it thickens noticeably with guide crystals. Then stir this fraction back into the remainder of the melted chocolate. If its temperature doesn't fall below 91°F/33°C, then repeat with a smaller amount of chocolate. If necessary, warm the batch back up to 88 to 90°F/31 to 32°C, where it will be in temper.

To test chocolate for temper, dip a knife edge or piece of foil into it and put it aside. Tempered chocolate will set in about 5 minutes to an even matte upper surface. Untempered chocolate will remain tacky for 10 minutes or more and develop streaks.

USING TEMPERED CHOCOLATE

Once you've tempered chocolate you need to keep it in temper while you work with it, with the correct proportions of crystals and liquid cocoa fat.

Keep tempered chocolate thin enough to work with by placing the bowl in a bowl of 90 to 93°F/32 to 34°C water, or nestled in a warm heating pad whose temperature you've checked well ahead of time.

If your tempered chocolate gets noticeably thicker, it has crystallized too much and won't coat and release properly. Rewarm it gently over a water bath or with just a few seconds in the microwave until thin again, but still no warmer than 90°F/32°C.

Don't scrape and stir in any chocolate that sets on the side of the bowl. This will speed cooling, crystallizing, and thickening in the tempered chocolate. Wait until you rewarm the bowl, then scrape the sides when the chocolate there remelts.

Warm other ingredients. Foods to be coated—candy fillings, cookies, nuts, fruit pieces—should be dry and at room temperature, 70 to 80°F / 20 to 27°C. Cold fillings will cause the chocolate to set prematurely and softly rather than developing snap.

Let freshly made chocolates or coatings set for 24 hours to develop the most mar-resistant surface and hardest snap. To make neat edges, trim them soon after the chocolate sets but before it becomes brittle.

CHOCOLATE SPREADING, COATING, AND CLUSTERING

The simplest ways to prepare chocolate are to spread it out on a surface to harden into morsels or sheets; to coat fresh or dried fruits, cookies, or other foods with it; or to mix it with toasted nuts to hold them together in clusters.

The surface of tempered chocolate preparations is attractive and resists marring and melting when briefly touched. When it hardens in air, tempered chocolate develops an even, matte appearance. When it hardens in contact with an object, it takes on the surface qualities of that object: matte if it's a piece of wax or parchment paper, glossy if it's a piece of glossy plastic or foil or polished stone, veined if it's a plant leaf.

The surface of untempered chocolate preparations is softer and less even and stable; it quickly becomes mottled and streaked.

To make chocolate pieces or coat or cluster foods with chocolate quickly and casually, simply melt the chocolate without tempering, spoon or spread it onto a surface or dip or stir a food into it, then let it cool and set. The chocolate won't have the best appearance or texture, but it will taste fine.

To speed the hardening of casual chocolates, chill them in the refrigerator or freezer in a covered container. When served they'll start to soften again, and in high humidity will become moist with condensation. Cold-set chocolate will be softer back at room temperature than chocolate set at room temperature.

To make chocolate pieces or coatings or clusters with an even, matte surface and good snap, temper the chocolate first. Allow several hours at room temperature after the chocolate sets to develop a snappy texture. Don't chill, which prevents true snap from developing.

Warm and dry fresh fruits before coating them with tempered chocolate so the chocolate will adhere and harden well. Wash and allow them to warm to room temperature before drying; air moisture condenses on cold surfaces.

GANACHE

Ganache is a soft but solid mixture of chocolate and cream, often flavored with spices or spirits. It's used as a filling in chocolate truffles, and as a filling or coating for cakes. Once made, a ganache may be whipped to make it lighter, or supplemented with butter to make it softer and slow the gradual firming of its cocoa fat. Recently some chocolate makers have been making "water ganaches," based on flavorful liquids without the fat that cream provides.

Ganache is made by melting chocolate and mixing it thoroughly with heated cream and other liquid ingredients, then letting the mixture set.

There are three basic methods for making ganache: mixing solid chocolate with preheated hot cream, mixing solid chocolate with cool cream and warming them together, and mixing melted tempered chocolate with warm cream.

Ganache consistency depends on the kinds and proportions of chocolate and cream you use, and how you mix and cool them. Ganache is essentially a sugar syrup filled and made firm with cocoa particles and droplets of cocoa fat. The more particles and droplets, the firmer the ganache. If the chocolate is kept in temper and cools gradually at room temperature, the ganache will be smooth and fine grained; if the chocolate loses temper or is chilled to set it quickly, it will be soft when warmed and will become grainy with time.

High-percentage chocolates provide more intense flavor and firmness in ganache than standard bittersweet or semisweet chocolate.

Heavy cream, around 38 percent butterfat, makes a richer and firmer ganache than whipping cream, at around 30 percent.

Double-check to make sure you're using the chocolate and cream specified in a recipe. The high proportion of cocoa particles in a high-percentage chocolate can soak up too much water and turn a firm standard-chocolate ganache recipe into an oily, streaky paste. Milk and white chocolates contain less cocoa fat than dark chocolate and make a softer ganache.

For a soft, creamy ganache for a mousse, pastry filling, or pot de crème, use more cream than chocolate, as much as double the amount.

For a medium-firm ganache that will hold its shape in cake icings and in truffles, use equal proportions of cream and chocolate.

For a firmer and more intense ganache, to 1 part cream use approximately 2 parts dark chocolate, 2.5 parts milk chocolate.

Prepare the chocolate by chopping it finely, to promote fast and even melting and mixing.

Prepare the cream by bringing it just to the boil. Heated cream gives the best shelf life for ganache, several days to weeks depending on the recipe. If it's to be infused with dry ingredients (spices, tea, coffee), add them to the hot cream, cover to avoid evaporation and skin formation, infuse 5 to 10 minutes, and strain the cream.

To make the ganache simply, pour the hot cream onto the chopped chocolate, wait 1 minute for much of the chocolate to melt, then stir to finish melting and combine. If some of the chocolate remains solid, warm the bowl over a water bath. For the best ganache consistency, keep chocolate in temper by allowing the cream to cool before adding it so that the mix temperature never rises above 93°F/34°C. When the ganache has formed, stir in any softened butter, flavoring extracts, or spirits.

To make tempered ganache another way, gently melt tempered chocolate to 90°F/32°C and no higher, cool the boiled cream and any other liquid ingredients to 105°F/41°C, and stir quickly to combine before the mix cools and begins to set. When the ganache has formed, stir in any softened butter, flavoring extracts, or spirits.

To set tempered ganache with the best consistency, pour it in a thin layer onto a slab or baking sheet, cover with plastic wrap, and allow to cool and gradually firm at room temperature overnight.

To set the ganache more quickly for shaping the same day, pour it out and allow it to cool until thick, then fold and mix with a few strokes, rest it for a few minutes, and repeat if necessary until the ganache is firm enough to hold a sharp ridge when scraped. Pipe or shape the firm ganache immediately.

Don't refrigerate ganache to speed its setting. It will be too soft when it returns to room temperature, and will become grainy.

To soften a ganache that has become too firm to shape, warm it gently.

To rescue a separated ganache, warm it with occasional stirring over a water bath until it reaches 90 to 92°F / 32 to 33°C, then whisk vigorously or blend with a prewarmed immersion blender or in a prewarmed food processor bowl until the fat disappears into the mixture. If this fails, then repeat with a small amount of added water or spirits to provide more volume in which the fat can be dispersed.

CHOCOLATE TRUFFLES

Truffles are balls of ganache coated with a thin layer of chocolate and/or dusted with cocoa.

The finest truffles have an even, snappy coating and cleanly melting interior. They require tempered chocolate for the ganache and coating, and a day or more of maturing.

Everyday truffles aren't as snappy or clean-melting, but are still delicious and can be made with less trouble and time.

Make the ganache filling an hour or more before shaping and coating, and let it firm at room temperature. If the ganache has been made ahead and refrigerated, allow it to warm to room temperature before shaping and coating.

Don't speed truffle making by refrigerating newly made ganache to firm it for coating. This will cause the chocolate shell to crack. Cold ganache expands as it warms, while the molten chocolate coating shrinks as it cools.

Form ganache balls in hands washed well and then rinsed with cool water; hot hands melt chocolate. Manipulate the ganache as little as possible. For a lighter truffle center, use a melon baller to scoop a continuous thin layer of ganache into a ball.

To coat the ganache balls with chocolate, temper the chocolate or melt it in a bowl or pan to 95°F/35°C, then dip the balls using a fork or special dipping utensil, shaking off as much excess as possible before placing them on a rack or clean surface to set.

For an especially thin coating, place a small amount of melted chocolate in the palm of one hand and roll the ball over it with the fingertips of the other hand. Allow the coating to solidify, then repeat if necessary to even it out.

For the best eating consistency, let truffles mature for several hours at room temperature. Immediate refrigeration prevents the cocoa fat from crystallizing fully and results in a soft, greasy feeling that becomes grainy with time.

MOLDED CHOCOLATES

When poured into a glossy candy or chocolate mold, tempered chocolate develops a glossy, hard surface that resists marring and melting when briefly touched. If the chocolate isn't tempered, its surface will be uneven, streaked, and greasy.

Keep tempered chocolate warm and relatively thin so it will be fluid and coat the mold evenly.

To keep chocolate in temper during molding, make sure the mold is slightly warm, 77 to 85°F/25 to 30°C, and any filling between 70 and 80°F/20 and 27°C.

Make cream fillings for molded chocolates with cooked fondants, or with uncooked sugar doughs made with fondant sugar, corn syrup, and flavors. Recipes that include invertase, an enzyme that slowly liquefies fondant, will produce a moister center with shelf life of several weeks at room temperature.

Let freshly molded chocolate rest at least 15 minutes at room temperature, so the guide crystals will dominate the setting and the chocolate will shrink slightly and release itself from the mold. Premature chilling prevents proper setting, shrinkage, and release.

Refrigerate the molds after resting at around 40°F / 4°C for 10 to 15 minutes, or until the chocolates have shrunk slightly and unmold easily. Solid chocolates take longer to shrink than filled chocolates.

Let freshly made chocolates set at room temperature for 24 hours to develop a hard, mar-resistant surface and snap. To neaten their edges, trim them soon after the chocolate sets but before it becomes brittle.

Avoid washing plastic molds with soap, which is hard to rinse away completely and can taint the next batch.

CHOCOLATE DECORATIONS AND MODELING CHOCOLATE

Chocolate is a versatile decorative material and can be formed into almost any shape while it's warm and malleable.

Make most decorative shapes with tempered chocolate, which will set quickly and to an even-surfaced, hard, durable mass.

Modeling chocolate is a claylike mixture of chocolate and corn syrup, made for forming into permanent decorative shapes.

To make modeling chocolate, melt chocolate, combine it with a third to half its weight of corn syrup, and knead the mixture until it's homogeneous and pliable. If it becomes too stiff to work, add more corn syrup. Once shaped and left to dry out, it will harden.

CHOCOLATE DRINKS, SAUCES, PUDDINGS, AND MOUSSES

Hot cocoa and hot chocolate can be made with water, milk, cream, or a combination. Chocolate will make a richer drink than cocoa due to its high fat content, while cocoa carries more concentrated chocolate aroma and bitterness.

For the purest chocolate flavor, heat the liquid just to serving temperature. Higher temperatures add a cooked-milk flavor. Whisk unheated liquid slowly into cocoa powder and sugar, then heat the mixture and stir or blend until it's thickened. Or grate chocolate, add it to the warm liquid, and stir or blend it in as it melts.

Chocolate sauces and chocolate fondue are similar to hot chocolate, and best made in the same way, with moderate heat.

Hot fudge sauce is a thick mixture of cocoa powder and chocolate with sugar and cream.

For a hot fudge sauce that gets chewy and candylike when chilled on ice cream, choose a recipe that calls for cooking the sugar into a concentrated syrup.

Chocolate pudding is another simple mixture of milk or cream and chocolate, thickened into a moist solid with cornstarch. For the best flavor and consistency, mix cold milk gradually into the cornstarch, heat the mixture until thickened and the starchy aroma has faded, and stir in the chocolate at the end.

To make a more intense chocolate pudding, thicken it with cocoa particles. Omit the cornstarch, replace with more chocolate or cocoa, and heat the mixture just until thick. It will thicken further and set when chilled.

Chocolate mousses are chocolate-flavored foams of egg whites, cream, or a combination, sometimes including gelatin. The egg whites or cream are whipped into a foam with sugar, then scraped onto a liquid mix of molten chocolate and egg yolk, and the mix carefully stirred or folded into the foam to minimize the loss of bubbles.

To fold, slowly and gently scoop up the chocolate base and trail it along the foam, repeating until base and foam are just mixed evenly.

Let mousses rest for up to an hour at room temperature before chilling several hours. This encourages the cocoa fat to set in crystals that will melt more cleanly and refreshingly in the mouth.

23

SUGARS, SYRUPS, AND CANDIES

Sugars are brilliant building materials, and sugar candies are marvels of microengineering. As foods they may be completely frivolous indulgences, but they feed more than the sweet tooth.

Manufactured candies can be very good, and they're what nearly everyone grows up on and has early and strong memories of. It was on a visit to France right after college that I encountered salted caramels in Brittany. That was my first taste of a candy that really invited savoring.

I've never really craved sweets, but I sometimes do crave the experience of making them. There's no other kind of cooking quite like it, starting with the same basic combination of table sugar and water and creating such different textures, from syrupy to creamy to chewy to crunchy to rocky. And one sugar preparation is my all-time favorite example of the alchemy of cooking. Start with pure table sugar, a single kind of molecule, colorless, odorless, and simply sweet. Add heat, and you create caramel: many hundreds of new molecules, brown color, rich aroma, sweet and tart and bitter.

Candy making is also unusual for the exacting nature of its recipes, which specify narrow temperature ranges for a given kind of texture. Monitoring the temperature of a scalding-hot, sticky syrup can be a little daunting. But a number of candies can be made casually and quickly, by heating the syrup in a microwave oven and using color changes as temperature indicators. The results may not be as consistent as you can get on the stove top, but they're still delicious. And the alchemy remains.

SUGAR AND CANDY SAFETY

Solid sugars and candies present little health hazard from microbes. They're cooked to high temperatures and contain little water for microbes to grow on. Liquid syrups can develop surface molds when stored for a long time.

Discard syrups with visible mold growth, or skim the mold off, bring syrup to the boil, and skim again before using.

Don't serve honey in any form to children less than one year old, who are susceptible to botulism spores that honey commonly contains.

Candy making can be hazardous. Sugar syrups get far hotter than boiling water, easily splatter and spill, stick to skin, and can cause serious burns instantaneously.

Take extra care when you make candy. Anticipate and think through every transfer of hot syrup from one place to another. Don't let children make candy without close supervision.

If you're burned by hot syrup, immediately place the injured skin under cold running water for several minutes before applying first aid.

CHOOSING AND STORING SUGARS, SYRUPS, AND CANDIES

Sugars and syrups come in innumerable types and variations. If you're following a recipe, choose the ingredients it specifies. Otherwise try out unfamiliar ingredients to learn about new flavors.

Store sugars for months at room temperature, tightly wrapped to avoid stickiness from humid air.

Store cooked syrups and maple syrup for months in the refrigerator. Molds can spoil them at room temperature. Corn and other manufactured syrups usually don't require refrigeration; check labels.

Store candies for weeks at room temperature. Wrap them airtight in humid climates.

Store candies for months wrapped airtight in the refrigerator or freezer. If they're frozen, allow them to thaw 24 hours in the refrigerator and then warm to room temperature before opening the package. Room moisture will condense on cold candies, making them sticky and mottled.

SPECIAL TOOLS FOR MAKING CANDIES

Several special tools help you make candy more easily, reliably, and safely.

An accurate thermometer is essential for cooking sugar syrups to specific concentrations. Inexpensive instant-read thermometers are not accurate or wide-ranging enough. Digital cooking thermometers are better. Special candy thermometers measure to 400°F/200°C; some clip to the side of the saucepan for continuous monitoring.

Don't use noncontact infrared thermometers in candy making. Their readings aren't reliable because they register the escaping water vapor, not the syrup.

A kitchen scale is useful for measuring ingredients with greater precision than cups and spoons allow.

Choose spoons made of wood or silicone, which don't conduct heat out of a syrup as you stir. This is good for the syrup (faster cooking, no undesired local cooling and crystallization) and the cook (a cool handle). Long handles help keep hands away from heat.

A pastry brush helps push crystallized sugar on the sides of a saucepan back down into the cooking syrup.

A marble or granite slab or countertop helps speed the cooling of hot sugar syrups and melted chocolate, and isn't damaged by vigorous scraping. A greased baking sheet or a silicone liner can be used instead.

Scrapers are large, flat blades of metal or plastic for manipulating sugar syrups as they cool on a countertop or stone slab.

Candy molds hold and set candy syrups into a variety of decorative shapes.

CANDY INGREDIENTS: SUGARS

The candy maker works with two sets of ingredients: sugars, and other ingredients that influence flavor, texture, or color.

Kitchen sugars contain three different chemical sugars: sucrose, glucose, and fructose.

Sucrose is good at forming crystals and provides the main solid substance of candies.

Glucose and fructose are smoothing agents. When dissolved with sucrose, they get in the way as sucrose forms crystals, and prevent the crystals from growing large and coarse. They help create both creamy and glassy candies.

Kitchen sugars come in two basic kinds. Standard white table sugar and brown sugar are entirely or mostly sucrose, but manufactured syrups and specialty sugars are mainly glucose and fructose.

White granulated table sugar is the standard sugar in candy making. It's extracted from sugarcane and sugar beets. Very rarely, beet sugar can carry off aromas or trace materials that cause foaming.

Confectioners' sugar is finely powdered white sugar together with some cornstarch. It's used more for dusting candies than making them.

Fondant sugar is powdered white sugar without cornstarch. Its particles are too small to feel grainy, so it can be mixed with a little water to make fudgelike candies without any cooking.

Brown sugars are less pure and more flavorful than white sugar. Their sucrose crystals are coated with a thin syrup layer of glucose, fructose, other flavors of caramel or molasses, and brown pigments. Brown sugars vary in color and flavor, from light and mild to dark and strong.

Corn syrup is about 20 percent water, 15 percent glucose, 10 percent other sugars, and the rest tasteless thickening molecules derived from cornstarch. It limits sucrose crystallization and smoothes candy textures. It tastes much less sweet than sugar or honey and often includes vanilla flavoring.

High-fructose corn syrup is mostly a mixture of glucose and fructose, with about 20 percent water and some long thickening molecules. It tastes much sweeter than ordinary corn syrup.

Glucose syrup is the professional version of corn syrup, available without added flavorings and in several sweetnesses. It can be very thick and almost tasteless.

Honey is a syrup made by bees from flower nectar, a mixture of fructose and glucose in water. It limits sucrose crystallization as corn syrup does, but its distinctive flavor also limits its usefulness in candy making.

Invert sugar is a texture-smoothing mixture of glucose and fructose, available from specialty stores.

To make invert sugar, gently boil table sugar with a little water and some acid, either lemon juice or cream of tartar, for 30 minutes. This converts sucrose into a mixture of glucose and fructose.

Molasses is a strong-flavored, syrupy by-product of cane sugar manufacturing, rich in texture-smoothing glucose and fructose.

OTHER CANDY INGREDIENTS

Invertase is an enzyme that slowly converts table-sugar sucrose into glucose and fructose, usually in creamy and liquid candy centers made of fondant or ganache. This conversion also slows mold growth and spoilage.

Always add invertase to a candy mix after it has been cooked and is no longer hot. High temperatures above 160°F/70°C destroy invertase activity.

Flavor and color ingredients are often concentrated into essences or extracts so that there's little or no water to cook off.

Milk, cream, butter, and egg whites contribute structure, fat, and flavor to many different confections. Their normal water content and tendency to scorch or curdle require long, slow cooking. Condensed milks and powdered egg whites are often used to shorten cooking times and avoid curdling.

Pectin is used to make fruit jelly candies. Use the concentrated powder form, not the liquid. Pectin is the component of fruit cells that causes jams to thicken with sugar and acid.

Gelatin is used to turn a concentrated sugar syrup into gummy candies, and to give chewy body to marshmallows. It's the dried animal protein used to make dessert jellies.

Cool hot sugar syrups before mixing with gelatin to avoid breaking it down with excess heat.

Starch is used to make Turkish delight and similar jelly candies, and to line the molds for molded candies. It's a fine carbohydrate powder extracted from corn and other plants.

THE ESSENTIALS OF MAKING CANDIES

Sugar candies are mixtures of sugar and water, along with minor ingredients. They're defined largely by their texture, which can range from a hard brittle to a luscious cream. Candy texture depends on two factors: their proportions of sugar and water, and the size of their sugar crystals.

You control the proportions of sugar and water in a candy by boiling them together in a syrup to a specific temperature.

The higher the boiling point of a syrup, the firmer the candy it makes. Boiling a sugar syrup evaporates water away and concentrates the sugar. As the sugar concentration rises, the boiling point does too.

The standard syrup boiling points for different candies are named by the consistency of the syrup when a little is dropped in cold water, or the sound it makes when the cooled sample is bitten.

CANDY SYRUP TEMPERATURES

SYRUP STAGE	TEMPERATURE, °F / °C (at sea level)	CANDIES MADE WITH THIS SYRUP
Thread	215–235/102–113	preserves, fruit jellies
Soft ball	235–240/113–116	soft fondant, fudge, caramel
Firm ball	245–250/118–121	hard caramel, marshmallow
Hard ball	250–265/121–130	soft taffy, fruit gums
Soft crack	270–290/132–143	hard taffy, firm nougat
Hard crack	300–320/149–160	brittles, butterscotch, toffee
Caramel	340/170 and above	caramel cages, spun sugar

Above about 300°F/150°C, sugar breaks down into caramel, a brown and aromatic mixture. As the temperature rises and caramel darkens, it becomes increasingly aromatic but also bitter.

You control how the syrup sugar crystallizes by how you handle the syrup as it cools down. When the syrup cools, the dissolved sugar molecules begin to rebond to each other into solid crystals or noncrystalline glass.

If you cool the syrup without stirring in the pot or kneading on

the countertop, the sugar forms large, grainy crystals and a coarse texture.

If you cool the syrup with vigorous stirring or kneading at the right stage, the sugar forms tiny crystals and a fine texture.

Other ingredients can limit sugar crystallization and help produce glassy, crystal-free hard candies, or tiny-crystal creamy ones. Corn syrups, honey, and invert sugar contain glucose and fructose sugars, which interfere with table sugar crystallization. Acid ingredients in a syrup can break down some of the table sugar into glucose and fructose, and also help smooth candy texture.

WORKING WITH SUGAR SYRUPS

Nearly all candies are made by cooking a sugar syrup to a specific high temperature, then manipulating it as it cools down and solidifies.

Candy making is normally done on the stove top, where the cook can observe syrups, measure temperatures, and adjust heat constantly to get the best results. Reasonably good candies can also be made in the microwave oven, which gives the cook less hands-on control, but cooks syrups more rapidly and evenly without the worry of scorching the pan bottom.

To make candies in the microwave, use a light metal mixing bowl, which won't be as heavy or retain as much heat as a microwave-safe glass bowl. Oven power levels vary, so check syrup temperatures frequently to avoid overcooking.

Be very careful when you cook sugar syrups. They get much hotter than boiling water, easily boil over and splatter, stick to the skin, and can cause serious burns.

Clear the stove top and enough counter or table space to handle hot syrups without obstacles. When pouring, hold the pot edge close to the new container or surface to prevent spills. Wear rubber or latex gloves to pull taffies and brittles or do pulled sugar work.

Cook syrups in a large pot with several times the volume of the initial ingredients, tall to allow plenty of room for the mix to boil up without boiling over, and broad to speed evaporation from the mix.

When measuring temperatures with a fixed or handheld thermometer, make sure the thermometer tip isn't close to the heated pot bottom or side to avoid misleadingly high readings. Take the pot briefly off the heat to get a stable reading.

Correct boiling temperatures for your altitude if you live significantly above sea level. Reduce recipe temperatures by 2°F/1°C for every 1,000 feet/300 meters of elevation.

Candy making is affected by the weather. It's difficult to make candies in a humid kitchen because sugars quickly absorb moisture from the air, making hard candies sticky and aerated candies soft.

To compensate for high humidity, cook syrups 2 to 3°F/1 to 2°C hotter than recipes specify.

Use a wet pastry brush on the pot walls to dissolve and wash crystallized sugar back into the syrup as it boils and spatters. If these crystals end up in finished syrup, they'll make the candy grainy.

Cook syrups with dairy products over moderate heat with constant stirring to avoid scorching on the pan bottom.

Don't try to shorten cooking times with high heat, or leave the pot unattended even briefly to do other things, or it may boil over or scorch. Cooking candy syrups can take a half hour or longer.

Lower the heat as the syrup temperature gets close to the target. Syrup temperatures rise faster toward the end of the cooking, and it's easy to overshoot.

To stop the cooking quickly, lift the pot off the burner and place it on a cool stone or tile countertop.

Add flavorings and colors to the finished syrup, to avoid losing or changing them as the syrup cooks.

To clean pots, fill them promptly with hot water and allow the hardened sugar to dissolve before scrubbing.

SYRUPS AND SAUCES

Sugar syrups can absorb and carry aromas from other ingredients, and their concentrated sugars give them a pleasing saucelike thickness.

To make "simple syrup" for cocktails or fruit ices, combine table sugar and water and heat until the sugar has dissolved. Store the syrup in a closed container. Refrigerate to keep for more than a few days and prevent spoilage by molds.

Simple syrup is made in two strengths. Equal volumes of sugar and water make a 1:1 syrup that's 45 percent sugar. Two volumes of sugar and one of water make a 2:1 syrup that's 63 percent sugar.

A 2:1 simple syrup is a handy liquid equivalent for table sugar, spoonful for spoonful. It provides the same weight of sugar in a given volume as table sugar itself does. (A spoonful of sugar crystals is almost half air.)

To make flavored syrups, prepare a simple syrup and infuse with fruits, fruit peels, herbs, or spices. To extract the most flavor, break the flavor ingredients into small pieces or crush the tissue, simmer until the syrup is well flavored, then strain.

Caramel syrups and sauces provide the flavor of sugar itself cooked very hot, to the point that it turns brown and aromatic.

To make caramel syrup on the stove top:

- *Have a bowl of water ready* for quick cooling of the pot bottom.
- *Heat the sugar* alone or with a small amount of water, stirring constantly to keep the pot bottom from scorching.
- *When the sugar colors, reduce the heat to low and watch carefully.* The sugar darkens quickly and can develop harsh flavors. When the color is right, turn off the heat. Use the bowl of water if necessary to arrest the cooking immediately.
- *Tilt the pan away* to avoid hot spatter, add water, and stir to mix.

To make caramel syrup in the microwave:

- *Use a light metal mixing bowl* and heat the sugar and any water on high power.
- *Stop the heating regularly* to check the color and stir.
- *Remove the syrup* from the microwave when it's done and cool the bowl briefly in a larger bowl of cold water. If you've used a heat-resistant glass bowl, don't cool it in water, which will cause cracking.
- *Tilt the bowl away* to avoid hot spatter, slowly add water to the syrup, and stir to mix.

To make caramel sauce, make stove-top or microwave caramel and thin with cream instead of water.

To make butterscotch sauce, cook sugar on the stove top or in the microwave until it begins to color, then add butter and continue to cook until it turns light brown and aromatic. Thin with cream as for caramel sauce.

HARD CANDIES: BRITTLES, LOLLIPOPS, TOFFEES, TAFFIES, AND SUGAR WORK

Hard candies are solid masses of sugar, most of them glassy and with little or no graininess. They're made from syrups boiled to a high temperature to remove almost all water, and often include large proportions of grain-preventing corn syrup. They can be difficult to make without stickiness in humid weather.

Stir syrups constantly to make sure the thermometer registers the true temperature. Reduce the heat as the temperature approaches 300°F/150°C to avoid undesired browning.

Brittles are thin, crunchy sheets of hard candy, usually embedding pieces of nuts. Baking soda leavens the syrup with crunch-amplifying bubbles, and deepens color and flavor due to its alkalinity.

Cook raw nuts along with the brittle syrup, or add cooked nuts as the syrup approaches 300°F/150°C.

Stir the brittle syrup rapidly when adding soda and butter at the end of cooking, so that the foaming doesn't cause it to spill over.

To make brittle less hard and more crisp, especially if the recipe doesn't include baking soda, make it thin. Pour the syrup out to cool, wait until it becomes pliable, then stretch it quickly in all directions.

Lollipops are hard candies stuck to a paper or wood handle.

To make lollipops, boil sugar and corn syrup to about 300°F/150°C, stir in concentrated flavorings and a food-coloring paste, and pour into molds that hold the handles.

To make lollipops without molds, cool the syrup until thick, around

240°F/115°C, and then pour spoonfuls over the ends of the handles on a greased surface.

Rock candy is masses of large sugar crystals that take days or weeks to grow. It's made without corn syrup or other ingredients that would interfere with crystallization.

To make rock candy, combine 2 parts sugar to 1 part water and cook the mixture to 250°F/120°C. Add food coloring paste, pour into a pan, and suspend strings or toothpicks in the syrup for crystals to grow on. Cover and leave in a cool corner undisturbed until crystals develop.

Toffees and crunches are brittle candies made rich with butter, which also helps limit graininess.

To make toffees and crunches, cook the syrup and butter to 300 to 310°F/149 to 154°C, then quickly cool without stirring until workable, and cut or shape individual candies.

Taffies are hard or soft candies that are worked hard to lighten them with tiny air bubbles.

To make taffies, cook the syrup to 290°F/143°C for a hard candy, 250°F/121°C for soft, cool until workable, then knead, fold, and stretch until stiff.

Sugar work includes spun sugar, sugar cages, and satiny pulled sugar ribbons, cords, and other shapes. They're made by manipulating the sugar base while it's still hot and either fluid or doughlike. Kneading and pulling sugar is hard, hot work.

Use a heat lamp and rubber or latex gloves for doing extensive sugar work. The heat lamp will hold the sugar base at working temperature. Gloves protect the fingers and prevent them from marring glossy sugar surfaces.

To make the base for sugar work, cook the mixture of sugar and corn syrup or invert sugar to 315 to 330°F/157 to 166°C. Make spun or poured shapes while it's still fluid, or cool it to 120 to 130°F/50 to 55°C for coloring and pulling.

SOFT CANDIES: FONDANT, FUDGE, PRALINES, AND CARAMELS

Soft candies are creamy, chewy, or crumbly. They're masses of tiny sugar crystals held together with thick sugar syrup, are made from syrups boiled to around 240°F/116°C, and usually include about one third corn syrup or some acid cream of tartar to limit crystal growth.

Fondant is the basic cream candy, and is also used to make cream centers and coatings. It's made only with sugars and sometimes an essential oil. Depending on the proportions of water and sugar, it can be crumbly and dry or creamy and moist.

To cook fondant, heat sugar, water, and corn syrup to 235 to 240°F/112 to 116°C, cool at room temperature without stirring to 125°F/52°C, then work the syrup with a scraper on a marble slab or countertop to make crystals, until it thickens, then turns opaque and crumbly. Knead it together into a single mass, working in any flavoring.

Fondant benefits from a day or more of maturing at room temperature after it's made. It becomes softer and easier to work with.

Store fondant at room temperature until needed, up to several months.

To rework or flavor masses of fondant or fudge, slightly warm them in the microwave oven until pliable.

To make fondant without cooking, mix fondant sugar or confectioners' sugar with corn syrup in a stand mixer until even and smooth.

Fudge is fondant made with the addition of milk or cream, butter, and often cocoa or chocolate.

Chocolate fudge has an added firmness and melting quality thanks to the chocolate's cocoa fat. Fudge made with cocoa powder lacks the fat and this melting firmness.

To make fudge, cook the ingredients to 235 to 240°F/113 to 116°C gradually, to avoid scorching or curdling. Cool the mixture to 110°F/43°C without stirring, then stir it to form crystals until thick, and pour it into a greased pan. Allow it to firm for at least 1 hour before cutting.

Make quick fudgelike confections by warming and mixing confectioners' sugar with dairy and chocolate ingredients.

Pralines are butter-enriched soft candies, either creamy or chewy.

To make creamy pralines, use more granulated sugar than corn syrup, cook the syrup to 240°F/116°C, add butter and beat until it thickens somewhat with crystals and looks less glossy, then spoon out to set.

To make chewy pralines, cook equal amounts of sugar and corn syrup, add butter and cream to the cooked syrup, and return to 240°F/116°C, then spoon out without beating.

Caramels are soft, chewy, caramel-flavored candies. Their flavor comes from the inclusion of milk, cream, and sometimes butter. They're usually grain-free thanks to a large proportion of corn syrup.

Traditional caramels take a long time to cook. Boiling whole milk or cream and sugar to 235 to 245°F/113 to 118°C can take an hour, and this produces a distinctive rich flavor.

Use very fresh milk and cream to make caramels. Long cooking can cause slightly soured dairy products to curdle.

Modern caramel recipes often replace whole milk with canned condensed milk, which takes much less time to cook.

To make caramels, cook the caramel mixture to 235 to 245°F/113 to 118°C over moderate heat and scrape the pot bottom frequently, to avoid scorching. Add butter toward the end to increase the sensation of juiciness when the candies are chewed. Cool without stirring.

FOAMED CANDIES: DIVINITY, NOUGAT, AND MARSHMALLOWS

Foamed candies are light, chewy, usually white confections filled with tiny air bubbles, which come from beating the syrup with foam-creating egg whites or gelatin.

When adding hot sugar syrup to eggs or gelatin in a mixer, pour it steadily down the inside bowl wall. Avoid pouring it directly onto spinning beaters, which will fling some of it out of the foam.

Divinity is a light version of fondant candy, creamy due to small sugar crystals initiated by a small portion of added fondant. For the smoothest candy, choose a recipe that includes a large proportion of corn syrup, honey, or invert sugar.

To make divinity, cook the syrup to around 250°F/121°C and pour it into egg whites whipped to stiff peaks. Add small pieces of premade fondant to the mixture and continue beating until thick.

Nougat is a chewy egg-foam candy that usually includes nuts. It's sometimes flavored with honey that is cooked and added separately to avoid flavor loss and inversion of the main syrup.

To make nougat, cook the syrup to 275°F/135°C, then pour onto egg whites beaten to a stiff foam and whip until cool but still spreadable, adding nuts at the end. To make sticky nougat easier to handle, spread out to set between sheets of edible rice paper.

Marshmallows are the lightest and softest foamed candies. They're usually made with gelatin. Egg whites make marshmallows that are fluffier, less chewy, and faster to dry and stale.

To make marshmallows, cook the syrup to 240°F/116°C for gelatin, 245°F/118°C for moister eggs, then allow to cool to 212°F/100°C. Pour the syrup onto presoaked melted gelatin or eggs whipped to soft peaks and beat for 5 to 15 minutes, stopping occasionally to scrape cooled mix from the walls back into the rest. Beat in any flavors and colors at the end. Spread the mix out and let it firm for several hours before cutting and dusting sticky surfaces with confectioners' sugar.

JELLIES AND GUMS

Jellies and gums are moist, sweet-tart, colorful confections given body by pectin, gelatin, or starch.

Fruit jellies, or French pâtes de fruit, are tender morsels with genuine fruit flavors and color.

To make fruit jellies, combine strained juice or puree with sugar and pectin, and cook the mixture to 225°F/107°C. Add lemon juice or other acid at the very end of cooking to set the pectin; adding earlier will break the pectin down and prevent setting. Pour into a pan lined with waxed paper and allow to firm at least 1 hour before cutting.

Fruit gums, or gummies, are chewy versions of the fruit jelly. They're made with a more concentrated syrup and low-moisture prepared flavors and colors, and thickened with gelatin instead of pectin.

To make fruit gums, cook a mixture of sugar and corn syrup to 250 to 275°F / 120 to 135°C. Cool it to 200°F/93°C without disturbing to avoid crystallization, then mix in soaked melted gelatin, flavorings, and color. Pour into molds to set overnight.

Starch jellies include firm jelly beans and tender Turkish delight (lokum). They're made by cooking a sugar syrup with starch and glucose to 235 to 265°F/113 to 130°C, depending on the desired consistency, then adding flavorings, allowing the mix to set, and shaping.

To make Turkish delight, cook sugar with water and lemon juice to convert some of it into crystal-limiting sugars, then add cornstarch and cream of tartar and cook slowly to 235°F/113°C. Add flavorings, scrape the mix into a greased pan, and allow it to set overnight before cutting and dusting with a mixture of confectioners' sugar and cornstarch.

CANDIED FLOWERS AND FRUITS

Candied flowers and fruits are flowers and fruits turned into confections, coated or impregnated with sugar.

Crystallized, or candied, flowers and petals maintain their original shape and some of their aroma. To make them, brush the petals with thinned egg white, then dust them with superfine sugar and allow them to dry for days at room temperature. To avoid concerns about salmonella, use powdered egg whites.

Candied fruits are whole fruits or pieces impregnated with sugar, which prevents them from spoiling and preserves their shape, color, and some of their aroma. Fruit pieces can be candied in a few hours. Whole fruits take days or weeks to progressively build up the sugar concentration throughout.

To candy fruit slices and citrus peels, cut thin pieces to speed syrup penetration. Remove the bitterness from citrus peels by bringing them to a boil in water and draining, two or three times if needed. Gently simmer slices or peels in syrup until they're translucent. To prevent the slow formation of sugar crystals during storage, include corn syrup in the cooking syrup.

To candy whole fruits and large pieces, immerse them in a light syrup, cook them through gently, and leave to soak. Every day over several days or weeks, remove the fruit, boil the syrup to concentrate it somewhat, and reimmerse the fruit. Continue until the syrup reaches about 75 percent sugars and microbes won't grow in it or the fruit.

Don't try to speed candying. Using too concentrated a syrup at any stage will dehydrate and toughen the fruit surface and actually slow sugar penetration.

24

COFFEE
AND TEA

C offee and tea are stimulating drinks, and caffeine isn't their only active ingredient. Their basic deliciousness, and the endless variations and subtleties in their making, inspire everything from simple liking to broad knowledgeableness to deep obsession.

Coffee and tea get yoked together because we make drinks with both, but they're very different ingredients. Coffee starts as a mature tree seed, a dormant, nutlike package of basic nutrients to nourish the seedling, bitter and astringent to deter animals from eating it. We give the seed intense flavors by roasting it with high heat. Tea starts as a newly opened leaf, also bitter and astringent to deter animals, but actively growing and full of enzymes to build and maintain itself. We provoke the enzymes to create new flavors by wilting and squeezing the leaf, and then preserve or modify those flavors with low or moderate heat.

Slumbering seed and heat, young leaf and its own liveliness. Flavors from two different realms.

When I came of caffeine-drinking age in the early 1970s, my standard choices were canned coffee grounds brewed in a percolator, and a few kinds of bagged teas, so dusty and quick to turn astringent that I measured infusion times in seconds. My first cup of freshly roasted, dark, drip-brewed coffee was almost too flavorful to finish. A few months later I bought the hand-cranked iron grinder that still breaks the quiet of my early mornings.

My son got off to a faster start on twenty-first-century coffee. He prefers his late-model Italian burr grinder to my Spong, and he's instructed me in the proper operation of his espresso machine, advanced milk-foaming techniques, and the better coffee-geek Web sites. He's also visited China and brought back unusual teas, one medicinally bitter, another like fallen leaves on a rainy day.

There's never been a better time to be stimulated by these familiar yet extraordinary leaves and seeds. The few pages of this chapter step back from the details to give the essential facts of their care and brewing.

COFFEE AND TEA SAFETY

Coffee and tea pose little risk of foodborne illness. They're made from dry ingredients and prepared in hot water, so they're relatively microbe-free.

Scalding and chronic irritation are the most common kinds of harm caused by coffee or tea. They're often served at temperatures that can cause serious burns in a few seconds. Habitual drinking of very hot liquids is also associated with an increased risk of mouth and throat cancers.

Take first sips cautiously to make sure you don't take a mouthful of burning-hot liquid. Don't drink coffee and tea when they're hot enough to hurt.

Caffeine is a stimulant chemical in coffee and tea that can also cause restlessness and insomnia. Once consumed it takes between 15 minutes and 2 hours to reach its maximum blood levels, and 3 to 7 hours to fall back again halfway. The caffeine content of prepared drinks varies widely. In general, a cup of tea contains half or less the caffeine in a cup of brewed coffee, and a shot of espresso coffee also contains somewhat less thanks to its small volume.

BUYING AND STORING COFFEE

Coffee beans are the seeds of small trees native to northern Africa. Today coffees are grown in many tropical and subtropical countries and shipped for roasting to the countries that consume them. "Fair-trade" coffees are meant to provide a higher price to farmers in developing countries. Coffees may be sold by their place of origin, or as blends. Arabica beans come from varieties of one coffee species and are valued for their fine aromas; robusta beans come from a different species and provide more body and caffeine than arabicas.

To try prized regional beans, buy from reputable sources. A number of regional coffees fetch high prices, and are sometimes counterfeited with cheaper beans.

Roasting creates coffee flavor. Medium roasting produces medium-brown matte beans with full body and flavor. Light roasting produces a lighter, more acidic drink with distinctive bean aromas; dark roasting produces oily beans with a more generic roasted flavor and some bitterness.

Buy coffee that has been roasted recently, within a few days for locally roasted coffee, or with the latest sell-by date for vacuum-packed coffees. Coffee develops stale, rancid flavors thanks to its polyunsaturated oils, which are vulnerable to attack by oxygen in the air.

Buy whole beans and grind coffee just before brewing for the fullest, freshest flavor. Coffee beans quickly lose aroma when they're ground into fine particles.

Store whole beans tightly wrapped at room temperature for a week, or freeze for a few months.

Store ground coffee tightly wrapped for a few days at room temperature, or freeze for a few months.

Before using a package of cold or frozen coffee, warm the package through at room temperature to avoid moisture condensation when you open it.

Decaffeinated coffee has had most but not all of its caffeine removed with water, carbon dioxide, or a solvent called methylene chloride, very small traces of which persist in beans but are thought to be safe. These treatments also remove substances that contribute flavor and body, so decaffeinated coffees generally brew into a less delicious cup.

Instant coffee is a dried concentrate of coffee flavor and color compounds, better as a flavoring ingredient in sweets and pastries than as a substitute for fresh-brewed coffee.

BUYING AND STORING TEA

Teas are the dried leaves of a species of camellia native to eastern Asia. Fine teas are now made in China, Japan, India, Sri Lanka (Ceylon), and Kenya, and come in a range of prices and qualities.

Inexpensive bag teas are made from small particles that brew quickly into a strong cup.

More expensive loose leaf teas and teas in silklike plastic sachets are larger pieces or whole leaves, and can make more distinctive, subtle cups.

Scented teas are made by storing the teas for some time with flowers, and may contain flower petals. Some versions are flavored with aroma extracts. Lapsang souchong is a Chinese tea lightly smoked with pine wood.

Choose teas from suppliers that sell a lot of tea and keep their stocks fresh.

Store tea for months in an opaque, airtight container in a cool place. Check older teas before serving; they slowly lose aroma.

White teas are made from the new buds of the tea plant before they have had a chance to unfurl into leaves. They brew into a very pale, delicate tea.

Green teas are made from young leaves of the tea plant, harvested and quickly heated to preserve at least some of their color. They brew into greenish to yellowish teas with an especially savory taste, some bitterness, and aromas that range from grassy to seaweedy to nutty.

Oolong teas are made from young leaves that are flavored and lightly colored by their own enzymes and by brief heat. They brew into yellowish to light amber, somewhat astringent teas with rich, flowery-fruity aromas.

Black teas are made from young leaves that are intentionally bruised and deeply colored by their own enzymes. They brew into amber to red, somewhat astringent teas with a complex, spicy floral-fruity aroma.

Puerh teas are made from Chinese teas that are fermented and aged. They brew into a deep red-brown, nonastringent tea with autumn-leaf, spicy, sometimes clovelike aromas.

Herbal teas are alternatives to standard teas from the camellia bush. They are mostly caffeine-free and made from a wide range of plant materials, including mints, hibiscus flowers, lemon verbena, rose hips, chamomile, and citrus peels. Many are manufactured with flavor extracts.

Rooibos, or red-bush, tea and honeybush tea are caffeine-free teas made from South African shrubs. Rooibos is especially rich in antioxidants.

Maté is a caffeine-rich tea made from a South American shrub.

THE ESSENTIALS OF BREWING COFFEE AND TEA

Coffee and tea are made by extracting flavorful substances from the dry beans and leaves into water.

Flavor extraction is influenced by the size of the coffee or tea particles, the water temperature, and the extraction time. Small particles and high temperatures cause rapid extraction. High temperatures extract more bitter and harsh tastes, but also more delicate aromas.

Both coffee and tea produce bland brews if they're not extracted enough. They produce harsh brews if they're extracted too completely.

The key to good coffee and tea is to adjust brewing temperatures and times to the character of the beans and leaves, to extract a pleasing balance of flavors.

Water quality affects the quality of coffee and tea, of which it makes up 95 to 98 percent.

Use filtered water to make coffee and tea, to remove any off odors that aren't driven off by heating the water.

Avoid using very hard, softened, or distilled waters to make coffee and tea. The abundant minerals in hard water interfere with flavor extraction and cause cloudiness and surface scum. Softened and distilled waters produce unbalanced flavors.

To remedy flat-tasting teas and coffee, try adding small pinches of acidic cream of tartar or sour salt to the brewing water. Many city tap waters are alkaline to slow pipe corrosion, and benefit from added acid. Or try bottled waters with moderate mineral contents.

BREWING AND SERVING COFFEE

There are several common methods for brewing coffee, and each produces a distinctive cup.

Drip filter cones give good control over the starting water temperature, but not over the brewing temperature or the brewing time, which is determined by how fast the water moves through the grounds. Paper filters remove nearly all residues and produce a sparkling, stable cup, but may contribute their own flavor. Metal filters and screens pass some residues, and these continue to be extracted in the cup and slowly increase bitterness.

Standard drip coffee machines usually give little control over either brewing temperature or time, and run at lower than ideal temperatures. Expensive models may brew with properly hot water.

Plunger, or French-press, pots give good control over brewing time, but the water temperature cools during the several minutes it takes to extract coffee from the coarse grind typically used. Plunger pot screens allow residues into the cup, and retain them in the pot, so the coffee becomes more bitter as it stands.

Stove-top moka pots give little control over brewing time or temperature, and the temperature is high, slightly above the boiling point. They make a full-bodied but bitter coffee, good for drinking with milk.

Inexpensive espresso machines force boiling water through ground coffee with relatively weak steam pressure. They also produce a full-bodied but bitter cup.

Genuine espresso machines actively pump below-boiling water through finely ground coffee at high pressures. Many are designed to optimize the brewing conditions, and the best give the operator significant control. They produce a cup with unparalleled fullness of body and flavor, in part because the high pressure forces the beans' oils into a fine, enriching emulsion. Special espresso coffee blends of arabica and robusta beans help optimize flavor, body, and the characteristic crema, or foam.

Turkish-style pots are used to boil very fine coffee grounds repeatedly, to get a very strong brew whose harshness is balanced by large doses of sugar.

Each brewing method extracts a particular grind of coffee for a particular time. In general, the finer the grind, the shorter the brewing time. Plunger pots extract coarse grounds for 4 to 6 minutes, drip and stove-top devices medium grounds for 2 to 4 minutes, espresso machines extract fine grounds for 30 seconds.

Evenly ground coffee beans make the best coffee. In a mix of large and small particles, some will be either underextracted or overextracted, and the coffee can end up weak, bitter, or both.

Avoid grinding coffee with a standard propeller grinder, which grinds very unevenly. Use hand-turned or electric burr grinders instead, or buy coffee preground every few days.

Brew coffee with water between 180 and 205°F/80 and 96°C. Water just off the boil extracts both more aromatics and more bitterness from the grounds. At cooler brewing temperatures, the coffee comes out with a smoother but less full flavor.

Experiment to find the right proportions of coffee to water for your tastes. Typical American drip coffee is made with a ratio of 1 part coffee to 15 parts water, or about 16 grams per 8-ounce/250-milliliter cup. The ratio for espresso is 1 to 5 or 1 to 4, 6 to 8 grams per 1-ounce/30-milliliter shot. It's better to make coffee too strong than too weak. Strong but balanced coffee can be diluted with hot water and remain balanced.

To brew coffee with consistent strength, measure the dry coffee by weight instead of volume. Coffee scoops are convenient but an unreliable measure. A standard scoop can contain between 8 and 12 grams of coffee depending on its fineness and how compacted it is.

To make a milk foam with the steaming wand on an espresso machine, use a well-chilled metal pitcher filled halfway with very fresh, well-chilled milk, at least ⅔ cup/150 milliliters. Immerse the steamer nozzle, turn on the steam, and move the pitcher down to maintain the nozzle just below the milk surface near the pitcher wall, where it will keep the milk circulating. Stop when the pitcher reaches about 150°F/65°C, to avoid a strong cooked flavor.

Preheat serving cups to prevent coffee from cooling too quickly.

Don't hold a pot of coffee on low heat or reheat it on high heat. The flavor balance of freshly brewed coffee is fragile. Further heat harshens aroma and increases acidity. To reheat cold coffee with the least damage to flavor, microwave it on low power.

To serve coffee over an extended time, brew or pour it into a preheated insulated pot.

Iced coffee can be made in several ways. To make it quickly, brew extra-strong coffee and pour it over ice, which will dilute it. Or brew normal coffee, chill it in the refrigerator, and add ice only when serving.

Cold-extracted coffee is a distinctively full-bodied but mild coffee, made by letting cold water percolate overnight through a bed of coarse coffee grounds, or letting water and coffee steep and then filtering off the extract. It's very smooth, with little bitterness or acidity, but it also has less aroma than hot coffee.

BREWING AND SERVING TEA

Teas are brewed in different ways in different parts of the world. You can brew a small portion of leaves once, or a larger portion several times to enjoy the changing flavors. Tea leaves are sometimes rinsed before brewing, or the first brew may be discarded.

Brewing proportions are flexible. The standard is a heaping teaspoon of leaves, around 2 grams, for 8 ounces/250 milliliters water, the equivalent of several small Asian cups, 1½ European teacups, or 1 American mug.

Brewing temperatures depend on the kind of tea. Delicate white and Japanese green teas are brewed at low to medium temperatures, 120 to 175°F/50 to 80°C, to moderate extraction of bitter and astringent compounds and retain greenish color and grassy fragrance. More robust Chinese green teas are brewed at medium temperatures, 160 to 175°F/70 to 80°C. Especially aromatic oolong, black, and puerh teas are brewed in water just off the boil.

Brewing times range between 15 seconds and 5 minutes, depending on the fineness of the tea pieces, the water temperature, and the number of times the tea has already been brewed. Inexpensive tea bags often contain very fine tea "dust" and become overextracted in a minute or two.

Experiment with brewing temperatures and times to get the flavor you like best. If the taste is flat, try a higher temperature and/or longer time. If the taste is somewhat harsh, try a lower temperature and/or shorter time.

Brew loose tea enclosed in a strainer, or use a one-serving pot, to be able to stop the brewing when the tea is ready. Continued contact between leaves and water will produce an overextracted, harsh tea.

Preheat the pot and cups with hot water so that the tea temperature doesn't fall too far during brewing or sipping.

When trying a loose-leaf tea for the first time, brew
- *white teas* at 175°F/80°C for 2 to 3 minutes,
- *Chinese green teas* at 175°F/80°C for 2 to 3 minutes,
- *Japanese green teas* at 160 to 175°F/70 to 80°C for 1 to 3 minutes,
- *oolong teas* just off the boil for 3 to 4 minutes,
- *black teas* just off the boil for 4 to 5 minutes,
- *puerh teas* just off the boil for 1 to 3 minutes.

Check tea flavor during the brewing by pouring small tastes at intervals.

Separate the liquid from the leaves as soon as the tea is ready. Either serve all of it into cups, or remove the leaves from the pot in their strainer or sachet or bag.

To enjoy teas at their best, drink them promptly. As they stand they cool and lose aroma. Green and oolong teas oxidize, changing both flavor and color.

If you drink black tea with milk, pour the milk into the cup first, then add the tea. This heats the milk gradually and makes it less likely to curdle.

Iced tea should be made with a stronger brew since it will be diluted as the ice melts. Use half again as much tea leaves per pot as usual.

To avoid cloudy iced tea, infuse cool or cold water with tea leaves over several hours. This extracts less of the materials that cause clouding when the tea is chilled.

WHERE TO FIND MORE KEYS TO GOOD COOKING

Here's a list of good, accessible sources of information about various foods and cooking methods. Treatises from culinary schools and specialist publishers can be excellent, but generally focus on large-scale preparation in professional kitchens. The following are directly relevant to cooking at home.

GENERAL COOKING

Harold McGee, *On Food and Cooking: The Science and Lore of the Kitchen.* New York, Scribner, 2004.

Shirley Corriher, *CookWise: The Hows and Whys of Successful Cooking.* New York. Morrow, 1997.

Nathan Myhrvold with Chris Young and Maxime Bilet, *Modernist Cuisine: The Art and Science of Cooking.* Seattle, The Cooking Lab, 2010.

Michael Ruhlman, *Ratio: The Simple Codes Behind the Craft of Everyday Cooking.* New York, Scribner, 2009.

GENERAL COOKBOOKS

Irma S. Rombauer, Marion Rombauer Becker, and Ethan Becker, *Joy of Cooking.* New York, Simon and Schuster, 2006.

Paul Bertolli with Alice Waters, *Chez Panisse Cooking.* New York, Random House, 1988.

Judy Rodgers, *The Zuni Cafe Cookbook.* New York, Norton, 2002.

KITCHEN TOOLS

Alton Brown, *Alton Brown's Gear for Your Kitchen.* New York, Stewart, Tabori and Chang, 2008.

Chad Ward, *An Edge in the Kitchen: The Ultimate Guide to Kitchen Knives.* New York, Morrow, 2008.

FRUITS AND VEGETABLES

Aliza Green, *Field Guide to Produce: How to Identify, Select, and Prepare Virtually Every Fruit and Vegetable at the Market.* Philadelphia, Quirk Books, 2004.

Elizabeth Schneider, *Vegetables from Amaranth to Zucchini.* New York, Morrow, 2001.

DAIRY PRODUCTS

Anne Mendelson, *Milk: The Surprising Story of Milk Through the Ages.* New York, Knopf, 2008.

MEATS AND FISH

Bruce Aidells and Denis Kelly, *The Complete Meat Book.* Boston, Houghton Mifflin Harcourt, 2001.

Hugh Fearnley-Whittingstall, *The River Cottage Meat Book*. London, Hodder and Stoughton, 2004.

Paul Johnson, *Fish Forever: The Definitive Guide to Understanding, Selecting, and Preparing Healthy, Delicious, and Environmentally Sustainable Seafood*. New York, Wiley, 2007.

SAUCES

James Peterson, *Sauces: Classical and Contemporary Sauce Making*. New York, Wiley, 2008.

BAKING, BREADS, PASTRIES, AND CAKES

Shirley Corriher, *BakeWise: The Hows and Whys of Successful Baking*. New York, Scribner, 2008.

Regan Daley, *In the Sweet Kitchen: The Definitive Baker's Companion*. New York, Artisan, 2001.

Jeffrey Hamelman, *Bread: A Baker's Book of Techniques and Recipes*. New York, Wiley, 2004.

Peter Reinhart, *Peter Reinhart's Artisan Breads Every Day*. Berkeley, Ten Speed Press, 2009.

Rose L. Beranbaum, *The Pie and Pastry Bible*. New York, Scribner, 1998.

Rose L. Beranbaum, *The Cake Bible*. New York, Morrow, 1988.

CHOCOLATE AND CANDIES

Peter P. Greweling, *Chocolates and Confections at Home with the Culinary Institute of America*. New York, Wilcy, 2009.

COFFEE AND TEA

Kenneth Davids, *Coffee: A Guide to Buying, Brewing, and Enjoying*. New York, St. Martin's, 2001.

Corby Kummer, *The Joy of Coffee: The Essential Guide to Buying, Brewing, and Enjoying.* Boston, Houghton Mifflin Harcourt, 2003.

Michael Harney, *The Harney & Sons Guide to Tea.* New York, The Penguin Press, 2008.

Mary Lou Heiss and Robert J. Heiss, *The Tea Enthusiast's Handbook: A Guide to the World's Best Teas.* Berkeley, Ten Speed Press, 2010.

ACKNOWLEDGMENTS

The key to good book making—at least for this book—has been having the best of colleagues, friends, and family.

I first met Bill Buford when I visited New York in May 2005. We got together for lunch, and before dessert arrived he had changed the way I thought about my life as a writer. I'm tremendously grateful to Bill for his counsel and friendship. And I thank Andrew Wylie, to whom Bill introduced me, for helping me plot my new course, and for finding such a good home for this book.

For sharing their deep knowledge of foods and cooking as I put this book together, I thank Fritz Blank, David Chang, Chris Cosentino, Wylie Dufresne, Andy and Julia Griffin, Johnny Iuzzini, John Paul Khoury, David Kinch, Christopher Loss, Daniel Patterson, Michel Suas, Alex Talbot, and Aki Kamozawa. I've been especially fortunate to work and play with the ever-questioning Heston Blumenthal and his team at The Fat Duck, including Kyle Connaughton, Ashley Palmer-Watts, and Jocky Petrie. My fellow writers Edward Behr, Shirley Corriher, Susan Herrmann Loomis, Michael Ruhlman, and Paula Wolfert plied me with acute questions and observations. I've learned much about cooking and science from conversations with Nathan Myhrvold, Chris Young, and Alain Harrus, and about chocolate and life from Robert Steinberg, a good friend whom I miss very much.

A special thanks to my teaching partners at the French Culinary Institute, David Arnold and Nils Noren, who have schooled me in and out of class on food and drink and much else.

For reading and commenting on drafts of this book I thank Shirley and Arch Corriher, Mark Pastore, and Daniel Patterson. David Arnold spent hours with me on the phone going over much of the text sentence by sentence. Of course I alone am responsible for whatever infelicities and errors remain.

At Penguin Press, Ann Godoff saw that this book needed to be more ample than the slim handbook it started out as, and has been wonderfully supportive throughout its prolonged gestation. Claire Vaccaro translated my ideas for the design into a model of clarity and utility. Noirin Lucas expertly shepherded the text through production, and Lindsay Whalen managed our communications with warm and tactful efficiency.

Then there's my family. I first learned what good cooking is from Louise Hammersmith's curries and Christmas cookies, and Chuck McGee's Sunday griddle cakes and roasts. My late sister Ann helped me visualize the invisible for my first book; and Joan, her husband Richard Thomas, and my brother Michael continue to hearten from afar. Harold and Florence Long, Chuck and Louise Hammersmith, and Werner Kurz gave me important lessons in the proper preparation and appreciation of fish, often after we'd caught them together. Sharon Long shared many enthusiasms and discoveries over the thirty years that we cooked side by side. And our young taste testers have grown up, generously forgiven the lutefisk experiment, and become valued collaborators. John improved the sections on tea and coffee and milk foams, and applied a keen eye to the page proofs. Florence carried out experiments on chocolate and baking, lent a critical palate to many others, and kept me fed when I couldn't leave the computer. My thanks and love to all.

INDEX

cakes (*cont.*)
  ingredients, 417–22
  leftover, 415
  mixing butter-cake batters, 425–27
  mixing sponge-cake batters, 427–28
  preparing and filling the pan,
    428–29
  safety, 414
  shopping for ingredients, 415
  special tools for making, 415–17
  sugar, 419–20
  texture, 12
  troubleshooting, 431–32
  two basic types, 425
cake testers, 417
candied flowers and fruits, 511–12
candies, 493–512
  candy thermometers, 45
  essentials of making, 499–501
  exacting nature of recipes, 494
  hard, 505–7
  ingredients, 496–99
  safety, 494–95
  soft, 507–9
  storing, 495
  sugars, 493–94, 496–98, 499–512
  tools for making, 47, 495–96
  working with sugar syrups, 501–3
  see also names of candies
cane syrup, 33
canned foods, 21–22
  beans and peas, 350
  fruits, 123
  legumes, 350
  sauce from canned tomatoes, 185
canning:
  fruits, 131–32
  vegetables, 164
canola oil, 24
can openers, 49
caramel, 493–94, 500
  making, 508–9
  syrups and sauces, 504
carbohydrates, 9–10
  see also pectin; starch; sugar
carcinogens, from high-heat cooking,
    99, 163, 246, 254, 278
cardboard packaging, 21
carpaccio, 240
carrots, 170–71
  "baby" carrots, 171

pressure-cooking, 156
  puree, 301
cashews, 365
cauliflower, 157, 171, 301
celery, 145, 171
celery root, 171
celiac disease, 325
Celsius temperature scale, 67
ceramic pots and pans, 44, 60–61
cereals (breakfast), 326, 330–31
ceviche, 279
charcoal, 56, 76, 98
chard, 172
charring, 99, 163, 254
cheesecake, 224–25
cheesecloth, 50–51
cheeses, 207–9
  aged, 207
  cooking with, 208–9
  fondue, 209, 304
  fresh, 207
  fruit, 128
  grated, 208
  low-fat and nonfat, 207
  melting, 208
  nonmelting, 208
  process, 207
  safety, 189
  sauces, 209, 304
  sourness, 13
  storing, 191
  stringy, 208
chemical leaveners, 390, 420–21, 444
chemistry, food, 6–11
cherries, 121, 137
chestnuts, 363, 365
chicken:
  cooking, 252
  with crisp skin, 243, 259
  oven roasting, 257, 258–59
chickpeas (garbanzo beans), 349,
    354, 387
chicories, 143
chiffon cakes, 427, 429
chillis, 179–80
  mole sauces, 302
  protection while handling, 36
  pungency, 14, 180
  reconstituting dried, 180
  relieving mouth and skin burning,
    37, 180

chocolate, 471–92
  bitter and semisweet, 477, 479
  "bloom," 474
  brownies, 439–40
  cakes and cookies, 422–23, 437
  compound coatings or
    nontempering, 478
  couverture, 478
  dark chocolate, 473, 474, 481, 482
  decorations, 490
  drinks, 491
  fudge, 508
  ganache, 485–88
  glazes, 435
  kinds, 477–78
  milk chocolate, 473, 474,
    477–78, 481
  mixtures, 479–80
  modeling, 490
  molded, 489–90
  mousse, 492
  pudding, 491
  safety, 473–74
  sauces, 491
  shopping for, 472–73
  spreading, coating, and clustering,
    484–85
  storing, 474
  substituting cocoa for, 423
  sweet, 477
  tempering, 472, 478, 480–83, 487
  tools for working with, 47, 474–75
  truffles, 488–89
  unsweetened, 477
  white, 473, 474, 478, 481
  working with, 478–80
chops:
  cooking, 252
  frying, 260–61
  grilling, 100, 254
  low-temperature cooking, 85
  preparing for cooking, 245
chopsticks, 54
choux pastries, 411–12
ciabatta, 379–80
cider vinegar, 29
cilantro, 147, 151–52
citric acid, 30
citrus fruits, 137
  candied peels, 512
  peeling, 125

flour (*cont.*)

cookies, 437

gravies and starch-thickened
    sauces, 309–10

griddle cakes and batters, 443, 444

nonwheat, 374

panfrying and sautéing, 90

pastries, 396–98, 399

pastry, 397

self-rising, 373, 418

shopping for, 371

soup thickening, 319

storing, 375

warm to room temperature after
    freezing, 23–24

whole-wheat, 374, 397

flourless chocolate cake, 423

flowers, candied, 511–12

foaming eggs, 228–29

foils, 55–56

grilling, 56, 99

microwave ovens, 102

oven baking, 97

folding method, 425

fondant, 507–8

divinity, 509

glazes and icings, 435–36

molded chocolates, 489

rolled, 435

fondant sugar, 497, 508

fondue:

cheese, 209, 304

chocolate, 491

foodborne illness, 109–10

fish and shellfish, 272

limiting risk, 112–15

low-temperature cooking, 84,
    263, 286

raw foods, 80, 189, 348

sprouts, 148

see also microbes; parasites; toxins

food mills, 50

food poisoning, *see* foodborne illness

food processors, 53, 380

forceps, 54

forks, 54

freezer burn:

fish, 276

fruits 125

ice creams and ices, 456, 463

meat, 244

pastries, 395

sauces and soups, 292

vegetables, 148

freezer canisters, 458

freezers, 22–24

freezing, 22–24, 453–54, 456–60

bean curd, 356

berries, 137

cooked dishes, 23

cookie dough, 438

fish, 276

fruits, 125

herbs, 148

ices and ice creams, 456–60

meats, 244

sauces, soups, stocks, 313

vegetables, 148

see also frozen foods

fregola, 343

french fries, 49, 181, 182

French-press (plunger) coffee pots, 520

frisée, 174

frittatas, 221–22

fritters, 391–92, 450–51

frostings, 434–37

frozen foods:

desserts, 453–66

fish and shellfish, 274

fruits, 123

peas, 179

safety, 454–55

thawing, 113

vegetables, 22–23, 146, 151

see also freezing

frozen yogurt, 204, 456

fructose, 14, 32–33, 497, 498, 501

fruitcakes, 433

fruit gums (gummies), 510–11

fruit juices, 127

ices, granitas, sorbets, and
    sherbets, 463–65

pasteurized for safety, 111

see also citrus juices

fruits, 119–42

acids, 29

allergic reactions, 116

baking and frying, 130

candied, 511–12

canned, 22

canning, 131–32

carbohydrates, 9

curds, 223

discoloration, 126

enzymes, 8

essentials of cooking with, 125–27

frozen, 123, 125

grilling and broiling, 131

jams, jellies, and preserves, 132–34

jelly candies, 510–11

pickling, 135

pie fillings, 407

poaching, 129–30

precut, 123

preserving in alcohol, 134–35

purees, sauces, butters, and pastes,
    128–29

raw, 120, 121, 127

refrigerating, 113

ripening, 121–22

safety, 120–121

shopping for, 122–23

storing, 124–25

see also dried fruits; fruit juices

frying:

batters, 94, 161–62, 450–52

butter, 203

deep- and shallow-, 92–95

eggs, 203, 219–20

fried breads, 391–92

fruits, 130

herbs, 152

leftover oils, 26

after low-temperature cooking, 84

meats, 260–61

oils, 25, 92–95, 451

panfrying and sautéing, 89–92

spatter, 89–90, 107

thermometers, 45

turkey fryers, 76

vegetables, 158–60

see also deep-frying; shallow-
    frying; stir-frying

fudge, 508

fumes, 107–8

funnels, 55

G

galettes, 447

game meats, 241

ganache, 485–88

garbanzo beans (chickpeas), 349,
  354, 387
garlic, 174–75
  aioli, 298
  preserving, 148, 174
  pungency, 14, 175
  salsas, pestos, and purees, 300
  sautéing, 175
  storing, 147
gas stoves:
  burners, 71
  gas flames, 69
  ovens, 71, 72, 96, 385, 429
gastrique, 317
gelatin, 8–9, 466–67
  aspics, 320–21
  candies, 499, 509
  cold jellies, 466–68
  consommé, 319–20
  fish, 285
  fish stock, 314
  fruit gums, 510–11
  ice cream, 457, 460
  liquefied by enzymes, 126,
    138–39, 141
  marshmallows, 510
  meat, 248, 252, 255, 256
  meat stock, 311–13, 317
  mousses, 465–66
  powdered and sheet, 467
  sauces, 308, 311
  vegetarian substitutes, 467
  whipped cream, 199, 434
gelato, 461, 463
Genoise, 428
geoduck clams, 282
ghee, 200, 202–3
ginger, 14, 36
glazes (cakes), 434–35
glazing vegetables, 159
gloves, 36, 99, 53, 107, 114, 502,
  506–7
glucose, 14, 32, 33, 420, 497, 498,
  501, 511
glucose syrup, 498
gluten, 373
  breads, 373–74, 378, 381–83
  cookies, 437–38
  fermenting dough, 382
  fried and baked batters, 94, 161,
    444, 451

griddle cakes, 444
  pastries, 396–97, 399, 401–3, 406,
    409, 410
  vital, 374
gluten-free foods, 10, 300, 320,
  332, 373
gnocchi, 344
goat's milk, 190, 194
gougères, 411–12
grains, 323–39
  allergic reactions, 116
  boiling, 81, 82, 329
  breads, 369
  carbohydrates, 9
  essentials of cooking, 328–30
  forms, 325–26
  grinding your own, 326
  "instant" and "minute" products, 326
  kinds, 331–39
  leftovers, 330
  oven baking, 97
  safety, 324–25
  shopping for, 325–26
  storing, 327
  toasting, 328
  see also rice; wheat; corn
granitas and granités, 463–65
granite slabs, 47, 395, 475, 496
granola, 326, 330
grapes, 138
  ripening, 121
  verjus, 29
grapeseed oil, 25
grass-fed meats, 241
graters, 49
gravies, 300–310
gravy separators, 55
Greek-style yogurt, 204
greens:
  beet, 169
  bitter, 169
  collards, 169, 172
  dandelion, 169, 173
  microgreens, 148–49
  wilting, 159
  see also mustard greens
green teas, 517, 522, 523
griddle cakes, 441–48
  crepes, 447–48
  ingredients, 443
  leaveners, 443, 444

  leftovers, 443
  pancakes, 445–46
  safety, 442
  storing, 443
grilling, 98–100
  barbecuing, 255
  foil, 56, 99
  fruits, 131
  after low-temperature cooking, 84
  meats, 99–100, 253–54
  pizza, 388
  vegetables, 163–64
grills:
  cast-iron, 99
  charcoal, 56, 76, 98
  clamshell, 100
  electric, 75–76, 98
  gas, 76, 98
  indoor, 75
  outdoor, 75–76
grinders:
  coffee, 50, 52, 514
  electric, 52–53
  hand, 50
  safety, 107
  spice, 50, 52
grinding:
  coffee, 521
  grains, 326
  meats, 247
grits, 338–39
ground meat:
  cooking, 252, 253
  fat content, 242
  grinding meats, 247
  safety, 106, 240
  vacuum-packed, 243
  see also hamburgers
guacamole, 168, 296
guar gum, 10
gummies (fruit gums), 510–11

H

hair dryers, 75
half-and-half, 197
halogen elements, 69
hamburgers:
  fat content, 242
  grilling, 254

metal pots and pans, 61–63
metric measures, 78, 79
mezzalunas, 49
microbes:
    antibiotic-resistant, 4
    batters for meat or fish, 452
    boiling water kills, 83
    dairy products, 188–90
    E. coli, 109, 188
    fermenting vegetables, 166
    fish, 109, 271–72
    food safety, 105–6, 109–10, 112,
        115, 117–18
    fruits, 120–121
    grains, 324
    legumes, 348–49
    listeria, 109, 188, 240
    meats, 238–40, 267
    sauces and soups, 290–91
    shellfish, 109, 271–72
    vegetables and herbs, 144–45
    viruses, 110–11
    see also botulism; salmonella
microgreens, 148–49
microwave ovens, 72–73
    candy making, 501, 504
    cooking, 102–3
    microwave heating, 69, 72
    milk foams, 196
    pasteurize egg yolks, 298
    power settings, 103
    soften ice creams and ices, 460
    toasting nuts and seeds, 363
    turntables, 103, 155
    uneven heating, 115
    vegetables, 155
milk, 187–96
    acidophilus, 194
    acids and tannins curdle, 126
    allergy, true, 190
    breads, 378–79
    candies, 499
    coffee, 196, 521
    condensed or evaporated, 194–95
    cooking with, 195–96
    cultured, 203–4
    essentials of cooking with, 191–93
    foams, 196, 521
    fresh, 193–94
    homogenized, 193
    low-fat, 188, 193

low-lactose, 194
nonfat, 193
pasteurized, 111, 189, 193
powdered, 195
problems cooking with, 195–96
raw, 189, 193
sauces, 303
separation, 192
shopping for, 190–91
skim, 193
stabilized and concentrated,
    194–95
sterilized, 194
storing, 191
structure, 192
sweetened condensed, 194–96
tea, 524
thickening and curdling, 192
UHT and sterilized, 189, 194
milk chocolate, 473, 474, 477–78, 481
milled grains, 325–26
miso, 27, 35, 318, 347, 357
mitts (gloves), 53, 107
mixers:
    electric, 52, 229, 380, 381, 416
    hand, 50–51
mixing and working bowls, 58
moist heating methods, 80–81
moisture:
    from fats and oils, 10
    from water, 7
moka pots, 520
molasses, 33, 353, 420, 498
mold:
    breads, 370, 372
    cheeses, 189
    nuts, 360
    preventing on berries, 124
molds:
    candy making, 496
    chocolate, 476, 489–90
moles, Mexican sauces, 302
molluscs:
    clams, 111, 275, 276, 278, 282
    essentials of cooking, 281–82
    mussels, 111, 275, 276, 282
    octopus, 275, 276, 277, 278, 282
    oysters, 35, 111, 275, 276, 279, 282
    preparing for serving or cooking,
        278–79
    scallops, 275, 279, 281–82

shopping for, 275
squid, 275, 276, 277, 278, 282
storing, 276
monosodium glutamate (MSG),
    14, 34
mortars and pestles, 50
mousses:
    chocolate, 492
    cold and frozen, 465–66
MSG (monosodium glutamate),
    14, 34
muesli, 330
muffins, 433–34
mung beans, 351, 354
muscovado sugar, 32
mush, cornmeal, 338–39
mushrooms, 176–77
    dried, 176, 177
    natural firmness, 150, 176
    sautéing, 177
    savory seasonings, 35
    truffles, 186
mussels, 111, 275, 276, 282
mustard, 14, 36
mustard greens, 177
    bitter greens, 169
    pungency, 15

N

naan, 387–88
napa cabbage, 170
navy beans, 354
nectarines, 122, 139
new potatoes, 180
nonstick pots and pans, 60
nonstick sprays, 26, 90, 416, 429
noodles, 340–44
    Asian, 343–44
    cooking, 341–42
    dried, 340
    making, 340–41
    rice, 343–44
    shopping for, 326
nougat, 509–10
nut butters and pastes, 359, 361–62,
    364, 437
nut milks, 364
nuts, 359–68
    allergic reactions, 116, 360

fish, 8, 270
food chemistry, 8–9
legumes, 347, 356
meats, 8, 237, 246–47, 248–49
milk, 187–88, 190, 192
sauces, 294, 304–7
soups, 318–19
texture, 12–13
see also gelatin; gluten
puddings, 345, 491
puehr teas, 518, 523
puff pastry, 393–94, 395, 408–9
pumpkin seeds, 367
pungency, 14, 36
 chillis, 14, 180
 garlic, 14, 175
 onions, 14, 178
 seasoning, 16, 36–37
purees:
 cooked sauces, 301–2
 fresh sauces, 299–300
 fruit, 128–29
 ices, granitas, sorbets, and
  sherbets, 464
 legumes, 353
 potato, 181–82
 tomato, 158, 185, 301–2
 vegetable, 157–58, 301, 318

Q

quail eggs, 214
quality of food, 3
quiches, 225, 407–8
quick breads, 390–91
quick cakes, 433–34
quick-cooking rice, 334
quick-pickling vegetables, 165
quick-rise yeast breads, 380
quinces, 141

R

racks, 58, 417
radiated heat, 68
radicchio, 182
radishes, 143, 182
raw foods, 80
 eggs, 111, 212, 213–15, 455

fish and shellfish, 111, 112,
  270–73, 279, 287
fruits, 120, 121, 125, 127
legumes, 349
meats, 111, 239, 240, 248–49
milk, 189, 193
nuts, 359, 360
safety, 105, 106, 111, 112, 115,
  183, 295, 348, 454
storing, 23
salads, 145, 149–50
sprouts, 148, 183, 348, 351
vegetables, 111, 145, 148
red beans, 353
red-bush (rooibos) teas, 518
red rice, 334
reductions, meat, 311, 313
refrigerators, 22–24, 113
 avoid habits that warm, 23
 check temperatures regularly, 23
 cleaning door handles, 118
 fat and oil storage, 24
 leftovers, 116
 perishable foods, 113
 setting for, 23
reheating leftovers, 116
 bread, stale, 20, 372, 391
 fish, 288
 meat, 267
 microwave oven, 102–3
 rice, 333
 steamer, 86
rhubarb, 141–42
rice, 332–37
 boiling, 334–36
 brown, 333, 335
 converted, 334
 cooking, 334–37
 kinds, 332–34
 noodles, 343–44
 pilafs, 337
 quick-cooking, 334
 risotto, 336–37
 safety, 324
 sushi, 324, 335, 337
 white (polished), 333
 wild, 334
rice cookers, 74, 336
rice flour, 373, 451
rice paper, 343–44
ricers, 50

rice wine vinegar, 30
risotto, 336–37
roasting, 95–97
 pan roasting, 89
 see also oven roasting
roasting bags, 57
roasts:
 cooking, 251–52
 oven roasting, 256–59
 serving, 266
rock candy, 506
rocket (arugula), 14, 167
rock salts, 27
roll cakes, 432–33
rolled fondant, 435–36
rolling pins, 396
rolling pin spacers, 396
rooibos (red-bush) teas, 518
root vegetables:
 boiling, 153
 shopping for, 145
 storing, 21, 147
rosemary, 148
roti, 387–88
rotisserie attachments, 76
rotisserie cooking, 256
roux, 310, 319
royal icing, 435
rutabagas, 183
rye, 332
rye flour, 374

S

sabayons, 51, 229–30, 307
saccharin, 34
safety, 105–18
 avoiding injuries, 106–8
 balancing with food quality, 112
 blenders, 52
 boiling water, 82
 breads, 370
 cakes and cookies, 414
 chilled and frozen desserts, 454–55
 chocolate, 473–74
 cleaning up and sanitizing, 117–18
 coffee and tea, 514–15
 dairy products, 188–89
 double-dipping, 296
 eggs, 212–13

ABOUT THE AUTHOR

Harold McGee writes about the science of food and cooking. He's the author of the award-winning classic *On Food and Cooking: The Science and Lore of the Kitchen*, and writes a column, "The Curious Cook," for *The New York Times*. He has been named food writer of the year by *Bon Appetit* magazine and to the *Time* 100, an annual list of the world's most influential people. He lives in San Francisco.

KITCHEN AND COOKING TEMPERATURES

	°F / °C
Freezer, maximum	0 / –18
Refrigerator, coldest corner	32 / 0
Microbe growth zone	40-130 / 5-55
Boiling water, sea level	212 / 100
Water for green teas	160-180 / 70-80
Water for black, oolong teas	200 / 93
Water for coffee	200 / 93
Water for pre-firming vegetables	130-140 / 55-60
Water for softening vegetables	212 / 100
Water for slowing berry spoilage	125 / 52
Braise, water bath for tender meats	130-150 / 55-65
Braise, water bath to cook tough meats in 12-48 hours	135-150 / 57-65
Braise, water bath to cook tough meats in 8-12 hours	160-170 / 70-75
Braise, water bath to cook tough meats in 2-4 hours	180-190 / 80-85
Pan for frying, sauteing	350-400 / 175-205
Wok for stir-frying	450 / 230 and up
Oil for deep-frying	350-375 / 175-190
Oil for french fries, first fry	250-325 / 120-160
Second fry	350-375 / 175-190
Oven for braising, grains and beans	200-225 / 93-107
Oven for large roasts, pan roasting	325-350 / 160-175
Oven for small roasts, vegetables	400-500 / 205-260
Oven for yeasted breads	400-450 / 205-230
Oven for cakes	325-375 / 160-190
Grill for slow barbecue	180-200 / 80-93

TARGET TEMPERATURES IN FOODS

	°F / °C
Chocolate in temper	90 / 32
Mixed-ingredient dishes, for safety	160 / 70 and up
Cooked-food holding temperature, for safety	130 / 55 and up
Tender eggs, fluid yolks	147 / 64
Firm eggs, firm yolks	153 / 67
Thickened creams, set custards	185 / 83
Moist fish, shellfish	120-135 / 50-57
Rare meat	125-30 / 52-55
Medium-rare meat	130-140 / 55-60
Medium meat	140-150 / 60-65
Medium-well meat	150-160 / 65-70
Well-done meat	160 / 70 and up
Vegetables	180-212 / 80-100
Sugar preserves	215-235 / 102-113
Fondant, fudge, soft caramels	235-240 / 113-116
Hard caramels	245-250 / 118-121
Soft taffy, fruit gums	250-265 / 121-130
Hard taffy, firm nougat	270-290 / 132-143
Hard candy, brittle, toffee	300-320 / 149-160
Caramel sugar, spun sugar	340 / 170 and up